Amelia Ann Blandford Edwards, 1831–92.

More Usefully Employed

Amelia B. Edwards, writer, traveller and campaigner for ancient Egypt

OCCASIONAL PUBLICATION 15

More Usefully Employed

Amelia B. Edwards, writer, traveller and campaigner for ancient Egypt

Brenda Moon

Foreword
Professor John Tait

EGYPT EXPLORATION SOCIETY
3 DOUGHTY MEWS, LONDON WC1N 2PG
2006

LONDON

SOLD AT

THE OFFICES OF THE EGYPT EXPLORATION SOCIETY

3 Doughty Mews, London WC1N 2PG

British Library Cataloguing in Publication Data

A catalogue record for this book is available from the British Library

ISBN 0 85698 1699

Typeset by Meeks & Middleton
Printed by Commercial Colour Press, plc

Frontispiece: Photographic portrait of Amelia Ann Blandford Edwards from a copy in Somerville College, Oxford (SCO Edwards 420)

Contents

List of illustrations

List of colour plates

Acknowledgements

This book has been many years in preparation, and could not have been attempted were it not for the kind help of many librarians and archivists who have gone out of their way to make their knowledge of their collections available to me. Here I shall name just a few of them.

Miss Pauline Adams, Librarian of Somerville College Oxford, has patiently accepted my visits, letters and, latterly, emails over not merely years but decades, and I owe her a special debt of gratitude; it has been a particular pleasure exploring the fascinating collection which the College holds, virtually the sole source for the first forty years of Amelia Edwards' life.

The archives of the Griffith Institute, and of the Ashmolean Library (now the Sackler Library), have provided an equally engrossing insight into the last twenty years of Amelia's life, especially through the albums of Amelia's watercolours of the Dolomites and Egypt, and through the account by Kate Bradbury (later Mrs Griffith) of Amelia's American lecture tour. Here I wish to record my grateful thanks not only to Dr Jaromir Malek, the present Keeper of the Archives at the Griffith Institute, and his assistants, Mrs Alison Hobby and Mrs Elizabeth Fleming, for their professional and enthusiastic help, but also to the late Miss Helen Murray, formerly archivist to the Institute, who first introduced me to its resources long before such information could be gleaned from the internet.

I wish also to acknowledge the helpfulness of the Keepers of the British Museum, in the Department of Ancient Egypt and Sudan and its predecessors, and of the Directors of the Departments of Printed Books and of Manuscripts in the British Library, and the Special Collections Librarians in University College London over more than thirty years.

I am especially fortunate in having enjoyed access to letters from Amelia Edwards and Kate Bradbury to Flinders Petrie, through the kindness of Miss Lisette Petrie; access to papers of Amelia's friend Marianne North through the hospitable help of the North family of Rougham, Norfolk; and access through the hospitality and kindness of Mr and Mrs J. Martin of Broadstairs to the diaries of Jenny Lane, the maid who accompanied one of Amelia's party in the journey up the Nile in 1873–74. To them I am especially indebted.

For the work for which Amelia is chiefly known, and rightly – the founding of the Egypt Exploration Fund, as it was first named – the

Society itself is naturally the unrivalled source. The nature of its archives will come as no surprise to any who have, like Amelia, dedicated their time to a cause: they reveal so much more than the chronological development of the Society in its early years. I have much appreciated the helpful and unstinting support of a succession of its Secretaries: Miss Mary Crawford, Mrs Shirley Strong, and most recently Dr Patricia Spencer, without whom this book certainly could not have been written. They have proved worthy successors to the first Honorary Secretary, Amelia Edwards herself.

In my research into the Society's archives I am fortunate indeed to have enjoyed the invaluable help and encouragement, especially in the early years, of Miss Margaret Drower, MBE, FSA, Vice-President and sometime Chairman of the Egypt Exploration Society, who kindly read the book in manuscript. I am also most grateful to Professor T.G.H. James, CBE, FBA, Vice-President of the Society and likewise formerly its Chairman, who encouraged me to approach the Society when I was seeking a publisher. I am delighted that the Society accepted; I am indebted to Professor John Tait, Vice-Chairman of the Society, and to the Publications Committee for undertaking this task, and wish to pay tribute to the hard work of Jenny Oates, Hilary Meeks and Caroline Middleton in bringing it to fruition. I can think of no more appropriate publisher for a biography of the Society's founder.

Behind all the help received from those whom I can name lie the painstaking efforts in so many libraries and archives of nameless collectors, cataloguers and indexers without whom my research would have been impossible. A complete picture of a life can never be given, especially after a century and more, and for missing or misplaced pieces in the jigsaw I must accept responsibility; but I hope that through this publication others may be encouraged to look further into the achievement of this remarkable woman, Amelia Edwards.

Brenda Moon
Edinburgh, October 2005

Note
In this volume, all illustrations originating from the Somerville College (Oxford) archives are reproduced by kind permission of the Governing Body of the College.

Sources and abbreviations

BL   British Library, Euston Road, London, NW1 4YD
BM   British Museum, Great Russell Street, London, WC1B 3DG*
BMFA   Boston Museum of Fine Arts, 465 Huntington Avenue, Boston, MA, 02115, USA
Boston PL   Boston Public Library, Boston, MA, 02117, USA
EES   Egypt Exploration Society, 3 Doughty Mews, London, WC1N 2PG
GI   Griffin Institute, Ashmolean Museum, Oxford, OX1 2PH
Houghton   Houghton Library, University of Harvard, Cambridge, MA, USA
Macclesfield Museums Trust and Macclesfield Borough Council, Macclesfield, SK11 6TJ
Martin   Mr and Mrs Martin, Broadstairs, Kent
The Trustees of the National Library of Scotland
North   Mr Tom North, Rougham, Norfolk
PP   Miss Lisette Petrie, Polegate, East Sussex
SAC   The Librarian of the Sackler Library, Ashmolean Museum, Oxford, OX1 2PH
SCO   The Governing Body of Somerville College Oxford, OX2 6HD
UCL   Libary Services, University College London, Gower Street, London, WC1E 6BT

*The abbreviations BM EAA, BM OA and BM WA refer to items in the former departments of Egyptian and Assyrian Antiquities, Oriental Antiquities and Western Asiatic Antiquities respectively.

Note
Where consecutive quotations are from the same document, reference to the document is given in a note only after the first quotation. Where dates of documents are not indicated in the text they are given in the notes, if known.

Foreword

The Egypt Exploration Society is proud to be the publisher of Dr Brenda Moon's biography of Amelia Edwards. By any reckoning, Amelia took a leading role in the founding of the Society as the Egypt Exploration Fund in 1882, and she served, jointly, as the Fund's first Honorary Secretary. Her educational, if not quite her social, background was very different from that of her chief fellow founders: Sir Erasmus Wilson, a wealthy surgeon, elderly at the time of the Fund's foundation but in just the previous year elected President of the Royal College of Surgeons and granted a knighthood, and Reginald Stuart Poole, who was then Keeper of Coins and Medals at the British Museum. Despite all the changes that have occurred in academic disciplines and in the climate of work in the field during the more than a hundred years since her death in 1892, it is to be hoped that there is still recognisable in the Society today the legacy of Amelia's enthusiasm, energy and dedication.

Amelia is in many ways an enigmatic figure. Her decision to devote herself, in the last two decades of her life, to the cause of the monuments and antiquities of ancient Egypt was only the last of several deliberate changes in the focus of her life and career. Unlike, say, her friend Flinders Petrie, or Wallis Budge, both a generation her junior, she did not become a personality wreathed around by colourful anecdotes. In her years as a campaigner for the scientific investigation of ancient Egypt, especially in her lecture tour of the United States in 1889–90, she developed into a public figure beyond her former fame as a novelist and writer, and yet she seems to have deliberately avoided all opportunities to push herself forward as a celebrity. She plainly fought a little shy of any conventional label as an activist for the rights of women.

Amelia's life has always been of significance for the history of the development of Egyptian archaeology and of Western and particularly British perceptions of Egypt, ancient and modern. Her work as a writer, and above all as a novelist has become ripe for academic study, both because of heightened interest specifically in women writers, and because of a new awareness of the social context in which her novels thrived. Dr Moon's biography is based on an unrivalled study of archival material, and her rounded account of Amelia helps us towards an understanding of a complex personality and a very varied life.

Professor John Tait
London, December 2005

Introduction

It is strange that Amelia Edwards, well known on both sides of the Atlantic at the time of her death in 1892, should thereafter have been largely forgotten for the best part of a century. In her own lifetime she first became known for her stories, essays and serials in the popular contemporary weeklies, and in particular for her ghost stories; then, during the 1870s, her travel writing became popular with the growing number of new tourists. In the last decade of her life she wrote for a different readership – for scholars, archaeologists, curators and public figures – as a campaigner for the preservation of the relics of ancient Egypt, developing a style that appealed to the leisure reader and the academic alike. A century after her death, however, her books had almost without exception been out of print for decades, and even in the field of Egyptology she was scarcely remembered outside the circle of the British Museum, the Egypt Exploration Society, which she had founded, and University College, London, where she had endowed a Chair.

The surge of interest in 'women's studies', and particularly in Victorian women, which began towards the end of the twentieth century, has brought Amelia Edwards renewed attention, although the wealth of information to be found in archive collections has not been fully recognised, while most discussion of her writing and her achievements has been confined to an examination of her published work.

Amelia Edwards' place in nineteenth-century fiction lies closest to that of the 'sensation novelists' such as Mrs Braddon, Mrs Henry Wood and Wilkie Collins. Some of the themes to be found in their novels also occur in hers, particularly in her early works. Sensation is present in all her novels – three of which (*Hand and Glove*, *My Brother's Wife* and *Debenham's Vow*) open with a death scene. Murder and suicide occur in her first novel, *My Brother's Wife* (1855); a secret identity is revealed in her second novel, *The Ladder of Life* (1856), when a village wood-carver proves to be a baron; a minister of religion in *Hand and Glove* (1858) turns out to be a convict, and commits suicide. In *Barbara's History* (1864) passionate kisses from an older man, a supposedly bigamous marriage, followed by a supposedly illegitimate baby, and a deranged wife locked in a secret room all feature, while deceit and robbery prevail in *Half a Million of Money* (1865). Battles in the cause of Italian liberty, and blockade-running in the cause of trade are the highlights of her next two novels. *In the Days of My Youth* offers flirtation with a *grisette*, gambling and a dual in quick succession, while in her last novel, *Lord Brackenbury*, the 'dark folk' give a brooding air of mystery.

At least one contemporary critic ranked her least popular novel, *Half a Million of Money*, as 'far above the Miss Braddon school'.[1] What set her above the rest was at least in part her 'word-painting', her ability to describe scenes and moods in an evocative way. The language of conversation in her novels is often old-fashioned but never stilted. Moreover, her novels are often set in an 'educated' environment, giving them an unusual 'tone': the leading characters, men and women, are acquainted with good literature; they have libraries, or long for access to them; they have artistic or musical talents; they visit art galleries and have an interest in antiquities. The plots are melodramatic and sometimes fantastic, but there is much to satisfy the serious reader. Archaeologists such as Gaston Maspero[2] and artists such as Gustave Doré[3] enjoyed Amelia's novels as well as her archaeological papers and her art criticism.

While some of her fictional work could now be seen as somewhat dated, the one genre of Amelia Edwards' writing that has never gone out of fashion is the ghost story. Composing ghost stories had come naturally to her since childhood, and the ghost story was in its heyday. Along with writers such as Mrs Braddon, Wilkie Collins, Elizabeth Gaskell and Mrs Henry Wood she contributed to the special Christmas issues of *All the Year Round* and *Tinsley's Magazine*, as well as others which sprang up after the repeal of the Newspaper Tax in 1855. However, Amelia's fascination with the macabre went deeper than the Victorian preoccupation with the trappings of death. It is part of a fascination with the past that gripped her in the catacombs of Rome and later in the tombs of Egypt, and led her to harbour some gruesome relics in her home in Gloucestershire in later life.

With the publication in 1873 of *Untrodden Peaks and Unfrequented Valleys*, the first travel book on the Italian Dolomites in English for the general reader, and four years later with the publication of *A Thousand Miles up the Nile*, Amelia found a new genre which gave her readers a longer-lasting satisfaction. Travel literature became immensely popular in the mid-nineteenth century as a medium for women writers. For the first time unmarried women were able to travel alone all over the world. (Amelia's friend Marianne North circled the world three times on her own between 1870 and 1890.)

Amelia lived through the early years of the women's movement, yet her attitude towards the cause is somewhat ambivalent. The press reports on her American lecture tour may need to be quoted with discretion, but some of the words which they put into her mouth ring true:

> 'Are you a woman suffragist?'
> 'I am one of those suffragists who believes the present condition of affairs is outrageous, but I am too much occupied with my studies to be interested in politics. I am an honorary member of the two leading suffrage societies in England. The ballot is something I don't want but think I ought to have.'[4]

As the *Sunday Herald* observed: 'She hoped to make friends for the advancement of Egyptian exploration, but in working for this result, she has wrought better than she yet knows in enlarging the sphere of American womanhood.'[5]

A Thousand Miles up the Nile did for Egyptian exploration all that *Untrodden Peaks and Unfrequented Valleys* had done for Italian tourism, and marked only the start of her writing for the cause. Almost every issue of *The Academy* from the late 1870s until shortly before her death in 1892 carried an article or a review by Amelia Edwards, sometimes unsigned, as were her articles in *The Times*. Some of her articles have become classics of archaeological reporting. Her greatest achievement in her writing was in combining scholarly reporting and readable, lively narrative. '[You] are reforming Egyptological literature', her friend Sir Erasmus Wilson told her, 'No more ponderous books!'[6]

The aim of this book is to present Amelia Edwards in a fuller light than has hitherto been directed upon her life, by drawing on a wider range of sources than previous writers have done. Even Kate Bradbury, her close friend of later years, only fully recognised the complexity of her personality after her death. The last word in the book has gone to Kate, but it could equally have gone to Emily Paterson, Amelia's secretary for the last four years of her life, who said, in a talk that she gave at the Egypt Exploration Society in 1931:

> Although very conservative in some ways, in others Miss Edwards was in advance of her time. She was one of the most ladylike women I have ever met, and yet she dressed in advance of her day in coat, skirt and waistcoat. She was also the most courteous person I ever met, no matter whether she spoke to a servant, a secretary or one of her friends. And she was the most delightful person to work for, as she gave full credit when one did anything to please her, and if she had to advise or correct, always did so in the kindest possible way.[7]

Notes

[1] *The Standard*, (London, 4 April 1866).
[2] SCO Edwards 151.
[3] SCO Edwards 454.
[4] GI Griffith Papers 2.
[5] *Sunday Herald* (Boston, MA, 30 March 1890).
[6] EES XVII.b.7.
[7] SCO Edwards 440.

The early years, 1831–52

It is no wonder that Amelia Edwards' cousin, Matilda Betham-Edwards, spoke of her as 'precocious of the precocious' when writing of Amelia's early years.[1] A memoir in Amelia's own hand headed 'Autobiographical Notes', written in the autumn of 1855 at the age of 24,[2] indicates something more than mere precocity: it shows a young woman who has 'resolved to be a writer' and intends to make her mark on the world.

Amelia Ann Blandford Edwards was born on 7 June 1831, at 1 Westmoreland Place, City Road, London, described as 'a dreary cul-de-sac' by her cousin, who writes: 'The situation suited her father who, in consequence of ill-health, had procured a post in a city branch of the London & Westminster Bank. Later, a much pleasanter house was taken in Wharton Street, Percy Circus.'[3] It is the house at 19 Wharton Street, Islington, about which Amelia writes when she describes her early childhood:

> My earliest recollections are of this quiet suburb, then divided from the city by a tract of meadows & gardens, but now a wilderness of shabby brick & mortar … My parents' means were small, & my father's health indifferent. I was an only child, & the child of old parents. They had been married fourteen years when I was born. I was in great part educated by my mother … & in part by masters. For some years I read with a tutor who prepared youths for college … I was a very idle child, very lonely & very quiet. My chief amusements as early as I can remember were drawing and reading. I used to sit, winter and summer, at a table at the farther end of the parlour, away from the circle round the fire. Then I used to cover sheets of foolscap with such rude pencillings as the stories I read suggested, or absorbed in the pages of *Sandford & Merton*, *Robinson Crusoe*, &c., &c.[4]

Many years later she wrote to Edward Abbott, editor of the *Literary World*:

> My good parents allowed me to read everything that came in my way; and I do not think that I was the worse for my liberty. Scott,

Fig. 1: 19 Wharton Street, Islington, Amelia Edwards' home until the early 1860s.

G.P.R. James, Fenimore Cooper, Marryatt, Miss Bremer, Harrison Ainsworth, Bulwer Lytton & Dickens (as far as then published) were all read before I was fourteen – besides many inferior works of the circulating library order of merit. Magazines of course, travels in abundance, memoirs, &c, shared my affections with the novelists. I well remember the enjoyment with which, when a very small child, I devoured Wilkinson's *Ancient Egyptians* and Stephenson's *Central America*.[5]

Matilda gives the only surviving physical description of Amelia as a child:

A beautifully shaped, by no means large head, a fine, rounded forehead, dark eyes and hair, a small, sensitive mouth ... Of medium height, she had nothing of the family spareness ... Even in girlhood she was of robust rather than slender proportions. She was always excessively neat in dress. A stranger would at once have noted her clear enunciation and correct, somewhat amplified English.[6]

Amelia's father, Thomas Edwards (1786–1860), served as an officer with the 20th Regiment of Foot in the Peninsular War. He entered the army as an ensign, receiving his first commission in 1809 at the age of 22, and was promoted to lieutenant in 1812. He served under Wellington from 1812 to 1814, and remained in the field after being slightly wounded at the Battle of Orthes in February 1814. Matilda Betham-Edwards records that when

> spending his yearly fortnight's holiday with [her] family near Ipswich … he would occasionally be drawn into a word or two about the battle of Corunna, at which he had been present … Oddly enough, he had made friends with a foeman, and in token of good fellowship the French officer, at parting, presented him with ten guineas to be spent on a ring, which was done.[7]

He later fell ill, however, and retired from the army on half pay in July 1819.[8] Amelia wrote that 'his War Medal with five clasps for the five battles in which he fought was 'one of my greatest treasures',[9] and her cousin records that it had the place of honour in her study. According to Matilda Betham-Edwards,

> No one ever set more store by lineage than Amelia B. Edwards. She rejoiced in her descent on her mother's side from the illustrious family of Walpole, and anything she could learn of the more modest paternal ancestry interested her extremely. It was not very much.[10]

In describing Thomas Edwards, Matilda talks of his taciturnity and his 'stern, unflinching sense of duty'. She continues:

> Admirable as were the moral qualities of the old Peninsular officer, his fireside influence was not inspiring. My uncle … combined with his quiet, almost pensive habits a regularity carried to excess. He rose, read *The Times*, breakfasted, started for the bank, supped, and went to bed by the clock. For society he had little taste. No wonder that his lively, high-spirited wife found some kind of stimulus necessary.[11]

He was the third of a large family, his father, also named Thomas, dying in 1816 and his mother, Margaret (née Dove) shortly afterwards. They 'belonged to the class called "gentleman farmers" i.e. occupiers of land on a large scale which they leased or rented'.[12] From 1825 he worked in the London office of the Provincial Bank of Ireland, and was at his desk until a week before his death. His widow, writing to the directors of the bank on 23 August 1860, the day after his death, commented that he 'had sedulously and honourably performed every duty of his situation'.[13] Records which she forwarded to the directors showed that he had in the course of 36 journeys to Ireland transported 830,000 sovereigns and 345 guineas. She begged the directors to consider some financial assistance for herself and her daughter: 'Beyond a very small sum for which his life was insured, we have nothing to look to in the future but our own labour.' Judging by its eloquent phrasing, the letter may well have been drafted by Amelia:

> His fidelity of long service could not be rewarded more gratefully to himself, could he be sensible of your sympathy, than in any generosity which you may be pleased to extend to the wife who has been for 44 years the partner of his fortunes, & the only child who was the pride & pleasure of his declining days.

Four years earlier, Thomas Edwards had written personally to Field Marshall the Right Honourable Viscount Harding pleading that he might be granted the honorary rank of captain:

> Your memorialist has lately seen the names of several retired Quartermasters on H.P. [Half Pay] promoted to the honorary rank of Captain in the Army. Your memorialist begs to lay his services before your Lordship, hoping that your Lordship will take them into your kind consideration and promote him to the honorary rank of Captain.[14]

There is no record that either plea met with success. Alicia Edwards survived her husband by only one week.

Thomas Edwards' reserve seems to have been more than offset by his wife's vivacity. Years later Amelia wrote of her mother that she was 'a very bright, clever woman'.[15] Alicia Edwards was the daughter of Robert Walpole, Barrister at Law, of Thurley, County Tipperary, Ireland. 'On my mother's side', Amelia wrote, 'I am also nearly related to the Fitzgeralds, Petty Fitzmaurices, & other good old Irish families.' Matilda Betham-Edwards gives a vivid picture of Alicia Edwards:

Fig. 2: Thomas Edwards, her father, aged 73, from her photograph album.

Fig. 3: Alicia Edwards, her mother, from a loose sheet in The Travelling Adventures of Mrs Roliston: *pencil drawing by Amelia Edwards.*

On the maternal side she [Amelia] inherited the more brilliant gifts
that made her famous – ready wit, a rare versatility, rapid powers of
acquirement and expression … From her mother also came
eminently practical qualities. The brilliant-complexioned, bright-
eyed, large-featured little Irish woman … descended of the Walpoles
– although accomplished, as the word accomplished was then
understood – possessed talents invaluable to the wife of an officer
living on half-pay. She was a skilled housewife and extraordinari-
ly clever in making the most of small means. As if prescient of her
only child's literary distinction, she forbore to give her the
domestic training she had herself received. I do not think that the
eminent Egyptologist ever threaded a needle or made a cup of tea
in her life.[16]

She adds later:

The child's teacher and companion was her mother … Mrs
Edwards must have been more than mortal, had she concealed her
pride in her darling. The achievements of the youthful story-teller,
artist and musician were freely vaunted in her presence … Means
were limited in these days, but first-rate housekeeping and rigid
economy gave the home an air of almost opulence. One relaxation,
and one only was freely indulged in, namely, the play. Sadler's
Wells and minor theatres were frequented … Perhaps theatre-
going may be regarded in the light of a reaction [to the taciturnity
of the husband and father].[17]

Amelia herself writes that 'I never went to any school & was educated
by Mama up to the age of six years.'[18] She describes at some length a visit
to Ireland with her mother in 1841 at the age of ten. In the previous
winter she writes:

I had a gastric fever lasting 13 weeks which nearly proved fatal, &
this journey was partly undertaken to recover me … This was my
first journey out of my native country … [It] made a profound &
lasting impression on my mind, cultivated in me the taste for fine
scenery, & left a series of ineffaceable pictures in my mind.

Mother and daughter sailed from London Bridge to Dublin harbour.

I remember now every passenger on board the steamer … every
incident of the voyage, every impression of sea-scenery: the flights

of gulls, the shoals of porpoises, the mean passenger who would not dine at the dinner table, the rich lady with her lapdog, the captain & all.

They stayed at Machin's Hotel in Dublin for three days, where they were visited by Aunt Henriette, then left by coach for Carlow, and thence by hired car to her uncle's house at Rathellan, ten miles further. 'There I found a little companion & friend in my cousin Dorinda. We called her Dorey. She was fair, wild as a young hare, full of fun & affection.' She describes the house at Rathellan, with its handsome stone portico, iron gates and sloping drive, and the mock ruin, 'built for the effect by my uncle' in the grounds:

> Here I spent three most happy months, visiting, riding, enjoying life as I had never before enjoyed it. At every ride or walk we came upon some old round tower or ruined castle … Respecting all of these there was some legend & all these I eagerly enquired after & stored up in my mind. Here I first wrote a complete tale – for I had begun endless stories & novels before this but finished none. This tale I called 'Lochlin Castle'. It was all love & fighting, was read to everyone, & gained me great applause.

From Rathellan they went to Enniscorthy, staying with the manager of the Enniscorthy branch of the Provincial Bank of Ireland, making a day visit to Wexford from there. In September 1841 they sailed for London 'in a terrible storm which nearly foundered the vessel off the Margate Roads'.

The deep impression which the visit to Ireland made on Amelia is seen in an amusing 'strip cartoon', entitled 'Patrick Murphy', which was created by her at the age of fourteen.[19] Witty as the captions are, the emphasis of the work lies in the 77 equally entertaining drawings. They give scope for Patrick Murphy to appear in diverse forms of apparel as the story progresses: sailor's clothes, riding habit, court apparel, opera dress, and so on. Matilda Betham-Edwards comments on Amelia's interest in clothes, saying that she 'loved to dress up in boys' clothes and one day thus disguised frightened a homely neighbour out of her wits'.[20] Again, in her sketch of Amelia's early years, she writes, 'there was no guessing what to expect from her love of fun – it must also be added, of mischief'. A sense of fun comes over strongly in 'Patrick Murphy', for instance in her presentation of an election, and of the behaviour of the gentry. The cartoons are sketchy, with spindly lines in pen and ink, yet the figures are expressive and attention is given to amusing background details such as elaborate chandeliers. The cartoon was never published and was probably intended simply to entertain family and friends.

'I was always drawing', Amelia wrote many years later, 'from the time when I could hold a pencil – caricaturing friends, strangers & public characters; illustrating the books I read, & so forth'.[21] Amelia's powers of caricature at an early age were recognised by George Cruikshank, who lived just round the corner from Wharton Street. In her letter of 1881 to the editor of the *Literary World* she relates an amusing incident:

> I had made some little story or article which I made bold enough to drop into the Editor's box at the office of *Cruikshank's Omnibus* – an illustrated serial of which he was himself editor, artist and proprietor. The story was no doubt bad enough – but I had chanced to scribble some pen & ink heads of the characters on the backs of some of the pages of my ms, & these attracted the great man's attention. The next evening he walked in, while we were having tea – introduced himself & asked to see 'the author & artist'. When he found that the important personage was a little girl in short frocks, he was greatly amused. By & by, he offered to take me as his pupil, gratuitously, & to train me for the profession. But my parents, with their old prejudice against the artist life, hesitated, objected, & finally let the opportunity drift by.[22]

Amelia continued to produce strip-cartoon stories: a second such story survives, dated February 1848, entitled 'The Travelling Adventures of Mrs Roliston'.[23] At the age of seventeen her drawings are bolder and more confident, but the style is similar to that of 'Patrick Murphy', with amusing detail both in the figures and in the background. The story on this occasion takes Amelia well beyond the basis of experience and draws on her reading as well as on her vivid imagination.[24]

Such juvenilia may be of trivial importance in terms of Amelia's career, but both 'Patrick Murphy' and 'Mrs Roliston' are of great interest in foreshadowing many features of her mature work. They present a racy chain of adventures in the manner of the picaresque novel; they show a love of storytelling, an interest in situations rather than in personalities, a love of travel, an amused and detached interest in current events, and an extravagant imagination. They were apparently produced for her own amusement and that of family and friends, and they are early examples of combining two of her life-long pleasures – sketching and story-telling.

In September 1851, on a visit to Suffolk, she sketched a two-yard-long cartoon of the landing of the Romans in Britain, in black chalk on the white wall of a spare room in her Uncle William's house, Hill Farm, Creeting, which still survived when Matilda Betham-Edwards wrote her 1893 memoir, and is reproduced there. Matilda calls it 'a presumptuous undertaking'[25] but Amelia herself judged it, at four years' distance, 'wonderfully well done for an amateur without any kind of knowledge … & the figures were so accurately drawn as to lead a surgeon who saw it to say that I must have studied the human figure anatomically.'[26] Throughout her teenage years Amelia enjoyed artistic activity, 'diversy-fying [*sic*] my time occasionally with a little amateur wood-engraving, & copying outlines given by Art Union, &c, &c. I also took to illuminating & filled the prayer books of my friends with emblazonings.'[27]

In her letter to Edward Abbott, Amelia describes how at the age of 14 she 'resolved to take up some one study & work in earnest. In an evil hour, I chose music – for I was considered too delicate to paint in oils & become, what I most wished to be, an artist.'[28] In her early autobiograph-ical essay she writes:

> In 1845 I began first to study music under Miss Mounsey[29] with whom, by the way, I remained till my twenty second year … I joined her musical class, studied the piano & theory of music, & turned my mind to composition. Under her tuition I became an accomplished pianist; played the most difficult music, & composed on an average eight or ten pages of music weekly … In 1849 I began to study the organ for the purpose of becoming an organist, also the Guitar, which I practised assiduously.[30]

Her musical ambitions were, however, thwarted for a time by 'a dreadful illness. It began in Novr 1849 & lasted till March 1850. I was 14 weeks in bed. It was the typhus fever.' The summer, however, brought better times, as she adds in a postscript:

> This summer [1850] I intended to become a professional singer. Went with Miss Cubitt to Guildford & sang with great success at the Town Hall … Passed a most delightful day there next day, driving about & seeing lovely country. Felt madly exhilarated all that day. Was intoxicated with success & dreamt dreams of fame & fortune. Lived in a rapture of pleasure & pride for some days.

Two months later she sang in a concert in Brentford, 'still a success, but rendered doubtful up to almost the last minute by several colds'. Sore throats and general poor health culminated in an illness which prevented her from singing in an oratorio in Exeter Hall just when she 'saw the very dawn of my fortunes ... This so disgusted me that I suddenly relinquished the public singing and resolved only to *teach*.' By September 1850 she had recovered sufficiently to take a post as organist of St Michael's Chapel, Wood Green, 'a pretty little village church 7 miles from London. I was very miserable. I knew no one & was constantly ill.'

Her wretchedness was due in part to illness, but in part to affairs of the heart, about which all too little is known:

> I had become engaged to a gentleman [a Mr Bacon] whom I had known for years, in the January of 1851 & he came round every Sunday to fetch me home from Church. This engagement was not a happy one. We were ill suited & though he loved me very much I could not really love him. I had accepted him out of regard and esteem & found that insufficient.

Amelia eventually broke off the engagement at the end of 1851. A comment by Matilda in her sketch of Amelia's early years may have a bearing on this episode:

> On the maternal side she inherited ... perhaps also the perilous dower of personal fascination. No one ever exercised stronger influence, and it was hardly her fault if she at times awakened interest or affection she could not return.[31]

As Amelia writes:

> This was the summer of the Great Industrial Exhibition one of my Irish cousins came over purposely to propose to me; but my unfortunate engagement prevented this chance.[32] I was ill all this summer ... I used to dread the journey to Wood Green so much that I had a nervous attack every Saturday night & diarrhoea every Sunday. At the close of the year for which I was bound by agreement to remain, I resigned the appointment.[33]

On returning to London in the autumn of 1851 Amelia had resumed her music teaching and tried to get an organist's situation near home. She 'played for testimonials to various distinguished professors ... & got fifteen first rate testimonials in all'. One reference from Sir John Goss, organist of St Paul's Cathedral, dated 13 September 1852 survives, stating that 'Miss Edwards having played a Psalm & fugue of her own composition to me on the organ in a very creditable manner, I have pleasure in stating that I consider her qualified to fill the situation of

*Fig. 4: Fugue composed by Amelia on her initials, from a copy given to her friend
Marianne North in 1871, from Marianne's scrapbook (RH39 fl 17v)
in the North archive, Rougham, Norfolk.*

organist.'[34] It is touching to note that in 1871, when she was famous, Goss
wrote to ask her for a signed copy of the fugue which she composed on
her initials.[35]

Matilda Betham-Edwards pays tribute to Amelia's ability as an
organist, displayed during one of her visits to Suffolk:

> One Sunday afternoon, to the intense admiration of the household
> and farming folk, she undertook the duties of organist at
> Witnesham Church close by. I well remember how she varied the
> cut and dried programme, and how the congregation lingered
> spellbound at the close of the service. She was playing us out with
> a voluntary of Bach's but nobody stirred till the magic notes
> ceased. Music of this impassioned kind was a novelty to the naive
> listeners. Hitherto the organ had seemed a mere necessary,
> befitting accessory to the service.[36]

Amelia herself was, at least in retrospect, under no illusions about the limit of her musical ability. In 1881 she wrote to Edward Abbott:

> Although I worked terribly in earnest, I virtually threw away another seven years of my life; for the divine gift of music was not mine; & although I became a thorough contrapuntist, a trained vocalist, pianist & organist, & covered reams of music paper with laboriously studied compositions, vocal, orchestral & instrumental, I never wrote anything worth a second hearing. And yet I took out first class testimonials from all our chief musicians, and seriously proposed to make music my profession. This brings me from 14 to 21 years of age. Then an accident turned the current of my life.[37]

Notes

[1] Matilda Betham-Edwards, 'Amelia Blandford Edwards (1831–1890)' [*sic*], in *Mid-Victorian Memories* (London: John Murray, 1919), pp. 110–18.
[2] SCO Edwards 439.
[3] Betham-Edwards, 'Amelia Blandford Edwards (1831–1890)', p. 111.
[4] SCO Edwards 439.
[5] SCO Edwards 351.
[6] Matilda Betham-Edwards, 'Amelia B. Edwards: her childhood and early life', *New England Magazine*, New Series, 7, 5 (Boston, MA, January 1893), p. 562.
[7] Ibid., p. 111.
[8] SCO Edwards 350.
[9] SCO Edwards 351.
[10] Betham-Edwards, 'Amelia B. Edwards: her childhood and early life', p. 557.
[11] Ibid., p. 560.
[12] Ibid., p. 550.
[13] SCO Edwards 470.
[14] SCO Edwards 484; 28 June 1856.
[15] SCO Edwards 351.
[16] Betham-Edwards, 'Amelia B. Edwards: her childhood and early life', p. 551.
[17] Ibid., p. 560.
[18] SCO Edwards 439.
[19] SCO Edwards 425. See also Appendix 3, pp. 275–77.
[20] Betham-Edwards, 'Amelia Blandford Edwards (1831–1890)', p. 112.
[21] SCO Edwards 351.
[22] Ibid.
[23] SCO Edwards 424.
[24] See Appendix 3, pp. 277–79.
[25] Betham-Edwards, 'Amelia B. Edwards: her childhood and early life', p. 556.

[26] SCO Edwards 351.

[27] SCO Edwards 439.

[28] SCO Edwards 351.

[29] Ann Sheppard Mounsey, 1811–94, an organist and composer, was a well known music teacher in London who held positions as organist in several London churches; see *New Grove Dictionary of Music and Musicians* (London: Macmillan, 2nd edn, 2001).

[30] SCO Edwards 439.

[31] Betham-Edwards, 'Amelia B. Edwards: her childhood and early life', p. 550.

[32] It is tempting to think that this Irish cousin was a Captain Fitzgerald of the Royal Scots regiment, the only cousin apart from Matilda who attended her funeral forty years later, according to obituaries, for example, in the *Bristol Mercury*, 22 April 1892; no other male Irish cousin is named in the Somerville archive.

[33] SCO Edwards 439.

[34] SCO Edwards 60.

[35] SCO Edwards 61.

[36] Betham-Edwards, 'Amelia B. Edwards: her childhood and early life', p. 562.

[37] SCO Edwards 351.

❖ 3 ❖

Early writing and travels, 1853–55

The 'accident' which 'turned the current of my life' was how Amelia described the success of her tale *Annette* (1853) (see Appendix 3, pp. 279–80). Yet *Annette* was not the first of her tales to be published, nor even the first for which she received payment. She had written stories from early childhood and had submitted some of her compositions to publishers, but, in her eyes, the offer of payment for publication in a respectable journal put her writing in a different category – it opened up the prospect of writing as a career.

When asked how she came to take up writing Amelia once answered 'I was born so', adding:

> I am quite certain that writing comes by nature. One of my very earliest recollections is of writing a story before I could write, that is to say, before I had even begun my pothooks and hangers. I in fact anticipated the type-writer, and executed my ms entirely in capital letters. I remember even the title of that prehistoric chef-d'oeuvre and the vignettes (highly coloured in blue, red and yellow) which illustrated it. I was then about four years old. It was in the reign of … shall I say William & Mary, or Rameses. I was always writing or drawing, when other children were playing with dolls or dolls' houses. I rushed into type at seven, and I still have the penny paper in which my first effort was published. That first effort was a poem in half a dozen stanzas called 'The Knights of Old' which my proud mother sent to the editor of a penny weekly & the said editor actually published it.[1]

Matilda Betham-Edwards reports that,

> when she was only nine years old she had seen in a penny journal announcement of a prize offered for the best temperance story. Fired with ambition, the authoress in pinafores went secretly to work, and to her own intense delight and the far intenser pride of her parents, carried off the palm.[2]

Matilda appends to her article a story which Amelia wrote at the age of twelve, 'The Story of a Clock':

> It is one of Amelia's earliest literary efforts. It is a story for children, written by a child, originally published in a cheap weekly … It was fortunately preserved by a friend of her mother's, and the number containing the story has been most kindly lent me by the author's early friend, Miss F.M. Sweeting of Clifton. The correctness of grammatical construction, the evident pains taken with punctuation, the conciseness of narrative, are very striking when we remember the author's age.[3]

About this time, Amelia writes, 'I began to write bosh for the public. I wrote two or three novels. One was called "The Gascon" & founded on the story of Edward II & his favorite [*sic*] Gaveston, which was published in a penny weekly, long since defunct, called the *London Pioneer*.'[4] Elsewhere she adds that 'for this publication, which ran for two years, I constantly wrote up to the date of its death, by which time my literary ardour (never being fed by *payment* of any kind) had grown so feeble that when it expired I wrote no more'.[5] She describes the work as 'a long historical novel … very strong in description of pageants, costumes, &c, &c.', and is sufficiently proud of it in later life to mention it to Edward Abbott, to whom she adds: 'A little later on I contributed stories – the poorest of poor stuff – to … other ornaments of the penny press.'[6]

In the autumn of 1851, while recovering in Suffolk at her uncle's farm, she 'amused [herself] by writing a critical work on the English poets' and in the new year, liberated from her engagement to Mr Bacon:

> I now began an earnest study & criticism of English poetry, kept working at my book, and began to accumulate books. I wrote my first essay in February 1852. it was on 'The Rainbow'.[7] I sent it to *Eliza Cook's Journal* & to my surprise received in a few days a proof & a guinea. This encouraged me. I wrote a tale founded on a dream (one of my best) called 'The Chateau Regnier'[8] & several others with the same result. Sent two papers to the *Magazine of Art* with the same,[9] & finding it strangely easy to get money by the pen resolved to keep it up & if possible give up music as a profession by degrees.[10]

However, not all her literary endeavours met with such easy success. In the spring of 1852 she offered her book, *Poets and Poetry of England* to a publisher and had it accepted, 'but in consequence of a question of copyright connected with the subject matter, found that it could not be published'. A letter dated Christmas Day 1851 which she wrote to Leigh Hunt while she was working on the book, asking his advice on the interpretation of stanzas of Shelley's *Adonais,* survives in the British Library.[11] Amelia was not dejected, feeling rather that she 'had gained facility & knowledge & was better prepared for the work which this publisher then offered me – viz. a translation in verse of the popular lyric poetry of Italy'.[12] That summer of 1852 she began the work of translation while at Creeting. She sent to Florence

> for a parcel of such common ballads as the poor there buy & sing, & passed all the remainder of that year laboriously occupied all the days with my [music] pupils – I had a great many – & spending my evenings at translation. I thus gained a great facility in versification & some of the poems I may say without vanity are admirable.[13]

Although she had learnt French from an early age, no doubt taught by her mother, it was only in 1851, according to her autobiographical note, that she began to learn Italian.

In February 1853 the translations were finished, and 'I took the book to the publisher, expecting to get it published immediately & to be paid at once. I was disappointed in both. His affairs were in a bad state & I had considerable difficulty in getting my money.' This time she was indeed dejected: 'When it was finished I was very ill from overfatigue of every kind.' Her disappointment was not simply in a commission to which she had devoted a year of her life not coming to fruition, but in the difficulty of obtaining payment. After failing to gain an organist's post in 1852 in any of the three churches to which she had applied, she had pinned her hopes on a writing career by which she could support herself financially. Literary criticism and translation had no doubt seemed a better prospect than poems and stories. One or two examples survive of her translations from Italian.[14] The book on *Poets and Poetry of England* which remained unpublished may well have been the basis for two anthologies which were published many years later with extensive critical notes.[15]

During the spring of 1853 she was 'yet on the sofa, very feeble & unwell, when I received a visit from a cousin and her governess who were going to Paris for a month to improve their accent & see that beautiful city'. It is possible that the cousin was Matilda, but there is no means of knowing, as the diary to which Amelia refers in her autobiographical note does not appear to have survived. 'On my return,' she adds, 'wrote the tale of "Annette" & ventured on sending it to *Chambers* [sic] *Journal*; when to my delight & surprise it was accepted. For this tale I received £9, & from this moment resolved to be an author.'[16]

No doubt it was not only the payment, far more than she had previously received for any story, but the standing of the journal that pleased her. *Chambers's Journal* had been published by the brothers William and Robert Chambers since 1832, beginning a new series in 1851. The essays and tales therein were almost all published anonymously. It continued in publication until 1859.

Over the next three years Amelia was to contribute ten other stories to *Chambers's Journal*, and tales or essays to various other popular magazines, including the *Literary World, Eliza Cook's Journal, Chambers's Repository of Tracts*, the *Illustrated Magazine of Art*, the *Magazine of Art, Household Words*, the *Art Journal*, the *Ladies' Companion*, the *Family Friend, Sharpe's London Magazine* and the *Illustrated London News,* and 'made a great deal of money' or so it seemed to a twenty-four year old. Her contributions to *Household Words* are more extensive than is often recognised. In the index to the magazine issued by the University of Toronto Press[17] only *The Patagonian Brothers*[18] is ascribed to Amelia, but in the Somerville archive there is a proof copy of *The First Poor Traveller's Story* with extensive alterations in her hand, with the effect of reducing the length.[19] Moreover Amelia writes in her letter to Edward Abbott that her later compilations *Miss Carew* (1865) and *M. Maurice* (1873) 'contain all the grim stories contributed to Dickens's Christmas Nos. – which, I believe, were reprinted in America under Mr. Dickens's name – a great error. For many years he relied upon me for his annual ghost story.'[20]

Modest success in print and growing financial independence brought Amelia to greater maturity in another respect. The 'quiet, lonely child' of her autobiographical note, and the teenage tomboy of Matilda's memoir had given way to a young woman at home with a wider range of friends, making the acquaintance of other writers and journalists on equal terms. She records that on her return to London in 1853 from an autumn holiday at Creeting:

> I was introduced by Miss Meteyard to my dear & valued friends, the family of the Du Bois, then resident at Hampstead. I became a constant & welcome guest & there formed the acquaintance of my kind friends, Mr and Mrs Stirling Coyne. All this winter [1853/54] I ventured in all seasons up to the pleasant house bordering on the heath & cemented a friendship with Etty du Bois, the invalid daughter, which has ever since been a happiness to me & which I trust may last my lifetime.[21]

Miss Meteyard can be identified as Eliza Meteyard (1816–79), who had moved to London from Norfolk in 1842 and had become a regular contributor of fiction and social articles to *Chambers's Journal, Eliza Cook's Journal* and *Household Words*. Her novel, *Struggles for Fame*, had been serialised in *Tait's Journal* in 1840 and reprinted in 1845. Joseph Stirling Coyne (1808–68) was an Irish writer who had forsaken a legal career for one in journalism and writing for the stage. He had met with considerable success on the Dublin stage before coming to London in 1836 and had joined the staff of the *Morning Gazette*, the first cheap daily paper in London. He was involved in the establishment of *Punch*, and contributed to the first issue. He also became the drama critic on the *Sunday Times*. It is easy to see why Amelia would value the friendship of Eliza Meteyard and Stirling Coyne, who had established themselves in the literary world to which she aspired.

It is somewhat less easy to identify the Du Bois family, but Amelia's friends may well have been the widow and family of Edward Du Bois (1774–1850), of Swiss descent, who was also a regular contributor to popular periodicals, and editor first of the *Monthly Mirror* and later of the *Lady's Magazine*. In 1833 he had been appointed Treasurer and Secretary of the Metropolitan Lunacy Commission, and the existence of a letter to the Commissioners in the Somerville archive[22] reinforces this identification. He left a widow and three sons, as well as the daughter, Etty.

Among the diverse literary essays to which Amelia turned her hand in the mid-1850s, when she was beginning to enjoy the society of such friends, it is intriguing to find three small books of etiquette not listed in any catalogue of her publications. They were published anonymously, and it is only the survival of a document, signed in her own hand, in the Routledge archive in University College London,[23] in which she sells her copyright in them, that identifies them as hers. These are *Etiquette for Ladies and Etiquette for Gentlemen*, with the *Ballroom Guide*. The assignation of copyright to Routledge is dated 15 July 1864, but the only publications which match the titles assigned were first published between 1855 and 1857, to judge from the accession dates of the British Library copies, and since this was the period during which Amelia was writing for women's magazines and other journals of a social nature the identification seems probable, although it cannot be proved. It is amusing to read, in *Etiquette for Ladies*:

> An afternoon at home is one of the necessities of London life. The distances are so enormous that but for this institution it would be virtually impossible to see anything of one's friends … It is not necessary to have more than two species of edibles to offer; and it

will generally be found more convenient to have only two things, such as cake and bread and butter, so you can hand them round simultaneously.[24]

Her comments on dress are of particular interest: 'A well-conceived toilette speaks for us at once, and consciously or unconsciously impresses everyone we meet … A woman has now … the power of impressing her own individuality on the dress she wears.' *Etiquette for Gentlemen*[25] holds equally forthright advice:

> Always negotiate with a lady *viva voce*, when you can. A woman does not like love-making by the intervention of pen and ink … Do not tyrannize over your mistress by your jealousies. You must not behave like a wronged man, if she dances with another, or is seen taking a walk with a male friend. All this is sheer barbarism, and it is one of the curses of English society.

Perhaps she had her own unhappy engagement in mind.

By the spring of 1854, Amelia writes, 'I had now imbibed the passion for travel, & this year… besought my father to let me visit the Rhine. We formed a party of five and visited all the most interesting Belgian cities, the Rhine, Baden, Paris, &c.'[26] The diary of this tour does not survive, and the names of the five in the party are not known. We do know, however, that she went with a letter of introduction from Mrs Du Bois to a M. Emile Stéger of Paris. In Emile Stéger, she says, she 'gained the dearest & most intimate of friends'. This friendship blossomed that autumn while she was staying at Westerfield: 'Every Tuesday brought me his letter, & every Wednesday I replied. I used to go out & meet the postman in the road when I expected them.'

On her return to England, she writes, 'I resolved to do something better than mere tales, & wished to write a novel.' Novel writing began not in London but in Suffolk, on her annual visit to the home of Matilda and her parents. Amelia describes that visit with enthusiasm:

> Came down to Suffolk for my annual visit & happening, for the first time in my life, to spend a few days at the house of an uncle at Westerfield of whose family I knew but little, I there mentioned my wish, & was so incited by my cousin Milly, that I forthwith began it on my return to Creeting. Here I wrote the first six chapters of 'My Brother's Wife'. The cholera was now raging in London, & when we left Creeting this Westerfield uncle kindly consented to let me stay with him till the violence of the disease

abated. Here we staid two months, & happy months they were for me. I gained four sisters in my four cousins, & my heart, closed from all young affections & youthful society in my childhood, now opened to the sweet friendship of relationship. I wrote everyday, and as each chap [*sic*] was completed, read it aloud. We spent our evenings in reading and music.[27]

Matilda, who was six years younger than Amelia, describes this same visit:

It was a somewhat alarming outbreak of cholera that gave us the society of our cousin and her mother for many weeks in the old manor house with my brothers and sisters ... Perhaps Amy and her mother never spent happier, more careless days. The warm harvest weather admitted of out-of door life ... She rode, drove, rambled, rusticated, the life and idol of the party.[28]

Matilda writes of following this period of 'close companionship' with six months in London for her education, during which Amelia gave her piano lessons. She writes with nostalgia of the Sunday evenings at the house of the Stirling Coynes, when the children acted in plays and charades produced by Amelia. Curiously, Amelia does not mention Matilda at this point, but writes that she was accompanied on her return to London by 'my young and dear cousin Alfreda. Passed the winter and entered this spring of 1855. She [Alfreda] studied drawing, I wrote my novel, and as before kept reading it to the little circle every night.'[29] Amelia was writing only six months later, and could hardly have forgotten which cousin had been staying in Wharton Street, whereas Matilda, writing many years later, may well have forgotten the year of her long visit to London.

Amelia had finished *My Brother's Wife* by the end of April 1855 and immediately began 'a child's book called *A Holiday Ramble through the North of Belgium* which occupied me only three weeks. Book was immediately accepted at a price of £40 and put in hand'.[30] By the time the proofs were ready she was again in Europe and they were posted to her in Paris. It was in fact not published until 1862, when it appeared under the title *Sights and Stories*.[31] It is interesting to note that it was printed by the distinguished printer Emily Faithfull, who established her press in Great Coram Street 'for the employment of women'.

Amelia departed for Paris in June 1855 with her father to visit the Exhibition, and remained there a month. At some point she was joined by her friend Fanny Sweeting, and her father apparently returned to England, for she tells us that after a month in Paris:

> We passed a week at an auberge, a farmhouse at Monthéry near St
> Michel, about 24 miles from Paris. F. Sweeting, Emilie & Emile
> Stéger & myself were the party. We spent a jolly time. Every day
> we went out to the forest of Genevieve or to the ruined Tour de
> Montery [*sic*] & lying in the shade, smoked & chatted, till the sun
> began to decline. We breakfasted at 11, dined at 6, went to bed at
> 10, lived well and enjoyed ourselves & were thoroughly happy.
> From here Fanny & I went down to … Burgundy & spent a week
> at the old chateau of M. Gauthey de la Flaulière, a gentleman of
> fortune & a considerable vine grower. Here we were very happy
> … Made an excursion to a ruined Gothic Chapel in a wood fifteen
> miles away; had lots of champagne & were very happy.[32]

From there the two friends 'started for home, going round by the Lake
of Geneva to the Rhine'. In three days they travelled by rail to Chalons,
by steamer to Lyons, by diligence to Geneva and Vevey, by 'private little
voiture' to Basle. 'We had a pleasant voiturier, a pair of good horses, light
hearts & lighter purses. Regretted not to have the command of more
money … Fribourg so delighted me that I resolved to write of it, & begin
the first scenes of my next novel there.' Amelia was eagerly trying new
experiences and her attraction to Emile Stéger must have heightened her
enjoyment. 'Began my new novel [*The Ladder of Life*] on August 12th but
in consequence of many delays progressed but slowly. In the autumn
came down to Westerfield.'[33]

Thus ends Amelia's autobiographical memoir written at the age of
twenty-four. No later account gives so vivid a picture of her personality:
hardworking, ambitious, the prospect of a successful career as a writer
bringing elation and excitement; vivacious and convivial, with a
growing circle of friends and a particular fondness for Emile Stéger;
enjoying the new experiences which continental travel afforded. The list
of 'studies' which she adds at the end of her memoir reveals a
remarkable breadth of interests in 1855, and marks her out as a
thoroughly modern woman: 'perspective, fencing, oilpainting, pistol-
shooting, riding, smoking, mathematics; begin German'. The memoir
was apparently intended to be written up more fully, for at one point she
adds in parenthesis 'Here describe Westerfield Hall & all the circle. For
this purpose collect letters written to E. du Bois, to Miss Meteyard &
others.' Unfortunately none of these letters survives.

On her return to England in August 1855 she found *My Brother's
Wife*[34] published and popular '& my name figuring on placards, in
newspaper criticisms, &c. &c'. The reviews were encouraging: 'It is one
of those tales, full of incident and passion, which excite general interest,

and which entrance the reader not less by the vivacity of the action represented than by the eloquence and enthusiasm of the narrator,' wrote the *Civil Service Gazette*.[35] 'A new story, told in a new way, by a new author,' wrote *The Globe*, adding:

> This author, were it not for the name of Amelia B. Edwards on the title page, we should pronounce to be a young man who has travelled, read, and experienced more of life in its widest sense, than the generality. We should presume the author to be of the male sex as much from the absence of certain literary characteristics as from the presence of others which are undoubtedly masculine, though they might be possessed by a woman with advantage. The construction of the story is good … Even those who scorn railway volumes … will do well to ask for 'My Brother's Wife'.[36]

Little wonder Amelia was pleased with her reception in print.

It may be appropriate here to comment on the relationship between Amelia and Matilda in later years. Matilda describes a visit in company with Amelia in 1869 or 1870 to their Aunt Maria at Claydon: 'I wish I had noted down our conversations during these strolls, never to be renewed on native soil … Many holidays we spent in after life together both at home and abroad.'[37] The only holiday abroad for which there is evidence that Matilda accompanied Amelia is a tour to Rome in 1857, although it has to be said that in such records of holidays in the 1860s as survive, Amelia does not name her travelling companions. It appears that their association was never again as close as in the 1850s. 'Not that we ever lost sight of each other for any length of time,' Matilda writes, ' She ever seemed so much more robust than myself … that … I never contemplated the probability of surviving her. And of course,' she adds pointedly, 'busiest of the busy ever, she was not very accessible. Habits of strict seclusion grew upon her with advancing years. Having from childhood arranged the plan of her daily life, she found it difficult indeed to diverge from routine.' Matilda's essay on Amelia's early life, and her note on Amelia in *Mid-Victorian Memories*, both contain thin strands of disapproval, within a web of eulogy:

> Had she attained the Psalmist's three score and ten years, quite certainly her next passion, Egyptology, would have been thrown to the winds and one or two other subjects as enthusiastically taken up. Who knows? She might have thrown herself heart and soul

into the Women's Rights agitation… Not only might we have had in her a powerful statesman and party leader, but a lady Prime Minister.[38]

Amelia's attitude to Matilda likewise seems to have been ambivalent. In spite of her early outpouring of affection for the Westerfield family which shared the birth-pangs of her first novel, she dissociated herself from her cousin in later life, when Matilda herself gained a reputation as a writer.

Fig. 5: Matilda Bentham-Edwards, Amelia's cousin, from Matilda's book Mid-Victorian Memories *(John Murray, 1919).*

Understandably, she was irked by the popular confusion in the public mind between herself and her cousin and repeatedly tried to dispel it. In a letter to *The Academy* dated 6 February 1882 she comments on Henry Morley's review of *A Thousand Miles up the Nile*:

I am sorry that Professor Morley, instead of merely noting the confusion which is supposed still to prevail ... did not use this opportunity to say something which might have aided the public in distinguishing between two writers whose opinions, convictions and lines of study have literally nothing in common.[39]

Notes

[1] SCO Edwards 438; a copy survives in the Somerville archive at SCO Edwards 351.

[2] Matilda Betham-Edwards, 'Amelia B. Edwards: her childhood and early life', *New England Magazine,* New Series, 7, 5 (Boston, MA, January 1893), p. 550.

[3] Betham-Edwards, 'Amelia B. Edwards: her childhood and early life', p. 560.

[4] SCO Edwards 438.

[5] SCO Edwards 439.

[6] SCO Edwards 438.

[7] *Eliza Cook's Journal,* 8, 204 (26 March 1853), pp. 339a–41a.

[8] *Eliza Cook's Journal,* 8, 207 (16 April 1853), pp. 387a–90b.

[9] They were 'The Brilliant Ring, in four parts' and 'The Painter of Pisa' in the *Illustrated Magazine of Art,* 1 (1853), pp. 49a–111b; 330a–31b.

[10] SCO Edwards 439.

[11] BL MS Add 38111 f.32.

[12] SCO Edwards 439.

[13] SCO Edwards 439.

[14] See for example, SCO Edwards 493: a translation of Dante's Sonnet 85.

[15] Amelia B. Edwards (ed.), *A Poetry Book of Modern Poets* (London: Longman, 1879); and Amelia B. Edwards (ed.), *A Poetry Book of Elder Poets* (London: Longman, 1879); see also Chapter 10, pp. 157–58.

[16] SCO Edwards 439.

[17] *Household Words: A weekly journal 1850–1859 conducted by Charles Dickens: table of contents, list of contributors and their contributions, based on the Household Words Office Book in the Morris L. Parrish Collection of Victorian novelists, Princeton University Library* (Toronto & Buffalo, NY: University of Toronto Press, 1973).

[18] Published in *Household Words,* 17, 494 (23 January 1858), pp. 126b–31b.

[19] SCO Edwards 522; it was published in *Household Words* (Extra Christmas Number 1854), pp. 1–10.

[20] SCO Edwards 351.

[21] SCO Edwards 439.

[22] SCO Edwards 114.

[23] UCL, Routledge Contracts 1850–78, 1, 295, dated 15 July 1864.

[24] *Etiquette for Ladies in Public and Private* (London: Warne, rev. edn, 1855).

[25] *Etiquette for Gentlemen, being a manual of minor social ethics and customary observances* (London: Knight, 1857).

[26] SCO Edwards 439.

[27] SCO Edwards 439.

[28] Betham-Edwards, 'Amelia B. Edwards: her childhood and early life', p. 562.

[29] SCO Edwards 439.

[30] Ibid.

[31] *Sights and Stories: being some account of a holiday tour through the north of Belgium, by Amelia B. Edwards, author of 'Hand and Glove'...&c, &c.* (London: Victoria Press, 1862); see also Appendix 3, pp. 281–308.

[32] SCO Edwards 439.

[33] SCO Edwards 439.

[34] Amelia B. Edwards, *My Brother's Wife* (London: Hurst & Blackett, 1855). In the case of this and the other novels, an account of their reception in the press is given in context, but for a synopsis and analysis see Appendix 3, pp. 282–84.

[35] SCO Edwards 434.3.

[36] SCO Edwards 434.5.

[37] Betham-Edwards, 'Amelia B. Edwards: her childhood and early life', p. 563.

[38] Matilda Betham-Edwards, 'Amelia Blandford Edwards (1831–1890)' [*sic*], in *Mid-Victorian Memories* (London: John Murray, 1919), p. 115.

[39] SCO Edwards 565.

❖ 4 ❖

Successful author, European traveller, 1856–59

Although Amelia now saw her career as that of a novelist, she continued to write for popular magazines, and in June 1856 she was contracting with G. Routledge & Co. for the publication of a school textbook, for which she was paid £18.[1] This was *A Summary of English History*.[2] In the preface she sets out the claims of history in a way which does not altogether ring true:

> The poorest as well as the richest, the lowliest as well as the loftiest, may learn from … the perusal of our English history … such a lesson of patience, courage and honest endeavour as will make their task of life easier to support under adversity, and teach them better to employ the advantages which Providence may have entrusted to their hands for the benefit of their fellow-creatures. The History of England is the history of progressive refinement.[3]

Amelia was nothing if not pragmatic, however, and this was no doubt what was expected of schoolbooks. She has no inhibitions in passing judgement on monarch or rebel: 'Thomas à Becket … was a man of inferior birth and brilliant talents who loved power and splendour better than anything in the world.'[4] Henry VIII 'upon life placed no value and for law he entertained no reverence'.[5] Chartism 'was formed in the year 1839, chiefly among the working classes, for the furtherance of a scheme of universal suffrage which they imagined was to redress all their grievances, and which they proceeded to enforce … with guns, pikes and other weapons'.[6]

That summer, one of the tasks which occupied Amelia's time was the preparation of text to accompany an exhibition of portraits of Mary Queen of Scots in the Archaeological Institute the following year. On 15 June 1856 she wrote to her mother from a friend's house in London: 'I am obliged to go down to Pall Mall on Saturday morning, to select the Photographs for part 3 that Caldesi may print in advance.'[7] The ensuing publication, now extremely rare, appeared in 1857.[8]

In the same year Amelia produced a work of an entirely different nature: *Home and Foreign Lyrics: a dramatic entertainment*.[9] This was the libretto for a presentation by an impresario, Miss Julia St George, 'consisting of the characters she has met with, and representative selections of the music she has heard on her travels in search of this entertainment'. The lyrics show the diversity of Amelia's style and her love of impersonation. Amelia herself thought the production worthy of mention in her letter of 1881 to Edward Abbott, writing that it was 'performed in every principal town of Great Britain'.[10] The verses do not appear to justify her judgement on their own; the musical accompaniment must have added significantly to the performance. The programme begins with Sappho on the rock from which 'the impassioned poetess' threw herself, with stanzas such as:

> Fare thee well, bright world of song
> Take my latest, fondest sigh!
> God of love, thine utmost wrong
> Human grief can yet defy.
> Pluto, open wide thy portals!
> Bear me, sea, to thine immortals!
>   Sappho only asks to die![11]

It ends with a 'characteristic English song' of one verse:

> Oh, wot can I do but die,
> All onder the willer tree
> For Sall doant care a jot for I
> But I still care for she.
> Yer heart I am sure is just
> Like a colly-flower run to seed
> for you doant care if mine do bust
> Thow I hope you'll be hanged for the deed.[12]

Trivial though this may seem, it became a popular production. It was first performed as a Christmas entertainment on 24 December 1856 in Liverpool and was still touring the provinces in July 1857. The *Sunday Times'* reviewer wrote that 'the poetry throughout the entertainment is flowing and graceful, and does great credit to the fair authoress',[13] while *The Era* yet more extravagantly claimed that the libretto was 'of very great literary merit'.[14]

Amelia's second novel, *The Ladder of Life*,[15] was published on 8 January 1857, and received modest reviews in the *Ladies' Companion*, the *Waverley Journal*, and *Bell's Life in London*.[16] According to *The Dispatch* on 2 February:

> This story, of the emotional order … is far superior in the plot and execution to the generality of dreary novellettes on which the lady writers of America have, for the most part, bestowed so much tediousness … It reminds us of the 'Consuelo' of Georges Sand, for the grand passionate genius of music breathes throughout the latter half … Its fault is an excess of the romantic element…[17]

while the *Sunday Times* commented that 'Miss Edwards is particularly felicitous in her pictures of Swiss life. … She writes with an ease and a freshness of style which give a wonderful charm to her work'.[18]

In the second week of January 1857, Amelia departed once again for Europe. Her extensive diary of this tour has fortunately survived in the Edwards Archive at Somerville College.[19] She left London on 16 January with 'Middy'. One hesitates to identify 'Middy' with her cousin Matilda Betham-Edwards, since the references to 'Middy' in the diary do not seem altogether appropriate to a girl of twenty – Matilda's age at the time. It is clear from the diary that Amelia felt in some way responsible for 'Middy'. On 23 January she writes: 'Middy very unwell. Kept her in bed all morning.' On 21 February she writes: 'Invited to tea with Miss Cushman, but Middy too poorly to go.' There are even more surprising references to 'baby', apparently referring to 'Middy': on 30 January, while travelling to Pisa by coach 'the door flew open & we lost the baby's railway wrapper & our store of oranges.' On 7 March she writes: 'Baby very poorly all day'; and on 23 March: 'Middy too poorly to go out. Staid [*sic*] in all the morning.' She went out with three friends in the afternoon, however, and 'got home to baby at 5.30'. On 11 March, returning from a visit to Rocca di Papa and 'in great danger from rocky roads on the edge of precipices' she records: 'Middy very alarmed' and when on 18 March they visit the 'private room' in the Museum of Natural History in Florence, Middy is 'greatly astonished'. If, as seems almost inescapable, 'Middy' is indeed Matilda, then it would seem that Amelia regarded her as unusually young and innocent for her age. It is interesting to speculate whether she was mothering Matilda and 'baby' was a term of endearment, or whether she found her cousin immature and her poor health a handicap. If the latter, it might help to explain her reluctance to maintain their early 'close companionship' in later life. That 'Middy' is indeed her cousin Matilda gains cogency, however, from the fact that Amelia, in her preface to her children's book about Cervantes (see p. 57) which she dedicates to Matilda, cites an incident in the Italian Tyrol one Easter Sunday which coincides with her diary entry for Easter Sunday 1857.

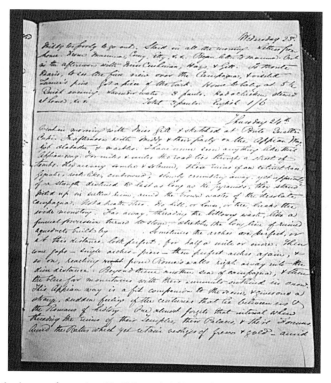

Fig. 6: A page from Amelia Edwards' diary, for 23 and 24 March 1857.

Both Amelia and Middy were ill on the crossing from Dover, but Amelia nevertheless enjoyed the 'capital supper' which Emile Stéger had prepared for them at 15 Rue de Kevise in Paris. They spent a week there before travelling overnight by rail to Lyon. From there they went by diligence to Chambéry, a 'very uncomfortable journey & objection-able company.' By 27 January they had reached the foot of the Mont Cenis Pass and prepared for the crossing. 'We went into a great rambling inn while our baggage was moved to the covered sledges. In the kitchen we all warmed ourselves, passengers of every class.' There follows a graphic account of the journey:

> Then entered the sledges past midnight and began the ascent ... to the grating, dreary wine [*sic*] of the sledges on the snow. Passengers of all classes together. Dreadfully hot & dark & miserable. Then we reached the top as morning dawned. Saw the dawn come up on our side while it was yet night & stars on the other. Peak after peak rose up & flushed first a warm amber & white, & then rose pink. (28 January)

They reached Turin and thence by rail to Genoa, by coach to Pisa, and on to Leghorn, setting sail for Civita Vecchia on 4 February. There they met 'the Blaikies', who accompanied them the next day to Rome. One can only speculate whether these were Alexander and Ruth Blaikie, both artists; Alexander was exhibiting at the Royal Academy and at the British Institution at this period. At four o'clock on 5 February 'we entered the gates of Rome. Passed St Peters, the Castle of St Angelo & the Tiber for the first time. Got greatly excited. Tried three hotels before we could find a bed. Came to Hotel d'Amérique. Called on Miss Cushman & dined with them' (5 February).

The month spent in Rome was to have a significant impact on Amelia. Rome was to provide the backcloth for much of the action of *Barbara's History*. It is clear from her diary that she was greatly moved and impressed by the monuments and even more by the paintings and sculptures. She also made the acquaintance of a number of British and American ladies who were residing in Rome at the time. This was no doubt the beginning of her lifelong affection for Americans. Charlotte Cushman, the tragic actress, with whom they had dined on their first night in Rome, was American by birth but had lived and worked in England in the 1840s and had taken the critics by storm. She was known to Mrs Ellen Braysher, the older woman who was to provide a home for Amelia after her parents' death, and was, with Amelia and Ellen Braysher, a member of the circle which gathered on Sunday evenings at the London home of the artist, Samuel Laurence.[20] Of two others mentioned repeatedly in Amelia's diary of her Rome visit, Emily Hays and Mary Duggan, little is known. Mary Duggan may have been the daughter of the Mr Duggan who set Amelia's early songs to music in 1854–58,[21] and Emily Hays may have been a sister of the Miss Hays on whose behalf Mrs Ellen Braysher sought a meeting with George Sand in Paris, the Matilda Hays who was also one of the Laurence circle.[22]

Amelia and Middy soon settled into 'nice little apartments'. It was to become Amelia's practice, when arriving in a new place for an extended stay, to book a room in a hotel for a night or two while looking for more modest accommodation. The routine of the day was to call on one or other of their acquaintances, or to await their calls, and to visit one or two of the sights of Rome together. They sometimes dined out, but more often bought food in the markets and ate it in their lodgings, or bought 'carry-out' meals from a local trattoria. They lived frugally and every penny was accounted for. Throughout the tour Amelia kept careful accounts, listing each day what she had spent, and recording visits to the bank to draw money; on 28 February, when she reviewed her travelling expenses, she found that the journey from London to Rome had cost £36. 4s. 4d and three weeks in Rome had cost them £20, including doctor's fees. They had £69 in hand.

Amelia records her impressions of the monuments, by no means uncritically, in a literary style, quite distinct from that of the abbreviated notes recording the details of daily routine. Of the Temple of Vesta she writes:

> In the midst of a dreary open space littered with straw, refuse & the debris of a neighbouring market & surrounding stables stands this little temple of Vesta. All that remains of its antique beauty is a circle of slender Corinthian columns. It has been patched here & there. A shabby little sentry box of a chapel has been built up within the circuit of the pillars … Still the imperishable grace & beauty reigns there still. Dirt, neglect, Catholicism cannot deface or degrade it. (10 February)

Of that quarter of the city she writes: 'Every inch of ground is history … but the life we encounter is melancholy, poor & dirty, the shops expose only offensive food, secondhand goods, or dusty worm-eaten furniture. A few steps farther & we enter the Corso – we pass the Capitol – we are in the centre of palaces, of wealth, of luxury & of art' (10 February).

They also spent happy days visiting artists' studios. On 12 February they visited a Mr Gibson's studio. He was working on the bust of a Miss Gill, and they made her acquaintance; she later accompanied them on some of their excursions. Here too Amelia was introduced to a Miss Hosmer. On 18 February they visited the studio of a Mr Litton, whose life story clearly held a fascination for her:

> A very clever young man of interesting appearance. Began life as a poor boy. Tried house painting and heraldic painting, & so by steps to art. Came to Rome & lived on chestnuts. He paints on what he calls a system of prismatic colouring … but his pictures are very dreamy, harmonious, singularly mellow. His Venetian views a combination of Canaletto & Claude … Long discussion upon *Tone* at Mr Litton's. I was the only person present who could define it. My view of it was that tone brought all the colours together, as a senate under a President, or a council under a King.

On 19 February she describes a further visit to the artists' quarter:

> Went to some studios in the Via Magritta – a melancholy little street full of stables & coach-houses & studios, hung across with

lines of washed linen & bridged over by a melancholy roofed gallery with bluish windows like the Bridge of Sighs. Up here congregate a multitude of artists & bad smells.

They visited three studios here: those of an Italian sculptor named Rosetti; an English landscape painter in oils named Mr Dessoulary, 'very communicative & obliging. Rather violent in colour & not very good'; and a Mr Holme Cardewell who had 'a very choice Venus Victrix in hand, & a charming Sabrina. Very gentlemanly & obliging.' None of these artists is remembered today, but talking with artists was clearly an important element in Amelia's visit to Rome.

On 15 February Amelia felt ill enough to warrant summoning an English doctor, but she recovered in time to enjoy the carnival of Mardi Gras which she describes vividly:

> The chief fun & excitement is among the English. The poorer Italians have no spirit for the Carnival, the nobler are too indolent & too haughty. It is the proud, cold English who breathe & enjoy the Carnival madness – who shower the confetti – pelt with bouquets – & casting utterly aside their grave island gravity, revel in liberties, impertinances & personalities … Some carriages are full of young men, some full of ladies, & the ladies pelt the men & the men the ladies.

On 20 February Amelia and Middy visited the Protestant burial ground to see Shelley's grave:

> Found Miss Hays & Miss Cushman there, to my surprise & somewhat to my annoyance … I would rather have been utterly alone. I beheld it with a new and unexpected sensation – I may truly say with the *first* emotion I have felt in Rome … I could have knelt down and kissed the stone. I would have done it, had I been alone, were it only in memory of the strange worship I once paid to the memory of that man. Much of my intense admiration, much of that untiring and all of that insatiable study that I gave to his works is past – but to that passion, to my earnest study of his poetry, I owe more than is perhaps known even to myself.

After this uncharacteristic confession, she adds: 'Made a capital little sketch in pencil, which I have since spoilt at home.' On returning to their lodgings, she 'wrote diary, read part of *Adonais*, and Keats' *Ode on a Grecian Urn*'.

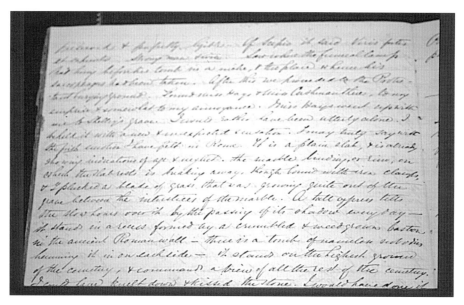

Fig. 7: A page from Amelia Edwards' diary, for 20 February 1857, describing her visit to Shelley's grave in Rome.

The wish to be alone was felt not only when contemplating Shelley's grave: on 6 February, their first morning in Rome, Amelia writes:

> the glorious view from the Pincio gave me great delight, but I find it absolutely a necessity that I should be alone when drinking in the sights & glories of a great locality – the admiration, the exclamations & the enthusiasms of others worries me.

It may be that for her companions a visit to Rome was simply a holiday, but for Amelia it was an emotional experience, a realisation of history, poetry and images that she had studied in books and in galleries, and was now visiting *in situ*.

Although her note book was used primarily as a diary in which to record daily progress on the tour, Amelia also used it increasingly as the tour progressed to record scenes or incidents which do not necessarily relate to a particular day but summarise impressions, which may be composite. Thus between the entries for 12 and 13 February there is a section headed 'A street in Rome' followed by another headed 'A Roman family of rank', and between the entries for 20 and 21 February there is a passage entitled 'Dining in Italy'. By far the most interesting of these interpolations are two untitled passages in which Amelia is clearly making rough notes for the novel which was to be published as *Barbara's*

History. These come between the entries for 3 and 8 April and amount to a detailed plan of the novel (see Appendix 3, pp. 291–92).

Amelia sometimes records the books which she was reading while abroad: on 7 March she 'began *Westward Ho!* & did not like it'. On 16 March she obtained, perhaps from a circulating library, *The Tenant of Wildfell Hall* but the next day she writes: 'changed my book for *Wuthering Heights'*.

Before leaving Rome Amelia and Middy spent a day at Tivoli on 1 March, driving there in two carriages with Miss Hosmer, Miss Hays, Miss Gill, Mr Wood and another, unnamed, gentleman. They explored the ruins, Amelia did a little sketching, and they 'dined in the shade of the circular temple very merrily.' They came home late, and Amelia 'told ghost stories all the way.' Then, after three further days of sightseeing, they left for Albano on 5 March, not perhaps without a pang, but their new friends would not be parted from them for long: Miss Hosmer and Miss Hays came over to Albano to visit them three days later. They 'would not go out', having had a stormy journey, so they all 'lunched merrily in our room off tongue, biscuit, figs, bread & butter, Marsala, coffee & cake. Miss Hosmer & I played Tiddleywinks & I lost 9 bajecchi. Went out to see them off.'

On 11 March Amelia and Middy went to Nenci via Rocca di Papa. 'Never saw I such a steep, dreary, poverty-stricken town as R. di P. – dirty, but very picturesque … Street so precipitous that I was quite nervous … In great danger from rocky roads coming home.'

They finally left Rome for Florence on 14 March, travelling overnight, Mr Wood seeing them off. On arriving at Florence, Amelia found a letter from Emile Stéger waiting for her. She had written to him on 8 February, and she now replied on 1 April. She was clearly still in frequent touch with him, though not as frequent as during their weekly exchanges of letters four years earlier. Florence delighted them as much as Rome had done: 'Saw the Grand duke, & also saw more fine horses & handsome equipages than I have seen before in this country – Young fellows on fine horses race in the meadows to display their skill' (16 March). They revelled in the treasures of the Uffizzi, staying until the gallery closed. Amelia was fascinated by the self-portraits: 'Deeply interesting to study these portraits of painters by themselves, & to trace in the manner of the work the little vanities or stern principles of the man' (18 March).

After a week in Florence they travelled 'a dreary journey across the wildest & most desert tract of the Appenines' to Bologna. Amelia comments that 'at every village a troop of the very young & the very old surrounded the doors [of the carriage] begging and following the vehicle for one or two miles' with 'importunate cries'. At one point the road was so rough that the loaded diligence could not pass. 'Then came a ridiculous sight. All the passengers were carried. I was absolutely taken pick-a-back by a stout merry young fellow who staggered under my weight & was several times obliged to set me down. I roared with laughter till I nearly fell off' (23 March). Clearly, she had not lost the sense of fun for which she had been known at Westerfield. They travelled from Bologna to Modena and Mantua, and by rail to Padua and Verona. 'Made the acquaintance of a young Venetian, Signor Silvio Bono, with whom I conversed all the way, much to the improvement of my French' (25 March).

The first day in Venice must have been a disappointment. 'Dreadfully wet day. Spent the whole seeking for lodgings, going to the Banker, &c, &c' (26 March), but the remainder of their stay was fine and Amelia devoted herself to the monuments and galleries with her usual enthusiasm and sense of humour: of a mosaic over one of the doors of St Mark's depicting the death of the saint and the removal of his body from the East she writes that 'in one of these a Musulman is depicted holding his nose, so I suppose the saint really did die in the odour of sanctity' (28 March). On 30 March they went to the Fenice Theatre to see an opera by Verdi ('Audience unnecessarily enthusiastic') followed by a ballet ('Very effective & well done'). Amelia was impressed by the magnificence of the theatre but not by the behaviour of the audience:

> Just between the two [performances] there was a shower of lithographs from the top boxes – portraits of three or four of the principal performers & the composer in the middle. These were eagerly caught up by everyone who could get one. A droll scene of excitement & noise, which would not be possible in any but a very mediocre English house. Between the acts lemonade & orangeade at 6d a glass is handed round!! this at the Opera House in Venice!

A robust scepticism was always part of Amelia's approach to religious relics, and never more so than in Venice, where they saw 'a pretended page of the Gospel of St Mark said to be written by himself … Also the knife used by Jesus Christ at the last supper' (3 April). Her reaction to Titian's house is somewhat more romantic: 'Nothing to see when we got there but a bare dismantled building occupied by a poor builder; brought away a piece of the balustrade' (3 April). At the Lido she was particularly affected by the tombs of the Jews 'banished even in death … I stayed by some to put aside the brambles & spell out the names & dates of those which were yet legible … Here, thought I, may lie what was once the dust of Shylock!' (5 April).

They left Venice on 8 April and travelled north through Riva, Trento, Botzen and Brixen to Innsbruck where, 'being Easter Sunday, expected to see something striking, but was greatly disappointed' (13 April). Her account is here illustrated with sketches.

They travelled down the Rhine, which 'looked very charming in its garb of pink & white spring blossoms. Quite a new aspect of the noble river to me, being my third journey upon its waters.' When they reached Brussels Amelia met her friend Fanny Sweeting and 'took her out for the day', leaving for Dover on 25 April.

Although there are records of later travels in the same note book, the diary of the 1857 tour is unique in its spontaneity, its intimacy and its personal detail. The later records, for 1859, 1862, 1871 and 1872 are mainly descriptive of scenery and art. The diary of 1857 gives a vivid picture of Amelia as a capable young woman, arranging travel tickets, engaging porters, finding acceptable accommodation, living frugally, managing a budget, conversing in French, German and Italian, making friends in Rome with American women and other English women, and looking after a younger woman whose frequent periods of poor health must have been an inconvenience as well as a worry to her. Her intense interest in art and her love of sketching are always evident. Her descriptions of scenery are the descriptions of an artist looking at a scene.

While she had been away, another of her books for children had been published. This was *The Young Marquis, or Scenes from a Reign*.[23] Although the book was noticed by the *Sunday Times*[24] and the *Ladies' Companion*,[25] it is unlikely that Amelia regarded it as a significant achievement. She later dismissed this and similar books as 'a few juvenile story and class books'.[26] It is, however, like *Sights and Stories*, a lively tale of adventure, in which the Paris of the 1780s is vividly portrayed.

Within two months of her return from Europe, Amelia appears to have been engaged as a regular contributor of a weekly column under the title of *Wanderings and Ponderings of a Man about Town*, beginning on 21 June 1857 and ending on 10 October 1858. The articles bear no attribution, but the style is Amelia's, and there seems no other explanation for their survival, systematically pasted up in a newscuttings book, along with her other papers in Somerville College.[27] Writing to Edward Abbott in 1881 she said: 'In earlier years I did my share of journalism in the way of musical, dramatic & art criticisms, reviews, leaders, &c. I was at the time on the staff of the *Saturday Review* & have done a good deal of work on the *Morning Post*. But all this ended 12 or 14 years ago.'[28] Neither the *Saturday Review* nor the *Morning Post*, however, were the vehicle for these essays, and the location has not yet been traced. The subjects of the series are extremely varied, from old

men in the public parks in the heat of summer to the sound of the muffin
bell in the suburbs as autumn comes 'and the paper ornaments in the
drawing-room fireplace are looking dull and dingy'; from the repulsive-
ness of the façades of butchers' shops to the ardour of teetotallers, of
whom she writes: 'Devoted to a more attainable end, the same organism
would effectually combat many of the social evils that affect our
happiness.' The articles are often forthright, often amusing, and
enlivened further from time to time with verses. There are numerous
literary allusions and parodies.

Before she had finished her weekly column in the guise of a 'man
about town', her third novel had been published. This was *Hand and
Glove* (1858),[29] to which she later refers, along with *My Brother's Wife*
(1855) and *The Ladder of Life* (1856), as one of 'three juvenile efforts'.[30] She
was, however, sufficiently happy with it at the time to send a copy to
Charles Dickens via a mutual friend. He acknowledged it non-
committally on 12 June, six days after its publication, writing that
'"Hand and Glove" and I are presently going down together into Kent,
there to become closely acquainted.'[31] It received considerable attention
in the press. *The Dispatch* reviewer wrote that it was 'elegantly and
forcibly told'[32] and the *Daily Telegraph* commented that it was 'original in
its character, striking in its situation'.[33] *The Athenaeum* was more critical:
'A slight but very readable and interesting story, not very sensible, but it
is romantic and easy to read ... *Hand and Glove* makes good railway
reading.'[34] It was a popular book, reprinted, no doubt in the light of the
subsequent success of *Barbara's History*, in 1865 by John Maxwell,
London, and in the same year published in a Tauchnitz edition, in their
Collection of British Authors, and in an Italian translation in 1872.[35]

Amelia's second school book, *A History of France*, was published in June
1858.[36] This was condemned unequivocally by *The Athenaeum*:

> Miss Edwards has evidently run through her task in a hurry ...
> What there is of mutilated narrative is of a most misleading
> tendency ... When dealing with recent events [she] absolutely
> forgets to notice the most important of all – that which overthrew
> the French Republic of 1848 ... We can imagine no class of persons,
> young or old, who will gain by becoming her readers.[37]

The Spectator commented that 'the writer is scarcely equal to the style of
composition adopted'.[38] Less discerning journals such as the *Ladies'
Companion*, however, were 'agreeably surprised ... an excellent and
readable little volume'.[39] The book was reprinted in 1880 in a new,

updated edition, but the supplementary material was not by Amelia, who wrote no more school books.

In December 1858 Amelia's translation of a French work, *The Adventures of Fanny Loviot*, was published.[40] The element of daring and adventure in the work was one to appeal to Amelia, and she provides a natural, colloquial translation. The *Sunday Times* commented cryptically that 'some parts of it will be read with breathless interest',[41] but the work soon sank into obscurity. It was reprinted as late as 1930, however, in the *Magazine of History* for its interest for Californian studies, the editor commenting that it 'is now very scarce – we have had to resort to the Library of Congress for a copy'.[42]

In the autumn of 1859 Amelia was again travelling in continental Europe. Unfortunately, no systematic diary of this tour survives, but in the same note book as that used for the 1857 diary there are eight pages of notes headed 'Impressions of Switzerland 1859. The Oberland, the Valais & Piedmont.'[43] The entries are in note form, and almost entirely descriptions of scenery. Personal names are sparse, and there is no indication of the identity of her travelling companions. Nevertheless, these pages give a fascinating glimpse of the impact of the Swiss countryside on Amelia. The description of watching the sunrise from the summit of the Righi on 2 October is vivid:

> Woke in the cool grey morning, & lay silently in my bed. Could see the mountains beyond the shuttered casement coming out slowly, one by one, clean, white, dead & ghostly. Presently the alphorn echoed along the corridors. Everyone sprang out of bed &, dressing hastily, ran out to the raised … ground behind the house. There we looked upon a sight surpassing words … Then the red light in the East grew brighter & wider, & a rose-hue flushed suddenly upon the snow peaks of the Schreckhorn & the Wetterhorn … After breakfast, to Kusnacht. A very easy & beautiful descent. Walked & ran nearly all the way down, buoyant with the fresh gladness of the mountain air. (2 October 1859)

She is able to convey a tingling sense of elation and excitement. Her description of an excursion to the glacier of Rosinlaui is equally vivid: 'The ice was a smooth perpendicular wall which we scaled, preceded by the guide. He with his axe cut footholds in the ice & we followed, holding hands in one long chain, & clinging against the face of the precipice' (5 October). When they were safely down, but not before, she 'made a little sketch' from the window of the inn where they rested.

As in 1857, she welcomes occasional solitude:

> The time of rest being over, I took my turn to walk [her companions were on horseback] & went on for a long distance in advance of my party. The heat was tremendous & I was heavily dressed, but the purity of the air, the sense of grandeur, & solitude, & freedom, gave me strange activity & caused me to fight fatigue & suffering. It was a strange half-savage feeling of exaltation, thus to be *alone*. (6 October)

Amelia suddenly seems older: she is no longer simply recording scenery for use in novels, nor as an *aide-memoire* for sketching; she is attempting to express in words what it felt like to be there.

On 9 October on an excursion from Kandersteg they mounted to a high plateau on horseback, and 'also hired two youths with a chair, to carry me down' from the summit of the pass, whereas the guides would be returning with the horses. At the top:

> The boys brought up the chair, the knapsacks were slung round the back & arms of it, the cloaks, books & bottles heaped on my lap, the chair hoisted, & away we went ... The next moment we were on the brink of a vertical wall we were about to descend ... The path is a mere zigzag groove, with often not even a balustrade at the side. To be carried down here where a false step, or a lurch, or an accident to the chair would have been instant destruction! It was the most agonising sensation of sickening terror that I ever experienced.

This may well be an experience to which she referred in her letter to Edward Abbott in 1881, when she wrote that she had 'nearly broken my neck once or twice'.[44]

They had a pleasant journey by carriage along the valley of the Rhone to Martigny, and there the recorded impressions end. From one of the few letters to her mother which survive, however, dated 25 October 1859,[45] we know that Amelia stayed in Paris at the Stégers' house on the return journey. She writes: 'My darling Mamma, tomorrow we leave Paris for London. I do not know yet by what train my société will make up their blessed minds to go ... at all events do not sit up for me after 12.' She adds that 'today they are all gone to Versailles & I have been all over the factories & workrooms of the Orhaus Railway Company with Stéger's brother, who is Chef de Station ... I have also been over the Hospital of Enfants trouvés & seen many things which will be very useful to me.' She was not simply a tourist, but keen to visit places which might help her in her writing. She also mentions a watch which she has bought in Paris for a friend: 'I shall tell her I got it in Geneva, as she desired. She will be all the better pleased, & I, by getting it here, have it at trade price through Stéger & can make £1 on it for myself.' Emile Stéger was treating her and Lizzie to 'a good dinner & stalls at the Opéra Comique to mark Lizzie's birthday'. She was evidently still on good terms with the Stéger family, who 'were very agreeable & hospitable & would have had me staying with them if I could'. Not all of them were acceptable company, however: 'Emilie Stéger has bored me to death since I have been in Paris,' she writes, 'fastening herself completely on me & perpetually talking of her love affairs.' One wonders whether talk of love affairs was especially unpalatable to Amelia at a time when she was the guest of one who only five years before had been her 'most intimate and dearest friend' and maybe had touched her heart.

This letter comes tantalisingly close to enabling us to identify other of Amelia's travelling companions on her Swiss tour of 1859. She writes:

> You must prepare Papa to have Lizzie & the Porteous's & Mr & Mrs Layard one evening at the end of this week, or the beginning of the next. After our long journey I being arrived at so much intimacy it would be impossible to avoid it. Indeed, Captain P. has repeatedly expressed a wish to know Papa & the rest (that is Mrs P. & her sister) are longing to see you. They call you 'the dear little woman' entirely on the faith of what Lizzie has told them.

By the end of the decade Amelia was well-established on a career as a writer, with three full-length novels to her credit. She was also becoming an experienced traveller, familiar with Paris and Rome, unattached, but with a wide circle of friends and literary acquaintances.

Notes

1 UCL, Routledge C, 1, 302.
2 *A Summary of English History from the Norman Conquest to the Present Time, with observations on the Progress of Art, Science, and Civilization ... for the use of schools* (London: G. Routledge, 1856).
3 Ibid., p. 5.
4 Ibid., p. 27.
5 Ibid., p. 44.
6 Ibid., p. 87.
7 SCO Edwards 456.

[8] *Series of Photographs from Portraits of Mary Queen of Scots* executed by Caldesi and Montecci from the collection exhibited by the Archaeological Institute, June 1857 (London: Caldesi, [1858]).

[9] SCO Edwards 526, pp. 169–80; the programme includes the libretto in full: *Miss Julia St George's Dramatic Entertainment. Miss Julia St. George will have the honour of presenting her dramatic entertainment, entitled 'Home and Foreign Lyrics'* (London: Hartmann, n.d.).

[10] SCO Edwards 351.

[11] 'Miss Julia St George's Dramatic Entertainment', p. 2.

[12] Ibid., p. 10.

[13] *Sunday Times*, 11 January 1857.

[14] *The Era*, 11 July 1857.

[15] Amelia B. Edwards, *The Ladder of Life: a heart history* (London: G. Routledge & Co. 1857).

[16] *Ladies' Companion*, February 1857, *Waverley Journal* 1857, *Bell's Life in London*, 18 January [1857].

[17] *The Dispatch*, 2 February 1857.

[18] *Sunday Times*, 18 February 1957.

[19] SCO Edwards 515; all subsequent references to the diary of 1857 are to this document, and are cited by the dates of the entries.

[20] Eliza Lynn Linton, *My Literary Life* (London: Hodder & Stoughton, 1899), p. 39.

[21] SCO Edwards 429.

[22] SCO Edwards 120. Matilda Hays had written a romantic novel (*Helen Stanley: a tale* (London: Churton, 1846) and had translated six novels by George Sand into English under the title *The Works of George Sand* (translated by Matilda Hays, Eliza A. Ashurst and E.R. Larken), 6 vols (London: Churton, 1847).

[23] Amelia B. Edwards, *The Young Marquis, or Scenes from a Reign* (London: J. & C. Brown, [1857]).

[24] *Sunday Times*, 5 April 1857.

[25] *Ladies Companion*, July 1857.

[26] SCO Edwards 351.

[27] SCO Edwards 607.

[28] SCO Edwards 351.

[29] Amelia B. Edwards, *Hand and Glove* (London: Brown & Co., 1858); see also Appendix 3, pp. 287–89.

[30] SCO Edwards 351.

[31] SCO Edwards 39.

[32] *The Dispatch*, 23 May 1858.

[33] *Daily Telegraph*, 10 June 1858.

[34] *The Athenaeum*, 19 June 1858.

[35] *Il Guanto Fatale* (Milan: Emilio Croce, 1872).

[36] *A History of France from the Conquest of Gaul by the Romans to the Peace of 1856* (London: Routledge, 1858).

[37] *The Athenaeum*, 3 July 1858.

[38] *The Spectator*, July 1858.

[39] *Ladies' Companion,* 2 August 1858.
[40] *Fanny Loviot, The Adventures of Fanny Loviot; a lady's captivity among Chinese pirates,* trans. Amelia B. Edwards (London: Routledge, [1858]).
[41] *Sunday Times,* 5 December 1858.
[42] *Magazine of History* (Tarrytown, NY: William Abbott, 1930), Extra Number 156.
[43] SCO Edwards 515.
[44] SCO Edwards 351.
[45] SCO Edwards 335.

❖ 5 ❖

From Islington to Westbury-on-Trym, 1860–65

'In 1860', Amelia wrote to Edward Abbott: 'the great misfortune of my life befell me, in the sudden death of my dear parents.'[1] Her father died on 22 August 1860, after a brief bronchial infection which lasted no more than five days,[2] and according to Matilda Betham-Edwards, her mother died within the week.[3] 'Long it was,' she writes, 'before Amelia recovered from the blow, if indeed she ever recovered.' For an only child to lose both parents within a week must indeed have been a blow. There is no reason to suppose that she lacked affection for her father: in a letter of 1860 to her mother she sends 'my fond love to Papa',[4] but she had been especially close to her mother. From a letter of 1856 it is apparent that she shared her friendships with her mother, whom she addressed as 'my darling'. This letter shows her planning a party or other form of entertainment with her mother: 'Don't you think we ought to invite Annie & Mrs Galbraith? I am sure we ought – & I have heard of two who will not come – so we might as well give them the vacant places … I will take two invitation notes with me to the class, ready written.'[5]

Amelia's friend Stirling Coyne, writing amusingly from Ilfracombe on 11 September 1860, shortly after her parents' death, about his holiday in Devonshire with his 'two task mistresses' (probably his wife and daughter), adds at the close,

> I find I am writing you such a posset of silly nonsense that I feel almost disposed to tear up the paper – only that I know you will have by the same post that takes this, a letter from Miss Philp in which you will find all that is kind, consoling, warm-hearted … We only wish you could participate our happiness with us.[6]

There is no other correspondence in the Somerville archive, nor elsewhere, to suggest how Amelia coped with the loss of her parents. In her letter of 1881 to Edward Abbott, after speaking of her parents' deaths, she writes:

> Since that time I have made my home with a very dear old friend, an aged lady who has within these 20 years lost her husband and her only child; so now we are all the world to each other. We lived

in Kensington while her dear ones yet remained; since then we
have lived at Westbury-on-Trym, where my friend purchased the
little property to which we give the name of The Larches.[7]

This 'very dear friend' was Mrs Ellen Drew Braysher. Amelia may
have made her home with the Brayshers immediately on her parents'
death, returning to Wharton Street only to move her own things and
clear the house. No letters from either of her parents survive, although
she kept many trivial notes from illustrious friends. She kept a few
photographs of her father, his commission documents and his medals,
but apart from her own pencil sketch, apparently of her mother, placed
loose at the back of *Mrs Roliston* (see Figure 3), no mementos of her
mother survive, although Matilda Betham-Edwards tells how 'to the
very last she preserved a fragment of pastry, the last made for her by
those deft little hands that ever busied about her darling',[8] an instance of
sentimentality not typical of Amelia.

From the tombstone in the parish churchyard at Henbury, near
Bristol, which records Amelia's death as well as the deaths of the
Brayshers, we learn that Mrs Braysher was born at Creen End, Hemel
Hemstead, on 9 April 1804, making her fifty-six years old when Amelia's
parents died. How and when Amelia came to know her can only be
surmised. If Mrs Braysher is indeed the 'Mrs Brazier' to whom Eliza
Lynn Linton refers in *My Literary Life*, Amelia may well have met her at
the Sunday gatherings at the home of the artist, Samuel Laurence. Eliza
describes 'a Mrs Brazier, made much of as a woman of large means
holding advanced views', and she is the only member of the circle not
mentioned by her first name, as would befit one of an older generation
respected by the younger company there.[9]

Amelia was staying with Mrs Braysher in June 1856: 'I have to go
down early to Pall Mall on Saturday morning', she writes to her mother
on that occasion, '& Mrs Braysher has begged me to remain till then,
which, as I have my work all with me, I may as well do'.[10] She also
appears to have been staying on holiday in Dorking with Mrs Braysher
in July 1860, just a few weeks before her mother's death, for she writes:

Dorking is lovelier than ever … I am immensely well & enjoying it
thoroughly … My darling, the woman who keeps this house has no
fresh lodgers coming in till Thursday week, so Mrs B. has agreed
with her to keep us a few days longer … On Sunday we are to have
the same chaise we have already had, & Mrs B. is going to drive to
Leith Hill. Yesterday we had it for 4 hours & went to Mickleham &
Leatherhead. Today we have been up for a stroll to the Tower.[11]

The letter suggests that Mrs Braysher did not know Mr and Mrs Edwards well, for Amelia adds:

> I read Mrs Braysher that part of your letter which referred to her. She seemed quite touched by it, & said you were a dear sweet thing & she quite felt to love you! She desires her kindest love to you, & said you need be under no apprehension lest I should fatigue her, as I have not yet found a single sketch to make, & except at Shere, do not seem likely to find one … We get such a nice chaise here, my darling, & a dear old quiet horse, & Mrs Franks cooks charmingly. We have such nice little dinners, plenty of fruit, vegetables, fowls, &c, &c, – & the Burgundy that Mrs B. brought with her as well.

The letter is clearly intended to reassure her mother that she was well and contented. Her mother, indeed her father too, may already have been unwell.

What little can be learnt of Ellen Braysher comes from the Edwards archive in Somerville College. It appears that her husband, John Braysher, was an educated man: on 3 December 1818 Coleridge wrote to him, sending him prospectuses of his historical and bibliographical lectures and expressing the hope that he would be recommending them to his friends.[12]

Ellen Braysher, although nearly thirty years older than Amelia, shared many interests with her. She counted actors and actresses among her friends. She corresponded over a period of years with Helena Faucit Martin (1817–98), the Shakespearean actress. Ellen Braysher also knew William Macready, the actor, and on one occasion had apparently written to him on behalf of a Miss Hays to ask whether George Sand would receive the girl; William Macready, in an undated reply, asks Mrs Braysher 'to communicate to Miss Hays that Madame Sand could not receive the girl as she was out of Paris for 10 months'.[13] It is interesting to note that Matilda Hays was also an acquaintance of Eliza Lynn Linton.[14] Ellen Braysher was herself an accomplished woman. Her commonplace book, bearing the date 15 February 1838, contains eighty-four pages of her poetry.[15]

Little enough is known about the Brayshers' one child who survived infancy, Sarah Harriet. In Ellen Braysher's commonplace book there is a letter in verse written upside down at the end, from 'Sally' to 'Polly'. It is possible that 'Sally' was Sarah's nickname just as, within the family, 'Polly' was Amelia's, and that the friendship between the two families was of long standing. There survives in the Somerville archive, a series of interesting letters from Giuseppe Mazzini, addressed to 'Miss Braysher', mostly written from 15 Andover Street, King's Road, Chelsea, in which he advises her on whom to meet in Italy, expresses a wish to see her before she leaves, expresses his gratitude to her and to Mrs Braysher and recommends histories of Italy.[16] In one letter he expresses a hope that he can do something for 'their imprisoned friend';[17] in another he addresses her as 'my fair victim'.[18] None of these letters is dated, but since John Braysher is not mentioned, they may well belong to the period between his death and Sarah's, 1863–64. They suggest that Sarah, and probably her mother with her 'advanced views', sympathised with Mazzini and his cause.

It is not known exactly when Mrs Braysher and Amelia moved from London to 'The Larches', Eastfield, Westbury-on-Trym, Gloucestershire. Amelia implies that they remained in London until after the deaths of John and Sarah Braysher, that is, until after June 1864,[19] but the house must have been purchased earlier and used at least intermittently, since Amelia was writing a letter from there on 27 April 1864.[20]

Fig. 8: The Larches, Westbury-on-Trym, Gloucestershire, Amelia's home from the early 1860s until her death in 1892. The house was destroyed during the Second World War.

Amelia will undoubtedly have found her writing a great help in her time of grief, and it gave her a continuing focus for her energy. She was young and resilient, and she was free of domestic commitments. By the following summer she was enjoying a holiday in Pangbourne. Acknowledging the gift of Oliver Wendell Holmes' new book, *Elsie Venner*, she wrote to the publisher, James Fields of Boston, Massachusetts: 'Intending to run away from London some time in May, I reserved the book to read under some great oak ... To read it in a place like Pangbourne – inhabited only by eels, swans and anglers – is like coming upon a dinner in a desert, or a wit at a quaker meeting.'[21] Some of her witty form had obviously returned by then.

By February 1862 she was contributing short stories once more to magazines, but now she was more aware of the value of her copyright. In contracting with Routledge for the copyright of a story entitled *Our First Great Sea Fight* for the sum of five pounds, she does so 'reserving to myself only the right of reprinting the said story in a collection of my miscellaneous writings'.[22]

Following the earlier publication by Colnaghi in 1857[23] Amelia had continued to work on the task of preparing text to accompany reproductions of miniatures of illustrious historical personages, which came at last to fruition in the publication of *The Photographic Historical Portrait Gallery*.[24] She referred to this work years later as 'a superb book issued only to subscribers, which never found its way to the public at all & for which I wrote some three or four hundred short lives'.[25] In her later list of her own publications she gave the date as 1860,[26] but it was published in parts and was not completed until 1864. This expensive book was dedicated by the publishers to the Duke of Buccleuch and Queensberry, and designed for display, but Amelia's text was at times uncompromising. Of the Lady Hunsdon she writes: 'Unknown to posterity for any achievements of her own, [she] may best be described by her position with regard to others.'[27] Her description of Sir Isaac Newton on the other hand conveys a typical sense of the dramatic:

> He now enjoyed the inexpressible delight of finding each fact develop itself, as he went on, in exact accordance with the hypothesis which he had previously laid down. As the end approached, his emotion became so overwhelming that he could proceed no further, and he had to call in the assistance of a friend to finish the working out of that great problem to which he alone possessed the key. This time no doubt, or room for doubt, remained. The secret of the universe was solved.[28]

That summer of 1862, the Brayshers were travelling abroad: a passport survives which was issued for 'Mr John Braysher, accompanied by his wife, daughter and Mrs H. Ryde [Mrs Braysher's sister] travelling on the Continent with a maid servant', dated 5 August 1862.[29] Whether Amelia accompanied them is not known, but she was certainly travelling in Europe in late August and September. She had her own passport, and may well have been with them. She wrote extensive notes on her travels of 1862, but as in 1859 they are almost entirely devoted to describing the scenery and give no clue as to travelling companions. Nor do they provide a continuous narrative, or diary of events, although some dates are given.[30] They are headed 'Impressions of Switzerland & Upper Rhine, 1862', and cover the period from 26 August, when she was at Rheinfelden, until 13 September, when she was in Bonn.

Amelia's descriptions are extremely detailed, and written with the eye of an artist. She sometimes compares the views before her eyes with a painting or drawing of the same scene; thus at Rheinfelden she writes: 'At the end of the street we find ourselves face to face with Ruskin's wonderfully faithful & beautiful sketch.' Her description of the river above the Schaffhausen Falls is typical of the detail in which she expresses her careful observation:

> Cross the river on a wooden side-path or annex to the great railway bridge … Leaning over the parapet to the right you look down into these pools, over the surface of which the flood hurries to the leap; but underneath which there seems to lie a still awful body of water, profound & dark as the grave. In other places you can see the pebbly bottom, the great flapping weeds which toss with the flood, like earth plants in a great wind storm. In others you see purply masses of rock – red in local colour, but purple by the blue wash of the water above. All this upper part of the river is a vivid, sparkling blue, broken through with rocky islets on which shrubs & little trees are growing & all broken, foaming, eager & leaping towards the fall. The effect of these broken rocks & wild shrubs is just as if all were in motion together: the very islets look as if they were being washed along with the current.[31]

Such detail suggests that she was writing while she was at the scene and leaning over the parapet, notebook in hand, but this was probably not so; she had an artist's eye, and may even have made a sketch at the time. The writing in this section of her notebook appears to be a fair copy: on one occasion a line has been omitted, and in the last sentence quoted above, the word 'look' replaces the word 'seem' which has been crossed out. Such descriptive passages in her notebook appear to be literary exercises, possibly written with a mind to future publication.

On 30 August 1862 they visited the baths at Pfeffers, first the baths then in use, in 'old whitewashed conventual buildings with enormous corridors & accommodation for all classes of invalids … No luxury anywhere, but perfect cleanliness & order', then the remains of the old baths, which involved walking with a guide along the side of a gorge, their only path 'a wooden shelf with a handrail, just clinging against the steep side of the rock'.

> Below, far, far below foamed & roared the Tamina; 300 feet overhead the great whitish, heavy rounded precipices … leaned together, shut out the sky completely, & revealed tiny openings far overhead, through which we could see the waving branches of the trees on the upper earth & a gleam of sunlight & blue sky … The terrible chill, the stupendous terror of this place, exceed description.[32]

From Pfeffers they went on to Rheichenau, and Amelia is equally at ease describing her room in the inn, formerly a convent: 'The furniture of the beds is snow-white; the floors, the blue china stoves, the white porcelain washing apparatus, all are of the cleanest & daintiest; little prints, illustrative of the great events of Swiss liberty, framed in black wood, hang on the walls.' On the Sunday they went up to the small Protestant church at the top of a hill nearby, but did not apparently attend the service. 'The school had all assembled before the coming of the congregation. The boys were playing in the church yard, the girls sitting on benches at the lower end of the church; but as soon as we had passed through, they came pouring out after us.'[33] She comments only on the appearance of the church, on its sign announcing that 'where there is God there is liberty', and on the graves in the churchyard. To Amelia, the village church is little more than part of the scenery.

By 3 September they were at Ulm, where by contrast Amelia gives a detailed account of the cathedral, and in particular of the sculptures on the façade depicting scenes from the Old Testament, including 'God with his hand on Adam's heart, giving him life; Adam looking astonished, as well he might.' There are other touches of humour, reminiscent of Amelia's love of caricature: 'The Angel flourishing his sword very much as if it were a rod, & Adam setting a right at him like a naughty schoolboy.'

On 13 September they were staying in Bonn, and made an excursion across the Rhine to a fair in the neighbouring village of Bühle. Amelia writes of the great crowd at the landing place:

> [They were] chiefly soldiers, women, young men of the lower
> classes & children. All in holiday clothes; the young men with gay
> neckties & gaudy china meerschaums & some of them with oak
> leaves bound round their hats – the girls with clean little 'buy a
> broom' caps, coloured handkerchieves pinned across the bosom, &
> earrings & necklaces of bright blue & red beads. The better sort of
> girls, such as the daughters of small tradesmen, &c. with hair
> turned back from the brow over a roll, dresses cut half-low, open
> sleeves, necklaces, rings, &c.

She is still fascinated by dress, as she was as a child when she drew her
cartoons of Patrick Murphy and Mrs Roliston. Amelia accepts the class
structure as she interpreted it, without any sign of concern for the poor
or envy of the rich; similarly she records the disabled without either
compassion or disdain: 'A great many beggars along the road: one a
blind man … telling his beads & praying loudly, with a hat before him
… Another without legs, grinding an organ.' She never takes up the
stance of the social reformer in her notebook; her aim is to record life as
she observes it. She describes market stalls at the fair in such detail that
one might conclude that she had never been to a market before, were it
not for the knowledge that she had bought her provisions at the market
in Rome only five years earlier. 'Here a stall of combs of all kinds, side
combs, back combs, pocket combs, curry combs, small tooth combs, &c.'
and later: 'then comes a stall for mock jewellery, china chimney
ornaments, purses, & so forth … then a toy stall, all the toys of the most
common description, wooden horses, poofs, squeaking birds, &c.' There
are occasional cynical comments, as on the game of chance at the
gingerbread stall, where the prizes are pieces of gingerbread: 'The owner
of the stall gives an impetus to a kind of … arrow balanced like the
compass needle on a roulette board. This arrow … stops opposite a blank
or a prize – generally a blank.' Some of the most interesting vignettes in
this description of a fair are of the 'merry-go-rounds … with alternate
sofas & wooden horses – sofas for the women & horses for the men, &
all ages enjoying it with the utmost gravity' and of the show booths – a
Punch and Judy show, a puppet theatre and a 'theatre for grown-up
actors, who stand outside in their gaudy ballet dresses' and a booth 'over
which is painted up "Tanz-musik", and there, through the open door of
the anteroom, we see couples polking & waltzing'. The whole essay is
lively and conveys a sense of excitement, but written more from an
observer's than a participant's point of view.

The Brayshers and Amelia must have returned from Europe by the
end of the year, for when Amelia signed the contract with Routledge,

Warne and Routledge for the copyright of her next publication, *The Story of Cervantes*, in London on 7 January 1863, her signature was witnessed by Sarah Harriet Braysher.[34]

The Story of Cervantes[35] was serialised in *Routledge's Every Boy's Annual* in 1863, and was dedicated to 'my friend and cousin, M. Betham-Edwards, whose admirable volumes for the young delight readers of all ages', an amiable gesture, but possibly also part of Amelia's campaign to distinguish her own works from those of her cousin. Routledge paid her no more than £5 for it. In the strangely inconsequential preface which is signed 'Amelia B. Edwards, Bonn, Sept., 1862' she recounts how some years previously, when travelling home from Rome, they had spent Easter Sunday in the Italian Tyrol and had seen a church procession including 'eighteen gorgeous beadles, two and two, with cocked hats and halberds, and crimson shoulder scarves, embroidered with gold, and then … a very little boy in a soiled surplice, several inches too long for him, who looked terribly frightened, and lit the candles! We had expected to see a bishop at the very least!' The book itself is, as she is keen to point out, 'truth or historical fact', drawing on Roscoe's biography[36] and other sources, which she declares in her preface. It is, however, in narrative form, imagination complementing fact when, for instance, Cervantes attends the Roman carnival, just as she had done 300 years later. She does not fail to point the moral, writing of foreign travel that 'every day brings some instruction with it … [We] learn how to love and appreciate our fellow-men, whatever be their dwelling-place or nation.'[37] Where fact about the life of her subject was hard to come by, she admitted the case, and she presents the last years of Cervantes' life in the form of glimpses, like tableaux on a stage. She comments on his romance *Galatea*:

> It is composed in the false taste of those days … It is doubtful if we could read the book at all nowadays. The taste for pastoral has gone by, and we moderns find it impossible to be interested in a race of imaginary beings … Peace be with them, and the reverend dust of antique libraries light upon them![38]

The Story of Cervantes represented a great deal of research, and dependent though she was on previous publications, it bears the unmistakable stamp of Amelia's mock-heroic style, and is presented as a very readable adventure story. Even *The Athenaeum* declares it 'well-written'.[39]

In March 1863 one of Amelia's ghost stories, *The Eleventh of March*, was included in an anthology published by Emily Faithfull[40] which included works by authors such as Harriet Martineau, Christina

Rossetti, Charles Kingsley and Anthony Trollope, as well as authors lesser known today. Amelia's contribution is written in the first person as a man sketching by the lake of Albano, 'not rising till there was only half an hour of daylight left', who sees a monk 'still young, still handsome, but so lividly pale, so emaciated, so worn with passion, and penance, and remorse, that I stopped involuntarily'. One recollects how Amelia had regaled her friends with ghost stories when staying at Rome and Albano six years earlier – she rarely let experience go to waste.

In April 1863 John Braysher died. This must have been a great shock not only to his widow but to their daughter, Sarah, to whom a letter of condolence from Theodore Martin survives, addressed to her at 4, Earl's Terrace, Kensington.[41] Yet perhaps Sarah's death the following year was an even greater blow to the widow. The monument erected in Henbury churchyard reads:

> To the beloved memory of Sarah Harriet, only surviving child of the late John Braysher, Esq., and Ellen his widow, who died at Paris in the flower of her youth on the 25 June 1864, this monument is erected by the bereaved mother in consecration of a grief that knows no ending and a love that knows no change.

Whether Sarah Braysher was in Paris with her mother or with friends – even with Amelia – is not known, but that her death was unexpected is seen from a letter of condolence from Helena Faucit Martin to Mrs Braysher written on 12 July 1864, saying 'how deeply I feel for you in this sudden & so sad bereavement … Will your sister be good enough to write a line & tell me how your heart is bearing up against all this terrible strain upon it?'[42] A letter to Mrs Braysher from the wife of Samuel Carter Hall, writing from Wexford on 6 July, also expresses sorrow at the death of her 'darling girl' and sympathy both to the widow and to Amelia.[43]

By the end of the year, the novel for which Amelia was to be principally known for the rest of her life, *Barbara's History,* and which she had been planning when in Rome as early as 1857, was ready for publication. The British Museum Library received its copy on 27 November 1863, but it was not formally published until January 1864.[44] It was reprinted in a Tauchnitz edition, and continued to be reprinted by Hurst and Blackett at least until 1911. It was widely reviewed, with mixed judgements: *The Athenaeum* wrote that

> if Miss Amelia Edwards goes on writing such stories … she will on some bright day of a lucky season wake up and find herself famous. She has made great progress since the publication of *The*

Story of Cervantes and her other books for children ... She has humour, insight into character, a somewhat extensive knowledge of books, and a mind thoroughly feminine in tone ...[45]

but then adds, 'She is greatly indebted to others for the plot, principal characters, and general tone of the book.' The reviewer refers with justification to *David Copperfield*, *Jane Eyre* and *Villette*, and continues: 'Consenting to humour the existing taste for bigamy stories, she was determined not to make too great a sacrifice of womanly dignity ... so has ... effected a compromise between her own sense of right and the depraved appetite of the public.'

The Times gave a mixed review: 'This is not a novel of the sensational class ... It is just a novel of passion, and sentiment, and character, which never once approaches the purlieus of the police court...'[46] Its reviewer thought highly of the portrayal of Barbara Churchill's character, but not of the characterisation of Hugh Farquhar.

The *Saturday Review* commented that 'we fancy we have met all these puppets before, and yet it is possible so to pull the wires that our interest is excited anew',[47] and the *Sunday Times* at the end of the year referred to it as 'already standard ... one of the best novels of the day ... Possibly she may at times be a little pedagogic or ostentatious in the display of her erudition.'[48]

Amelia was abroad in Switzerland at some time in 1864. Although there are no entries in her notebook for her travels this year, five dated water-colour sketches survive in Somerville College: two views of Grindelwald, the Bernese mountain range from the Albis, Bex (Canton Vaud) and Thun.[49] She was still in England in July[50] and it seems most likely that she did not travel abroad until the autumn. It is not known whether she travelled with Mrs Braysher, or indeed, with any other companion.

By the end of 1864 Amelia had returned to England and had received from the publisher the first copies of a compilation of her poetry. There were twenty-four original ballads, and four translations from the French and Italian with erudite notes on the context of three of them. The manuscript survives, with instructions to the printer.[51] None of the ballads is dated in this copy, but another manuscript in the Somerville College archive[52] contains thirty-five ballads, including three translations, with dates of composition and an indication of who set them to music (mostly a Mr Duggan) and where they were first published (mostly in the *Englishwoman's Journal*). The earliest date back to 1854, the latest to 1864. Many of the ballads are love songs, and some had also been used in her early novels. They have a certain charm, with fluent rhythm, natural flow of words and apparently effortless rhyme. They do not express novel experiences nor deep emotion, and Amelia recognised their limitations when she wrote in the preface:

> The few ballads here gathered together were nearly all written for music. Perhaps I scarcely knew till now how much of their melody they owed to the composers who set them … In their present form … they are too effectually disenchanted to leave me in any doubt as to the slenderness of those intrinsic merits upon which my rhymes must now stand.

Ballads[53] was not formally published until the following year, but in late November and December 1864 Amelia was sending out copies to her friends, sometimes adding dedications in verse. To C.M. (probably Miss Constance Murray, daughter of Sir Digby Murray, whose photograph had a place in Amelia's album) she wrote on 14 December 1864:

> I wish my rhymes were better worth
> These names inscribed above,
> Had more of sparkle in their mirth
> More music in their love,
> More point, more pathos & more wit
> More skill of verse & fable –
> In short, I wish they were more fit
> To lie upon your table.[54]

She also sent a copy four days later to 'John Addington Symonds, MD, FRS, Author of the Principles of Beauty, &c &c &c' with a sonnet ending:

> I mark thy progress through the realms of thought
> And ask how I dare pay to taste like thine
> So poor a tribute as these songs of mine?[55]

This is the first evidence of her friendship with him.

Two acknowledgements of such gifts survive, from W. Frith and Lord Lytton. The latter wrote of the collection shrewdly as,

> a volume of charming verse, with which at first glance I have been delighted … What I have read of your verse is peculiarly to my taste, which is somewhat old-fashioned and requires for the utterance of genuine poetry tones modulated to tasteful music & expressing ideas which it does not expect the learning of a

schoolmarm to criticise, & if the schoolmarm be well educated, to despise.[56]

The published book of *Ballads* was dedicated to 'my most beloved friend, Ellen Braysher' and Amelia gave her a copy on New Year's Day with a sonnet ending:

> … and may ev'ry month
> As it steals by in shade and sunshine, lend
> Its ministering virtues to restore
> Bloom to thy cheek, strength to thy fragile form,
> And all that full content of heart and spirit
> that I (were love omnipotent) would fain
> Endow thee with, Belov'd, for evermore.[57]

Ballads, with its attractive frontispiece by Birket Foster, was well received by the press. 'Viewed as words for music', *The Athenaeum* reviewer commented, 'they have great merits – emotion, melody and far more picturesqueness than is usual in such compositions',[58] but there were also more critical voices, such as the reviewer in *The Examiner*: 'They often portray a mood happily, but have … but little originality either of imagery or thought. Like half the poetry of the day, they are quite unexceptionable … hardly worthy of the writer'.[59]

By the end of 1864 Amelia and Mrs Braysher were beginning what was to prove nearly thirty years of close companionship in what must have seemed to both of them a quiet rural retreat. Why they chose to live in Westbury is not known. Neither family had, as far as can be discovered, any previous connection with the village, but it is clear from Amelia's essay about her home that she was happy there.[60] The essay belongs to a later period, and the routine described there no doubt evolved over the years. When they moved to the village, Amelia was thirty-three and Ellen Braysher was fifty-nine; when they died there, Amelia was sixty-one and Ellen eighty-seven.

In the early years there, Amelia gained a wide circle of new friends in and around Westbury. She knew the Ames family, one of the leading families of the area, who lived at Cote House. She had in her album photographs of Henry St Vincent Ames, who built the village hall with its organ and its library at his own expense in 1870, and of Mrs Ames and Mr Reginald Ames.[61] She also knew the Caves at Burfield House, although not well at first, for on 30 March 1871 she needed 'courage to write to' Mrs Cave, on holiday in Penzance.[62] In this letter she gives Mrs Cave news of mutual acquaintances in Westbury; of being driven by Mrs

Heyworth to call on Mr Harford of Stapleton; of being taken by Mrs Sillifant for a drive to Shirehampton; and of Mr and Mrs Heyworth and Mrs Parish going to London to see the opening of the Albert Hall. She reports Mrs Buchanan's imminent departure for Cheshire and Mr Ames' likely return from Madeira in May. She thanks the Caves for their repeated gifts of fruit during her recent illness.

In the same letter to Mrs Cave, Amelia writes with emotion of the departure of the Rev. and Mrs Byrne from Westbury: 'I shall spend the summer, autumn and winter abroad … I suppose I shall start very soon after Mr and Mrs Byrne go away – for I must go somewhere to get over that great blow – the greatest that could befall me …' Later in the same letter she adds: 'No doubt you have heard that Mr Byrne's district is changed, and they are compelled to leave. They are to be in Surrey and will probably make Guildford or Dorking their place of residence. It is like a death-blow to me.' It seems probable that she was writing of the Reverend John Rice Byrne, who was a close contemporary. On graduating from Oxford in 1850 he went into the the Church, but by the time Amelia was writing he was serving as one of Her Majesty's Inspectors of Schools.[63] He still preached on occasions in the Bristol area, as is seen from another letter from Amelia, undated, in University College London[64] addressed to Miss Cave: 'Mr Byrne preaches tomorrow morning at Horfield & if it is fine I mean to go. Would you like to go with me? Mr Elton is such an affliction that I thought you might be glad to exchange him for a really good preacher with a really good accent.'

A memorandum dated 11 November 1865 in her commonplace book tells a story of a visit which she received from the Byrnes:

> NB. I had fastened some artificial roses to a rosebush in our garden, Nov. 10th, when the flowers were long since all off. The Rev. Rice Byrne and Mrs Byrne coming to call on me, observed the deception, & much amused by it, sent me a bouquet of lovely roses next day. I sent this parody on 'Drink of this Cup' in acknowledge-ment of the Gift.[65]

This would suggest an easy, close friendship in which Amelia could count on the Byrnes sharing her sense of humour. Her verse response was an apt acknowledgement:

> Bend o'er this bouquet – the pleasure of smelling
> Its perfume is almost too pure for mortality –
> Talk of the roses that bloomed near my dwelling

Those roses were fiction but these are reality! …
Mine had no scent – but the soul of a flower,
Be sure, is the perfume shut up in the heart of it;
Mine had no thorns, but, by beauty's own power!
Who loves it & seeks it must bear with the smart of it.
Then give me the thorns and the perfume together
For such is a type of the joys of mortality –
No fiction that ever was penned weighs a feather
When balanced, I fear, 'gainst the claims of reality.

It is hardly surprising that Amelia was dismayed at the thought of losing such good friends. Her association with them continued long after they had left Westbury: Robert Browning acknowledged an invitation from Amelia, made apparently from the Byrnes' home and on behalf of Mrs Byrne, in July 1869,[66] and in June 1871 Gustave Doré, writing to Amelia, sent his 'compliments bien cordiaux à Monsieur et Madame Byrne' and expressed the hope of seeing them again one day in London.[67]

Joan Rees, in her biography of Amelia, comments that '[Amelia's] reaction to their impending departure from the district suggests an over-excited state of mind'. She assumes that the Mrs Byrne to whom reference is made in these letters is the Mrs Byrne to whom Amelia's friend Marianne North referred when she wrote in 1870: 'When the Byrne bullies you too much, come here.'[68] She suggests that Mrs Byrne fulfils Amelia's need for a 'mother-figure'.[69] The Mrs Byrne to whom Marianne refers may well be Mrs Julia Clara Byrne, a writer and contributor to the periodical press, and widow of William Pitt Byrne, editor of the *Morning Post* until his death in 1861. It would be natural for Amelia to have been acquainted with one with similar literary ambitions. Moreover Marianne's advice needs to be read in context. Her letters to Amelia, as to others, were always uninhibited and their language idiosyncratic. In another letter a few days later Marianne warns Amelia against 'being bullied day after day … for your friend will not like doing without you a bit better a month hence than she does now'.[70] It would appear that Mrs Byrne was urging Amelia to stay longer with her, and Amelia was torn between accepting the invitation, and going to stay with Marianne in her flat in London. The widowed Mrs Byrne may well have in Marianne's eyes been making too great demands on Amelia's time. In the absence of Amelia's reply neither interpretation can be proved conclusively.

Early in 1865 the publication of *Miss Carew*[71] met with a predominantly disappointed press. It included many of Amelia's most successful ghost stories, such as *The Eleventh of March* and *The Patagonian Brothers*, reprinted with only a loose connecting thread. The book was inadvertently advertised as 'a new novel'. Amelia did her utmost to correct this[72] but the mistake caused 'much pother'. The *Daily News* reviewer adds, however, that 'Miss Edwards appears to stand perfectly clear of mercenary imputation'. *The Athenaeum* gave the book a mixed reception: 'No part of the compilation is poor, with the exception of the new portion … Miss Edwards is a cultured woman, and capable of great things in her special department of art; but this compilation will not raise the reputation which she achieved by an excellent novel.'

During the year, Amelia's genuinely new novel, *Half a Million of Money*, was published as a serial in *All the Year Round*, and re-issued as a serial in *Harper's Weekly* in America. The novel was published in three volumes in 1866. Inevitably the press compared it with her best-known work, *Barbara's History*, and for the most part unfavourably. It is 'far more improbable and sensational,' wrote *The Standard*, 'but it ranks far above the Miss Braddon school.'[73] While there were some favourable reviews, the journals which Amelia most cared about were damning: 'Not without regret is it,' wrote *The Athenaeum* reviewer, 'that we lay aside *Half a Million of Money* with diminished confidence in Miss Edwards's power to originate as well as to reproduce … Every now and then her ignorance of London betrays itself by a laughable slip.'[74] The *Saturday Review* commented that 'Miss Edwards' scenes of club and bachelor life are amusing, and much more lifelike than is usual with lady-novelists', but added, 'Miss Edwards forgets that there are two parties to every love affair.'[75] The *Pall Mall Gazette* is sceptical:

> Why is it that lady novelists take delight in writing on subjects of which they must almost necessarily be ignorant? … In future a lawyer should be consulted just to check her law. The characters and incidents are so exaggerated as to be simply amazing. When our authoress ceases to exaggerate she becomes painfully tame … [However] … The language is not ill-chosen, and the style unusually grammatical for a lady.[76]

Such reviews seem to have hurt Amelia badly: years later, when meeting the request of a journalist for a list of her works, she omitted *Half a Million of Money*, and that work alone, from the list.[77]

Aware of the criticism of improbability in the plot, Amelia considered revisions for the publication in book form. On 28 May 1866 she wrote to William Tinsley, the publisher,

I had at one time thought of writing a new chapter in place of the one entitled 'What pity is akin to', but after hammering over it for a week, & trying all manner of ways to devise some plan by which my lovers should fall in love more leisurely, I have been forced to give it up. I really see no other way for them to act – & love at first sight does happen.[78]

By the mid-1860s Amelia had published five of the eight novels which she was to produce in her lifetime, and numerous short stories, essays and ballads. She was able to keep herself by her writing. Her life had changed dramatically with the death of her parents and her removal with Ellen Braysher to Gloucestershire, where she had settled into a new way of life and a new circle of friends. She could not afford, however, to lose the stimulus of London and the inspiration of foreign travel, and was resolved not to forego these, content though she appears to have been in her country home.

Notes

[1] SCO Edwards 351.
[2] SCO Edwards 470.
[3] Matilda Betham-Edwards, 'Amelia B. Edwards: her childhood and early life', *New England Magazine*, New Series, 7, 5 (Boston, MA, January 1893), p. 564.
[4] SCO Edwards 458.
[5] SCO Edwards 456.
[6] SCO Edwards 37.
[7] SCO Edwards 351.
[8] Betham-Edwards, 'Amelia B. Edwards: her childhood and early life', p. 563.
[9] Eliza Lynn Linton, *My Literary Life* (London: Hodder & Stoughton, 1899), p. 39.
[10] SCO Edwards 456.
[11] SCO Edwards 458.
[12] SCO Edwards 36.
[13] SCO Edwards 120.
[14] Linton, *My Literary Life*, p. 39.
[15] SCO Edwards 427.
[16] SCO Edwards 213–20.
[17] SCO Edwards 217.
[18] SCO Edwards 219.
[19] SCO Edwards 351.
[20] UCL Ms Misc. 3E/1.
[21] Houghton, fms AM 201.
[22] UCL Routledge, c1850–c78, Vol. 1, p. 306.

[23] SCO Edwards 456.

[24] *The Photographic Historical Portrait Gallery, consisting of a series of portraits, principally from miniatures in the most celebrated collections in England* (London: P&D Colnaghi, 1864).

[25] SCO Edwards 351.

[26] SCO Edwards 394.

[27] *Photographic Historical Portrait Gallery*, p. 73.

[28] Ibid., p. 88.

[29] SCO Edwards 423.

[30] SCO Edwards 515.

[31] Ibid., 28 August 1862.

[32] Ibid., 30 August 1862.

[33] Ibid., [31 August 1862].

[34] UCL Routledge Contracts, c1850–c78, Vol. 1, p. 308.

[35] Amelia B. Edwards, *The Story of Cervantes, who was a scholar, a poet, a soldier, a slave among the Moors and the author of Don Quixote* (London: George Routledge, [1863]).

[36] Thomas Roscoe, *Miguel Cervantes Saavedra, The History and Adventures of the Renowned Don Quixote ... to which is prefixed a memoir of the author*, 3 vols (London: Effingham Wilson, 1833).

[37] Edwards, *The Story of Cervantes*, p. v.

[38] Ibid., p. 195.

[39] *The Athenaeum*, no. 1831 (29 November 1862).

[40] *A Welcome: original contributions in poetry and prose* (London: Emily Faithfull, 1863).

[41] SCO Edwards 134.

[42] SCO Edwards 462.

[43] SCO Edwards 67.

[44] Amelia B. Edwards, *Barbara's History*, 3 vols (London: Hurst & Blackett, 1864).

[45] *The Athenaeum*, no. 1888 (2 January 1864), pp. 15–16.

[46] *The Times*, 23 March 1864.

[47] *Saturday Review of Politics, Literature, Science and Art*, 24 May 1864.

[48] *Sunday Times*, 25 December 1864.

[49] SCO Edwards W32,W75, W79, W80, W81.

[50] UCL Routledge Contracts c1850–c78, Vol. 1, p. 245.

[51] SCO Edwards 513.

[52] SCO Edwards 429.

[53] Amelia B. Edwards, *Ballads* (London: Tinsley, 1865).

[54] SCO Edwards 565, no. 5.

[55] Ibid.

[56] SCO Edwards 118, undated.

[57] SCO Edwards 565, p. 9.

[58] *The Athenaeum*, no. 1954 (8 April 1865), p. 488.

[59] *The Examiner* (London), April 1865.

[60] Amelia B. Edwards, 'My home life', *Arena*, 4 (4 August 1891), pp. 209–310.

[61] SCO Edwards 524.

[62] UCL Mss Add 182.9.

[63] *Crockford's Clerical Directory* (London: Horace Cox, 1872).

[64] UCL Mss Add 182.3, undated.

[65] SCO Edwards 565, no. 14.

[66] SCO Edwards 15.

[67] SCO Edwards 446.

[68] SCO Edwards 237, 3 June 1871.

[69] Joan Rees, *Amelia Edwards: Traveller, Novelist and Egyptologist* (London: Rubicon Press, 1998), p. 23.

[70] SCO Edwards 236, 17 June 1871.

[71] Amelia B. Edwards, *Miss Carew*, 3 vols (London: Hurst & Blackett, 1865).

[72] SCO Edwards 434.96.

[73] *The Standard* (London), 4 April 1866.

[74] *The Athenaeum*, no. 1969 (9 December 1865), pp. 801–2.

[75] *Saturday Review*, 30 December 1865.

[76] *Pall Mall Gazette*, 10 January 1868.

[77] SCO Edwards 394.

[78] Houghton, Autograph File, Wendell Bequest 1918.

❖ *6* ❖

The dark years, 1866–71

The second half of the 1860s is the least well documented period of Amelia's life. Part of each year was certainly spent in Westbury with Mrs Braysher, but she also went up to London from time to time. Writing on 28 May 1866 to William Tinsley who was publishing the American edition of *Half a Million of Money*, she said: 'I have been sadly idle this spring & am going up to town before long to be still more idle, I am ashamed to say, but I am going to work very hard during the autumn and winter.'[1] Writing much later to Edward Abbott, the editor of the *Literary World*, describing her 'life of a cabbage' in Westbury, she adds: 'I do not, of course, imply that I have never mixed with the world or gone into society. I have, on the contrary, done my London seasons, & undergone the usual treadmill of … driving, dressing & the rest of it, till I became too weary of the wretched round to submit to it any longer.'[2]

She was not yet tired of London in the 1860s, and appears to have taken every opportunity when in town of entertaining, usually in the house of a friend with whom she was staying. On 16 June 1868 she wrote from 19 Gloucester Place, Portman Square, inviting Henry Wadsworth Longfellow to tea, uninhibited by never having met him.

> I have the pleasure of knowing many of your personal friends & fellow countrymen & perhaps I may almost hope that my desire to meet you is not altogether misplaced or unreasonable. It would be a source, indeed, of grievous regret & disappointment to me, if you were in London & I had not the honour of receiving you.[3]

She tempts him with an indication of her other guests:

> Monsieur Gustave Doré, who is here for only a few days and leaves England on Sunday, has promised to come on Saturday next (the 20th inst.) to afternoon tea, between 4 & 5 o'clock, to meet Professor F.D. Maurice, Mr Grant Duff (Rector of the University of Aberdeen & M.P. for the Elgin Burgh), Lady Emily Foley, Lady Hastings, and some other friends. If you are disengaged & will give me the honour of a visit that afternoon, it would give me the greatest possible pleasure to welcome you & make your acquaintance.

It is not known whether he accepted. The following year Robert Browning was prevented from 'obeying your kind invitation' by the unexpected arrival of a 'very old friend' from Florence 'just as I was leaving the house ... and I was obliged to await his exit at five o'clock, and no earlier'.[4] This, apparently, was another afternoon tea-party.

Amelia received invitations in return: later that month, on 20 July 1869 when she was still staying at 19 Gloucester Place, Anthony Trollope wrote from Waltham House, Waltham Cross:

> Would you do me and my wife the honour of coming to us next Saturday and staying until Monday morning? I am aware, as is my wife painfully, that duty would strictly require her to call on you first; but as she lives down here, and as she is averse to come up to London, especially in this hot weather, she thinks that perhaps you will consent to waive the strict law.[5]

He too tempts her with his other guest: 'Millais will be with us'. Amelia refers to her acquaintance with Trollope in an article which appeared in the *Literary World* in 1883:

> I was living in London when I knew Trollope and he was living at Waltham Cross, Hertfordshire. He used to be frequently going to and fro between town and country, dropping in at his club and his publisher's, and not disdaining, after the manner of men in general, to now and then make an afternoon call at the hour when ladies take tea ... Though twice invited, I was to my regret on each occasion unable to put aside the pressing work which tied me to the desk.[6]

On 24 November 1869 Lord Lytton wrote to her: 'I much regret that you could not visit me at Knebworth', curiously adding: 'though there was no need of your scruples considering Lady Bulwer & Mrs Villiers being there at the same time.'[7]

There seems little doubt that Amelia, at this period in particular, sought to cultivate the acquaintance of the great names in literature and art. Few of her letters have survived in their papers, as far as is known, but from their letters to her in the Somerville archive it is clear that she was accustomed to write and congratulate authors on their new publications, and to send them copies of her favourite reviews. 'I am highly flattered', wrote Lord Lytton in the same letter, 'by your approval of my translation [of Horace] – I could scarcely hope it would have any attraction for a lady, however accomplished.' Four years earlier

Theodore Martin had written, 'I wish I had sooner become aware of your wish to have a copy of my volume [of translations from Goethe]. You should not have had any trouble about getting it.'[8]

Amelia's cultivation of famous personages is exemplified by her habit of collecting their autographs. It is, in fact, largely due to this habit that so many often inconsequential letters to her survive in the Somerville archive; indeed the earliest manuscript account of that archive refers to 'an envelope marked autograph poems … a miscellaneous collection of letters & odd little poems …' which have subsequently been dispersed. It is clear from a letter which she wrote to a Mrs Grove on 9 November 1867 that she not only collected autographs but also exchanged them: 'I enclose a few pen & ink scrawls & autographs – two of Mr Yates, & one of Frith – the 'Derby Day' Frith – May you barter mine for others of more worth!'[9] On 8 May 1868 James Holland, the water-colour painter, sent her a drawing 'for your collection',[10] and there are various other examples which cannot be precisely dated.

In some cases the acquaintances with the famous which Amelia cultivated flourished into friendships. Her friendship with Gustave Doré appears to have begun with her favourable review of his exhibition in London in 1869:

> Dear Mademoiselle, I am writing to thank you for the infinite favour you have done me in reviewing for your readers the new works that I am exhibiting in London and … for such kind and flattering lines. Once more a thousand thanks, dear Mademoiselle, and in the hope of seeing you soon, for I have in mind before the end of the month, to make a brief visit to London and to have the pleasure of shaking your hand.[11]

This was the beginning of a continuing correspondence in the course of which Doré described the siege of Paris and its aftermath.[12] There survives in the Somerville archive a small sketchbook with signed sketches of London life which he gave to Amelia, possibly on this first visit.[13]

Not all whom she approached were willing to comply with her requests for autographs. 'My dear Miss Edwards,' wrote Anthony Trollope on 26 April 1871:

> I never keep letters addressed to myself, and therefore had to look about me before I could send you ought of what you want. I now enclose a note of Dickens, one of Carlyle, and the signature cut out of a note from George Eliot to myself which I happened to receive

the other day. I could not send the note itself as its contents were not such as should be shown to all the world. And now I grieve to say I cannot do what you ask of me about my own writing. I could not copy a bit of my own work for the sake of making an autograph, as I cannot assume [as if to soften the rebuff] that what would be so written would have any subsequent value.[14]

E.F. Fowler was likewise reluctant to oblige her, since she had apparently asked, or purported to ask, on behalf of friends: 'I don't like to refuse your request, tho' I do very much dislike giving an autograph to strangers, but as they are friends of yours you shall have these scribbles.' He enclosed a sketch of his children on the sands at Crouch, which remained in Amelia's collection – he could hardly have done otherwise, for he adds in a postscript: 'Thank you for your kind promise of a Doré. I shall be charmed to have something of his.'[15] Edward Lear was more gracious, when Marianne North approached him for an autograph on Amelia's behalf. He wrote from San Remo: 'I doubt if your friend will think the drawings worth her keeping. I fancy I have already had the pleasure of making Miss Edwards' acquaintance (at Mrs G. Scrivener's) … I shall always be glad to know any friend of yours.'[16]

While autograph hunting and bartering was a popular pastime among ladies in the Victorian age, in Amelia's case it is perhaps also indicative of her reverence for fame. Ever since her youthful elation at the success of her singing in 1850 she had not been content with a woman's ordinary lot. In two decades she had worked hard to become a successful novelist: her journalism was her bread and butter, but she saw her novels as her greatest achievement, and it was these that she posted to notable writers of the day with graceful compliments. She was genuinely attached to 'a few dear friends in our own neighbourhood, some much loved American friends in Rome, and a circle of old friends in London,'[17] but acquaintance with the famous held a special attraction. There is in the Somerville archive a sheet headed 'List of Remarkable Persons I have met, known, conversed with or corresponded with', containing ninety two names, of which seventeen are names of women.[18] It is undated, but must have been completed at a later date, since it includes a number of Egyptologists whose acquaintance she did not make until the 1880s; it does, however, include many artists and writers whom she knew in the 1860s. She collected notables just as she collected books, and would later collect antiquities.

During the late 1860s Amelia continued to contribute to anthologies, annuals and journals. In 1867 her story *The Four-Fifteen Express* which had appeared in *Routledge's Annual* was reprinted in *Mixed Sweets*, along with contributions from her friends Stirling Coyne and F.C. Burnand among others. The book was published as 'a Summer Volume, to be read and enjoyed in the country or at the seaside'.[19] In 1868 she regularly reviewed art exhibitions, theatrical performances and books for the *Morning Post*. This was the vehicle for her notices of Doré's engravings,[20] Frederick Church's 'gorgeous but never gaudy' oil paintings[21] and those of Bierstadt and Holman Hunt. In a letter to Edward Abbott she wrote,

> An author I have remained but the old passion for art has never died out. I am half an artist even now. I spend my holidays in sketching … My sketches altogether fill many folios, & form a consecutive record of my travels … I have carried my notebook & colour box far & often afield …[22]

Her holidays in the late 1860s can be traced mainly from her few dated sketches which survive: Hastings in September 1866,[23] West Somerset in 1867.[24] She was staying at Atlantic Terrace in November 1867,[25] at the Westminster Arms Hotel, Malvern, in September 1868[26] and in Devon in 1870.[27] There is no record, however, that she travelled abroad in these years. This may have been due to the political unrest at the time in both France and Italy, or to poor health. Writing of a serious illness in the winter of 1870/71 she comments that she has suffered from it twice before, though not so badly.[28]

Her one major literary achievement of these years was her sixth novel, *Debenham's Vow*, which first appeared during 1869 as a serial in *Good Words*, and was published in three volumes by Hurst & Blackett with an 1870 imprint. It was well reviewed, and Amelia must have been pleased that the critical reception which *Half a Million of Money* had provoked was now reversed. The *Contemporary Review* described *Debenham's Vow* as

> an exciting story and a satisfactory work of art … One or two faults of treatment present themselves … But the book as a whole is an admirable, we might almost say, a noble work. Its characterisation is profound. Our sympathies are unsparingly given to Juliet … De Benham is painted with unusual care and is a masterly study.[29]

The book was translated into German and published in Leipzig in 1876, and reprinted in the Tauchnitz series, in Harper's *Library of Select Classics*, and in a cheap edition by Smith & Sons, London. As was her custom, Amelia sent complimentary copies to her literary friends shortly before

Christmas 1869, and must have been gratified by Anthony Trollope's response:

> The man's character is admirably kept up, and is, as you no doubt intended, the pearl of the book … All the American scenes are excellent and full of life … To my seeming the only fault of the story – for there always is a fault – is the want of sympathy with Debenham.[30]

When she sent copies to Robert Browning a year later he replied that he was 'continuing to cheer *cent per cent* [*sic*] at your very bright, very beautiful story. All the perils by sea are capitally done, but, do you know, the delicater touches of the last volume are even more to my mind.'[31]

Names on a list, mere acquaintances, could not wholly satisfy Amelia, however friendly and hospitable such acquaintances might be. There is no evidence to suggest that she still thought of marriage; as she neared the age of forty she must have thought that such a future was unlikely. She must have yearned for companionship of friends of her own generation, such as she had enjoyed on her childhood visits to Westerfield and on her travels abroad in her twenties. Two people, it would appear, seemed able in different ways to provide for such yearnings: they were John Addington Symonds and his sister-in-law, Marianne North.

One of the literati among Amelia's local acquaintances was the poet and philosopher John Addington Symonds, who lived at Clifton with his wife Catherine, whom he married in 1864. An anonymous note with the Edwards papers at Somerville College refers to:

> Long correspondence, beginning about 1864, with J.A. Symonds, distinctly intimate & personal in character – conversation of 2 intimate friends between whom the bond of intimacy is principally an intellectual one. V. interesting – allusions to his work in the making or to hers, here & there his views on art or Lit. Much that is of purely family interest. A few poems in ms., some of which are contained in 'Many Moods' – some not traced. Beside these a large packet of proof copies of his poems.[32]

Unfortunately almost no correspondence answering this description survives with the Edwards papers. There are proof copies of poems, but the earliest letters from John Symonds to Amelia are dated 1871. The nature and duration of their friendship can only be surmised. That Amelia enjoyed his company and that they met regularly is, however, clear from an undated letter from Amelia asking him to send her copies of two of his poems, presumably for her compilation of *A Poetry Book of Modern Poets*.[33] 'Pray bring this one, and the one I last mentioned, when you next come for a talk, as I have so much to say about them.'[34] There were once three photographs of John Symonds in Amelia's photograph album, but all are now missing. There are two signed but undated poems by John Symonds in the Somerville Archive, and seven others unsigned but probably his.

The most revealing document in John Symonds' hand which survives is a letter, addressed to Amelia on 17 September 1871, when she was about to leave for Italy, enclosing a poem with the note:

> My dear friend, I sat up late last night finishing & writing out these lines – some of which are very unpolished. When I am the great poet you prophesy, this sheet will have an additional value from the lines I am now writing! (The influence of your autograph book, you see, is still upon me) ... I wanted to send this to you at 'Albergo delle due Torri, Verona', but Catherine has dissuaded me, saying Florence will be safer. You are probably on the sea as I write this. I am writing in the room where my dear father died so lately – 6 months since ... Some of the above stanzas, I should tell you, were written years ago for him; but the whole poem is altered so as to be yours. I often think of that crested ring & wonder what it all means. [The allusion is unknown.] Go cruel egotism – or passion remorseful & yet stubborn in its pride. Ever yrs, J.A.S.[35]

Amelia's admiration for John Symonds dates back at least to 1864, when she sent him a copy of her book, *Ballads* (see page 60). The poem in twenty stanzas, to which he refers above, 'To A.B.E. leaving England Sept: 16.1871', has a morbid tone, and it seems somewhat odd that he should offer her an amended poem first written for his father, but that this is preserved when most of his letters to her are lost suggests that it was acceptable to her:

> ... Pale autumn leaves us to the lingering grief
> Of melancholy winter; while you fly
> On summer's swallow-wings to Italy ...
>
> The mighty names & memories of those
> Who lived & died to die no more, shall close
> Your happy pilgrimage; & you shall learn,
> Breathing their ancient air, the thoughts that burn
> Forever in the hearts of after men ...

Farewell: you pass, we tarry; yet for us
Is the long, weary, penitential way
Of thought, that souls must travel, dubious,
With tottering steps …

There is no rest except in death
For him who stays and him who journeyeth.[36]

How long Amelia's correspondence with John Symonds was maintained is not known, nor when they ceased to meet 'for a talk', but as time went by, John spent more and more time abroad in Switzerland 'for his health', as the *Dictionary of National Biography* puts it, or because he was driven by his homosexuality to seek a more tolerant country. His marriage to Catherine North was not altogether a happy one. 'I always think it is good for both to be apart sometimes,' wrote Marianne to Amelia in May 1871.[37]

Although she had many eminent acquaintances, after the death of Sarah Braysher in 1864 Amelia had no close woman friend of her own generation, and this may well have led to a sense of loneliness and depression, but in the summer of 1870 this was to change, when she met Marianne North. The beginning of their friendship can be dated from Marianne's autobiography *Recollections of a Happy Life*. 'I made friends with Amelia B. Edwards that year [1870]' she wrote, 'whose bright companionship and varied interests did me a world of good when she stayed with me. Her home was near my sister's at Clifton, in the house of a kind old lady who treated her like a daughter.'[38] The occasion of their meeting is not known, but may have been at the Symonds' house in Clifton. They were almost contemporaries: Marianne was nine months older than Amelia. Unlike Amelia, Marianne had been born into a landed family which had over several centuries made an illustrious contribution both to political and to academic life. She had been brought up in a home frequented by scientists and artists, politicians and writers. Her father had been the Whig Member of Parliament for Hastings for many years, but had died in October 1869, and his loss to Marianne was as great as the loss to Amelia of her mother nine years earlier. Their common grief may well have been a factor in their attraction for each other, and they had much in common. Like Amelia, Marianne had both musical and artistic talents, but had chosen to devote herself to art. They may well have recognised kindred spirits in each other on first acquaintance.

Marianne was no hoarder, and none of Amelia's letters to her survives, but there is a lively series of letters from Marianne to Amelia, written over more than a decade, which reveal an intimate friendship.

*Fig. 9: Marianne North from her scrap-book at Rougham Hall, Norfolk,
where it has the title 'Pop', her nickname.*

Within months of their meeting Amelia had apparently declared her
fondness for Marianne and her hope that it was reciprocated, for
Marianne replied: 'Dear Amy, thank you so much for your letter. I will
write you one tomorrow – at present I am driven! I only scrawl this to
tell you that I do love you without any blarney. Ever yrs as always,
Pop.'[39] There is no indication that there was a sexual side to the
friendship which speedily developed between the two women. It would
appear to have been no more than a very close, platonic relationship.

Marianne was true to her word, and posted a second letter on 15 May
1871, thanking Amelia for a gift of writing paper. In the course of the
letter she describes a visit to friends 'in part of Queen Anne's Palace of
Camden in an odd old house … that would suit you & me some day'.[40]
Amelia apparently responded by return of post with a heady
enthusiasm for a closer relationship, proposing to give her a gold ring,
for Marianne writes four days later:

> Bless you! What love letters you do write, what a pity you waste
> them on a woman! Don't waste your money on 'massive gold
> garter rings'. I never wear them out of England … I shall not forget
> you in a hurry though I can't write sentiment …
> Goodbye & don't go & sentimentalise in damp meadows about
> your affectionate friend Pop …
> [PS] She is not worth it & you will get your feet wet & cold & then
> you will not be able to come & stay at the flat never no more.[41]

Marianne was about to leave on her longest journey yet in search of
exotic flowers to paint, and Amelia must have felt a particular urgency
in establishing a bond with one whose friendship she so much
cherished, but Marianne was unprepared for her demonstrative manner,
and wrote a few days later:

> My dear Amy, what an unmitigated goose you are! There you have
> my whole opinion of you frankly. What's the use of giving me
> rings – do you think I have no memory for friends & want
> playthings to remind me of them? & besides I have not the
> slightest intention of marrying you or anybody else & shall have
> you bringing me up for a 'breach of promise' case next. – I don't
> wish to lose my money in paying lawsuits. If you are dull & bored
> at the Larches (as you must & ought to be) come up here & I will
> not flatter you when I say you will make me very happy.[42]

Marianne wanted to visit her father's grave before leaving for America,
and added 'in all truth, Amy, I have no love to give you or anyone – it is
all gone with him – it would be untrue to pretend otherwise, but that is
no reason why you & I should not be true friends as long as we both live
& bring much happiness to one another also'.

Although Marianne's letters often give an impression that she was
less prepared than Amelia for intimacy, there was a genuinely mutual
fondness. After Amelia had seen her off from Clifton on the London train
after a visit to her sister, Marianne writes: 'It is so nice to be home & nice
to have your petting at the last moment – for I do like it – rather – though
what should put it into your head to do it I can't think!'[43] The usually
bright and cheerful style of her letters belied an underlying depression,
and she felt the need to apologise to Amelia for her 'stingy grumbles of
yesterday in return for those wonderful long letters of love you wrote
me'.

They did indeed remain friends, but Marianne's travels worldwide
over the next two decades meant that they rarely met after the summer

of 1871, and the later letters do not show the same intimacy. Amelia kept Marianne's name alive in Britain by reporting her travels in the papers, by mutual agreement, but this eventually strained their relationship to the limit. In one of her last letters Marianne writes from South Africa:

> I wish you had not put that thing in the Academy,[44] it is full of things I never wrote & which are untrue & has been copied into local papers & turned me into a joke … Please do not print anything more about what 'she writes' unless you put the very words … The idea of Queenstown being 6000 ft above the sea![45]

Amelia was evidently forgiven, for the following year Marianne comments on Amelia's article about her in *The Queen*:[46] 'What a grand story you have made of me … I have hardly studied it, but saw no mistakes of consequence [here she draws attention to three mistakes] … & am so glad you have put your name to it.'[47]

It is doubtful whether Marianne could ever have coped for long with a bosom friend. She was thankful to escape from Mrs Skinner, her travelling companion in America, and thereafter always travelled, and lived, alone. 'I never repent of being alone,' she wrote to Amelia.[48]

During the winter of 1870–71 Amelia was very ill. All that is known of her illness is what she writes in a letter of 30 March 1871 to Mrs Cave who was wintering in Penzance:

> I have been very ill – ill for three months – but this I dare say you do not know. First I had a very dangerous throat attack (laryngitis) & when I was just beginning to recover from that, an attack of pressure on the brain. I have had the latter twice before – but never so badly as this time. It brought with it a sort of half-paralysis & *not* being brought on by overwork or over-application of any kind, alarmed me the more. But I am now much better – if not yet quite well.[49]

The symptoms which she described might indicate that she had suffered a stroke, but there is nothing in any of the available documents to suggest that she suffered any of the frequent after-effects of a stroke. Joan Rees suggests that,

> The special stress of this period may well have owed something to years of sexual abstinence or frustration and if she became passionately heated in her feeling for Marianne, her emotions inflamed further by the prospect of long periods of absence, it

would not be surprising. Diagnosis in all the circumstances must needs be cautious.[50]

There is, however, no evidence that she was so consumed with a sense of frustration that it caused a pathological condition. It seems incompatible with the 'bright companionship and varied interests' which cheered Marianne three months later when Amelia went to stay with her and was busy writing again.[51] All that is certain is that Amelia could not understand her illness and was alarmed by it.

Having recovered from her long illness by the summer of 1871, Amelia planned to travel to Europe for the first time in nine years. She wrote to her friend and neighbour, Mrs Cave:

> I shall soon be going away ... for a long time. I shall spend the summer, autumn and winter abroad, remaining away perhaps nearly a whole year ... I was engaged already [i.e., presumably, before she was taken ill] to spend the winter with my dear friends Sir John and Lady M[urray] in Florence – & now I shall throw the summer into the scale, & try what Switzerland can do to re-establish me first.[52]

In the event she did not leave England until mid-September, two months after Marianne had left for America. On this occasion Amelia travelled alone. She took with her the notebook which she had last used when travelling abroad in 1862, and began a new page with the heading *Reminiscences & Notes of a Tour in Germany, Bavaria, Tyrol & Italy*. The first entry was made in Oberammergau on 23 September 1871, and describes the carriage ride from Munich, mentioning people whom they passed on the road, and in particular 'a withered old crone [sitting] on a heap of stones by the wayside, lifting her blind eyes to the carriages as we pass. A party of peasant men coming up on foot with eagles' feathers in their hats drop each a small coin into her lap as they pass.'[53] Her power of meticulous observation and her ability to record with the minimum of sentimentality, had not diminished since her last journey abroad.

Amelia's long description of the Passion Play at Oberammergau is of particular interest as one of very few accounts of religious observances in her writing. She would have been drawn to the performance by her love of theatre rather than from a sense of pilgrimage, yet her account is not simply that of a theatre critic but a record of both a physical and a spiritual experience.

She describes the theatre, and notable members of the audience: 'Prince and Princess Leck, Lord and Lady Stanhope, Archbishop of

Munich present', but soon the audience is forgotten. 'Nothing could describe the beauty of these [the Old Testament] scenes in the bright daylight – the absence of artificial aids, of painted faces & gaslight – the green hills behind the theatre … the real shadows cast by the personages.' She did not wholly suspend disbelief, writing: 'The Pharaoh & Red Sea scene, the Jonah & some of the others, were beyond the reach of the village artist & simply ludicrous', but with the scene of the entry into Jerusalem she was overwhelmed by Joseph Mayer, the actor who played Christ:

> He is graceful, beautiful, dignified … His eyes are large, soft, dark grey & very gentle – his smile is the sweetest I ever saw – a perfect *gentleman*, God-made – he lifts his hand with a grace no nobleman could surpass, & his manner is all courtesy, kindness, simplicity & unconsciousness. He is a confectioner & woodcarver, married to a wife some years older than himself & somewhat plain – has three children – lives in a good house in the village where I called on him. (p. 68)

Fig. 10: Joseph Mayer in the role of Christ, Oberammergau, 1871, from Amelia Edwards' photograph album.

Joseph Mayer was included in Amelia's list of 'Remarkable Persons I have met'[54] and she kept two photographs of him in the role of Christ in her photograph album.[55] She found the scene of Christ scourged particularly affecting:

> He stands bound to the low pillar as in some painting by an old master ... This is the first time we see his beautiful form – in the light flesh-coloured garment. His face expressed pain & sadness, but the resignation of one pre-ordained & prepared to suffer. This scene produced a thrilling & breathless sensation (which was [over] in about 2 and a half minutes) – all silent. I looked at my next neighbour & drew a deep breath & she the same at me.

This last strangely incoherent and scarcely grammatical sentence is without precedent in her notebook. Of the Crucifixion scene she writes that she 'saw where the main support was, at the back of his neck' but this artifice in no way distracted her attention from the man:

> He looked marvellously beautiful, & his form more beautiful than I had supposed any man's form could be; full & yet not fat, every limb rounded, every line grace ... His voice when he spoke to Mary and to John ... was truly sonorous & plaintive. Then his head dropped & it was over. They were another 20 min. taking him down ... A beautiful, peaceful, tender close to a terrible scene.

Amelia is describing a deeply emotional, one might say an erotic, experience – she is seeing Joseph Mayer, 'the Christus', as a man, rather than as the Son of God; yet it appears to have been a rare religious experience for her too:

> The effects of the weather all through were fine, as if so arranged by a miracle ... One could consider the natural scenery beyond as belonging in some way to the play ... High as I sat, I could see the outer life of the fields going on beyond ... During the scene before Pilate I saw a man going up the stream fly-fishing – & during the crucifixion scene (it being now near five & the day turning to storm) the country folk some way off ... were clearly seen driving home their oxen from pasture.[56]

It is wholly in character that her highly emotive description of the play is followed by the prosaic entry: 'Outside the theatre were scores of stalls for the sale of rosaries, holy prints, medals, fruit, cakes, photographs, wine, &c. &c. ... & people of all nations & classes crowding & surging about between the parts & at the close of the performance.'[57]

After the description of the Passion Play the notebook contains shorter entries on the various places visited as she travelled south to Rome, with descriptions of the architecture, landscape and customs of the region; scenes to be sketched or written into novels. The villa of the Marchesa della Stufa at Castagnola, the Palazzo Visconti at Padua, the House of the Capulets at Verona, the cities of Bologna and Genoa all receive her attention, but with the exception of Genoa where she recounts an amusing incident in the cathedral where children are being taken through their catechism, there is little of personal interest in the descriptions.

By mid-October Amelia had reached Rome, her goal for the winter. In her notebook she describes the view 'from my window'. She was staying in a lodging house overlooking the Piazza di Spagna and describes the scene below: 'The models [for her sketches], picturesque fellows six feet high, black-haired olive-skinned women, little children & old men with white beards, group themselves on the great steps of the Trinità del Monte, close against my window. I sketch them for nothing, & they scowl at me picturesquely – also for nothing.'[58] She describes the flower-seller, the roast-chestnut vendor, the newspaper kiosks, a troupe of youths 'from some religious seminary' and:

> Just opposite, on the same floor as myself, lodges a young musician. His room is so small that when the window is thrown open *à deux volants* I can see almost into every corner ... I see him in the very act of composition ... He is rather good-looking & I am sure very poor, but he looks like a gentleman.[59]

Matilda Betham-Edwards writes that 'During her winter in Rome, 1872–3 [an error, her winter in Rome was 1871–72] she attended the classes of an Italian artist'[60] and this may well account for the unusually close observation of people and her reference to the youths in the Piazza as 'models'. In the Somerville archive there is a scrap-book pasted up with sketches, some of them dated, including a sketch of a man asleep 'on the steps, Novr 10th/71', and four sketches of priests dated December 21st. In all there are thirty pages of drawings of figures in picturesque garments which, though unsigned, can be ascribed with reasonable certainty to Amelia and from which her progress through Italy can be dated.[61]

Fig. 11: Sketches in Italy, from Amelia Edwards' sketch-book of 1871–72.

Writing from Boston to Amelia in Rome, Marianne reported that she had met their mutual friend, Miss Cushman, who had 'talked affectionately of Mrs Braysher'. She added: 'I wish you could have had her with you abroad – poor old lady, she will miss you sadly I fear.'[62] Marianne was clearly somewhat worried about Amelia's solitary travels. Her letter was forwarded to Amelia from Florence, where it was addressed to the care of Sir John Digby Murray, and forwarded again from Verona, reaching her in Rome on 19 November. By the time Marianne wrote again, on 7 November, she had heard from Amelia in Florence, and was reassured: 'It is so funny your finding Mrs Ross – my mother's godchild & namesake… So you expect to be quiet in Rome! possible but not probable! but I am glad you have relations near you & may be a great help to your poor blind cousin by your pleasant talk.'[63] The identity of the blind cousin has not been traced. Matilda and one of her sisters may have been in Rome that winter, but there is no reference to them in Amelia's notebook, nor to any visits made or received. There is, however, between vivid descriptions of the Corso and of the Appian Way, a uniquely introspective passage, which reveals Amelia's mood, and the numbness and melancholy which beset her during that winter in Rome. It needs to be quoted in full:

> As life goes on, one's heart deadens & wearies from many disappointments, & one ceases to look for heart in others. My heart no longer beats faster at the sight of a new or kindly & beautiful face. I hope nothing from it. I have come to the turn in the road of life when I expect no more love, when an act of genuine kindness, or an expression of genuine interest startles me & surprises me & fills me with gratitude, but ceases to give me hope. That it should last, or increase, or be anything but a pleasant, passing incident seems impossible. I go through the world now as one goes through the Hall of Busts at the Capitol, seeing only heads and looking for hearts no longer. To me my fellow creatures are busts only. I have come to ask nothing and expect nothing from them but a certain amount of intellectual stimulus. That a person should be clever is the only merit I ask, & all the difference I seem to observe between this person or that is his or her greater or lesser degree of intellectual culture & innate cleverness. Thus I think I appreciate wit & critical faculty above every other now – simply because it sparkles more, plays more on the surface, & rouses me for the moment. Men & women are not to me like my fellow creatures any longer, but as animate books, or pamphlets, or daily papers – talking shadows – things so far from & apart from me, that except as they

amuse me they do not seem to exist. In fact, to paraphrase Berkeley's theory, they exist only as I perceive them to be entertaining. They are, briefly, busts – busts alive, thinking & speaking & nothing more. Whether the bust is that of a good or a bad person, a Christian or Pagan, a man or a woman, matters nothing. To me it is a work of art only, & so are my fellow-creatures. Sometimes I feel as if I also were a mere bust – or worse still, a terminal statue – head above & a marble column below. At other times I am scarcely conscious of even my head, & feel like a shadow moving among shadows – emotionless, passionless, unimpressed, almost without the consciousness of thought. I have to look for things, in order to see them, & to listen, in order to hear. My senses are no longer open & ready as of old. Moving to & fro among the sights & sounds of this wonderful city, I have to fix my attention upon objects – to compel myself to observe, or I should see nothing. This is real age – it is thus I know how the years have gone over my head. And yet it is only fourteen years ago – it seems like a century.

Notes

[1] Houghton Autograph File, Wendell Bequest, 1918.

[2] SCO Edwards 381, undated.

[3] Houghton bMS AM 1340.2 (1778).

[4] SCO Edwards 15, 1 July 1869.

[5] SCO Edwards 318.

[6] *Literary World*, 25 February 1883, pp. 93–95.

[7] SCO Edwards 609.

[8] SCO Edwards, 135, 14 December 1865.

[9] UCL Ms Misc. 3E/2.

[10] SCO Edwards 70.

[11] SCO Edwards 443, 'Chère Mademoiselle, Je viens vous remercier de la grace infinie que vous avez eu de rendre compte à vos lecteurs des oeuvres nouvelles que j'expose à Londres, et … pour les lignes si obligantes et si flatteuse. Encore mille fois merci, chère Mademoiselle, et à bientôt j'espère, car je pense bien avant la fin du mois faire une petite visite à Londres et avoir le plaisir de vous serrer la main.'

[12] SCO Edwards 445, 17 February 1871.

[13] SCO Edwards 512.

[14] SCO Edwards 319.

[15] SCO Edwards 52, undated.

[16] SCO Edwards 96.240.

[17] SCO Edwards 351.

[18] SCO Edwards 565.32.

[19] *Mixed Sweets*, from Routledge's annual, by Mrs H. Wood [and others] (London: Routledge, 1867).

[20] *Morning Post*, 29 June and 24 December 1868.

[21] *Morning Post*, 27 February 1868 and 24 June 1868.

[22] SCO Edwards 351.

[23] SCO Edwards W57.

[24] SCO Edwards W36, W58.

[25] UCL Ms Misc. 3E/2.

[26] SCO Edwards 518.

[27] SCO Edwards W14, W55, W3, W88.

[28] UCL Mss Add 182.9.

[29] *Contemporary Review*, December 1869.

[30] SCO Edwards 318, 9 December 1869.

[31] SCO Edwards 17, 27 March 1871.

[32] SCO Edwards 613, undated.

[33] Amelia B. Edwards, *A Poetry Book of Modern Poets* (London: Longman, 1878).

[34] SCO Edwards 559.

[35] SCO Edwards 500.

[36] Ibid.

[37] SCO Edwards 229, 22 May 1871.

[38] Marianne North, *Further Recollections of a Happy Life* (London: Macmillan, 1894), p. 313.

[39] SCO Edwards 226, 13 May 1871; 'Pop' was the nickname her father had given her.

[40] SCO Edwards 227.

[41] SCO Edwards 228, 19 May 1871.

[42] SCO Edwards 239, 26 May 1871.

[43] SCO Edwards 233, 1 June 1871.

[44] 'Miss North in South Africa', *The Academy*, Vol. 23, No. 567 (17 March 1883), p. 188.

[45] SCO Edwards 259, 30 April 1883.

[46] Amelia B. Edwards, 'Miss Marianne North', *The Queen* (15 December 1883), pp. 603–4.

[47] SCO Edwards 242, 30 January 1884.

[48] SCO Edwards 249, 10 September 1871.

[49] UCL Mss Add 182.9.

[50] Joan Rees, *Amelia Edwards: Traveller, Novelist and Egyptologist* (London: Rubicon Press, 1998).

[51] SCO Edwards 221.

[52] UCL Mss Add 182.9.

[53] SCO Edwards 515, p. 68.

[54] SCO Edwards 565.32.

[55] SCO Edwards 524.

[56] SCO Edwards 515, p. 67.

[57] Ibid.

[58] SCO Edwards 515, p. 81.

[59] SCO Edwards 515, p. 82.

[60] Matilda Betham-Edwards, 'Amelia B. Edwards: her childhood and early life', *New England Magazine*, New Series, 7, 5 (Boston, MA, January 1893), p. 555.

[61] SCO Edwards 433.

[62] SCO Edwards 251, 7 November 1871.

[63] SCO Edwards 252, 23 November 1871.

7

Lucy Renshaw and the Dolomites, 1872

Amelia began the year 1872 in a melancholy mood. There are two poems headed 'Verses written in Rome' in her notebook, both of them signed, which are love poems. The first in the book, though it has the title 'An Answer', is dated 30 January 1872 and begins:

> Last night, sweet, in a jesting hour
> You bade me tell you where my skill
> Fell short to execute my will
> And where the limit of my power.
>
> I'll tell thee. First of all, my sweet,
> I cannot choose but lay my heart,
> My life, and what I have of art,
> And all my future at thy feet.
>
> I cannot, loving thee so well,
> Unlove thee for a single day
> I cannot, even when I pray,
> Unloose the magic of thy spell.[1]

It is tempting to speculate whether Amelia was addressing the verses to Marianne North, remembering a conversation of the previous summer, or whether she had in mind one of her friends in Rome, or whether she was writing without reference to her own situation but simply envisaging a context for the poem in a future novel or book of ballads. The second poem, undated, is equally enigmatic:

> My love, in dark & lonely years,
> When life was all too sad at times,
> I wrote these melancholy rhymes
> And wrote them, not in ink, but tears …

I never thought the sun could rise,
The roses bloom again for me
How could I dream I should love thee
And find my heaven in thine eyes?

But so it is, & the drear Past
Is dead & buried. Let it go
I love thee & am loved, & lo!
The sun shines in God's heaven at last!

Again, one can only speculate on whether this was an expression of Amelia's own feelings at the time, or merely a poetic exercise with a view to future publication. The sense suggests that it was written some time later than the first, but the use of the same form and metre show that they were intended to be read as a pair.

A water-colour painted in Rome and dated 19 March[2] shows that Amelia remained in Rome until the early spring, but she then travelled south, reaching Salerno by 10 April, and it was while staying there that

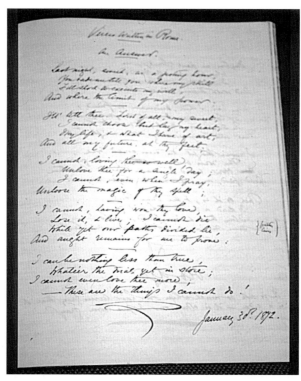

Fig. 12: Verses written in Rome, from Amelia Edwards' diary, 1872.

she witnessed an eruption of Vesuvius. There is a full account of the event in her notebook,[3] and a second manuscript account in a separate document also survives in the Somerville archive.[4] Her power of vivid and meticulous description is nowhere more clearly seen than in the account in her notebook, beginning 25 April.

> Rose at 5 AM & looked out of the window & saw a rosy golden cloud hanging over the mountain & went to bed again. Looked again at 6 AM. Large volumes of smoke were now rising rapidly, in curling white & golden columnar masses against an inconceivably clear blue sky. This cloud kept developing with marvellous rapidity, pouring upwards from the crater, changing form with every second, now assuming shapes of capes, promontories, arches, towering higher & higher, piling up height above height, & by 9 AM reaching over half the horizon. At 10 AM I heard the first low thunderous rumble of the coming eruption – more like the dull ominous throbbing of a deep organ pipe than like any storm sound I ever heard.

That afternoon she went with friends into Naples for a better view:

> At the station Castellamare found a crowd of women & children & old men, loaded with household goods, sitting on piles of bedding, all talking, raving, gesticulating. These were the people from Portici and Torre del Greco who had fled from their homes for fear of the lava. At every station along the line we saw the same pitiable sight – old, old women, old men, little children, waiting for the gratuitous trains to carry them away … Driving through Naples … all the quays, housetops, street corners, balconies which commanded the view were crowded with spectators … As we sat at dinner the windows rattled & the deep thundering never ceased.

She describes a procession of priests and acolytes, followed by 'a vast crowd of the poorest and dirtiest of the population'. As they passed, the onlookers

> dropped on their knees, parting before them like the waves of a troubled sea, & closing up behind. It was strange in the dark night, with the glow of the burning mountain & burning villages for background, to see the flaring yellow torches, the upturned, agonised, imploring faces, the clasped hands, & to hear the wild, harsh, unmusical chant … Thus the procession swept on & passed

out of sight, & immediately the sound of frivolity & laughing …
burst out afresh.

The interest in Amelia's essay on the eruption of Vesuvius lies,
however, not only in the vividness of her description both of the physical
phenomena and of the human impact, but also in the first mention of
Lucy Renshaw, the friend who was to share her travels in the Dolomites
and in Egypt. It seems probable that it was at this time, when staying in
Salerno, that Amelia first met Lucy, for she is 'Miss Renshaw' and not
'Lucy' or 'L', the initial by which alone she is identified in the published
accounts of their travels. She is mentioned casually in the notebook,
along with other British people staying in Salerno at the time:

> Said here in South Italy (Mrs Somerville's mutterings among
> others) to be the greatest eruption since 1572 … Miss Renshaw &
> the Davidsons had been up to the cone on 23rd, & I sketching that
> day at Pompeii, had observed several shoots of very black smoke

Fig. 13: Lucy Renshaw, from Amelia Edwards' photograph album.

go up from the cone. One of the guides pointed out this appearance to me two or three times. Still no one attached any special importance to it.

Little can be deduced from Amelia's account of Mrs Somerville, other than that she is portrayed as something of a local authority: 'Mrs Somerville told Mrs Davidson that it was often very difficult to get the contadini to leave their homes & vineyards.' She was probably resident in the south of Italy, or a regular winter visitor. The Reverend Henry Davidson of Edinburgh and his wife were on an Italian tour with their son, Randall Thomas, who in 1903 became Archbishop of Canterbury. He was to write to Amelia more than a decade later from Lambeth Palace, shortly after his father's death, reminding her of their first meeting in Rome.[5] Miss Renshaw, on the other hand, was to share Amelia's most exciting and productive journeys, and to become the second of the three close women friends of her mature years.

Born in 1833, Lucy Renshaw was two years younger than Amelia. Very little is known about her, although by great good fortune the diary of her maid during their travels with Amelia in France, Egypt, Syria and Greece survives and reveals that at that time, 1873–74, Lucy Renshaw was living, or staying, at 'Broome Park'.[6] The location of Broome Park has not been identified, but was probably in the home counties. There is no evidence that she ever lived in Broome Park in Kent, later the home of Lord Kitchener. In 1898, according to her Will, she was living at South Frith Lodge, Tunbridge, Essex, but by July 1913, shortly before she died, she was living at 27 Clifton Crescent, Folkestone. She died on 28 September 1913, at 'Pekes', Hellingly, Sussex, aged 80. Neither of her parents is named on the death certificate, on which she is described as a 'spinster, of independent means'. She appears to have had no surviving relations at the time of her death. 'Renshaw' is a name found predominantly in the Manchester area, and it is perhaps significant that her bequests, apart from one to a friend in Drogheda, Ireland, were to Manchester friends and Manchester charities. It is possible that it was she who introduced Amelia to the families of the north west of England who were to play so important a part in the early years of the Egypt Exploration Fund and established an interest in Egyptology in that area which continues to this day.

There are scant references to Lucy in the Somerville archive. On 4 November 1880 Giuseppe Ghedina, the innkeeper in Cortina d'Ampezzo where they stayed in 1873, wrote to Amelia: 'I was very pleased to have the pleasure of seeing Miss Lucy, and some other time I hope to see the two of you together',[7] from which it would appear that Lucy Renshaw returned to the Dolomites later, without Amelia. She seems to have revisited Egypt too, without Amelia, for there is in the Martin archive a photograph of a party 'leaving Cairo for the desert' clearly dated 1876, and not 1874 when they made the trip up the Nile together.[8] They remained lifelong friends, however, travelling about Britain together and entertaining together when Amelia was in London. Amelia wrote to a Miss Worrall on 6 November 1881: 'We will certainly try to call on you before we again start away on our travels – for Miss Renshaw and I are flitting about the country, making excursions, paying visits, &c. &c...',[9] and a letter from Robert Browning dated 16 July 1881, addressed to Amelia at Bailey's Hotel, Gloucester Road, SW, declines 'your kind invitation and that of Miss Renshaw' which he would 'most cheerfully obey' had he not been 'otherwise unluckily engaged'.[10] Although Lucy is not listed among the mourners at Amelia's funeral in 1892, she sent a tribute of flowers.[11] She may have been indisposed at the time; 'Pekes', where she died in 1913, was a mental hospital, and it is sad to contemplate her probable drift into dementia in her old age.

In her book *With Passport and Parasol*, Julia Keay writes of Amelia's decision to go up the Nile: 'There was really no need to consult L. Amelia knew from long experience that her friend would agree to whatever she suggested.'[12] She also writes that 'L., if Amelia is to be believed ... spent most of her time knitting.'[13] There is no evidence for these statements. Joan Rees, in her book *Amelia B. Edwards: traveller, novelist and Egyptologist*,[14] refers to this 'pathetic picture of L. in Egypt as a down-trodden woman, always overridden by a dominating and bullying Amelia' as 'Julia Keay's mistaken picture' and is right to do so.

Joan Rees speculates, however, on 'the true nature of the relationship' beween Lucy and Amelia in the context of a passage in *Untrodden Peaks and Unfrequented Valleys* in which four peasant women, finding that the two friends are travelling alone, shake their heads and say '" Eh! poverine! poverine! [poor things, poor things] ... Are you married? ... Come! Not married? Neither of you?" "Neither of us" I reply, laughing'.[15] 'Is it', Joan Rees asks, 'implied that Amelia and L experience a marriage which not only has no need of a man but is so far superior that they cannot but laugh at the idea that they are to be pitied?' She also speculates on:

> a curious photograph of Lucy Renshawe [*sic*] ... in which she appears with severely cropped hair and wearing a cravat and a masculine jacket. The photographer has even brushed in shadows along her cheeks to represent sideboards! The photograph may

have been merely a joke but perhaps it indicates that Amelia and Lucy Renshawe embarked for a time on a relatively serious campaign to test the liberating effects of masculine attire.

The identification of the photograph[16] to which Joan Rees refers may, however, be questioned. It is not the photograph[17] of Lucy reproduced in her book (plate 2), which is found in the same album in the Somerville archive. The photograph of a person in a man's dress is indeed slotted into a 'window' in the album which bears the caption 'Miss Renshaw' but this caption is somewhat blurred as if in an attempt at erasure. It is the very first 'window' in the album. Some of the other windows have captions but no photographs; there are on the other hand several loose photographs, and it would appear that at one point they were removed, and maybe some were wrongly replaced. In one window, at any rate, the photograph of Andromeda Schliemann as a child, named on the reverse, appears in the window with the caption 'Miss Wade' which is clearly wrong.[18] It is therefore doubtful whether the photograph in question is of Lucy Renshaw in a man's clothes or, as seems at least as likely, of an unknown man, wrongly captioned.

There is no evidence from the two books in which Lucy Renshaw appears as 'L' to suggest a lesbian relationship, nor that Lucy ever dressed as a man. If anything, Lucy is portrayed as the more feminine of the two. In Egypt, when Amelia is preoccupied with sketching the newly discovered temple at Abu Simbel, and Mr McCallum and Mr Eyre are busy surveying it, 'L. and the Little Lady [Mrs Eyre] took their books and knitting there and made a little drawing room of it.'[19] Mrs Eyre and Lucy go shopping for basketwork;[20] they also miss the first sight of a crocodile because they are in the cabin 'indulging in that minor vice called afternoon tea'.[21] On both journeys Lucy was accompanied by a maid. In the Dolomites her maid is referred to as 'S', who 'being delicate, was less able for mountain work than ourselves'[22] and remained at Cortina while Lucy and Amelia made an excursion by foot and saddle to Pieve di Cadore,[23] and again at Caprile, when they embarked on a circular tour into the more exacting mountain tracks of the central Dolomites.[24] S. 'had never before mounted anything more spirited than a Sorrento donkey.'[25] For the Nile voyage Lucy took a new, younger maid, Jenny Lane, about whom more is known from her surviving diary of the voyage. Lucy may well have been brought up in a wealthier home than Amelia's, and have been more thoroughly accustomed to the life of a lady.

Lucy nevertheless appears to have been an extremely capable and intelligent woman. Amelia tells us that she 'is better up in her maps than myself and knew something of the distances',[26] and she also appears to have had more botanical knowledge than Amelia: at Caprile 'she found specimens of unusual wild flowers' which Amelia names in Latin;[27] no other reference to wild flowers seen by Amelia on her travels are so named, and the references to flowers are often far from specific. When it was necessary to inform the courier whom Lucy had engaged in Sorrento, 'a gentleman of refined and expensive tastes, who abhorred what is usually understood by "roughing it"', that they planned to venture into a little known and barely accessible area, 'the Writer, never famous for moral courage, ignominiously retreated; and L., the dauntless, undertook the service of danger … Of that tremendous interview no details ever transpired. Enough that L. came out of it composed but victorious.'[28]

Lucy was fond of animals, and possibly the more experienced rider of the two: 'L. and her mule', Amelia writes, 'are the best friends in the world. She feeds him perpetually with sugar, and he follows her about like a dog. My mule and I, on the contrary, never arrive at terms of intimacy. Perhaps he knows that I am the heavier weight …'[29] When they finally part company at Atzwang 'L., albeit unused to the melting mood, exchanges quite affecting adieux with fair Nessol.'[30] In Egypt, Lucy nurses an injured bird on board the dahabiyah.[31] It may well be that Lucy had been brought up in the country and was more at home with animals than Amelia was.

Lucy was as eager and stalwart a traveller as Amelia. Of all Amelia's friends she was the one with whom physically demanding excursions were possible. In *A Thousand Miles up the Nile* Amelia wrote, 'L. and the Writer had done some difficult walking in their time, over ice and snow, on lava cold and hot, up cinder slopes and beds of mountain torrents; but this innocent looking sand-drift proved quite as hard to climb as any of them.'[32]

Amelia was still in the south of Italy on 6 May 1872, when she was sketching at Sorrento[33] but by the beginning of June she had travelled with Lucy north to Bologna. From this point the entries in her notebook cease, but her progress can be followed from her published account, *Untrodden Peaks and Unfrequented Valleys*. By mid-June, having escaped from 'the steaming lakes … Como, Lugano and Maggiore' they had reached Monte Generoso, where they were staying in 'a pleasant hotel… numbering among its guests many Roman friends of the past season'.[34] They had intended to proceed from there to tour the Engadine, but 'we began, somehow, to look more and more longingly to the north-eastern horizon; and to dream … of those mystic mountains beyond Verona which we knew of, somewhat indefinitely, as the Dolomites'. Amelia says that fifteen years earlier she had seen sketches of the Dolomites by 'a great artist not long since passed away' and had been 'haunted by them ever since, and that 'fortunately my friend … had also read and dreamed of Dolomites'.

Very few British travellers had visited the Dolomites at that time, and the only book in English dealing with them at any length was Gilbert and Churchill's scholarly book of 1864.[35] It was no doubt in part the attraction of the unknown which lured Amelia. She must also have looked forward to sketching these most spectacular mountains, and her love of art will have drawn her to the region which had inspired Titian.

In making their plans for the journey they had 'some difficulties to be overcome'. They knew that accommodation could present problems so far from the usual tourist areas; then too, Lucy's maid, 'being delicate, was less able for mountain work than ourselves', and there was 'the supreme difficulty of the courier' who would not be happy with their change of plans. They left Monte Generoso on 27 June 1872 and 'went down in all the freshness and beauty of the early morning' to Como by carriage, and thence by steamer to Bellagio. The next day they continued by boat to Lecco, by carriage to Bergamo and by train to Venice:

> For the traveller who has gone over all this ground at his leisure and is familiar with each place of interest as it flits by, I know no greater enjoyment than to pass them in rapid review. What a chain of memories! I had not thought, when I turned southwards last autumn, that I should find myself threading the familiar waterways so soon again. … It was a gayer, fuller, noisier Venice; a Venice empty of English and American tourists; full to overflowing of Italians.[36]

Amelia's mood is different too: gone is the melancholy of the solitary autumn and winter in Rome. She has a friend prepared to share an adventure.

After shopping for provisions to sustain them in emergencies they left Venice by train on 2 July, still accompanied by the courier, 'sulky and silent', and alighted at Conegliano 'with our pile of bags at our feet and all our adventures before us. We look into each other's faces.'[37] The sense of shared excitement is unmistakable. They travelled to Longarone that evening by carriage, catching a glimpse on the way of their first Dolomite mountain. The next day they reached Cortina, which was to be their base for the next week, and stayed at the Aquila Nera, an inn run by the Ghedina family, a father and two sons. One day at Cortina they watched through field glasses as two British gentlemen, who were staying at the same inn with their wives, made the first ascent of the Bec di Mezzodi, and enjoyed the sense of 'being there' as the history of alpinism was made. They also enjoyed the Sagro, or patronal festival, which took place while they were there, and Amelia sketched the country people in their traditional costumes.

On the third morning of their stay in Cortina their courier tendered his resignation. 'Our vagabond tastes were too much for him and he deserted us … just at the time when the protection of a trustworthy and respectable man had become an indispensable condition of our journey.'[38] They summarily rejected the fortnight's notice which he offered, and he was paid off immediately. 'As for L., by whom he had been retained for months before we joined forces in Naples, she transacted the whole affair with … withering sang-froid.'[39]

The dismissal of the courier, satisfying though it was, presented them with a dilemma: 'Could we possibly go on only with guides, and no courier?' Before long the problem was solved when their landlord's nephew, Giuseppe Ghedina, 'a tall, fair-haired young man of about twenty-eight or thirty… a farmer, lately married, well to do',[40] agreed to travel with them. They would pay for his travel and subsistence but not for his accommodation. 'A more fortunate choice could not have been made. Faithful, honest, untiring, intelligent , [he was] … always at hand but never obtrusive, as economical of our money as of his own.'[41]

An unexpected problem was the difficulty in securing side-saddles. 'In the event of our being able to carry out our journey, they were of more real importance than a whole army of couriers. Without them, certainly, we could do nothing in the way of peaks or passes',[42] and they needed three. They learnt that Madame Pezze, the innkeeper at Caprile, had one, and arranged to borrow it. Their landlord also possessed a side-saddle but was clearly reluctant to lend it or even show it, but Amelia 'followed him into the stable one day' and caught sight of it. As for a third saddle for Lucy's maid, he said, 'We'll dress up a *basta* for the *cameriera* [maid] and all shall be well'. Amelia explains:

> This promise of the Basta was obscure but comforting. I had not the sightest idea of what a Basta was and Ghedina could only tell me what it was not. It was not a side-saddle. It was not a chair. It was not a railed seat with a foot rest … It had to be made when required.[43]

When they eventually arrived at Caprile, probably on 14 July, they spent the first day

> getting rid of the two Ghedinas, who were returning to Cortina with their horses, but not, if we could help it, with their side-

saddle. How this delicate and difficult matter was negotiated matters little now. Enough that, being simple men with but few words at command, they were ultimately talked out of their convictions… We promised of course to pay for the hire of it … We promised everything possible and impossible, and were crowned with that success which is not always the reward of virtue.[44]

Their determination to have their way was indeed ruthless. '"The Padre will be furious with us", said the younger Ghedina … It occurred to me that this was highly probable.' The incident is described with humour and in no sense as a confession.

Amelia gives few dates in her published account, but from clues in the narrative it is possible to reconstruct with reasonable certainty the passage of time. She describes the days meticulously, usually giving an idea of the time of departure, hours spent riding or walking, and the time of arrival at the day's destination. Her book was certainly intended to provide practical hints for other travellers, although primarily designed to entertain. For such purpose the actual dates of their excursions were of little significance.

From Cortina they made two day-long excursions before Giuseppe joined them, one on 6th July to the Falzarego Pass, from which to see the Marmolada, and one to Landro and the Dürren See on 9 July. On the first occasion their landlord provided a '*caretta*' which was 'simply a wooden trough on wheels … with a crosswise plank to sit upon',[45] and they had a rough ride. On reaching the inn at the pass, and finding there was nothing but dry bread, butter and 'a coarse, uneatable mountain cheese' to be had, Amelia undertook 'in a moment of happy inspiration' to concoct a dish of '"buttered eggs", or more politely, … "hasty omelette"' which proved so successful that she was thereafter known at the inn as 'Signora Cuoca'.[46] This culinary episode seems to belie Matilda Betham-Edwards' remark that 'I do not think that the eminent Egyptologist ever … made a cup of tea in her life'.[47] For the second excursion 'our landlord provided a comfortable little chaise on good springs, with a seat in front for the driver; and the chestnut appeared in smart harness, with red tassels on her head and a necklace of little jingling bells.' Signor Ghedina had no doubt learnt that the ladies expected more comfort.[48]

When Giuseppe joined them as 'travelling attendant', probably on 10 July, they made a two-day excursion to Pieve di Cadore, Titian's birthplace, breaking their journey at Auronzo. 'L's maid, mournful enough at being left behind in a strange land, watched us from the balcony' as they set out.[49] At Pieve they stopped for lunch at an albergo 'quite as indifferent as its reputation' where 'the landlady's youngest daughter, an officious little girl of about twelve, volunteered as guide, and, being rejected, followed us pertinaciously from a distance.'[50] The following day, returning by a different route from Auronzo, they came to the end of the road, 'its future course being marked off with stakes across a broad plateau of smooth turf' which 'sinks away into a wooded dell down which a clear stream leaps … To our amazement the driver [of the carriage] coolly takes the leader by the head and makes for the steep pitch … ' They are horrified. '"But the horses will break their legs, and the carriage will be dashed to pieces!" "Come lei piace, Signora" [As you please, Madam] says the driver … Now it pleases neither of the Signoras,' and they insist that Giuseppe fetch a 'reinforcement of navvies, the horses are taken out, and the carriage is hauled across by men.'[51] This is one of many examples of the concern for animals which Amelia and Lucy shared. Then, a few days later, they left Cortina for Caprile, accompanied by Giovanni, Giuseppe and the Ghedina brothers, the ladies riding horses, the maid a mule with the *basta*, 'little more than a bundle of cushions and sheepskins strapped upon a man's saddle, with no real support save a stirrup'.

They spent 'two or three weeks' at Caprile, or rather with Caprile as their base, staying at the Aquila Nera, run by Signora Pezze and her two sons. 'In the sitting room … were Ball's Guidebooks, and Gilbert's *Dolomite Mountains* presented to Signora Pezze by the authors. On the walls … we found portraits of F.F.T[uckett] and his sisters; in the visitors' book, the handwriting of J.A. S[ymonds] … and of other friends.'[52] While at Caprile they made day excursions to the hamlet of Rocca and the gorge of Sottoguda, and took a boat on the lake of Alleghe, before engaging a local guide, Clementi, for a more demanding excursion to the Sasso di Ronch, which had intrigued Amelia from afar one day as she was sketching. These one-day excursions were no doubt a useful way of testing Clementi and his mules before setting out with him and with Giuseppe on the more adventurous extended tour though the central Dolomites 'with Alpenstock and saddle'.

For this more arduous part of the tour Lucy's 'delicate' maid was left behind, to keep their rooms at the inn until their return. However lonely she felt, she can scarcely have relished the prospect of many long days of riding without a proper saddle. Their programme was exacting: they left at 6.30 a.m., probably on 22 July, and rode for twelve hours before reaching Primiero for the night. Their first day at Primiero was a Sunday, and Amelia describes how the

> church bells began ringing merrily before five A.M., and went on till
> ten. The streets were thronged with peasants in their holiday clothes;

and in the piazza sat a group of country women with baskets of crimson cherries … for sale. The men with their knee-breeches … and jackets loosely thrown over one shoulder like a cloak looked as if they had just stepped out of one of Pinelli's etchings.[53]

Later in the week they left Primiero via San Martino and Paneveggio. The pass beyond Primiero was steep, 'our upward path being indicated by the giddy windings of a little handrail, which scales the face of a huge rock straight ahead. It is here too steep and slippery for riding, so we dismount and walk.'[54] Torrential rain drove them to seek shelter in 'a tiny chapel not much bigger than a sentry box' on their way down to Predazzo, where they stayed at the Nave d'Oro for two nights. The next lap of their route was by the Val di Fassa to Vigo, which they were glad to leave at 6.30 the next morning, possibly 30 July, via the Fedaia Pass, for Caprile, where 'a warm welcome awaits us, a heap of English letters, and rest'.[55]

There was one ambition not yet achieved: to make the first attempt of the Sasso Bianco, which they had seen from the foot of the Sasso di Ronch when they were first in Caprile.[56] They left at 3 a.m. on the fourth morning after their return to Caprile for this their most exacting climb, partly by mule, partly on foot, and reached the summit at 11.30 in mixed weather. They had not eaten since five, and were glad of their picnic lunch before taking time to identify the surrounding peaks with the aid of field glasses. Clementi was just able to make out Lucy's maid on the Cordevole bridge far below on the outskirts of the village[57] before they descended, reaching Caprile just after five.

They made one further excursion from Caprile, to 'the little white church' of Zoppe, near Forno di Zoldo, 'which contains the Titian which is the glory of all this countryside … There [it] hangs, uncurtained, dusty, dulled by the taper-smoke of centuries of Masses.'[58] They stayed overnight at Zoldo and left at 5.30 the next morning, returning to Caprile at six in the evening.

It was probably mid-August when they finally left Caprile, travelling first to Corvara in the Val Badia, the next day to St Ulrich (Ortizei) with its flourishing toy trade, the 'toytown' of Amelia's narrative, the next day to Ratzes, where they stay at the 'bath-house', and then to Atzwang, where they part with sadness from Clementi and the mules and take the train to Bolzano. 'Here is Atzwang; here is the railway; here is the hot, dusty, busy dead-level World of Commonplace again!'[59]

Both Amelia and Lucy must have had stamina, determination and good constitutions to travel over such rough ground, day after day, for several weeks with very few rest-days. It seems likely that Lucy was the more confident in the saddle. Amelia's humour is nowhere seen to better effect than when describing her relationship with her mule: 'Fair Nessol is L.'s mule – a gentle beast, weak but willing, given to stopping and staring at the landscape in a meditative way ... Dark Nessol being bigger and stronger, is assigned to me. He is a self-sufficient brute; one who ... invariably prefers his own opinion to that of the rider.'[60] When they leave Caprile

> it takes some time to strap on the bags ... and to induce dark Nessol to receive me upon any terms. He has a hypocritical way of standing quite still till the very moment Giuseppe is about to put me up, and then suddenly ducks away, to my immense discomfiture and the undisguised entertainment of the neighbourhood. When this performance has been repeated some six or seven times ... I mount ignominiously at last by the help of a chair.[61]

Fig. 14: The Sasso di Ronch: watercolour by Amelia Edwards, 1872.

Within a year of her Dolomite tour, Amelia's account of it was published by Longmans as *Untrodden Peaks and Unfrequented Valleys: a midsummer ramble in the Dolomites,* and was an immediate success. The reviews, too, were good: 'Our authoress is quite a match for Mr Ruskin, without a particle of his egotism or his cynicism', wrote *The Rock*.[62] The *Westminster Review* praised the 'pleasant ease of Miss Edwards's style'. All praised the engravings, which were made from her own sketches. She herself played down the quality of her drawing in her preface:

> Why, my dear American friends to whom this volume is inscribed, had I not some of those gifts that make your paintings more eloquent than words? Could I have seized the weirdness and poetry of those scenes, Vedder, ... tones of trees and skies and mountain-summits ... with your fidelity, [Coleman]? – could I

Fig. 15: Cover of Untrodden Peaks and Unfrequented Valleys, *2nd edition, 1890, depicting the Sasso di Ronch.*

have dipped my brush, Tilton, like you ... what sketches mine
would have been![63]

The book has, indeed, a charm which is not found in her novels, nor in
the diary entries of other travels in her private notebook. The humour is
sometimes found in no more than happy phrases, such as: 'Every
insignificant little town... has its *pretended Titian* to show'[64] or 'a party of
country girls with red handkerchiefs on their heads, wading knee-deep
through the wild-flowers of a wayside meadow, look like a *procession of
animated poppies*'.[65] The incident of the second omelette is an example of
her mock-heroic style:

> Again... the 'Signora Cuoca' was welcomed with acclamations.
> Again, leaving the public room for the use of the men, we took
> possession of the padrona's bright little kitchen; again the eggs and
> butter, the glittering brass pan, the long brass ladle and the big
> apron were produced; and again the author covered herself with
> glory. It may have been the peculiar quality of the air on this
> particular pass, or it may have been the result of an exaggerated
> degree of self-approbation; but those Falzarego eggs did certainly
> seem ... to transcend in delicacy and richness of flavour all other
> eggs.[66]

There is practical advice in the book, but it is given obliquely:

> One soon learns not rashly to venture on strange meats and drinks
> in these remote villages. We now habitually provide ourselves
> before starting in the morning with fresh bread and hard-boiled
> eggs ... When we are unusually tired, or minded to indulge in
> luxuries, we light the Etna, and treat ourselves to Liebig soup, or
> tea.[67]

There are numerous 'pen-portraits' of people encountered on the way,
such as Santo Siorpaes, who had been recommended as a possible guide:

> a bright-eyed, black-haired mountaineer about forty; a mighty
> chamois-hunter; an ex-soldier in the Austrian army, and now a
> custode of forests, and local inspector of roads; an active, eager
> fellow, brown as a berry, with honesty written in his face, and an
> open, vivacious manner that won our liking at first sight.
> Unfortunately, however, this jewel of a guide was pledged for the
> next six to eight weeks.[68]

Then there was old Signor Ghedina, who 'grinned from ear to ear – he had a large, brown, flat face that looked as if it had been sat upon – and patted me on the shoulder with a paw like a Bengal tiger'.[69] At Primiero there was Signor Prospero,

> whose glory it is to be a member of the Italian Club Alpino; who believes the British nation to be the most enlightened that the sun shines upon; who so worships the names of Ball and Leslie Stephens that he all but takes his hat off when he mentions them … Shall I ever forget that blazing afternoon when, gaitered, white-hatted, his garments all awry and a striped silk umbrella under his arm, he escorted me to Signor Sartoris's museum and apiary?[70]

There is a warmth about these characters which is almost entirely lacking from her other writings, although it was to reappear in *A Thousand Miles up the Nile*. In travel-writing Amelia had found her forte, and *Untrodden Peaks* is in some ways her finest achievement. Although she herself judged *A Thousand Miles up the Nile* to be 'my best book, by far',[71] it does not have the same sustained lightness of touch. It is puzzling that she had not previously attempted to make a travel-book out of any of her earlier journeys, although she frequently drew on her experiences in her novels. True, the Dolomites presented a virtually new subject for British readers, but the spur on this occasion may also have been the company of Lucy, who features as a wholly sympathetic yet independent-minded companion: '"Don't you think we have taken a great deal of trouble for nothing", says L., in a tone of disappointment,' when they reach the Sasso di Ronch, 'I would not acknowledge it for worlds, but I have been thinking so myself for some minutes.'[72]

Amelia was apparently in no hurry to return home. She remained in Bolzano with Lucy for a further week, but their paths may have diverged for a time after that. In an album of sketches of various periods which belonged to a friend, Miss Emily Burbrook, are two sketches by Amelia, signed and dated, the one 'Interlaken Ocr. 11 1872' and the other simply 'Ocr 14 1872'. There is also one last brief isolated entry in her notebook headed 'Floods in France, 1872 Novr' describing flooding in the Chalons–Macon–Dijon area. It might seem surprising that she would linger in Europe beyond the summer which she had planned as the last phase of her tour. There is, however, in the Somerville archive a passport[73] for Mrs Braysher 'travelling on the Continent' dated 10 July 1872, and it is possible, although there is no evidence for the speculation, that rather than return to an empty house she had arranged to join her old friend in France in the autumn of 1872.

The Dolomite tour was the peak of Amelia's physical achievement, and 'roughing it' at times gave her much satisfaction. Fifteen years later she wrote to Flinders Petrie, who had hesitated to recommend somewhat basic accommodation to her,

> Of course I will go to your primitive hostelry – & thankful. Have I not slept in a loft with cheeses & corn sacks for my companions, in the Dolomite days? Yea, – & occasionally with livelier & worse society in a bedroom so dirty that my friend & I had to go to bed with our shoes on & take them off when up there, rather than touch the ground with our feet? And have I not dined where they sent the peas to table boiled in their shells, & the chickens with their head feathers on, & their interiors not removed? – Such is travel – but I like it. It is part of the fun.[74]

Notes

[1] SCO Edwards 515, p. 83.

[2] SCO Edwards W22.

[3] SCO Edwards 515, p. 85.

[4] SCO Edwards 428.

[5] EES III.j.33.

[6] Martin 1.

[7] SCO Edwards 473: 'Con gran piacere o avieto la fortuna di vedere la signora Lucia, e unaltra volta spero di veder le tutte due insieme.'

[8] Martin 3.

[9] UCL Mss Add 181/11.

[10] SCO Edwards 28.

[11] *Bristol Mercury*, 22 April 1892.

[12] Julia Keay, *With Passport and Parasol* (London: BBC Books, 1989), p. 53.

[13] Ibid., p. 56.

[14] Joan Rees, *Amelia Edwards: Traveller, Novelist and Egyptologist* (London: Rubicon Press, 1998), pp. 32–35.

[15] Amelia B. Edwards, *Untrodden Peaks and Unfrequented Valleys: a midsummer ramble in the Dolomites* (London: Longmans, Green 1873, repr. London: Virago, 1986), p. 322.

[16] SCO Edwards 524, no. 1.

[17] SCO Edwards 524, no. 58.

[18] SCO Edwards 524, no. 89.

[19] Amelia B. Edwards, *A Thousand Miles up the Nile* (London: Longmans 1877, repr. London: Century Publishing 1982), p. 333.

[20] Ibid., p. 248

[21] Ibid., p. 315.

[22] *Untrodden Peaks*, p. 3.

[23] Ibid., p. 101.

[24] Ibid., p. 197.

[25] Ibid., p. 145.

[26] Ibid., p. 72.

[27] Ibid., p. 174.

[28] Ibid., pp. 4–5.

[29] Ibid., p. 184.

[30] Ibid., p. 356.

[31] Martin, 1.

[32] *A Thousand Miles*, p. 236.

[33] SCO Edwards 433.26.

[34] Ibid., pp. 1–2.

[35] Josiah Gilbert and G.C. Churchill, *The Dolomite Mountains: Excursions through Tyrol, Carinthia, Carniola & Friuli in 1861, 1862 and 1863* (London: Longman, Green 1864).

[36] *Untrodden Peaks*, p. 9.

[37] Ibid., p. 17.

[38] Ibid., p. 65.

[39] Ibid., p. 65.

[40] Ibid., p. 87.

[41] Ibid., p. 88.

[42] Ibid., p. 68.

[43] Ibid., p. 69.

[44] Ibid., p. 164.

[45] Ibid., p. 70.

[46] Ibid., p. 78.

[47] Matilda Betham-Edwards, 'Amelia B. Edwards: her childhood and early life', *New England Magazine*, New Series, 7, 5 (Boston, MA, January 1893), p. 551.

[48] *Untrodden Peaks*, p. 91.

[49] Ibid., p. 101.

[50] Ibid., p. 103.

[51] Ibid., p. 134.

[52] Ibid., p. 153.

[53] Ibid., p. 229.

[54] Ibid., p. 268.

[55] Ibid., p. 275.

[56] Ibid., p. 187.

[57] Ibid., p. 287.

[58] Ibid., p. 309.

[59] Ibid., p. 356.

[60] Ibid., p. 183.

[61] Ibid., p. 199.

[62] *The Rock*, 31 October 1873.

[63] *Untrodden Peaks*, pp. xxxvi–xxxvii.

[64] Ibid., p. 232.

[65] Ibid., p. 29.

[66] Ibid., p. 146.

[67] Ibid., p. 202.

[68] Ibid., p. 67.

[69]Ibid., p. 69.

[70] Ibid., p. 243.

[71] SCO Edwards 351.

[72] *Untrodden Peaks*, p. 187.

[73] SCO Edwards 423.

[74] PP 9.iv.31 (14 September 1887).

8

To Egypt, 1873–74

By January 1873 Amelia was back at The Larches, Westbury-on-Trym, in time to read the New Year reviews of her seventh novel, *In the Days of My Youth*.[1] As early as 8 January 1873 she had received proofs of specimen pages of *Untrodden Peaks* indicating the proposed form of printing,[2] and she was soon immersed in her writing activities again. She was staying at the Langham Hotel, Portland Place, in February[3] but appears to have spent most of the spring and summer of 1873 at home in Westbury-on-Trym. From letters written to her by Robert Browning and others[4] it is evident that she suffered a period of poor health again, and probably for this reason spent a month at Carbiswater, Cornwall, in July and August, but she was back at The Larches by the end of August.

When she had written *In the Days of My Youth* is not known, but possibly in 1871, when she was recovering from her illness and spending some time in London, or possibly in the winter of 1871–72 when she was staying in Rome. The reviews will not have given her much pleasure. According to the reviewer writing for *The Athenaeum*, the work was:

> A most singular novel, wholly different from the other works … The first and third volumes may be described as dull … The second volume is coarse … In the whole work there is neither plot nor character nor life … Miss Edwards is not free from … attempting to increase the interest by impossible situations of a sensational kind.[5]

'Her men talk like clever girls', wrote the *Daily News*.[6] The *Morning Post* was somewhat kinder: 'Miss Edwards relates [tales of the Latin Quarter] as if she had been herself a student and had entered into their pranks and pastimes.'[7] The *Saturday Review* had similar qualms to those of *The Athenaeum*:

> It is difficult to conceive that Miss Edwards can have had any personal experience of these scenes and of these characters … Miss Edwards, we are thankful to admit, injures the dramatic prose of her story by omissions which would certainly not have occurred in Balzac. But though her story is thereby rendered more moral, yet

it loses to the same degree in truthfulness … It is bad enough for English gentlemen and ladies to sit gazing at women dancing for hire in such a way … It is still worse, however, when an English authoress of fair repute, speaking in the person of the hero, upholds public indecent dancing, however modified… Had this book been the work of a man, we should have had little fault to find with its morality.[8]

The suspicion of the critics that Amelia had derived her knowledge of the less acceptable incidents from writers and not from personal experience is unwarranted. Amelia was far more experienced in the ways of the world than her critics imagined. As a girl she had accompanied her mother to 'Sadler's Wells and minor theatres', as Matilda Betham-Edwards records with a hint of disapproval;[9] she had spent months as a young woman in the Latin Quarter, staying with the Stégers; she had seen side-shows at country fairs and carnivals, had visited bath-houses and had attended art classes in Rome. The first thirty years of her life had been less constrained than would probably have been the case if she had had a more well-to-do upbringing. Acute observation, supplemented by wide reading, are sufficient to explain the passages which were regarded by her critics as 'coarse' and 'immoral'.

It was in 1873 that she began to collect material for an anthology of contemporary English poetry, to complement one of earlier masters, although the two volumes were not published until 1878.[10] Robert Browning, in giving his permission to use any of his poems which she pleased, wrote on 17 June 1873: 'I am sorry to hear that you have been out of health – but the quietude with which one is bound to set things right again is some compensation, I should say.'[11] This is the only reference to a further period of poor health. On the same date Christina Rossetti wrote with permission for *Uphill* to be included,[12] while Richard Monkton Houghton wrote: 'All I have written is at your disposal.'[13] William Morris took rather longer to reply, but wrote on 18 June: 'You may do as you please.'[14] Matthew Arnold wrote on 25th July: 'You are quite welcome to use the two pieces [*Saint Brandan* and *Growing Old*] for which you ask,' adding, 'I hope you will not leave off writing novels because you edit poetry.'[15]

Not all correspondents were so accommodating. Caroline Norton wrote on 2 August: 'I absolutely forbid the insertion of "Love Not" as a specimen of my poetry', but she sent two other poems, 'little known and not yet generally published' for inclusion instead (one of which, *In the Storm*, Amelia used), and she added that she usually charged 'a fine on the employment of my verses in collections … That I do not do so in this case will I hope be accepted by you as a proof of sympathy in your literary industry & admiration of your own literary talent.'[16] Algernon Swinburne also had other of his poems to suggest than 'the boyish *Rondel*' which she proposed.[17] She was apparently not happy with his alternatives, for he wrote again on 2 August enclosing *In San Lorenzo* (which she used), adding somewhat ungraciously that he had 'transcribed it in great haste amid the agonies of packing. I only hope it will not make me miss the train.'[18] In the event she used neither *Rondel* nor those he suggested, but four others.

Amelia's month at Carbiswater near St Ives in July was certainly not an idle holiday. Apart from preparing the anthology of contemporary poetry, she visited antiquities in the county. Three years later she would write to *The Academy* expressing concern that 'there was no mention of the early antiquities of Cornwall' in the list of monuments marked out for preservation under the new bill then going through Parliament.[19]

In September 1873 a second collection of her tales was published under the title *Monsieur Maurice*.[20] The publishers perhaps saw this as a companion to *Miss Carew*. Both collections were reprinted in Tauchnitz editions. The 'novelette' which gave the book its title was a new work, but most of the other stories included in the book had appeared in magazines over a period of years: *An Engineer's Story*, *Sister Johanna's Story* and *In the Confessional* in Christmas numbers of *All the Year Round*; *The Cabaret at the break of Day* in *Chambers's Journal*; *A Service of Danger*, *The Four-fifteen Express* and *A Night on the Borders of the Black Forest* in *Routledge's Christmas Annual*; *The Story of Salome* 'written some seventeen years ago', in *Tinsley's Annual*; and *The Tragedy in the Palazzo Bardello* in *The New Eclectic*. All of these tales were essentially ghost stories, and, unlike any of her full-length novels, several of Amelia's ghost stories have retained a degree of recognition well into the twentieth century. *Monsieur Maurice* itself was reprinted in *Five Victorian Ghost Novels* in 1971.[21] The genre was one in which Amelia had indulged since she was a girl. The contemporary reviews were good: 'In each story', wrote *The Times* reviewer, 'there is a supernatural appearance … [but] it is kept in its proper place throughout, and made subordinate to the real purpose and interest of the story.'[22] 'Each sketch is a feast in itself,' wrote the *Morning Post*, 'The Engineer's Story … is an excellent illustration of prevailing spiritualistic opinions. The author, however, does not profess actual belief in such theories.'[23] Amelia added four exclamation marks to this sentence in the extract in her newscutting book.[24] More recently, E.F. Bleiler's verdict has been that 'No other Victorian author of ghost stories surpassed her in conveying in brief form the color and romantic atmosphere of the mountains of Italy, the ancient monasteries of Central Europe, or the hidden secrets of the forests of Germany.'[25]

Amelia was back in Westbury by the end of August 1873,[26] still collecting material for her anthology of recent poetry. *Monsieur Maurice* was published at the beginning of September and *Untrodden Peaks* at the beginning of October. By that time she was travelling in Europe again for a second winter abroad, and one which was to change the direction of the rest of her life.

In *A Thousand Miles up the Nile* Amelia writes from Cairo:

> We had drifted hither by accident, with no excuse of health, or business, or any serious object whatever, and had just taken refuge in Egypt as one might turn aside into the Burlington Arcade … to get out of the rain. Never was distant expedition entered upon with less premeditation.[27]

This amusing statement has been quoted in virtually every biographical note of her life ever since, but it was not strictly true. A visit to Egypt was certainly not a completely novel idea. She appears to have contemplated Egypt two years earlier when she left for her winter in Rome. Marianne North, who had herself visited Egypt with her father and sister in the winter of 1865–66, wrote to her on 16 August 1871: 'I should like nothing better than to pass a winter at Thebes taking tents & camping alternatively at Karnac, Medinet Abou, Memnonium, & other places – for a month at a time – it has been one of my life's dreams – but I fancy you would find it a little *langweilig* …'[28] Moreover Gustave Doré, writing on 23 August 1873, when she was still at The Larches, to compliment her on her artistic talent which he first recognised in the advance copy of *Untrodden Peaks* that she had sent him, wrote: 'I see you now, Mademoiselle, in all the fervour of labour and productivity that you command, in the magnificent new mine that you have open. I am referring to your travels in Africa; I am sure that on your next return home we shall see a book that brings you honour.'[29]

For the journey to Egypt Amelia once more enjoyed the companionship of Lucy Renshaw. Lucy was again accompanied by a maid, but a younger and healthier maid than the delicate 'S' who had been something of a worry and an encumbrance to them in the Dolomites the previous year. By great good fortune the diary of Lucy's new maid, Jenny Lane, survives in private hands.[30] In an unsigned and undated note kept with the diary, Jenny's niece, Mrs Dorothy Martin, wrote:

> Jenny Lane was the eldest daughter of George Lane, a market gardener in Pulborough, Sussex. Miss Renshaw must have known

her as a little girl in the local school, which Miss Renshaw visited from time to time. Broome Park, Miss Renshaw's home, was not without the usual balls, dinner parties and other entertainments … for which the teenage daughters of local tradesmen and farmers were called upon to help the domestic permanent staff. Miss Renshaw … when quite young … had visited most of the countries in Europe, attended only by her personal maid and companion. But now, contemplating travel in the Middle East, she felt a younger and more active companion was needed, and her choice fell upon Jenny Lane. A third traveller on these journeys was the artist and authoress, Miss Amelia B. Edwards, for many years a friend of Miss Renshaw.

Fig. 16: Jenny Lane, Lucy Renshaw's maid during the Nile voyage.

This passage suggests that the visit to Egypt was no more simply a change of plans for Lucy in the middle of 'a few weeks' sketching' in central France than it was for Amelia.

Jenny's diary is the only surviving source for their travels in France and through Italy before boarding the *Simla* at Brindisi for Alexandria, apart from a few references to these months in the introduction to *A Thousand Miles up the Nile*, and a single pen and ink drawing signed by Amelia. Miss Renshaw and Jenny left Broome Park on 4 September for Charing Cross, and then took the train to Dover. Whether Amelia had been staying with Lucy or joined her in London is not known, but they certainly crossed the channel together. 'It was a rather rough crossing … Miss Edwards like myself felt good for nothing'. Jenny wrote. They took the train to Paris, and the next day went on by train to Vichy. From there they travelled two days later to Clermont-Ferrand, and stayed at Royat a little way out of the town.

Royat was their base for two weeks, and from there they made several day excursions, following the pattern which had proved so successful in the Dolomites. On 11 September they visited Volvic and the Castle of Tournoit. The next day they climbed the Puy de Dôme and the Puy de Panion with a guide in a thunderstorm. 'We keep very good hours at Royat', wrote Jenny, 'We go to bed about 8 o'clock and get up soon after 5 o'clock. I am now getting accustomed to it.' The following week began with 'very unsettled, very wet and cold' weather. Lucy had a cold and sore throat, but this did not stop them driving out, although on the Wednesday, 19 September, Lucy stayed in while 'Miss Edwards and self walked to Clermont & did a little shoping [*sic*].' By the Saturday the weather was again fair, and on Monday 23 they made the ascent of the Pic de Sancy: 'Miss Renshaw was taken up in a chair, Miss Edwards & I rode … the last half hour had to do on foot with the assistance of guides.' On Thursday 25 September they drove to St Nectaire for the night, stopping on the way at Murol to visit a country fair, where 'we caused quite a sensation'. Jenny mentions seeing a dolmen standing in a field at St Nectaire; Amelia's signed pen and ink sketch of this survives in Jenny's album.[31] They returned the next day to Royat, a journey involving ten hours on the road, a 'very hot but pretty drive'.

After three more nights at Royat they left at 5 a.m. for Murat, where they stayed for three nights. On Tuesday 30 September they rose at 4 a.m. to catch the train for Le Littons, where they alighted and took a guide for a five-mile walk to the Plomb de Cantel, 'rather hard work – a rough mountain road'. From Murat they also made an excursion by train to Aurillac, 'a very dirty old town, & the people appear to be a century behind …' On 2 October they returned to Clermont-Ferrand and the next day took the train to Le Puy. 'The excessive heat', wrote Jenny, 'makes it very fatiguing. It is quite like an English July day.'

They spent two weeks at Le Puy, staying at the Hotel de l'Europe, 'considered the best in Le Puy', making day excursions to places of interest in the vicinity before leaving on 20 October at 5 a.m. by 'a very mountainous road which required three horses' then taking the train for Nîmes, where they stayed for four weeks. On 22 October Jenny wrote of Nîmes: 'The weather here is very warm and bright, that people are sitting out like summer', and again on 24 October: 'A very fine day. The sun quite hot … Mosquitos are very troublesome here.' She wrote, on 28 October, 'Miss Renshaw is very busy making arrangements for our trip to Egypt.'

Jenny's contemporary account belies Amelia's humorous statement that they decided to go to Egypt 'to get out of the rain' in France:

> Having left home in September for a few weeks' sketching in central France, we had been pursued by the wettest of wet weather … At Nismes it poured for a month without stopping. Debating at last whether it were better to take our wet umbrellas back at once to England or push on farther still in search of sunshine … the talk fell on Algiers–Malta–Cairo; and Cairo carried it.[32]

The romantic had clearly the upper hand over the journalist, to good literary effect.

By 10 November Jenny was writing: 'We are very busy preparing for our trip to the East' and on 15 November that 'Miss Edwards has given me a very nice album for my views'. Two days later they left Nîmes for Marseilles, and on into Italy the next day, spending relatively comfortable nights in Genoa and Bologna, and a night on the train to Brindisi, where they stayed at the Grand India and Orient Hotel, 'close to the pier,' Jenny records, 'which I look on with a kind of sinking feeling.' The crossing to Alexandria on board the *Simla* was indeed rough, and took three days, and after berthing they still had to endure three days of quarantine before they could land. On 29 November, however, they disembarked at last, and were met by their dragoman, Mr Tolhamy, 'a very nice-looking fellow' in Jenny's eyes.

At this point Amelia's published account[33] becomes the primary source for their adventures. She begins her narrative with 'the first appearance of L. and the Writer' (this was Amelia's designation for herself throughout the book), 'tired, dusty, and considerably sunburnt' in the crowded dining room of Shepheard's Hotel, Cairo.

> People asked each other, most likely, where these wandering Englishwomen had come from; why they had not dressed for dinner … We had not dressed for dinner because, having driven on from the station in advance of the dragoman and luggage, we were but just in time to take our seats with the rest.[34]

It seems strange that Amelia should think it necessary to include such a trivial detail, as if she needed, even three years later when her book was published, to justify her first bedraggled appearance to the former fellow-travellers who might be reading it.

Jenny's diary is of particular help in matters of chronology and identity. Very few dates are given in *A Thousand Miles up the Nile* and Amelia admits at one point: 'I do not very distinctly remember the order of our sight-seeing in Cairo.'[35] It is also good to have Jenny fill out the tantalising initials of Amelia's companions. It is from her diary that we have confirmation that the 'L' of *A Thousand Miles*, and also of *Untrodden Peaks*, is Miss Lucy Renshaw; that we deduce that 'the Painter' or 'the Artist' is Mr Andrew McCallum (although this can be gleaned from 'Appendix I' of the book where his signed letter to *The Times* on his discovery of a painted chamber at Abu Simbel is reprinted); and that we identify 'the Happy Couple', comprising 'the Idle Man' and 'the Little Lady', as a Mr and Mrs Eyre. The 'M.B.s' of Amelia's book remain, however, 'the Bagstones ladies' to Jenny.

They stayed two weeks in Cairo. Amelia first describes the bazaars: 'One should begin in Cairo with a day in the native bazaars; neither buying, nor sketching, nor seeking information, but just taking in scene after scene … Every shop-front, … every turbaned group, is a ready-made picture.'[36] As always, she saw with the eye of an artist.

On 4 December, Jenny reports: 'Miss Renshaw [was] very busy settling about our trip up the Nile.' To Jenny, it is Lucy and not Amelia who is in charge of business matters, just as in the Dolomites. Amelia describes how they visited Bulaq, 'a desolate place by the river', to look at boats, and found that 'the miseries of dahabeeyah-hunting' were far worse than those of househunting, and adds that 'for the first ten days or so some three or four hours or so had to be devoted every morning to the business of the boats'.[37] This was something of an exaggeration, for Jenny records on 6 December, only a week after their arrival in Cairo, 'it is settled that we start for the Nile on the 12th. Miss R. has engaged a charming boat called the *Philae*.'

Meanwhile they saw the sights of Cairo and its neighbourhood. 'To remember in what order the present travellers saw these things would now be impossible; for they lived in a dream, and were at first too bewildered to catalogue their impressions very methodically',[38] Amelia admits. On Friday 5 December, according to Jenny (12 December according to Amelia) they visited the Convent of the Howling Dervishes. This was a regular tourist attraction. 'All Shepheard's Hotel was there', wrote Amelia. Her account of the furious dance is vivid and touched with humour. At the end of the performance 'there was a murmur of relief and a simultaneous rising among the spectators. It was announced that another zikr … would soon begin; but the Europeans had enough of it.'[39] They also visited the Mosque of Sultan Hassan, which draws a rare comment on piety from Amelia: 'This was the first time we had seen Moslems at prayer, and we could not but be impressed by their profound and unaffected devotion.'[40] One of the earliest excursions from Cairo, dated by Jenny to 11 December, was to the Pyramids of Giza, but 'we did not go to *see* the Pyramids. We went only to look at them',[41] Amelia explains. On this occasion they had only a short time at the site, but on their return they revisited Giza and climbed to the top of the Great Pyramid. Amelia goes out of her way, on both occasions, to speak well of the Bedouins there, who 'have been plentifully abused by travellers and guide books, but we found no reason to complain of them now or afterwards. They neither crowded round us, nor followed us, nor importuned us in any way',[42] and later: 'As for the men, they are helpful and courteous, and coax one on from block to block in all the languages of Europe … They offered to sing "Yankee Doodle" when we reached the top; then, finding we were English, shouted "God save the Queen!"'[43]

Unlike the Dolomites, by the mid-nineteenth century Egypt was firmly on the tourist trail, and most tourists went up the Nile. Cook's steamers took those with limited time to spare up and down the Nile in three weeks, but the more leisurely way was to make a winter of it and travel by chartered dahabiyah. This was how Marianne North had travelled in 1864–65, and likewise their mutual friend, Edward Lear, on his three visits to Egypt, in 1849, 1853–54 and 1866–67. 'As a very small child', Amelia once wrote, 'I devoured Wilkinson's "Ancient Egyptians"',[44] and it was no doubt a similar curiosity about the lost civilisation and its monuments read of in books that drew many tourists, but others, like Edward Lear and Andrew McCallum, came primarily to sketch and paint; some, like Alfred Brocklehurst and the Idle Man, came to shoot game, especially crocodile; and some, like Lucie Duff-Gordon, whose *Letters from Egypt*[45] had been published in 1865, came for their health.

Amelia writes of the excursions to the pyramids at Giza and to see the pilgrims leave for Mecca: 'I have been able … to remember quite circumstantially the dates, and all the events connected with these last two days. They were to be our last two days in Cairo, and tomorrow morning, Saturday 13 December, we were to go on board …'[46] Jenny's diary shows, however, that they embarked on Friday 12, 'after a luncheon party'. On the Saturday 'Miss Renshaw and Miss Edwards went ashore to get letters.' They left Cairo at 2 p.m. 'Great excitement at starting, the Bagstones, a female friend's boat, leaving at the same time.'[47] This was the boat chartered by Miss Marianne Brocklehurst, daughter of John Brocklehurst of Hurdsfield House, Cheshire. She was accompanied by her companion, Miss Booth, and the two are referred to as 'the M.B.s' by Amelia, and as 'the Bagstones ladies' by Jenny. Marianne's nephew, Alfred, and manservant, George, were also of their party, and figure frequently in *A Thousand Miles*. George is the only servant whom Amelia names; there is no mention of Jenny.

Fig. 17: Marianne Brocklehurst, from Amelia Edwards' photograph album.

Marianne Brocklehurst and Mary Booth lived in a house called 'The Bagstones' on the estate belonging to Marianne's brother, Sir Philip Brocklehurst, at Swythamley Park near Winkle. Marianne's diary of the voyage up the Nile survives, and provides useful confirmatory and sometimes complementary detail.[48] It is kept in the Silk Industry Museum, Macclesfield, while trophies of the Nile journey are preserved in West Park Museum, Macclesfield, which was built at her expense to hold her collection of Egyptian antiquities. They had set out from home on 11 November with Alfred and George, reaching Brindisi on 21 November, and had made the same crossing as Amelia and Lucy in the *Simla*. When in quarantine at Alexandria they had, according to

Fig. 18: Girga, Middle Egypt:
watercolour (sepia) by Amelia Edwards' 1874.

Marianne, 'made friends with pleasant people: the MacCallums, Miss Edwards, Miss Renshawe [*sic*] and others' on 28 November. Two days later, she recorded that 'we go by railway to Cairo: we join Miss Edwards and friend and "find each other out"'. This was the beginning of a friendship which long outlasted the Nile voyage. While in Cairo the M.B.s had visited the Bulaq Museum with Amelia and Lucy, and had made the excursion to see the howling dervishes with them, so that by the time Amelia and Lucy set sail in the *Philae* and the M.B.s in the *Lydn*, which they promptly renamed the *Bagstones*, as a 'home from home', the four were well acquainted.

The *Philae* appears to have been chartered in Mr McCallum's name: Jenny refers to it as Mr McCallum's boat. Amelia writes:

> in place of a small boat, we had secured one of the largest on the river; and instead of going alone, we had decided to throw in our lot with that of three other travellers. One of these [Mr McCallum] was already known to the writer. The other two, friends of the first, were on their way out from Europe, and were not expected in Cairo for another week. We knew nothing of them but their names.[49]

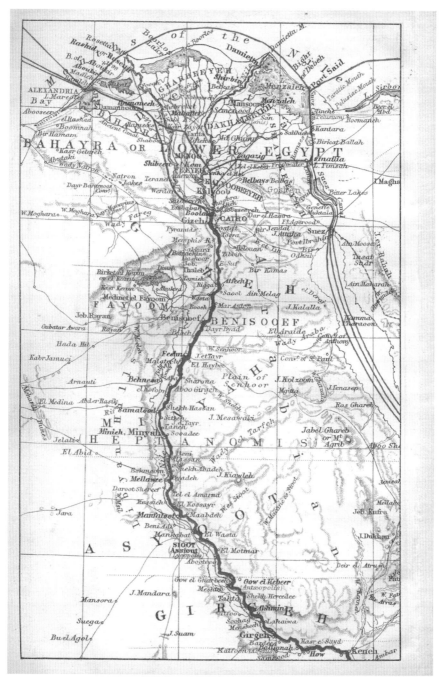

Fig. 19: Map of Lower Egypt, from E.A.W. Budge, The Nile: Notes for Travellers in Egypt, *2nd edn, London, Thos Cook & Son, 1892.*

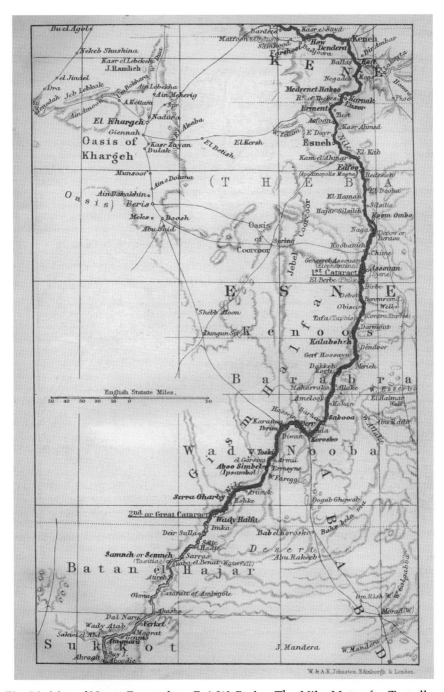

Fig. 20: Map of Upper Egypt, from E.A.W. Budge, The Nile: Notes for Travellers in Egypt, *2nd edn, London, Thos Cook & Son, 1892.*

For the first ten days, however, Amelia and Lucy had sole possession. 'These ladies have the boat to themselves', wrote Marianne, 'and are proportionately jolly.'

The details of the Nile journey are well documented, with Amelia's literary account tempered by both Jenny's and Marianne's diaries. They set sail from Bulaq on Sunday 14 December and reached Bedreshayn after dark. On 15 December they went on shore to visit Saqqara, dismounting when they came to cliffs 'through compassion for our unfortunate little donkeys.' At Saqqara, Amelia writes, 'the first thing we observe is the curious mixture of debris underfoot … And then, with a shock which the present writer, at all events, will not soon forget, we suddenly discover that these scattered bones are human …' Their shock was soon overcome: they found themselves looking for relics among the debris. 'These are experiences upon which one looks back afterwards with wonder, and something like remorse … Most Egyptian travellers, if questioned, would have to make a similar confession.'[50] Passages describing the history of the monuments which they visit, for example at Saqqara and Memphis, and the story of their excavation, the legends of the gods and the lives of the pharaohs, are interspersed in Amelia's narrative with domestic and personal detail: 'How pleasant it was,' she writes, 'after being suffocated in the Serapeum and broiled in the tomb of Ti, to return to Mariette's deserted house and eat our lunch.'[51] The contrast between the magic of Saqqara and the disappointment of Memphis is well drawn: 'Memphis is a place to read about, and think about, and remember; but it is a disappointing place to see.'[52]

For the next few days they were hampered by contrary weather: the wind dropped, and the crew had to abandon sail and proceed by 'tracking' which 'looks like slaves' work.' The M.B.s sometimes dined on the *Philae*, and sometimes Amelia and Lucy dined on the *Bagstones*. During the day 'the ladies', to use Jenny's collective term, 'sat on deck writing letters and reading'; while waiting for the weather to change they went for walks and sketched. On 17 December, when they were moored at Beni Suef, the ladies on both boats were alarmed to hear a man swimming round the boats at night. The guards whom they had been advised to engage by arrangement with the governor of the town, slept through it, but the swimmer was scared off when Tolhamy, the dragoman, loaded his gun.[53] On 20 December they were almost blinded by a sandstorm. On 21 December a Moslem 'holy man' came on board, to the enthusiastic welcome of the crew. He blessed the boat, and 'from that moment the prosperity of our voyage is assured'. Later in the day, a Copt from a neighbouring convent swims up and is less well received by the crew, though sympathetically by Amelia, for he is 'one of those whose

Fig. 21: Luxor Temple, pylon, colossi of Ramesses II, and obelisk:
watercolour (sepia) by Amelia Edwards.

remote ancestors exchanged the worship of the old gods for Christianity
… Remembering these things it is impossible to look at him without
feelings of profound interest.'[54] During these early days Amelia and Lucy
were fast learning the 'manners and customs' of the modern Egyptians.

By Christmas Eve they had reached Minieh, where they had arranged
to meet the rest of the party, and were duly joined by Mr McCallum,
whose wife remained behind in Cairo, and by his friends Mr and Mrs
Eyre, 'the Happy Couple' on their honeymoon, accompanied by their
maid. The M.B.s came to dinner on the *Philae* on Christmas Day, and the
boat was decked with 150 lanterns and flags. The crew of the *Philae*
invited the crew of the *Bagstones* to coffee, and afterwards 'they danced,
they dressed up, improvised a comic scene, and kept their audience in a
roar. George, Tolhamy and the maids sat apart at the second table and
sipped their coffee genteelly.'[55] Amelia, who had enjoyed home
theatricals and dressing up as a child, clearly enjoyed it.

The following week they suffered from adverse weather, running into
a sandbank on 27 December. Two days later they reached 'that fairy
town of Siût' which 'seemed always to hover at the same unattainable
distance',[56] and visited the market and the 'big mud town as ordinary
and ugly as its fellows … So our mirage turns to sordid reality.'[57]

Fig. 22: Dabod Temple, Lower Nubia: watercolour by Amelia Edwards.

By 5 January they had reached Dendara, and with 'an escort of three or four sailors' they set off on foot across country 'without paths or roads of any kind' until 'the last belt of palms was passed ... and the temple, islanded in that sea of rippling emerald [of young corn], rose up upon its platform of blackened mounds'.[58] Amelia's description of the temple is precise, with quotations from Wilkinson and Mariette, yet also romantic: 'surely there must be some weird night in the year when they [the sculptured procession] step out of their places and ... pace the moonlit roof in ghostly order!'[59] Returning to the *Philae*, they lost their way in the dark, and only when Tolhamy fires his last cartridge does an answering shot signal salvation. Amelia depicts their relief at seeing the crew who had come out searching for them, by commending each one by name.[60]

On 9 January they reached Luxor, which they intended to visit at more leisure on their return journey. Nevertheless the first visit left a strong impression on all the travellers: 'It would be a glimpse, yet that glimpse was essential ... It enables one to put things in their right places; and this after all is a mental process which every traveller must perform for himself.'[61] Marianne Brocklehurst records only 'Karnak's immense halls and gorgeous ruins', while Amelia, after describing the impressive ruins and their history, adds:

> But it was the magnificence of a splendid prologue to a poem of which only garbled fragments remain. Beyond that entrance lay a smoky, filthy, intricate labyrinth of lanes and passages. Mud hovels, mud pigeon-towers, mud yards and a mud mosque,

clustered like wasps' nests in and about the ruins ... Buffaloes, camels, donkeys, dogs and human beings were seen herding together in unsavoury fellowship ... all the sordid routine of Arab life was going on.[62]

The journey from Luxor to Aswan was enlivened by friendly rivalry between the crews of the *Philae* and the *Bagstones*, and by the proximity of other boats such as the *Fostat*, with 'five English gentlemen' on board. On 17 January they reached Aswan with its noisy and importunate peddlers, and visited the market, where 'L., who is given to vanities in the way of dress', bought a fringed leather girdle, the traditional dress of the local girls. Here they needed to arrange with the Governor for the Sheikh of the Cataract to be engaged to take the boat up the rapids above Aswan. Amelia gives an amusing description of the Nubian governor's visit to the *Philae*. He was 'a tall young man, graceful, good-looking, and black as a crow.' They inadvertently struck a discordant note by asking to see the slave-market, the existence of which he denied, and by offering him 'unholy liquors', which he refused, but the situation was redeemed when Mrs Eyre pleased him by playing extracts from 'Tannhäuser' on the piano in the saloon. The governor, 'who talked of going to England shortly, asked for all our names and addresses, that he might come and see us at home'.[63]

By 21 January they were through the First Cataract and reached the island temple of Philae, its colonnades and the surrounding palms reflected in the water of the lake above the rapids. Amelia writes,

> It is one of the world's famous landscapes and it deserves its fame ... yet it bears putting neither into words nor colours. The sketcher must perforce leave out the atmosphere of association which informs his subject; and the writer's description is at best no better than a catalogue raisonnée.[64]

Continuing through the desert of Nubia, visiting temples on the way and exploring villages, they came on 31 January to Abu Simbel, where they were to remain until 18 February. It was night when they moored just below the temple, but,

> the Painter and the Writer had no patience to wait till morning. Almost before the mooring rope could be made fast, they had jumped ashore and begun climbing the bank ... They felt as if the whole scene must fade with the moonlight and vanish before morning.[65]

Abu Simbel marked the high point in Amelia's Egyptian journey, although it was not the most southerly point of their journey: they continued to Abusir and the lower end of the Second Cataract where, on 3 February, the sails of the dahabiyah were taken down and the boat was converted to a galley for the northward journey downstream. By 11 February they were again mooring at Abu Simbel for a further week, which proved to be the most exciting of all: on 15 February Andrew McCallum discovered what they took at first to be a burial chamber, and later concluded must have been a temple library. They were, they believed – and Amelia devotes many pages to the proof of it – 'the first to enter the place, at all events since the time when the great sand-drift rose as high as the top of the fissure'.[66] With the help of official reinforcements they excavated what they could, and before leaving they wrote their names and the date on 'a space of blank wall over the inside of the doorway; and this was the only occasion upon which any of us left our names upon an Egyptian monument'. As soon as they reached Korosko, the nearest town, Andrew McCallum sent a letter to *The Times*, published a month later on 18 March, announcing the discovery.

During their journey on the Nile, Amelia had become more and more aware of what might remain to be discovered of the ancient Egyptian civilisation, and how urgent it was to record and preserve its art. No event on the journey did more to fire her enthusiasm for archaeology and preservation than their chance discovery of the painted chamber at Abu Simbel. Three years later she wrote

> I am told that our names are partially effaced and that the wall-paintings which we had the happiness of admiring in all their beauty and freshness, are already much injured. Such is the fate of every Egyptian monument, great or small … The work of destruction, meanwhile, goes on apace.[67]

Two days later they left Abu Simbel and proceeded downstream, visiting temples on the way. As they were nearing the First Cataract again on 4 March, an incident occurred which is variously reported by Amelia and by Jenny Lane: Mr Eyre, the 'Idle Man', while shooting quail on shore, accidentally hit a small boy. The *Bagstones'* party were not in the neighbourhood when this incident took place, so that it is not possible to refer to an eyewitness version of the event from Marianne, but the seriousness of the incident can be judged from Jenny's diary. She writes:

> Mr Eyre went out shooting and shot a boy. Did not kill him. We heard the screams and wondered what was the matter. The whole

Fig. 23: 'Digging for mummies': watercolour (sepia) by Amelia Edwards.

village fell onto Mr Eyre and the sailors who were with him. They took his gun and knocked him about dreadfully & tore nearly all the things off the poor sailors. Mr Tolhamy rushed out to help and brought Mr Eyre on the boat looking more dead than alive. We had the boy brought on the boat. He was about 7 years old and perfectly naked. He was not very badly hurt. A few shots went into his body & one or two into his head and face.[68]

Five days later she reports that Mr Eyre and Mr Tolhamy went to Aswan to see the Governor and

> settle the row with the natives for attacking Mr Eyre when he shot the boy. He got his gun again and about 6 men were bastonarded. Both Mr Eyre and Mr Tolhamy had to stand and see it done. Horrible. Poor wretches. I don't suppose they will want to attack another English gentleman.

In contrast to this straightforward and serious account, in which sympathy is expressed for both parties, Amelia's account is theatrical and almost playful:

> Hapless idle man! – hapless but homicidal. If he had been content to shoot only quail, and had not taken to shooting babies! We

> heard our sportsman popping away presently in the barley. 'Every
> shot,' said we, 'means a bird.' We little dreamt that one of those
> shots meant a baby.[69]

There are some inconsistencies, but the most striking difference between
the two accounts lies in the tone. Amelia's wry and ironic tone seems
badly misplaced on such a subject.

On 15 March they descended the First Cataract. According to Jenny
Lane, both Lucy Renshaw and Andrew McCallum avoided the
unnerving experience by hiring donkeys and riding across the desert to
Aswan, although Amelia says only that 'our Painter ... preferred rolling
up his canvasses and carrying them round on dry land',[70] and does not
mention Lucy. Below Aswan, the Nile flowed once again at a calm pace
and the journey continued without further drama, opportunities being
taken to visit sites not fully explored on the way south. They reached
Luxor on 21 March, and spent some days exploring the ruins of Thebes,
sketching, and watching excavation in progress. The *Bagstones* had
joined them again by this time, and Amelia describes a pleasant
'luncheon with the M.B.s in the second hall of the Ramesseum. It was but
one occasion among many, for the Writer was constantly at work [i.e.
sketching] and we had luncheon in ... one or other of the western
Temples every day.'[71] But their stay at Luxor was not all sketching and
exploring. 'A morning among temples is followed by an afternoon of
antiquity-hunting; and a day of meditation among the tombs winds up
with a dinner-party on board some friend's dahabeeyah, or a fantasia at
the British Consulate.'[72] She admits that they enjoyed 'the pleasures of
the chase: the game, it is true, was prohibited; but we enjoyed it none the
less for that'. The 'game' was antiquities, and mummies and papyri in
particular. She disclaims an interest in acquiring a mummy, but coveted
a papyrus, and was somewhat aggrieved to find that the successful
bidders both for a mummy and for a papyrus were none other than the
M.B.s, who bought both at 'an enormous price'.[73] Marianne records in a
discrete section of her diary how they acquired these treasures and
smuggled the mummy case and the papyrus out of Egypt; they may
now be seen in the West Park Museum, Macclesfield.

Amelia describes at some length one of the fantasias given by
Mustapha Aga on their last evening in Luxor. The exact date is not
known, because Jenny's diary finishes abruptly after 24 March.
Marianne records that the *Bagstones* party left Luxor on 29 March, and
the governor's fantasia must have taken place after that, for Amelia
writes that 'even the faithful *Bagstones* had long since vanished
northwards; and the *Philae* was the last dahabeeyah of the year'.[74] The

friendship of the M.B.s had added considerably to the pleasure of the voyage for Amelia and Lucy. Slipped between sheets of Marianne's diary is a verse in Amelia's hand:

> Day by day & mile by mile,
> As I journeyed up the Nile
> Pen in hand,
> Taking sketches, making notes
> Of temples, tourists, boats,
> Palms & sand;
>
> Labyrinthine tombs exploring,
> Climbing pyramids, adoring
> Gods of old;
> 'Antikah-hunting'; trying
> My prentice hand at buying;
> Being 'sold';
>
> In the midst of these excursions
> 'Fantasias' & diversions
> Without end
> I bought a tiny scarab
> One morning from an Arab
> For my friend.
>
> It was once a sacred token
> Of eternity unbroken
> And divine;
> Some long-vanish'd priest or king,
> Lord or lady, owned the thing.
> Now 'tis thine.[75]

One of their last visits before leaving Luxor was to a Coptic church service, sympathetically described, 'because it represents, with probably but little change, the earliest ceremonial of Christian worship in Egypt … No traveller in Egypt should I think omit being present at a service in a Coptic church.' It was partly the language which attracted her: 'In another fifty years or so', she predicted, 'the Coptic will in all probability be superseded by the Arabic in the services of this church'.[76] It was not only the vulnerability of the monuments which concerned her; she was equally anxious to see preserved the languages and traditions of Egyptian civilisation.

Fig. 24: Saqqiya for irrigating palm-groves near the Temple of Derr, Lower Nubia: watercolour by Amelia Edwards.

The journey downstream was uneventful. The weather was hot and their energy was flagging, but they stopped at Abydos and again at Beni Hasan, and at both sites the ruins are recorded with customary diligence. Then at Ayserat, below Girga, they 'paid a visit to a native gentleman … to whom we carried letters of introduction'. After showing off his fine horses and entertaining them with the usual pipes, coffee and sherbert, 'L., the Little Lady and the Writer were conducted to the harem and introduced to the ladies of the establishment'.[77] Amelia adds, that Lucy also 'visited some of the vice-regal harems at Cairo, and brought away on each occasion the same impression of dreariness.' Amelia was dismayed at the restricted lives of the women in Egypt, and one visit was apparently enough for her: 'It seemed to us that the wives of the Fellahin were in truth the happiest women in Egypt. They work hard and are bitterly poor; but … they at least know the fresh air, the sunshine, and the open fields.'

At last they reached Cairo, and the 'big rooms' of Shepheard's Hotel, and the pleasures of sightseeing and shopping in a city again, but their last recorded excursion was not in the city but at Giza, where they climbed the Great Pyramid, and gained the view from which they could see 'the measureless desert in its mystery of light and silence … the Nile where it gleams out again and again, until it melts into that faint far distance beyond which lie Thebes and Philae and Abu Simbel.'[78]

In Egypt Amelia had found what no other journey had given her: a mission for life. Her account of her travels ends at Giza, but she did not immediately return home. With no surviving record of hers, and no longer a parallel diary of Marianne Brocklehurst – for the M.B.s had left Cairo on 18 April – nothing would be known of the rest of Amelia's eastern journey were it not for a second diary of Jenny Lane's, beginning on 1 May, when Amelia and Lucy, and apparently Mr and Mrs Eyre, left Cairo for Ismailia, travelled the next day by steamer to Port Said, and then on 3 May boarded a French steamer for Beirut. They still had Tolhamy as guide, and he was as attentive as ever: at Jaffa he 'went ashore and bought the ladies some pottery'.[79]

The day after arriving at Beirut they were up at five: 'Our caravan consisted of 9 mules, 6 muleteers, a cook, one waiter, Habib who was with us on the Nile, the mules carrying our luggage and lanterns. We had five horses – all Arab breed but one.' They rode through Lebanon, camping at night in tents: 'Miss Renshaw and I sleep in one tent, Miss Edwards sleeps in the dining tent. Then we have a kitchen tent and two small ones besides.' On 8 May they reached Damascus, where Jenny was 'pleasantly surprised to find my friend and Nile companion, Miss Urquhart'. Lebanon, Syria and Palestine were frequently visited by European travellers before or after Egypt, and tourists – and their servants – often met, parted, and met again thus on their tours. From Damascus they had a rough ride 'up mountains, through rivers and over stones, most disagreeable' to camp at Wadi Barada. The next day they stopped for luncheon in a small garden 'for Miss Edwards to make a sketch'.

On 15 May they reached Baalbek after another early start and a 'shockingly rough ride', and camped in the ruins. 'Two parties besides us here, altogether about 10 tents up. Rather an impressive sight amongst these old walls.' They spent a day exploring the ruins of the five temples, and on the 17th began their journey back to civilisation, with one last night in tents, to Jenny's disappointment, for 'it is a glorious life, & should have liked to live in tents the whole summer'. They reached Beirut on 18 May, and left the next evening by a French steamer 'leaving Mr Tolhamy behind, which I am very sorry for he has been with us 6 months & he was a very kind fellow'.

They were at sea for a week, calling at Rhodes on 26 May and reaching Smyrna the next day. There they boarded another French boat three days later for Constantinople. On 1 June they parted from the last two of their fellow travellers on the Nile, Mr and Mrs Eyre, who left for Athens. 'The ladies', however, had yet more sightseeing planned: they spent the day on a steamer trip up the Bosphorus, and 'came back very cold'. They spent several days exploring Constantinople, visiting churches and mosques and bazaars, where 'Miss Edwards bought some pottery'.

They left Constantinople on 6 June, changing boats at Syra, where Lucy engaged a guide for their visit to Athens. As ever, it is Lucy who attends to the business of their travel arrangements. At Athens they spent several days exploring the sights, staying 'some hours on the Acropolis, where Miss Edwards sketched' and watched excavation in progress. While in Athens, Amelia met Heinrich Schliemann and his wife Sophia; this is known from a letter which he wrote to her three years later: 'Ever since I had the pleasure of meeting you in Athens you have been in my heart and on my lips.'[80] They left for Corfu on 19 June by Greek steamer, crossing the isthmus by carriage. Lucy and Jenny slept on deck, but there is no mention of 'Miss Edwards' doing likewise. They were detained in Corfu first by quarantine regulations and then by the late arrival of the Austrian Lloyd steamer for Trieste, which was full when it arrived. It was not until 20 June that they finally parted with their guide and set sail for Trieste, which they reached on 25 June. There they took a train for Vienna, whence they had intended to sail up the Danube, but the weather was cold and windy and they 'felt too wretched', so they took a train for Frankfurt instead. From there it was a matter of only four days to travel via Cologne, Brussels, Calais and Dover to the Langham Hotel, London, which they reached at 11 p.m. on 29 June 1874. 'Very pleased to see dear old England again once more, & thankful we have arrived safe and well', wrote Jenny, and her words were no doubt echoed by Amelia and Lucy. For Amelia, this was to be the last overseas travel for twelve years.

Notes

[1] Amelia B. Edwards, *In the Days of My Youth*, 3 vols. (London: Hurst & Blackett, 1873).
[2] SCO Edwards 434.145.
[3] SCO Edwards 116, 26 February 1873.
[4] SCO Edwards 310, 475, 287.
[5] *The Athenaeum*, 4 January 1873, p. 11.
[6] *Daily News*, 7 January 1873.

7 *Morning Post*, 8 January 1873.

8 *Saturday Review*, 11 January 1873.

9 Matilda Betham-Edwards, 'Amelia B. Edwards: her childhood and early life', *New England Magazine*, New Series, 7, 5 (Boston, MA, January 1893), p. 562.

10 Amelia Edwards, *A Poetry Book of Modern Poets* (Leipzig: Tauchnitz, 1878).

11 SCO Edwards 18.

12 SCO Edwards 281.

13 SCO Edwards 74, 26 June [1873].

14 SCO Edwards 222.

15 SCO Edwards 3, 25 July 1873.

16 SCO Edwards 268.

17 SCO Edwards 310.

18 SCO Edwards 310, the reference is to Sir John Gardner Wilkinson's *Manners and Customs of the Ancient Egyptians*. First series, 3 vols.; second series, 3 vols. (London: John Murray, 1837–41)

19 SCO Edwards 434.146.

20 Amelia B. Edwards, *Monsieur Maurice, a new novelette, and other tales*, 3 vols. (London: Hurst & Blackett, 1873).

21 E.F. Bleiler (ed.), *Five Victorian Ghost Novels* (New York: Dover, 1971), pp. 245–96.

22 *The Times*, 5 December 1872.

23 *Morning Post*, 4 September 1873.

24 SCO Edwards 434.132.

25 Bleiler, *Five Victorian Ghost Novels*, p. ix.

26 SCO Edwards 288, 28 August 1873.

27 Amelia B. Edwards, *A Thousand Miles up the Nile* (London: Longmans 1877, repr. London: Century Publishing 1982), p. 2.

28 SCO Edwards 247.

29 SCO Edwards 448: 'Je vous vois d'ici, Mademoiselle, dans toute l'ardeur de travail et de production que vous puissez dans la nouvelle et magnifique mine que vous vous êtes ouverte; je veux dire votre voyage en Afrique; je suis sur que nous allons voir retour prochainement un livre qui vous fera honneur.'

30 Martin 1. Jenny Lane's diary of travels in France and Egypt, 1873–74. This and other documents are in the hands of Mr and Mrs J. Martin of Broadstairs. All references in this chapter to Jenny Lane's diary are to the relevant dates in this document, unless otherwise stated.

31 Martin 4: Jenny Lane's album, chiefly of photographs, 1873–76.

32 *A Thousand Miles*, p. 2.

33 *A Thousand Miles*.

34 Ibid., p. 2.

35 Ibid., p. 23.

36 Ibid., p. 3.

37 Ibid., p. 12.

38 Ibid., p. 11.

39 Ibid., p. 30.

40 Ibid., p. 20.

41 Ibid., p. 13.

[42] Ibid., p. 17.

[43] Ibid., p. 488.

[44] SCO Edwards 351.

[45] Lucie Duff Gordon, *Letters from Egypt, 1863–1865* (London: Virago Press, 1983, first publ. 1863).

[46] *A Thousand Miles*, p. 35.

[47] Martin 1.

[48] In the Macclesfield Museum; the diary has recently been published (Disley: Millrace, 2004).

[49] *A Thousand Miles*, p. 34.

[50] Ibid., p. 51.

[51] Ibid., p. 62.

[52] Ibid., p. 67.

[53] Ibid., p. 75.

[54] Ibid., p. 80.

[55] Ibid., p. 90.

[56] Ibid., p. 98.

[57] Ibid., p. 101.

[58] Ibid., p. 118.

[59] Ibid., p. 139.

[60] Ibid., p. 132.

[61] Ibid., p. 136.

[62] Ibid., p. 141.

[63] Ibid., p. 179.

[64] Ibid., p. 232.

[65] Ibid., p. 261.

[66] Ibid., p. 353.

[67] Ibid.

[68] Martin, 1.

[69] *A Thousand Miles*, p. 382.

[70] Ibid, p. 392.

[71] Ibid., p. 417.

[72] Ibid., p. 449.

[73] Ibid., p. 451.

[74] Ibid., p. 466.

[75] Published after Amelia Edwards' death under the title 'With a Scarab to a Friend', *Academy*, Vol. 42, No. 1057 (6 August 1892), pp. 110–11.

[76] *A Thousand Miles*, pp. 464–65.

[77] Ibid., p. 479.

[78] Ibid., p. 492.

[79] Martin, 2; all subsequent quotations in this chapter are likewise from the second diary of Jenny Lane, 1874.

[80] SCO Edwards 48.

9

'My best book by far'

Amelia reached London on 29 June 1874, and was presumably at home at The Larches within a few days, after her absence of ten months. In earlier years she had come home with plots for novels in her notebook, but this time her thoughts were all of Egypt: to learn all she could of the civilisation which she had glimpsed, and to bring its magic to a wider public. Back in Westbury, she resumed the threads of her quiet life with Ellen Braysher. On 6 December she was writing to Miss Cave to congratulate her prettily on her engagement.[1] Her friend John Symonds was ready to pick up their friendship again, sending her on its publication a copy of his book *Sketches in Italy and Greece*[2] with a sonnet inscribed on the fly-leaf:

> Pencil & pen, dear friend, alike are thine:
> The hand which answers to the guiding brain
> With hues of morn & eve, with tints divine
> Expressed from flower or gem, the page where shine
> Thy written idylls …
>   yea thou shalt draw
> Through fancy on my margin meadows green
> Still seas, & ancient towers, & temples vast,
> Dreaming far lovelier places than I saw.

It may be that when she set out for Egypt she envisaged writing a travel book on the lines of *Untrodden Peaks and Unfrequented Valleys*, but by the time she had been up the Nile and back she had apparently determined to write something more than simply an account of her travels; she wanted to urge the desperate need to preserve what remained of the ancient civilisation of Egypt on those who could act to save it. There were numerous guide books for travellers and scholarly works on ancient Egypt with which she herself had been familiar since childhood, but there were no books which incorporated a scholarly account of current archaeological and historical research within a lively and amusing narrative such as to attract the growing number of educated readers at home. This would be an altogether different proposition from writing a novel, and would require considerable research, which she lost no time in undertaking.

Within two weeks of her return she was writing to Dr Samuel Birch, Keeper of Oriental Antiquities at the British Museum:

> I enclose with this a facsimile of the hieratic inscription I copied from the walls of the rock-cut chamber at Abu Simbel ... I need not say that I have copied every break in the flow of the ink, & every uncertain wavering of the pen – thinking it better to be slavishly correct than to err in the opposite direction. I fancy I recognise many of the forms – birds, asps & the like. I wonder if I am right in supposing that I see a dot & line man in the last long line?[3]

Dr Birch acknowledged receipt two days later, writing 'I will see if I can make it out.' On 25 October she was writing to him again, this time from Torcross, South Devon, where she was staying for about a week:

> I wonder if you will kindly tell me the meaning of the two inscriptions enclosed, taken partly from rubbing, & then defined in ink. The one is from a sepulchral cone, the other from an alabaster canopic vase in my possession. I should be exceedingly obliged to you, & think it very kind. Have you ever been able to make anything of the Demotic inscription?'[4]

She was perhaps a little too familiar with Dr Birch: after expressing regret at being unable to attend the Orientalist Congress, she adds: 'I ought long since to have written to congratulate you on the French decoration you received. I hope it is handsome to wear, as well as an honourable distinction.'

Amelia looked forward to examining the Egyptian antiquities which she had collected abroad. 'My last case, I hear, has arrived from Cairo,' she writes, 'since I left home. If all has come safely, there is in it a very interesting painted stele on sycamore wood, & a bas relief in green marble of a curious table of offerings – both of which I shall hope some day to show you.' The M.B.s' victory in the papyrus hunt clearly still rankled a little: 'I tried hard to get a specimen of papyrus when I was in Egypt, but Miss Brocklehurst and Miss Booth carried off the only one on the market. Is there any place in London where a small, but fairly good specimen could be picked up?'[5]

By June 1875 Amelia was preparing *A Thousand Miles up the Nile* for the press, and was writing to Dr Birch with increasing frequency. 'Before sending off the proof of my hieratic inscriptions to press, I wish to ask you the meaning of two things – & shall be very grateful if you will kindly tell me … I am sure I don't know how I am ever to thank you enough for your kind & invaluable help. I don't know what I should do without it.'[6] Three weeks later she wrote again, repeating her queries:

> If you could very kindly oblige me by an explanation of 'Ammon Ra Harmachis' & of the meaning of 'the god at the first time', you would release me from a worrying printer … I am so sorry to bother you, but worry is like electricity – it is communicated by successive shocks. Perhaps somebody worries the printer; then he worries me. Can't you worry somebody else? It would be only fair. To save you all needless trouble, I enclose an envelope ready directed.[7]

On 18 October she wrote once again, asking whether he had leisure to glance at four pieces of inscribed pottery which she had sent to him. Her book on Egypt was progressing well:

> The chapter relating to Assouan & Elephantine is ready to go to the printer as soon as I know what to say about the tiles … I feel like a monster in human form to torment you thus; but … unless I remind you about the potsherds you cannot be expected to remember their existence. Did you ever get a letter that I addressed to you partly in hieroglyphics?[8]

Samuel Birch replied on 30 October[9] and Amelia responded the next day thanking him heartily, with a cartoon of two men in oversize hats ('elephantine tiles', in the slang of the time).[10]

Samuel Birch was not amused by her playfulness: 'Your tiles are so fragmentary that they are really not worth being engraved. One alone of your four pieces is complete and that illegible', adding gratuitously: 'Your letter reached me after my return from Oxford, where I went after my election as honorary fellow of the Queen's College.'[11] Amelia, writing from Weston-Super-Mare, did not miss her cue: 'I saw in *The Times* that you had been receiving honours at Oxford – only the honour is theirs … What I should really like is to see you a K.C.B. – though in truth the university honours are better worth having.'[12]

On 17 January 1876 Amelia wrote yet again to Dr Birch, having read in a paper in the *Revue archéologique* of a Homeric fragment found at Elephantine, which she would like to mention in her book: 'I hope you will not think me an importunate bore. I have tried all I could to find it

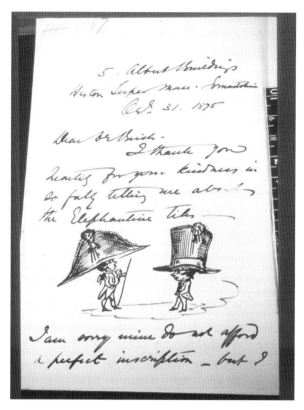

Fig. 25: 'Elephantine tiles', part of a letter from Amelia Edwards to Samuel Birch.

without asking you.'[13] There is little doubt that Samuel Birch did indeed find her tiresome, and this was to lead to a rift between them with lasting consequences. For the present, however, she continued to pester him with queries:

> By the way, when I was in Thebes Mustapha Aga gave me two pieces of a painted wooden mummy case bearing a cartouche [here she added a drawing of it]. I conclude it must be of Eustipaa III. Does Eustipaa mean 'The Great He'? My minute progress in Egyptian seems to lead me to this translation – but I have so little time for carrying the study.[14]

Such an approach may have been galling to the authority who had been so tied to his duties at the British Museum that he had never had the time to visit Egypt himself; moreover, Amelia was unwise enough to offer him advice in the same letter: 'It seems a pity that the British Museum should not effect an amicable exchange with the Louvre, & the

Fig. 26: Dr Samuel Birch, from a portrait in the British Museum.

Cambridge collection get the earlier sarcophagus – it loses half its interest in being divided.'

Amelia met a more kindly response from Joseph Bonomi, the draughtsman of vast experience of Egypt who had illustrated many of Birch's treatises and designed his hieroglyphic type. He was currently Curator of Sir John Soane's Museum, although then in his eighties. He wrote to her from 'The Camels', Wimbledon Park: 'I think your discovery of the small temple … was a most fortunate circumstance',[15] and again, a week later, answering her questions about Abu Simbel, 'the whole case could be easily unravelled from data existing in Europe; perhaps the British Museum could furnish sufficient to a young and active person like yourself'.[16]

If Amelia was importunate with her questions to the Egyptologists of the day, she was also on the receiving end of queries from others. She drew W.E. Gladstone's attention to an article by Vicomte de Rougé in 1869 on the question of Homeric synchronisms, and added: 'Should you at any time be returning to this subject & desire a list of references, it will give me much pleasure to furnish you with them.'[17]

It was fortuitous that Amelia could undertake the work of preparing her book for the press from home, because it appears that Ellen Braysher's health was giving her concern. 'I do hope', wrote her friend, Elihu Vedder, the American artist, 'that when you get your book finished that your friend may be strong enough to travel & that we may see you – not in a hurried & feverish way but so as to get a little comfort out of each other.'[18] Gustave Doré had written earlier in the year: 'Dear Mademoiselle, I can see that your head must be stocked full of projects impatient to see the light of day … I know you well enough to think that you will not take many years, nor even many months, to produce them, and that we shall soon see!'[19]

In August 1876 Amelia wrote to Dr Birch again: 'I should think you must have been hoping I was dead or mummified, as I have been quiet for some little time. Now, however, I rise again to torment you.' She needed his help with her description of two cartouches, because:

> Being so much pressed for time [when in Egypt], taking notes, copying hieroglyphic inscriptions, hieratic *do*, heads, cornices, &c., I delegated a little of the work to a friend [Lucy?], such as noting colours of garments, &c., &c. This friend wrote me down the details of these two cartouches – & now that I know more about such matters than I did then, I am ready to tear my hair that I did not copy them myself … My book, & my long task, are now drawing to a close. I am bound to finish completely in less than 9 weeks, & the book is to be published the first week in November.[20]

Some weeks later she sent him proofs of inscriptions in hieroglyphic type, asking him to correct one and send it to Longmans. 'I think the type a great improvement,' she wrote soothingly, 'I am so glad you suggested it.'[21] A few days later, sending him part of the original sketch which he asked for, she wrote: 'I hope to write that happy word "Finis" in about a fortnight, & to have a holiday in London in November.'[22]

Amelia did not quite meet the original deadline – she was still referring a query to Samuel Birch on 1 November. One worry, however, was removed: by 19 October Ellen Braysher was well enough to 'walk out daily, even if not far'[23] and a holiday could be contemplated with an easy mind. The book appeared in December 1876, with the imprint 1877, and on Christmas Eve Amelia wrote to a friend, Mary Davidson – maybe the Miss Davidson whom she had met in Naples in 1872:

> A poor prisoner, but just released & very weary … My long task is at last completed & the book (of which I enclose you an announce-

ment for Longman written by myself) was *out* within a fortnight from the day I wrote the last lines. They were actually sewing up the early sheets while I was writing the preface, & we only saved the Christmas season by 5 days! It nearly killed the writer.[24]

A Thousand Miles up the Nile was an immediate success with the reviewers, although their response was not necessarily of the kind that Amelia would have wished. 'A delightful gossiping book, written in a bright, light and genial style ... a book to be read as well as to impart a new dignity and grace to the drawing-room tables on which it reposes,' wrote *The World* reviewer;[25] and according to *The Athenaeum*: 'We are forced to allow this to be a charming book of its kind ... Her forte undoubtedly lies in bringing before the eyes the passing scene ... Her historical observations are generally correct; a great merit in works of the ornamental class.'[26] The *Saturday Review* described the work as:

> A very bright and agreeable picture ... The author writes in such an easy, good-natured, chatty way, and her simple unaffected enjoyment of the tour is catching ... We get, of course, quite a woman's view of the subject; for Miss Edwards, unlike some other literary ladies, is evidently the last person in the world to think of renouncing her sex, and assuming a masculine swagger.[27]

There were inevitably some critics: the *Morning Post*, with good reason, commented that 'The episode of the Idle Man and his baby victim is perhaps just a trifle cool.'[28] *The Times* made an interesting point:

> As to the people, the author is not quite consistent. She likes the boatmen – and who does not? – but she shrinks from the squalor and noise of their towns and villages. It is difficult for an English lady to encounter for the sake of knowledge and humanity a life which is nearly as wretched as some of the districts of London, but it cannot be impossible. Had Miss Edwards known more Arabic, her love of character and kindness of heart would have got the better of her instinctive shrinking from the disagreeable.[29]

The Academy reviewer observed that, 'It is enthusiasm for old Egypt, running powerful and deep throughout the volume, that gives its real charm to the work.'[30]

Amelia had set herself a difficult task, to be popular and scholarly at the same time, and in general she succeeds. Visits to major sites are made the occasion for learned discourses on Egyptian history, art or religion,

Fig. 27: 'Tunis Bazaar; Cairo': watercolour by Amelia Edwards, 1874.

as at Thebes in chapter 8, Philae in chapter 12, Abu Simbel in chapters 15 and 16, chapter 15 being entirely given to the history of the reign of Ramesses II. The descriptions of antiquities, however, are rendered as personal and casual as possible by reference to the beholder, and any suggestion of the academic is played down. The emphasis is always on personal discovery, as for instance when describing the fallen colossal statue at Thebes:

> How this astounding mass was transported from Assouan, how it was raised, how it was overthrown, are problems upon which a great deal of ingenious conjecture has been wasted. One traveller affirms that the wedge-marks of the destroyer are distinctly visible. Another, having carefully examined the fractured edges, declares that the keenest eye can detect neither wedge marks nor any other evidence of violence. We looked for none of these signs

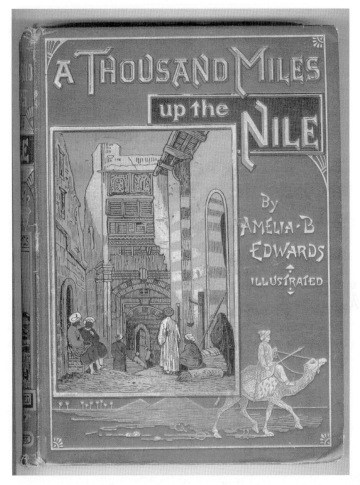

Fig. 28: Cover of A Thousand Miles up the Nile, *second edn, 1889,*
depicting Tunis Market, Cairo.

and tokens. We never asked ourselves how and when the ruin had
been done. It was enough that the mighty had fallen.[31]

Amelia was always conscious of the risk of boring the reader with too
much detail, 'for it is of temples as of mountains – no two are alike, yet
all sound so much alike when described that it is scarcely possible to
write about them without becoming monotonous'.[32] The impact of
history is, however, sometimes conveyed by detail, as when she
describes how Mariette entered a vault in the Serapeum at Saqqara 'and
there, on the thin layer of sand that covered the floor, he found the
footprints of the workmen who, 3700 years before, had laid that

shapeless mummy in its tomb, and closed the doors upon it, as they believed, for ever'.[33] Amelia's sense of the dramatic and mysterious had full scope for expression in describing antiquity; on the other hand, her description of antiquities is frequently enlivened by her humour and playfulness , as when she writes of a sarcophagus in the catacombs of the Serapeum: 'Four people might sit in it round a small card-table, and play a rubber comfortably.'[34]

There are fewer descriptions of purely scenic beauty in *A Thousand Miles up the Nile* than there had been in her earlier travel writing, but they are presented with equal skill, and again, a sense of mystery often creeps in. Describing the sunset as they approach Minieh, she writes:

> Such is the sunset we are destined to see with scarcely a shade of difference for many a month to come. It is very beautiful, very tranquil, full of wonderful light and most subtle gradations of tone … but it lacks the variety and gorgeousness of our northern skies … however, we never weary of these stainless skies, but find in them, evening after evening, fresh depths of beauty and repose.
> …
> As for that strange transfer of colour from the mountains to the sky, we had repeatedly observed it while travelling in the Dolomites the year before, and had always found it take place, as now, at the moment of the sun's first disappearance. But what of this mighty after-shadow, climbing half the heavens, and bringing night with it? Can it be the rising Shadow of the World projected on the one horizon as the sun sinks on the other?[35]

She seems to have found sunset and its aftermath an unusually moving experience on more than one occasion. Sixteen years later, a friend with whom she was staying at Olana in the Hudson Valley was to write: 'Miss Edwards came for me to my room, and found me doing just what she had been doing, sitting spell-bound at the window … She said "It might be the end of the world. This sunset looks as though there would be never be another."'[36]

Amelia's description of moonlight on the Nile is equally vivid and the effect is heightened by her reference to common-place objects:

> Colour neither deadened nor changed; but softened, glowing, spiritualised. The amber sheen of the sand-island in the middle of the river, the sober green of the palm-grove, the Little Lady's turquoise-coloured hood, were clear to the sight … The oranges showed through the bars of the crate like nuggets of pure gold.

L.'s crimson shawl glowed with a warmer dye than it ever wore
by day.[37]

In spite of her lively style and her popular approach to historical
subjects, the book does drag at times, not only because one temple is
much like another, but also because the characters remain shadowy and
the confines of the party on the dahabiyah are somewhat restrictive. The
characters of her story are, for the most part, placed there for
amusement, and their behaviour, when it receives comment at all, is
used to offset and relieve descriptions of landscape and ruins.

Lucy Renshaw, always referred to as 'L' no doubt for her own
protection, features chiefly as the ship's doctor: 'L., with her little
medicine chest and her roll of lint and bandages, soon had a small but
steady practice, and might have been seen about the lower deck most
mornings after breakfast, repairing these damaged Alis and Hassans.'[38]
At Esneh they bought 'a big bottle of rose-water to make eye-lotion for
L.'s ophthalmic patients'.[39] The words 'little' and 'big' simply press the
humour home. L. is always ready for a bargain, eager, for example, to
buy a sample of the famous basketwork at Derr.[40] Her susceptibility in
this respect may have been encouraged by the Little Lady, with whom
she is at one point found 'indulging in that minor vice called afternoon
tea',[41] and in whose company at Philae she writes 'no end of letters'.[42]
Lucy and Amelia were by no means inseparable on the journey. Lucy is
depicted as a capable, sociable lady, sharing with Amelia a love of
'antikas', and accompanying her on most though not all of their shore
excursions; but she is never found sketching. Jenny Lane's diary adds a
little to the picture of Lucy gleaned from *A Thousand Miles up the Nile*,
but the strangest incident which Jenny records of 'Miss Renshaw' is one
which goes unrecorded by Amelia: the episode of the eagle, or, as
Marianne Brocklehurst's diary calls it, the hawk. 'Miss Renshaw bought
an eagle', writes Jenny on 14 January, a day on which otherwise
'nothing very particular occurred'. On 19 January 'Miss Renshaw's
eagle escaped and settled on a rock, but was caught again by an Arab.'
On 30 January it escaped again 'and flew to the desert … Mr McCallum
and Mr Tolhamy went with their guns to try and get it, only by shooting
it to wound it, and brought it back with a broken wing.' When the *Philae*
was moored, they sent to a neighbouring boat with a doctor on board,
asking him to come and set the wing, but he refused, 'much to the
ladies' disgust'. Two days later Jenny records that 'the eagle is very bad
and bound up like a mummy. Miss Renshaw gave it a dose of medicine.
Awful fuss.' By 3 February she is writing: 'Miss Renshaw nursing the
eagle … Dreadful fuss over it. Miss Renshaw has given it beef tea and

sherry. I wish it could die.' The next day Mr McCallum shot it to put it out of its misery, and it was buried in the sand with some ceremony. It is astonishing that Amelia, who records every other incident found in Jenny's diary, makes no mention of this episode. Bird-lover that she was, it seems most likely that she regarded the whole incident, including the purchase of the eagle in the first place, as thoroughly disreputable, even too shameful to treat humorously, as she treats the wounding of a boy. It may be that she omitted it to protect her friend Lucy; Mr Eyre, who shot the child, was not one whom she would feel disposed to protect.

The 'Idle Man' and the 'Little Lady' who comprise the 'Happy Couple' are not depicted in an entirely sympathetic light. Amelia establishes at the outset, before they join the dahabiyah at Minieh, that they are friends of 'the Painter' but that she and Lucy 'knew nothing of them but their names'.[43] Her description of them when they arrive is cynical:

> In point of fact they have not yet been married a month. The bridegroom is what the world chooses to call an idle man; that is to say, he has scholarship, delicate health, and leisure ... Of people who are struggling through that helpless phase of human life called the honey moon, it is not fair to say more than that they are both young enough to make the situation interesting.[44]

The Little Lady does not make many independent appearances in the book. She shares Lucy Renshaw's attachment to wildlife, feeding the chickens and other poultry on board. She entertains the governor of Aswan on the piano in the saloon,[45] and while the rest of the party are measuring and sketching the newly discovered 'temple' at Abu Simbel, 'L. and the Little Lady took their books and their knitting there and made a little drawing room of it'.[46] With her husband, the Little Lady went out in the *felucca*, a dinghy attached to the *Philae*, and 'managed to see the little rock-cut Temple of Ferayg, which the rest of us unfortunately missed', Amelia writes enviously,[47] and the Eyres prefer to visit the Rock of Abusir by boat, while Lucy and Andrew McCallum go by donkey. The 'Happy Couple' never quite come up to the mark which Amelia expects of her fellow travellers:

> There are fourteen temples between Abou Simbel and Philae; to say nothing of grottoes, tombs and other ruins. As a rule, people begin to get tired of Temples about this time, and vote them too plentiful. Meek travellers go through them as a duty; but the greater number rebel. Our Happy Couple, I grieve to say, went

over to the majority. Dead to shame, they openly proclaimed themselves bored. They even skipped several temples.[48]

However, the Idle Man eventually comes in for positive approval for his changing attitude to wildlife in the course of the book. His purpose, as that of Marianne Brocklehurst's nephew, Alfred, in undertaking the journey up the Nile, is sport. There had been rumours of crocodile for some days before they found a trail on an island at Abu Simbel:

> As for the Idle Man he flew at once to arms and made ready for the fray. He caused a shallow grave to be dug for himself … then went and lay in it for hours together, morning after morning, under the full blaze of the sun … with his gun cocked and a *Pall Mall Budget* up his back.[49]

Yet later, when he finally does see two crocodiles from the dahabiyah while they are having breakfast, he does not pursue them: 'We had heard of so much indiscriminate slaughter at the Second Cataract, that he was resolved to bear no part in the extermination of these old historic reptiles.'[50]

During the excavation of the new 'temple' at Abu Simbel, the Idle Man was investigating an unusually thick wall, when he 'thrust his fingers into a skull! This was such an amazing and unexpected incident, that for the moment he said nothing, but went on quietly displacing the sand, and feeling his way under the surface.'[51] Throughout the book the Idle Man is depicted as of a languid, unexcitable temperament. One of his tasks during the voyage was to read the morning service on a Sunday.[52]

The Painter, by contrast, is a somewhat flamboyant character. When they reach Aswan, it is he, 'arrayed in a gorgeous keffiyeh and armed with the indispensable visiting cane' who sprang ashore and hastened to call upon the Governor'.[53] His one purpose in the journey is to paint, and to paint a big picture. He is shown frequently wandering off alone, bent on sketching; he is 'our indomitable Painter, who is always ready for an afternoon excursion'.[54] The Painter is always the ladies' champion when some degree of forcefulness seems to be required. Waiting to go up the First Cataract, they felt their 'time and money were being recklessly squandered, and … resolved to bear it no longer. Our Painter therefore undertook to remonstrate with the Sheykh.'

> [The Sheikh] shrugged his shoulders and muttered something about 'destiny', but the Painter, 'being of a practical turn, had compiled for himself a little vocabulary of choice Arabic maledic-

tions, which he carried in his note-book for reference when needed
… So he whipped out his pocket-book, ran his finger down the
line, and delivered an appropriate quotation. His accent may not
have been faultless, but there could be no mistake as to the energy
of his style or the vigour of his language. The effect of both was
disastrous.[55]

There can be little doubt that the Painter's stature was enhanced in
Amelia's eyes by the fact that it was he who discovered the new 'temple'.
The event is introduced in her narrative with the precision and gravity
of a testimony:

> The day was Sunday, the date February 16th 1874; the time …
> about eleven A.M., when the Painter, enjoying his seventh day
> holiday after his own fashion, went strolling about the rocks.' The
> others waited lunch for him, and had eventually sat down without
> him, when two of the sailors arrived with a message from him: 'I
> have found the entrance to a tomb. Please send sandwiches.[56]

Amelia cleverly conveys the excitement of discovery, while maintaining
the light humorous touch which is the hallmark of all her characterisation in *A Thousand Miles up the Nile*, and Andrew McCallum, 'our
Painter', emerges as the hero of the hour.

As the book progresses, the message gradually emerges that the
monuments and civilisation of ancient Egypt need to be protected from
nature and from man. At Memphis, while Alfred shot pigeons and
Amelia sketched, 'the others grubbed among the mounds for treasures,
finding many curious fragments.'[57] No condemnation is implied. On
Elephantine island they

> picked up several bits of inscribed terracotta … Believing them to
> be mere disconnected scraps to which it would be impossible to
> find the corresponding pieces, we brought away some three or
> four pieces as souvenirs of the place and thought no more about
> them. We little dreamed that Dr Birch, in his cheerless official room
> so many thousand miles away, was at this very time occupied in
> deciphering a collection of similar fragments … brought from this
> same spot … Six months later, we lamented our ignorance and our
> lost opportunities.[58]

It may well have been the discovery of the chamber at Abu Simbel
which convinced Amelia that much remained to be found, and needed

to be preserved for scholarly examination and not merely as trinkets. That much had been lost she knew well – at Thebes she comments on the many empty tombs:

> We may be certain that the splendid Pharaohs who slept in the Valley of the Tombs of the Kings went to their dark palaces magnificently equipped for the life to come ... It seems far more wonderful that the parure of one queen should have escaped rather than that all the rest of these dead and gone royalties should have fallen among thieves.[59]

Scholars may decipher inscriptions in their studies, travellers rescue, for their private or public collections, rare fragments or commonplace objects of everyday life, but when it comes to monuments, Amelia realises that rescue is a matter for governments. She writes of the fallen colossus at Memphis: 'This, it seems, is the famous prostrate colossus of Rameses the Great, which belongs to the British nation, but which the British Government is too economical to remove. So here it lies, face downward; drowned once a year by the Nile.'[60] She saw that the preservation of ancient Egypt demanded not only enthusiasm and scholarship, but the power to change national attitudes and marshal national resources, and that would mean a campaign. '*A Thousand Miles up the Nile* is my best book, by far', Amelia wrote to Edward Abbott, editor of the *Literary World*. It marked the beginning of her campaign.

Notes

[1] UCL Mss Add 182/4.

[2] John A. Symonds, *Sketches in Italy and Greece* (London: [privately printed], 1874, 2nd edn, London: Smith Elder & Co., 1879) from the copy in Somerville College Oxford Library.

[3] BM OA 1868–81, 1690, 11 July 1874.

[4] BM OA 1868–81, 1691, 25 October 1874.

[5] BM OA 1868–81, 1691.

[6] BM OA 1868–81, 1693, 10 June 1875.

[7] BM OA 1868–81, 1694, 2 July 1875.

[8] BM OA 1868–81, 1695.

[9] SCO Edwards 8.

[10] BM OA 1868–81, 1679.

[11] BM OA 1868–81, 1698, 3 November 1875.

[12] BM OA 1868–81, 1699, 4 November 1875.

[13] BM OA 1868–81, 1701.

[14] BM OA 1868–81, 1702, 9 April 1876.

[15] SCO Edwards 12, 10 April 1876.

[16] SCO Edwards 13, 18 April 1876.

[17] BL Ms Add. 44450, f.46, 18 May 1876.

[18] SCO Edwards 320.

[19] SCO Edwards 450: 'Je vois d'ici, chère mademoiselle, que vous devez avoir la tête toute meublée des projets impatients de voir le jour ... Je vous connais assez pour penser que vous ne mettrez à les produire ni de longues années ni même de longues mois, et que nous verrons cela bientôt!'

[20] BM OA 1868–81, 1704, 22 August 1876.

[21] BM OA 1868–81, 1705, 27 September 1876.

[22] BM OA 1868–81, 1706, 1 October 1876.

[23] SCO Edwards 465.

[24] Houghton, Autograph file, Wendell Bequest 1918.

[25] *The World*, 6 February 1877.

[26] *The Athenaeum*, 2573 (17 February 1877), pp. 219–20.

[27] *Saturday Review*, 13 February 1877, pp. 58–59.

[28] *Morning Post*, 10 February 1877.

[29] *The Times*, 4 January 1877.

[30] *The Academy*, New Series 247 (27 January 1877), pp. 65–66.

[31] Amelia B. Edwards, *A Thousand Miles up the Nile* (London: Longmans 1877, repr. London: Century Publishing 1982), p. 421.

[32] Ibid., p. 423.

[33] Ibid., p. 63.

[34] Ibid., p. 57.

[35] Ibid., p. 82.

[36] GI, manuscript journal of Kate Griffith, entry for Christmas Day 1889.

[37] *A Thousand Miles*, p. 114.

[38] Ibid., p. 107.

[39] Ibid., p. 158.

[40] Ibid., p. 248.

[41] Ibid., p. 315.

[42] Ibid., p. 382.

[43] Ibid., p. 34.

[44] Ibid., p. 88.

[45] Ibid., p. 178.

[46] Ibid., p. 333.

[47] Ibid., p. 306.

[48] Ibid., p. 354.

[49] Ibid., p. 193.

[50] Ibid., p. 358.

[51] Ibid., p. 334.

[52] Ibid., p. 379.

[53] Ibid., p. 176.

[54] Ibid., p. 238.
[55] Ibid., p. 198.
[56] Ibid., p. 326.
[57] Ibid., p. 71.
[58] Ibid., pp. 182–83.
[59] Ibid., p. 448.
[60] Ibid., p. 65.

Plate 1: Cairo, Bab el-Nasr.

Plate 2a: The Nile near Asyut.

Plate 2b: Abydos, the necropolis and Kom el-Sultan.

Plate 3a: Naqada, Coptic convent.

Plate 3b: Temple of 'Amada, Lower Nubia.

Plate 4: Temple of Dakka, Lower Nubia.

❖ 10 ❖

A campaign, 1877–82

The task of completing *A Thousand Miles up the Nile* may have left Amelia weary and in need of a holiday, but she appears to have spent the early months of 1877 quietly at home. Writing some years later, in 1888, to Richard Bowker, editor of *Harper's Magazine*, she described her life at The Larches:

> I have no special working hours, because I work simply all day, all the morning, all the afternoon, all the evening – from the time I get up till I go to bed – saving and excepting only such times as I am at meals, or taking exercise. At the Larches I have a straight path under the larch trees reaching from the entrance gate to the end of the lawn, which I have had measured. A register dial fixed on the greenhouse at the lower end tells off 22 turns (I moving the index hand each time I reach the bottom). The 22 make one mile. Winter and summer, rain, snow or sunshine, I walk half a mile before breakfast and ditto after breakfast, before beginning work. When tired of the desk, I rush out and do one quarter of a mile at various intervals during the day. In the afternoon, if my invalid is well enough, I go out with her for a couple of hours' drive, in the course of which we alight and walk a little. Besides this, I get another mile on the measured path before, or after, dinner – sometimes in the dark. I always make sure of two miles a day exercise; but generally get more. When Mrs Braysher is not well enough to go out, or the weather is not fit for her, I sometimes walk only in our own little domain, for weeks and weeks together, without once going outside the gates. My friends marvel how I can stand it; but the absolution from hat or bonnet is delightful, and I am quite happy.[1]

In her letter of 1881 to Edward Abbott, editor of the *Literary World*, Amelia paints a pleasant picture of life at The Larches at this time:

> The house is small, & contains only one really large room – my library, built out for the purpose of housing my 3000 odd books which I have been accumulating for the last 25 years, & for which it has been my amusement to design all sorts of quaint & charac-

teristic bindings. Then I am a collector of miscellaneous rubbish –
Greek and Etruscan pottery, antique glass, autographs, etchings,
engravings, paintings, drawings, Egyptian antiquities & the like.
These hobbies, together with my ferns, flowers & gardening, give
me abundant entertainment – to say nothing of the wild birds,
whom we feed all the year round, & who come by hundreds for
their meals. My thrushes drop fearlessly into the library to be fed,
& the robins perch on my stationery-case & the tops of my
bookcases, & even on my feet when in summer I lie reading or
writing in a long Indian chair under a shady tree.[2]

It is a pretty picture, and one which was paraphrased in the article
which duly appeared in the *Literary World* five months later.[3] Life at The
Larches was, however, not always as well ordered as this account
suggests. On 9 March 1880 Amelia wrote to a local paper warning
readers of

a gang of three men who were prowling about this neighbourhood
on Sunday evening last … Two of our maid servants, going to
church, met these men in the lane … The second, our cook, became
uneasy. About a quarter of an hour later there was a ring at the side-
door … The housemaid went round and asked who was there.[4]

It is interesting to note that there were at least three women servants at
The Larches, and from another letter in which she refers to 'our boy' it
appears that there was a boy too.[5] After describing the incident in detail,
and warning other local residents to secure their windows, she adds:

And where, it will be asked, were the Westbury police all this time?
Where are the Westbury police at any time? I sometimes see one on
the Down, but in these Eastfield lanes, and in the meadow paths
beyond – never … Roughs of all kinds, many of them carrying
guns (probably unlicensed) and shooting our few remaining wild
birds, hang about here on Saturday afternoons and Sundays. [In]
my own experience of the Westbury police, they adorn the village,
awe the little boys, and never concern themselves with anything
which does not take place on the high road.

Almost nothing is known of Amelia's activities during the spring of
1877, but she was evidently taking an active part in Westbury society, for
on 20 January she wrote to Frank Tuckett, the alpinist, about a talk which
he was to give at Westbury:

> I was dining on Thursday at Cote House [the home of Sir
> Vincent Ames, Westbury] and having just received your letter,
> took it with me. They were greatly pleased at its contents … I
> have read the three papers … & I agree with you that the Eagle
> adventure is best adapted for reading. I think it will be very
> effective indeed. I wld however suggest the omission of all
> foreign & technical words. It is well in these readings to make
> the style as simple & Saxon & forcible as possible. You can read
> for 20 minutes – or, in the case of a reading of thrilling interest,
> even a little longer.[6]

Amelia's advice is particularly interesting in that it shows that she was
herself accustomed to giving talks, and to the same audience:

> I have found it the best way to read the thing several times
> aloud to myself, just at the pace & with the pauses I intend to
> read it with in public, with the watch before me. Each time
> omitting the least interesting & essential matter, till at last I
> succeed in cutting it down to exactly the right length. It seems
> to me the only way to preserve the best & excise the worst of a
> paper & get it exactly right in length.

Amelia had no doubt learnt the art of holding an audience from reading
chapters of her early novels aloud to her cousins, and telling ghost
stories to her travelling companions in her youth. 'I am sure you will
enjoy your visit to Cote', she continues, 'and that we shall enjoy your
reading. You will find it a very pleasant & sympathetic audience – at
least, I have always found it so; but I have not read for it for 2 years now.
I don't suppose, however, that they have changed.'

Francis Fox Tuckett was a Gloucestershire Quaker, a near contemporary of Amelia, and a friend of the Symonds. By 1877 his alpine
expeditions were over, and he was devoting more of his time to his
interest in archaeology. He was a keen member of the Gloucestershire
Archaeological Society. Amelia may well have been introduced to Frank
Tuckett by John Symonds or by Marianne North, who knew him and his
sisters well.[7] Amelia had never lost touch with Marianne, and resumed
her friendship in 1877. Marianne had reached London on 23 February,
after travels which had taken her round the world, and Amelia went to
stay with her at her flat in Victoria Street that summer. She was there on
7 June when she wrote to Dr Schliemann inviting him and his wife to dine
with them.[8] Whether the dinner party ever took place seems doubtful.
Neither Heinrich Schliemann nor Edward Lear, an old friend of the

Norths who had also been invited, were free to come.[9] It is interesting to note that it was Amelia, and not Marianne, who issued the invitations.

Amelia remained at Marianne's flat for at least a month, even in Marianne's absence. During her stay she was introduced to Kate Field, an American journalist and in her youth a singer, known as 'a woman of great powers of intellect and remarkable versatility'.[10] Amelia seems to have found the company of American friends particularly enjoyable: the first edition of *Untrodden Peaks and Unfrequented Valleys* had been dedicated to 'my American friends in Rome', and the second edition, 1890, was dedicated to 'my American friends in all parts of the world'. There was clearly no difficulty in obtaining Amelia's publications in the United States – among the letters of thanks which she received in 1877 for the copies of *A Thousand Miles up the Nile* which she had despatched or offered to friends, is one from Frederick Church, the American artist, writing from his home on the Hudson. He comments on 2 September:

> I purchased some time ago an American Edition of *Untrodden Peaks* and read it with avidity. It is a great book, it is full of splendid landscapes, and breathes the spirit of *Nature*. It was not illustrated, and was consequently very *imperfect*. But we all enjoyed it. Another of your books – strangely different – I have read several times – *In the Days of My Youth*. I have not gotten over the astonishment I experienced at the diversity of the subjects ... when lo! you appear with the lantern of science casting its rays into the gloom of the Tombs of the Pharaohs ... I am daily expecting a copy which I ordered some time since, but I cannot resist the temptation of your kind offer.[11]

An indication that Amelia may at this time have been involving herself in the cause of women's employment is found in a letter of 3 May 1878 to Kate Field. 'I am so sorry not to be a subscriber to the Fund you canvas for so ably – but my purse is *washed* clean out. I have put all my pennies into the Laundry, & all my precious working time too, for the past eight months, & now I have neither days nor pennies to spare.'[12]

This allusion to a laundry is clarified somewhat by a paragraph in the *Paddington Times*, possibly submitted by Amelia herself, reporting that:

> On 21st July 1877 a garden tea was given by the lady-manager of the Great Western Laundry to the employés of that establishment, and held in the extensive grounds of the Old Manor House ... Paddington-Green. Tables were spread under the trees, and some seventy work people connected with the laundry, many of whom

are French blanchisseuses *en fin*, sat down … to a substantial meal … There were also present, among the private guests of the lady-manager, a considerable number of literary, artistic and musical celebrities, among whom was remarked in the course of the day, M. Gustave Doré, Mr C.C. Coleman, the Rev. Pender and Mrs Cudlipp (Annie Thomas), Miss E. Philp, Mr and Mrs Adolphe Smith, and Miss Amelia Edwards.[13]

It would appear that Amelia was investing in the Laundry as a charitable cause rather than as a profitable enterprise. That she gave more than money to the cause is borne out by a note addressed to her at the Great Western Laundry by the journalist George Sala, who had written to complain of 'an unfounded accusation made against his wife'. He writes somewhat irritably:

> Mr Sala has the honour to present his compliments to Miss A.B. Edwards. Matters connected with the wash-tub are clearly not within his province, and he only interfered in this celebrated question of soap-suds because he considered that his wife had been subjected to very great annoyance … and had not the remotest idea that Miss Edwards (of whose literary and artistic genius he has long had a high appreciation) was in any way connected with the Great Western Laundry … He is now heartily sorry to learn that she has anything to do with it.[14]

Little is known of Amelia's movements in 1878. She spent the winter at home, but was staying at 8, Albert Buildings, Weston-Super-Mare, at the end of March,[15] and did not return home before 8 April.[16] A letter from M. Inchbold written on 8 November has the remark 'I trust you have enjoyed your French visit', of which there is no other record.[17] For much of the year she was busy working on her two anthologies, the *Poetry Book of Modern Poets*[18] and the *Poetry Book of Elder Poets*.[19] They were published more or less simultaneously in London by Longman and in Germany by Tauchnitz at the end of 1878, although the London editions bear the imprint 1879. The German edition involved her in further correspondence with some of the poets whom she had already approached in 1873. Replies from Robert Browning,[20] Matthew Arnold,[21] Jean Ingelow,[22] Christina Rossetti,[23] Edward Bulwer-Lytton[24] and Algernon Swinburne[25] survive. She had evidently decided not to include poems by Roden Noel, excusing this on the ground of their length, for he wrote on 23 December 1878 hoping that he 'may observe without indiscretion that the critics think my short lyrics my strong point … Should you make another edition you might, if you cared, see if any were suitable to your purpose – in my Red Flag volume.'[26] Robert Browning in his letter of 25 March 1878 highlighted the problems of copyright which Amelia's request for permission to reprint poems of his had raised:

> Ah, dear Miss Edwards, this application of yours makes me sorry indeed, for I have no power to grant it. The poems belong to Baron Tauchnitz already ... no doubt certain pieces have so often been made use of that it is hardly worth while noticing any fresh infringement of the law. I fear there will be no way but an arrangement between the respective publishers.[27]

Amelia was increasingly concerned about the inadequacy of international copyright law and the effect of the growth of free public libraries on the welfare of authors. Years later, when she was lecturing in America in 1890, she was reported as saying:

> It is not right to expect that men will write books as a matter of sentiment. If authors are not encouraged they will naturally seek employment in other directions. In England, in contrast to the American practice, the circulating libraries, supported by subscriptions, are leading patrons of authors. Those libraries purchase large numbers of new books, for which the authors and publishers receive fair prices ... We have free libraries, but they are patronised almost exclusively by the poor people ... Nearly all the books in the course of time are issued in cheap editions and reach the free libraries, but this is not until they have been in the subscription libraries and the authors have received a fair recompense.[28]

When the *Poetry Book of Modern Poets* was published, a number of errors came to light. Jean Ingelow[29] and Christina Rossetti[30] wrote to point out errors of fact, and Robert Browning[31] to comment on an error of interpretation. The most serious error related to Christina Rossetti's year of birth, which Amelia gave as 1816 and not 1830. Her brother had pointed out the error to Amelia in a letter of 17 January 1879 suggesting an erratum note or a cancel leaf.[32] The mistake was picked up by *The Athenaeum*, hearing which her brother wrote on 14 February to assure her that 'the objection on a matter which I know is receiving your kind attention has not come in any way through me or mine'.[33]

Amelia seems to have resumed novel-writing as soon as *A Thousand Miles up the Nile* was off the press, with what was to be her last novel, *Lord*

Brackenbury (see Appendix 3, pp. 303–6). It was six years since the publication of *In the Days of my Youth* (see Appendix 3, pp. 301–3), and although she had since made a name for herself as a travel writer, she may well have feared that she might lose her reputation as a popular novelist, or that her lucrative readership might evaporate. There is no evidence as to when she began writing *Lord Brackenbury*, but that its publication was delayed is evident from a note in *The Queen* that 'Miss Amelia Edwards' new novel, promised some time back for the first week in January, has been postponed till the first week in February, when it will begin and continue weekly in *The Graphic*.[34] The first part appeared on 14 February 1880, and the delay was almost certainly due to the illustrator, the eminent artist Luke Fildes; he was still preparing the illustrations required for the early numbers when he wrote to Amelia on 14 January:

> Anything you may have in the way of photographs or sketches that you think would be useful to me, if you will kindly send them, I promise will be most religiously preserved and returned … Any scribbling of your pen giving the outline of a moor, the shape of a window, or anything, however roughly, may be invaluable to me.[35]

Amelia had apparently made a number of suggestions for illustrations, which he was happy to take on board. She had also asked him if he would make a drawing for a story in *Good Words*, but he declined:

> My legitimate work is to paint pictures and, as greatly as I am interested in illustrating your story [*Lord Brackenbury*], than which a more picturesquely suggestive one could scarcely exist (I am really charmed and delighted and perhaps a little surprised to find a story so teeming with artistic suggestions) still I miss my painting very much.

The book was immensely successful. It was published in three volumes by Hurst & Blackett in December 1880, and within a year it had

> gone through 15 editions, including translations … it is translated into Russian, German & French & has not yet done running as a serial in Australia & New Zealand. Messrs Hurst & Blackett are now preparing *their* fourth edition, to form a volume of *The Standard Library*.[36]

Generous as ever, Amelia sent copies to her friends. Gaston Maspero wrote from Paris on 18 August 1880: 'I don't need to tell you how delighted I should be to receive your book. I read many novels.'[37] He wrote later, having read the book, to point out two errors, but added: 'All this is merely a detail and a matter for a correction. The description of Verona and Genoa is charming and the interest well maintained.'[38] Marianne North wrote from New Zealand on 9 May 1881 to say 'I like your Lord B. very much.'[39] Earlier, when staying in New South Wales, she had seen copies of some of the parts in serial form on the bookstalls.[40] Gustave Doré in a letter of 1 May 1881 commented on the resounding success of the novel.[41]

While Luke Fildes was still preparing the illustrations for *Lord Brackenbury,* and before its serial appearance in *The Graphic,* Amelia was busy laying the foundations of a work which was to occupy her for the rest of her life, and to have a more lasting impact than any of her novels. On 20 January 1880 she wrote to a number of Egyptologists of her acquaintance, informing them that,

> the Editor of the *Morning Post,* being particularly interested in Egyptian research, permits me to inform you that he is willing to promote the interests of science in this direction by throwing open the columns of his influential daily paper to correspondence on Egyptological subjects ... Such correspondence, as you are aware, has hitherto been mainly restricted to the pages of the *Academy* and the *Athenaeum,* publications limited as to space, & issued but once in each week. Egyptologists who take advantage of the opportunity now hospitably placed at their disposal will therefore find in the *Morning Post* such a medium of communication with the public as Assyrian & Greek archaeologists command in the *Daily Telegraph* and *The Times.*[42]

She was concerned to bring the question of Egyptian antiquities into the popular domain, and had approached an editor whom she knew well, for she had written reviews and reports for the *Morning Post* herself for some years. She signed her letter 'Amelia B. Edwards, Member of the Society of Biblical Archaeology', of which she was 'one of the first Lady Members', as she proudly told Edward Abbott.[43] Knowing that Dr Samuel Birch had used the Society of Biblical Archaeology, of which he had been the founder and first President in 1872, as a forum for Egyptological reports, she took the precaution of writing to him on the same date, 20 January, enclosing a carbon copy of her circular letter, and telling him of 'the good will of the Editor of the *Morning Post* ... This may lead to the start of the excavation fund.'[44]

Dr Birch was not enthusiastic. In a letter dated 28 January he wrote:

> Dear Miss Edwards,
> At the present moment I find it quite impossible to write any
> articles about future excavations in Egypt … The first step towards
> a successful advocacy is to ascertain that the results of the
> excavations will be sent to the British Museum not that of Boulaq,
> the ultimate destiny of which is not clear. A public subscription in
> these bad times would be quite inadequate and better days must
> be waited for.[45]

He signed his letter 'with kind remembrances' but it was, to say the least,
discouraging.

Ernst von Bunsen's response was no more encouraging:

> I have before me a very short but pithy paper on … the ethnical
> relations of the Hyksos, connected with the date of the Exodus. I
> intended to send it to … our Bib. Arch. Soc. & I shall probably do
> so. Did I think that it could be worked out in a more popular form
> – fit for the *Morning Post* – I would gladly send it … I really believe
> that no real advance will be made in Egyptology till chronological
> and ethnological questions with regard to Egypt shall have
> received that attention which seems now to be imperatively
> demanded.[46]

Ernest (later Sir Ernest) Budge wrote the following day claiming to
know 'but very little of Egyptian matters … If there is anything I can
ever do for the *Morning Post*, will you please ask it? But it must be
connected with Assyrian.'[47] A kindly but scarcely more helpful reply
came from Dromana, from Henry Villiers Stuart, MP for Waterford. He
had read *A Thousand Miles up the Nile*, and had met Marianne
Brocklehurst when she was visiting Ireland: 'I shall bear in mind what
you say about the *Morning Post*. I take deep interest in Egyptology, but
I regret to say that at present Rich Landlords have very little leisure for
literary pursuits.'[48]

By the same post, however, came a letter from Stuart Poole, then
Keeper of Coins and Medals at the British Museum, but a student of
Egypt from boyhood. He promised to write a letter to the *Morning Post*
but added that contributions should be selected by 'some one who is at
once acquainted with the scientific literature of the subject and knows at
the same time how much the public can understand… I know no one so
well qualified as you are …'[49] Amelia's reply has not survived, but she

was clearly flattered and pleased, for he wrote again on 2 February, 'I did no more than you deserve – you do not know the popularity of your book,' adding in a postscript: 'don't be discouraged by Birch. I have been, for 28 years come the 27th February.'[50]

Fig. 29: Reginald Stuart Poole, Keeper of Coins and Medals at the British Museum.

Amelia was not discouraged by Dr Birch. She wrote to him on 29 January with perhaps a little sarcasm, thanking him for 'making time to answer my letter,' adding:

> there are one or two promises of very liberal contributions, in case a fund can be organised, & if a few more such promises come in, the rest I think should not be difficult. But it would [be] idle for any mere Rush of Enthusiasm to start such a thing, unless there was a nucleus of solid cash to begin upon. But if this nucleus is assured – then perhaps you would lend the great support of your name to the

enterprise? … You see, excavations in Egypt cost very little – labour
is so cheap … The object of getting up a little publicity in the
Morning Post is solely to secure public attention to pave the way.[51]

A letter from Archibald Sayce, an Assyriologist then working on the Old
Testament at Queen's College Oxford, encouraged Amelia further. 'I
have found your book [*A Thousand Miles*] such delightful reading …
Your names & c. are still as perfect as when they were first written in the
chamber you discovered at Abu Simbel … One thing is clear', he wrote,
'that only about one third of what may be found and done in Egypt has
yet been found and done.'[52] Heinrich Brugsch, writing from Berlin on
6 March, also agreed to write a weekly article for the *Morning Post*.

Amelia's approaches had extended to Egypt. On 4 April she received a
long letter from Mariette Pasha, the renowned French archaeologist who
had been working to arouse concern in Europe at the destruction and theft
of Egyptian antiquities. He told her that the museum at Bulaq which he
had founded had suffered from the Nile floods a year ago and that a new
museum was now to be built.[53] But Stuart Poole was wary of bringing
Mariette into the British campaign. On 7 May he wrote to Amelia:

> I am very sorry you are overworked and would gladly do all in my
> power to take the Egypt Exploration off your shoulders, and I
> think I could get efficient help, but … I cannot move unless Dr
> Birch has the first offer. In order to avoid complicating the affair by
> introducing M. Mariette, I would advise your first writing to Dr
> Birch asking if he will undertake to carry on the work for you.[54]

He was perhaps concerned that Mariette might take the British
campaign out of their hands, and was no doubt protecting the interests
of his superior. It was by no means the last time that he would stay
Amelia's hand when she made what he thought inadvisable
approaches. So she wrote again to Dr Birch the next day, reminding him
of 'the nascent scheme having for its object to raise a fund for the
prosecution of further excavations in Egypt', indicating that Erasmus
(later Sir Erasmus) Wilson, who had defrayed the cost of transporting
Cleopatra's needle from Egypt to London, had agreed to 'begin a subscription list with liberal donations'. She made no mention of Mariette,
but added:

> M. Naville … was the first to propose this undertaking point
> blank, as it was, to the English nation. He is profoundly interested
> in the success of the effort, & is willing to take any amount of

trouble, personally, in advance of it. He will be in England in about three weeks from now, & he proposes that a meeting should be convened of those who would be most interested and most likely to push the work.[55]

Amelia then put her request before Dr Birch, using all her persuasive charm:

> Will you, as the 'Father of Egyptology in this Country'... assume the direction and leadership of this movement? Will you, dear Sir, convene the meeting and organise the proceedings?... An eminent *savant*, a man of world-wide reputation, alone can take the initiative in such a matter.

Perhaps sensing that her own position needed an explanation if he were to be persuaded, she added:

> Up to this time I have done the very subordinate work of stirring up various Egyptological correspondents to write letters to *The Academy* and the *Morning Post*, & I have sounded many wealthy & influential persons as to money help. But I am obviously not qualified to organise meetings or to set a large movement finally going. It would be presumptuous & unbecoming on my part to attempt to do so.

She offered to book a room in the Langham Hotel in one or two weeks' time, but ten days went by without a reply, and she wrote again, not now expecting a positive answer. 'Pray be quite sure that I should be neither so forgetful nor so ungrateful as to attribute your refusal to any disinclination to be kind to me personally.'[56]

Eventually, Stuart Poole wrote to her to say that his colleague, Charles Newton, had persuaded Dr Birch to give 'nominal support, and will try and get Lord Carnarvon as chairman or president'. He added: 'We think we could do everything without a public meeting, by a private committee.'[57] Amelia was always for doing things with a flourish, while Stuart was more circumspect. On 7 June he wrote to propose a somewhat clumsy arrangement: a small meeting at the British Museum with himself, James Cotton, archaeologist and editor of *The Academy*, and Villiers Stuart, while she would invite 'a few more' for Wednesday 16 June after 5.30 p.m. He was still looking for 'an influential president' and comments on names which Amelia had suggested: 'I don't think M. de Bunsen will give much. I know he will talk more. S.C. is a fidget. L. is ...

I'm not even sure human … Avoid these unsettled parsons. But I do want a wealthy Hebrew.'[58]

The 'small meeting' took place on 11 June in the Department of Coins and Medals, with Edouard Naville, a Swiss Egyptologist, also present, while Amelia lost no time in inviting possible donors and participants to the meeting on 16 June. Lord Carnarvon sent his apology but offered 'every possible sympathy with the object of it'.[59] The meeting was reported in *The Academy* of 19 June, no doubt in Amelia's words: 'Last Wednesday several ladies and gentlemen interested in Egyptology held a private meeting in the Council Room of University College London, to consider the desirability of promoting research in Egyptology.'[60] To her press cutting of the report in the Somerville archive she has added in manuscript: 'This was the first meeting convened on the subject, in consequence of the steps I had taken … to open the subject in the *Morning Post* & to gain the ear of the English and foreign Egyptologists in favour of an English Fund. Mr Stuart Poole & Mr Bunsen did me the honour to call me the foundress of the infant society.'[61] She was justifiably proud of the success of her efforts. The meeting was indeed a landmark in the history of Egyptology in Britain, and the praise which she enjoyed was no more than she deserved.

One friend who had not responded to her initial approach was Gaston Maspero, but now, prompted by her enquiry, he wrote to her on 18 August after a gap of ten months. He had been overwhelmed with writing, having to correct the proofs of Mariette's third volume on the excavations at Abydos, in addition to his own work, because Mariette was seriously ill.[62] The news of his illness was a real blow to the cause: Mariette's favour was vital to any English scheme for excavation. Stuart Poole wrote to Amelia on 24 August: 'What you say about Mariette's health I know already, and it makes it all the more our duty to do what is kind to him.' ('Dear fellow!' wrote Amelia in pencil on the letter, 'how sweet and good'.) He had discussed the next step with a contact in Egypt, a Mr Waddington, telling him that he would like their results to appear simultaneously in Paris and London. The latter was 'very kind about our scheme and will try Mariette on the subject … As soon as the preliminaries are settled I will draw up a prospectus and send it round our little Committee for approval.'[63]

When Maspero wrote to Amelia again on 26 December 1880 it was to tell her that Mariette was gravely ill, and that the French government had decided to establish a school of archaeology in Egypt, analogous to those in Athens and Rome, and had asked him to go out there, taking selected students as his assistants. He was anxious that his mission would not be construed as a political one, when he was nothing other than 'un homme d'étude', a scholar.[64] Maspero's appointment as Director of Antiquities based in the French School of Archaeology in Cairo was to prove invaluable to the infant Society. Mariette was approaching seventy years of age, the doyen of French Egyptology, not known personally to Amelia; Gaston Maspero was thirty-five, a man of wide cultural interests and as good a correspondent as she was. He kept her informed of developments in Egypt from 1881 until 1886, when he resigned his post and returned to Paris because of his wife's poor health. He continued to write to her from Paris until 1891. She valued his friendship greatly and depended on him in the early 1880s, as she depended later on Flinders Petrie, for despatches from the scene of action.

Learning of Mariette's illness and Maspero's new appointment, Amelia wrote at once to Dr Birch, that she had received 'a long letter [from M. Maspero] … on his plans & hopes as regards the new French College at Cairo'.[65] She was no doubt keen to display her familiarity with the French plans. 'I also learn with great satisfaction from Mr R.S. Poole', she continued, 'that you have given your invaluable support to the movement set on foot by Mr V. Stuart, M. Naville & others'. She was always careful to suppress her own name when writing to Dr Birch. However, she knew how to touch a vulnerable spot.

> This gives me great hope that something may at last be done in the way of co-operation with the French on Egyptian soil. If we do not cooperate, there will be a German invasion of the Delta, & English scholars & lovers of Egyptology will be nowhere … It certainly seems very desirable in the interests of science that this should be anticipated by the English and the French.

With rather less than her usual diplomacy, she then added,

> The French can supply young and active *savants* & excavators – we English can supply money … I venture to hope that you will lend your immense influence, & the weight of your great name, to the furtherance of this object … by taking this opportunity of opening the subject to Prof. Maspero & so paving the way for combined operations on a large scale in the Delta.

Mariette died on 19 January 1881, and one reason for delay in pursuing the scheme for British activity in the Delta was thereby removed. Maspero's next letter, dated 20 March, was from Bulaq. It reported his discovery of the pyramid of Unas; his first excavations had been 'fructueuses' (fruitful) but overthrew several of Mariette's hypotheses. It was, however, 'l'argent qui manque … L'argent que vous m'offrez sera le bien-venue, s'il vient' (money which is lacking … The money you are offering will be welcome if it materialises). He arrived, he said, with ideas very different from those of Mariette. He explained that he had to consult the Egyptian authorities before accepting her proposition, but now had Riaz Pasha's permission to accept it on her terms, which were that any finds should be published simultaneously in Paris and London:

> I beg you therefore to press on with the negotiations as far as you can … We shall decide the points of detail … and when everything is agreed I shall submit your scheme for a contract to the Egyptian government for approval. It is a formality which will not take long to complete.[66]

This was good news. Stuart Poole was eager for a second meeting, and wrote to Amelia on 1 April recommending a number of names, mainly of academics: 'My plan would be to submit our scheme of corporation leaving the whole question of publication to Maspero, who should give us a *compte rendu* simultaneously with Paris. I am against Birch as Secretary … Why not Miss Adair who is a student of Egyptian and has time and money?'[67] What Amelia thought of this last suggestion is not recorded, but one suspects that she might not have appreciated another woman's involvement. 'A report', Stuart added in a separate letter four days later, 'would not draw subscriptions unless an Englishman were put under M. Maspero… An English engineer would be a capital assistant.'[68] He developed this idea in a letter of 18 May, urging that it was desirable for 'M. Maspero … to receive an English student who should report to him and to the English Committee and expend their funds. Professors Newton and Gardner agree with me.'[69] They left it to Amelia to put the proposal to Maspero. He replied on 8 June from Naples, thanking her for the news, but adding: 'Certains détails m'embarrassent un peu' (There are certain details which trouble me slightly). He had discussed the original proposal with the Egyptian government, but now the terms had been 'un peu changé' and he must refer it to the Ministry again. He suggested that they meet and discuss it in Paris and draw up an agreed plan which he would submit to the government. He hoped that it could be settled by the start of the season for excavation in the middle of November. 'I beg your pardon for this slight delay. I have business in Egypt with such particular people that I can't take too many precautions to protect myself from their touchiness. Correctness governs everything.'[70] As he saw it, 'the majority of the subscriptions which you are able to collect will come from Jews or others interested in Biblical archaeology, for whom the interest of excavations in Egypt would be greatly aroused if one found monuments relating by and large to the history of the Jews'. He proposed to devote the English subscriptions to the exploration of the eastern Delta, establishing his main base at Tanis. In this way 'the subscribers would have the justifiable satisfaction of being able to say that they have given their country a new scientific glory'.[71]

As yet, however, the British funds were promised rather than held, and no public appeal had been launched. The need for the preservation of the Egyptian monuments was raised at a meeting of the Society for the Preservation of Ancient Buildings at which both Stuart and Amelia were present on 27 June 1881 and met a sympathetic reception but no more. Maspero, however, was remarkably philosophic about the delays: 'I think the monuments, having waited many centuries, can wait a few months longer.'[72] He hoped, however, that if the enterprise were postponed a little, the Society could nevertheless send him 'a young Egyptologist who is well enough prepared to give me serious help.'[73] He already had an Italian and two German students sent by their respective governments to work with him in Paris, and would happily offer the same service to an Englishman.

Maspero had hoped to attend the Congress of Orientalists in Berlin to read a paper on his impressive discoveries at Deir el-Bahri but was unable to attend in person. Lepsius read his paper at the Congress, but Maspero asked Amelia to review it in *The Academy* or *The Times*, if not in both. She had lost no time in doing so, with articles in *The Academy* on 13 and 24 August.[74]

The find of royal mummies at Deir el-Bahri was an exciting and important discovery, and one to fire popular as well as academic imagination. The journalistic instinct inspired Amelia to write it up in *Harper's New Monthly Magazine*.[75] She wrote to Maspero for photographs of the mummies with which to illustrate the article, and he sent them in October 1881. By the time it was published the following April they were on display in Bulaq, lying, as she wrote, 'shoulder to shoulder ... a solemn company of kings, queens, princes and priests of royal blood ...'.[76] It was this dramatic style of narrative that was to prove so successful in her American lectures eight years later, and that from the start was an immense asset to the Society in helping to popularise the cause. She did not fail to stress the vulnerability of the mummies:

> Even at Boolak, although the structure has lately been rebuilt, and
> is now being enlarged, it is doubtful whether they are really safe.
> An unusually high Nile, a fire, a popular revolt, may at any

moment sweep them away, leaving to future generations only the strange story of their discovery and the memory of their fame.[77]

Amelia had asked Maspero to give *Harper's* exclusive rights in the photographs, but this he naturally declined to do, adding: 'I have to protect my freedom to publish my own work.'[78] He was most generous, as Petrie was later, in supplying Amelia with information and allowing her to publish it, but he believed in wide dissemination of knowledge and not in exclusive rights.

By this time Amelia was deeply involved in plans for the establishment of an Egypt Exploration Fund. It was more than a year since the informal meeting on 19 June 1880 and still no public appeal had been launched, and no president chosen. She sent the draft prospectus to Maspero and he replied from Bulaq on 22 October 1881 giving his complete approval.[79] As to Dr Birch, he added, she was a better judge than he: 'He has not always been very courteous towards me, but he is an old man and has done good service to science; I am not offended.' Stuart Poole was not so confident, however. He wrote to her on 9 December 1881:

> 1. Maspero's coolness [towards Birch] enormously increased my difficulty in acting without Birch, the natural leader of the project. Birch must be asked to join, and I think you should ask him.
> 2. A committee should be formed including yourself, Birch, me, Newton, Sir E. Wilson, Gardner, and whoever good we can get.
> 3. It would be well to have a meeting and choose a secretary. Then an appeal could be issued. Would it be possible to put the whole matter in the hands of the Society for Biblical Archaeology?[80]

It is easy to see his dilemma. Samuel Birch was his senior colleague and the Society of Biblical Archaeology was Birch's creation. Amelia had no such scruples about forming a new society without him. Stuart Poole did not know Gaston Maspero as Amelia did: writing to her with 'the great news' that the pyramid of Maidum had been opened, Maspero asked Amelia to pass a letter to 'M. Poole' because he did not know the correct way to address him.[81]

The year 1881 had been a year of hard work, but not without leisure moments. On 8 November Amelia wrote to a friend in Westbury who had been ill: 'Miss Renshaw & I are flitting about the country making excursions, paying visits, &c., & have been to Ilfracombe, Lynton, Stratford-on-Avon, Sudeley, &c., &c.. In a day or two we are off again, to Salisbury & Lymington.'[82]

Amelia began the year 1882 busily soliciting support for the proposed scheme. She was delighted to learn on 21 February that the Archbishop of Canterbury 'gladly appends his name'[83] and that Sir Erasmus Wilson approved of the prospectus and sent 100 pounds. By 25 February their supporters included a number of eminent scholars. 'I think after all you have taken aback Birch,' wrote Stuart Poole, 'He is like a portcullis blocking a pyramid.'[84] On 4 March Robert Browning sent his support: 'How can I have any objection to contribute my poor name to the list of movers, under your inspiration, in so good a cause.'[85] Stuart was, however, still nervous: 'You want a large meeting and a great success thereby ... If you call a large meeting you must have the signers as speakers. They will feel their coming will pledge them to give',[86] and five days later, on 13 March, he wrote again: 'I have secured some of the list names by distinctly disavowing all intention to ask for money. It would be impossible to ask poor men, or men not rich who are purely scientific.'[87]

Amelia was by this time staying at Weston-Super-Mare, no doubt with Mrs Braysher. They frequently spent short periods there during the winter or early spring, but this did not in any way interrupt her correspondence on the question of an Egypt exploration fund. A letter from Professor Sayce at Oxford gave her the impression that Maspero had told him that he was prepared to see antiquities which were discovered in the course of excavations by the new Society transported to the British Museum, subject to the approval of the Bulaq authorities. Such a *volte face* would have been likely to change Dr Birch's attitude to their project and to make the raising of funds much easier, but Mr Poole disbelieved such a rumour; it would be 'a tremendous change of point.'[88] He was right to doubt.

Among others approached by Amelia for signature to the proposal was Heinrich Schliemann, who wrote to her from Troy on 20 March that he had read her letter

> with profound interest. As you desire that I should sign the paper I have done so and return it enclosed, though I am perfectly certain that the funds for the excavation you contemplate could not be raised in your country ... But I shall no doubt be able to finish the Troad until [sic] August, and how would it be if you, Mrs Schliemann and I dig up Naukratis next winter? If you could persuade Mrs S., who has remained at Athens, I am quite ready to undertake this, or Goshen ...[89]

This was an unexpected suggestion, and though Amelia may have felt flattered by it, there is no reason to suppose that she was tempted. She forwarded the letter to Stuart Poole, after copying it for her own records. It was Stuart who wrote to Maspero asking if he had any objection to Schliemann's suggestion.[90] As he remarked to Amelia:

> Perhaps you did better in not writing to Maspero, as it is a kind of matter on which he might like to hear from me. He should be sounded rather officially than from a personal friend lest it be thought you were fussing him, and he would suppose that as an official man I could more easily put off important questions, though for real nature I should say you were far the better diplomatist.[91]

Schliemann's letter had not been received by the date of the crucial meeting on Monday 27 March, in Stuart Poole's room at the British Museum, and he is not listed among the thirty-five men and two women (Miss Jane Harrison, the historian, and Amelia) named in alphabetical order as supporters who were present, in the account submitted to *The Times* and published there three days later announcing that:

> A Society has been formed for the purpose of excavating the ancient sites of the Egyptian Delta, and the scheme has started with a reasonable prospect of success … A meeting was held on Monday last at which Sir Erasmus Wilson took the chair, supported by Mr H. Villiers Stuart M.P. Sir Erasmus Wilson was appointed hon. treasurer and Miss Amelia B. Edwards and Mr Reginald Stuart Poole hon. secretaries. The society is already in correspondence with M. Maspero with the object of beginning its operations so soon as sufficient funds are provided.[92]

The attractions of the Delta, then 'rarely visited by travellers', where 'must undoubtedly lie concealed the documents of a lost period of Bible history' were described. The announcement ended: 'It must be directly understood that by the law of Egypt no antiquities can be removed from the country.' The style of the announcement is unmistakably Amelia's.

The new society, with the title 'The Egypt Exploration Fund', was thereby made known to the British public, and Amelia took on a formal role within it as Joint Honorary Secretary.

Notes

[1] SCO Edwards 438, June 1888.
[2] SCO Edwards 351.

[3] *The Literary World* (Boston, MA), 4 June 1881, pp. 196–97.

[4] SCO Edwards 565, no. 38.

[5] PP 10.iv.8; in 1892 when Amelia died there were three servants at The Larches.

[6] UCL Ms Misc, 3E/4.

[7] Marianne North, *Recollections of a Happy Life* (London: Macmillan, 1893), vol. 1, p. 14.

[8] SCO Edwards 90.

[9] SCO Edwards 97.

[10] Boston PL, MS KF 187.

[11] SCO Edwards 32.

[12] Boston PL MS KF 1080.

[13] *Paddington Times*, London, 1 August 1877.

[14] SCO Edwards 294.

[15] SCO Edwards 19, 25 March 1878.

[16] SCO Edwards 283.

[17] SCO Edwards 616.

[18] Amelia B. Edwards (ed.), *A Poetry Book of Modern Poets, consisting of … works of the modern English and American poets selected and arranged by Amelia B. Edwards* (London: Longman, 1879); the Tauchnitz edition was published under the title *A Poetry Book of Songs and Sonnets, Odes and Idylls. Second series … Copyright edition* (Leipzig: Tauchnitz, 1878).

[19] Amelia B. Edwards (ed.), *A Poetry Book of Elder Poets, consisting of songs and sonnets, odes and idylls selected and arranged by Amelia B. Edwards* (London: Longman, 1879); the Tauchnitz edition was published under the title *A Poetry Book of Songs and Sonnets, Odes and Idylls. First Series* (Leipzig: Tauchnitz, 1878).

[20] SCO Edwards 19.

[21] SCO Edwards 4.

[22] SCO Edwards 87.

[23] SCO Edwards 282.

[24] SCO Edwards 11.

[25] SCO Edwards 311.

[26] SCO Edwards 225.

[27] SCO Edwards 19.

[28] *Cleveland Plain Dealer*, Cleveland, OH, 5 February 1890.

[29] SCO Edwards 88, 10 January 1879.

[30] SCO Edwards 285, 8 January 1879.

[31] SCO Edwards 21, 14 January 1879.

[32] SCO Edwards 290.

[33] SCO Edwards 292.

[34] *The Queen, the Lady's Newspaper*, 17 January 1880.

[35] SCO Edwards 49.

[36] SCO Edwards 351, 18 January 1881.

[37] SCO Edwards 150: 'Je n'ai pas besoin de vous dire combien je serais enchanté de recevoir votre livre… Je lis quantité de romans.'

[38] SCO Edwards 151, 26 October 1880: 'Tout cela n'est qu'un détail et matière à errata. La description de Verone et de Genes est charmante et l'interêt du roman de mieux soutenus.'

[39] SCO Edwards 256.

[40] SCO Edwards 254, 15 September 1880.

[41] SCO Edwards 454.

[42] EES III.j.1.

[43] SCO Edwards 351.

[44] BM OA 1868–81.1711.

[45] EES III.j.3.

[46] EES III.j.2.

[47] EES III.j.1.

[48] EES III.j.6.

[49] EES IV.a.1.

[50] SCO Edwards 565, no. 5.

[51] BM OA 1868–81.1712.

[52] EES XVII.a.3, 5 February 1880.

[53] SCO Edwards 122.

[54] EES IV.a.2.

[55] BM OA 1868–87.1713, 8 May 1880. Edouard Naville was a Swiss Egyptologist who had first visited Egypt in 1865 and had published on Egyptian texts and monuments.

[56] BM OA 1868–87.1715, 19 May 1880.

[57] EES IV.a.3, 21 May 1880.

[58] EES III.j.24.

[59] EES XVII.a.2.

[60] *The Academy*, Vol. 17 (19 June 1880), p. 455.

[61] SCO 565, no. 29.

[62] SCO Edwards 150.

[63] EES IV.a.4, 24 August 1880.

[64] SCO Edwards 151.

[65] BM OA 1868–81.1716, 4 January 1881.

[66] SCO Edwards 152: 'Je vous prie donc de vouloir bien engager les négociations dès que vous le pourrez. Nous réglerons les points de détail … et quand tout sera bien convenu, je soumettrai à l'acceptation de gouvernement égyptien votre projet de contrat: c'est une formalité qui ne sera pas longue à remplir.'

[67] EES IV.a.5.

[68] EES IV.a.7.

[69] EES IV.a.8.

[70] SCO Edwards 153. 'Je vous demande pardon de ce petit retard: j'ai affaires en Egypte à des gens si méticuleux que je ne saurais prendre trop de précautions pour me garder de leurs susceptibilités. La forme domine tout.'

[71] SCO Edwards 154. 'La plus grande partie des souscriptions que vous pourrez recueillir me viendra de personnages israelits ou autres qui s'interessent à

l'archéologie biblique, et pour qui l'interêt des fouilles en Egypte serait grandement éveillé si l'on trouvait des monuments les souscripteurs auront cette satisfaction très légitime de pouvoir dire qu'ils ont donné a leur pays une nouvelle gloire scientifique.'

[72] SCO Edwards 154. 'Je crois que les monuments après avoir attendu beaucoup de siècles peuvent attendre encore quelques mois.'

[73] SCO Edwards 155. '[U]n égyptologue jeune et assez bien préparé pour m'aider sérieusement.'

[74] Amelia B. Edwards, 'The discovery at Thebes' *The Academy,* Vol. 20, No. 484 (13 August 1881), p. 127; and Amelia B. Edwards, 'The archaeological discovery at Thebes' in *The Academy*, Vol. 20, No. 486 (27 August 1881), pp. 167–68.

[75] Amelia B. Edwards, 'Lying in State in Cairo', *Harper's New Monthly Magazine* (April 1882), pp. 185–204.

[76] Ibid., p. 185.

[77] Ibid., p. 204.

[78] SCO Edwards 158. 'Quant à ma propre publication, je dois garder ma liberté.'

[79] SCO Edwards 159. 'Il n'a pas toujours été très courtois à mon égard; mais c'est un viellard et il a rendu de grandes services au science, ne suis-je jamais offensé.'

[80] EES IV.a.10.

[81] SCO Edwards 161, 16 December 1881.

[82] UCL Ms Add. 181/11.

[83] EES III.j.33.

[84] EES IV.b.1.

[85] SCO Edwards 22.

[86] EES IV.b.3.

[87] EES IV.b.5.

[88] EES IV.b.8, 16 March 1882.

[89] EES III.j.35.

[90] EES IV.b.16, 5 April 1882.

[91] EES IV.b.17, 9 April 1882.

[92] *The Times*, 30 March 1882.

'More usefully employed', 1882–86

When Amelia was asked whether she would be writing more novels, she replied: 'That I shall sin again in the way of storytelling I do not doubt, but I venture to think that, for the present, I am more usefully employed.[1]

With her election as an Honorary Secretary to the infant Egypt Exploration Fund, Amelia's life changed in ways which perhaps she herself had not foreseen. She knew what it was to work under pressure, meeting the deadlines of editors and publishers, but until now her work had not led her into complex relationships with others: now she was one of a team. She was also entering a world of men and a world of politics. She had known men as guests, as hosts, as her publishers, as correspondents, as friends and husbands of friends, but never before as colleagues. The big names in her autograph album had been writers and artists; now she would be adding scholars and politicians, government officials and industrialists. Along with frustration and stress she would find much satisfaction in this new environment.

A few days after the foundation of the Fund was announced in *The Times*, Amelia received a reassuring letter from Edouard Naville. He was writing from Cannes, shortly after returning from Egypt, where he had spent some time with Maspero on his boat. 'He has always said that he intended to leave the Delta to the English. What Maspero does not want', he wrote, 'is for people to dig with the commercial aim of finding objects and selling them ....'[2] Both Stuart and Amelia wrote to him asking whether he would be willing to act as an 'agent' of the Fund, and he was clearly delighted: 'I cannot conceive anything more interesting for an Egyptologist', he wrote to Stuart Poole on 12 April 1882, 'than to make excavations.'[3]

As to Schliemann's offer, however, Maspero was not happy: 'M. Schliemann's intervention seems to me unfortunate in every respect … M. Schliemann does not include discretion among his virtues. He likes a fuss, articles in sensational papers', he wrote on 15 April.[4] He was anxious to respect the 'vanité nationale' of the Khedive and the Ministry, who regarded Egypt as 'la mère de civilisation ancienne et moderne'.

On reading Naville's letter, Stuart Poole had begun to hope that Maspero would allow the transfer to Britain of some of the monuments which Naville might discover: 'It would not do to show our hand, or frankly fist, but of course the prospect of having a sphinx or two of Joseph's Pharaoh would be most attractive', he wrote to Amelia on 17 April 1882.[5] Maspero's letter of 14 April to Amelia destroyed this hope:

> On principal, every monument found belongs to Egypt. Now I very much hope that the Egyptian Government, bearing in mind the generosity of the subscribers, would offer them, as a grace and favour, several monuments of their choice: I shall ask it as soon as I can. But it is a favour, and one could hardly demand anything but a favour.[6]

'I see we must go on the old lines and I fear for our subscriptions', Stuart Poole wrote three days later.[7]

Naville had written to Poole on 30 March about his activities during the winter. He had spent two weeks with Maspero on his boat, and the last week of his stay in an excursion to the Delta. He was especially enthusiastic about San (Tanis), 'a scene of striking desolation. I am convinced that there is much to do at San.'[8] He enclosed a report in English, which survives with annotations in Amelia's hand, as she prepared it for publication.[9] Stuart was anxious, however, that they should not publish anything which might disclose promising sites until the Fund's plan was secured. 'We all feel we must wait and keep quiet', he wrote to her on 28 April. 'It will never do for you to write to Maspero while we are negotiating …'.[10] Amelia knew that 'we' meant the 'sub-committee' consisting of himself, his assistant (Barclay Head) in the Department of Coins and Medals, and Charles Newton, Head of the Department of Greek and Roman Antiquities, all three of them colleagues at the British Museum, who could so easily meet in Mr Poole's room there at short notice. She saw all too clearly that her distance from London excluded her from the day-to-day discussions among the 'savants' in the metropolis. At the same time her independence from the Museum circle gave her a freedom which her friends could not enjoy. She could write to Samuel Birch in an almost frivolous manner, asking, for example, where to find 'Miss Harris of papyrus fame. I thought she was mummified ages ago… If she is dead, I suppose we must advertise for her Ka.'[11]

Maspero's suggestion that the Society should send out a young man as his pupil and assistant did not please either Amelia or the London colleagues; as Stuart put it in a letter to Naville: 'We must have an archaeologist of our choice.'[12] The London trio had an 'informal meeting' on 10 May and agreed to write to Maspero that 'much as we desired to help him we found his terms would hopelessly discourage our subscribers'.[13]

Amelia was eager to see the Society begin excavations in the Delta, and was no doubt frustrated by Stuart's circumspection, but in July 1882 the political situation caused a halt to their plans. Following riots in Alexandria and elsewhere on the part of the Egyptian army, a British naval force had been sent to the port on 11 July. The French had intended to act with the British, but when the Khedive, Arabi Pasha, declared war, they declined to join forces, and British forces acted alone, landing in the Canal zone. Times were not auspicious for Egyptian excavation. On 5 September Maspero wrote to Amelia, describing how his workers had been called up for military service and he had had to suspend his excavations. Provisions had become scarce and 'the position was becoming untenable'.[14] He was obliged to close his school of archaeology and he left with his sick wife for Paris, reaching it on 2 September. The government of Egypt effectively passed to the British, but the Archaeological Service remained in the hands of the French. Maspero's own position was uncertain. 'I intend to return to Egypt,' he continued,

> If the English Government has no objection to leaving me in charge of the excavation, the French Government will not oppose my remaining in the Egyptian service for several years yet. Uncertain as I am about the future, I dare not raise the question of the new Society and write on this subject to M. Stuart Poole. You can advise me on this.

He went on to propose that they used the enforced hiatus in archaeological work in Egypt to make detailed plans for the coming season's work

On receipt of Maspero's distressing letter, Amelia hastened to write to friends who might be able to help him, among them Sir Erasmus Wilson, who replied cautiously:

> What amount has the French Government been in the habit of spending, per annum, on the explorations in Egypt? What is Maspero's estimate of the probable cost per annum of what he proposes …? It is a scientific question, not a French or English question.[15]

Stuart Poole, however, was not pleased at her hasty approach to such a benefactor: 'I wish you had consulted me before taking so very serious a step.'[16] After two days' reflection and a long discussion with his colleague Charles Newton, he wrote a little more calmly: 'We feel that the present position is so delicate both as to Maspero and the French Govt. that the wisest thing would be private help.'[17] Amelia was justified, but Stuart Poole still objected to two of her suggestions: that British soldiers should be employed on excavations ('any but the Royal Engineers would be a great error') and that Sir Erasmus be elected as President of the Fund forthwith ('We cannot elect until the Society is constituted and some subscriptions have come in: as yet we are entirely a private club'). He was anxious to secure fair terms for excavation, but 'this must be done by our Government, but the difficulty is that Birch is the natural channel'.[18]

In her frustration Amelia turned again to her friend Sir Erasmus, who could, however, only echo Poole's advice: 'We must admit, as Egyptologists the French take the first place in Egypt … Maspero is awkwardly placed and he might find a difficulty in receiving a commission from "perfide Albion"',[19] he wrote on 11 October. Two weeks later, however, he wrote to her again, in the light of a letter from Naville which she had forwarded:

> I seek for knowledge & scientific enquiry – not for dolls [statuettes] to be stored up uselessly in a museum … It would certainly be best that our efforts should be backed by some kind of association; but I am quite ready to give £500 for a commencement of our work of excavation if some equitable arrangement could be made with Maspero.[20]

Amelia conveyed the news to Stuart by telegram. He called a meeting of his Museum colleagues at once to 'get a decision to engage Naville'.[21] He sounded out Naville, who was 'enchanted … quite prepared to go out to Egypt this winter',[22] and he drafted a letter to Maspero for Amelia's comments. 'I will not act without your consultation', he wrote.[23] She had not been well, but she lost no time in sending her comments.[24] By 21 November Maspero was re-established at Bulaq, and writing to Amelia of his intention to visit the Delta and decide 'l'emplacement des ateliers'; excavation could not start before December because of the flooding.[25] 'So you have won!' Stuart wrote to Amelia on 28 November, adding: 'We ought to make Wilson president next meeting – no doubt at all of this.'[26]

Stuart Poole's mood had swung to one of pleasure at progress made after months of frustration, and he wrote on 27 November to the still ailing Amelia a letter of unusual warmth:

I am sorry you are so overworked and in such a tangle … You lose time in various ways. 1. by writing letters when p. cards wd do as well … 2. Go to bed at 11.30. 3. Trust to events … 4. If you have to choose between pleasing the many and the few, between doing kind things and producing books, don't be too goodnatured. You write as on the point of tearing yourself up and throwing yourself into a waste-paper basket which but for Mrs Braysher you would do. Let her treat you like a sad child and coax & and make you … take up one of your oldest novels and think how clever you were and how much more you are *if you give yourself a chance* … I send you a kiss, so does [*sic*] L[izzie] and S[ophy],[27]

thus including his wife and daughter in his expression of affection.

Amelia's other interests at this time were not completely submerged in the joint honorary secretaryship. From a letter of 16 December 1882 we learn that she had recently crossed the Downs twice to have dinner with friends, though the severe chill which she caught on the latter occasion deterred her from further evening excursions. 'To be laid up seriously would be a very grave matter for me – & wld throw me out in all my engagements with my publishers.'[28] She spent more and more time in London, usually combining business and pleasure. She had been in London for much of July 1882[29] staying at Bailey's Hotel, Gloucester Road for at least part of the time, enjoying the company of Lucy Renshaw, entertaining and being entertained.[30] She may have visited Marianne North while in London. Marianne would shortly be leaving for South Africa and Amelia asked her to tell her something of her life story which she could write up in the context of Marianne's newly opened gallery at Kew.[31] She was back at The Larches in August, busy with work for the Fund, and building up her collection of Egyptian antiquities: when Stuart Poole mentioned Cairo lattices which a friend was wishing to sell, she was quick to express an interest.[32] It may be that these are the lattices visible in the surviving photograph of her hall at The Larches.[33]

The year of 1883 began well. Stuart Poole wrote to Lord Dufferin, Special Commissioner in Egypt for the British Government, alerting him to the existence of the Fund and its intentions, and received a kindly reply. He called a meeting for 9 January 1883 to elect Sir Erasmus Wilson as President, and the stage was set for Naville to go out in the new year and begin excavations under Maspero's aegis on behalf of the Society.

Sir Erasmus Wilson always had a special place in Amelia's heart. He was a wealthy surgeon who had in 1877 met the cost of transporting Cleopatra's Needle from Alexandria to London. He had long been interested in ancient Egypt and had published a popular book, *Egypt of the Past*, in 1881.[34] Amelia had reviewed it in *The Academy*.[35] At seventy-three years of age he had virtually retired from medical work and lived with his wife in Westgate-on-Sea. Amelia had consulted him unofficially and no doubt unprofessionally in 1880 about a young man, possibly a servant, whose health gave her much concern, and he had replied helpfully and kindly.[36] He was old enough to be her father, and did not hesitate to give her kindly advice: 'You are the coming as well as the present woman', he wrote on 18 March 1883, 'only take care of your health, and confine yourself as much as possible to general topics [in your writing]. They never do harm, but are a pleasant recreation to the mind.'[37] Sensing her frustration at her isolation from the London members of the committee, he encouraged her to make writing her particular role in the Fund: on 6 February 1883 he sent her a cutting of a leader from *The Times* of the previous day, urging the need for the preservation of Egyptian antiquities, and citing her own recent contributions, among others, by name.[38] In an accompanying letter he wrote,

> This leader puts you in a position of responsibility to which you are quite equal. In the first place, you must take seriously with consideration the publication of your papers on Rameses with a *popular* title. You must make it your 'pied de terre' [*sic*] until you have leisure to do something more. But this leader ... must be followed up smartly – the ground is your own, the battle is won. Academising and journalism are excellent; they give you a status among experts; but you must show yourself as a writer for the Public as well. You, and at a humble distance I, are reforming Egyptological literature – no more ponderous books![39]

Two days later he wrote: 'Please don't work too hard; and above all, don't worry – smoke your cigarette and trust somewhat in providence.'[40]

Sir Erasmus Wilson was a modest man, and accepted the Presidency 'perhaps because, as you say', he wrote to Amelia, 'there is nothing to do but look sweet and pleasant, but I am horrorstruck to be called "a sound Egyptian scholar" who am only a day-boy... [but] I can keep the seat warm for a better man.'[41] In the event he held the office for no more than a year and a half, dying after a short illness on 7 August 1884. 'He was one of the best & dearest friends I had in the world – or ever shall have in the world – and this loss seems to change all my life', Amelia wrote to Flinders Petrie on 19 August. 'He is a terrible loss to the Fund, to you, to M. Naville, & to all of us, & especially to myself who wrote to him & heard from him three or four times in every week, & to whom he was like a second father.'[42] To Mrs Petrie she wrote on 27 August: 'It is impossible to say what a gap this bereavement makes in my life. I have lost the only companion I had in Egyptological study … I always helped him with the proofs of his history [*Egypt of the Past*] & I have the unfinished task on my hands.'[43]

On 8 January 1883, the day of the meeting to elect Sir Erasmus as President of the Fund, Edouard Naville sailed from Brindisi. He reached Cairo ten days later, called on Maspero before setting out for the Delta,[44] and on Maspero's advice went first to Tell el-Maskhuta 'with the special purpose of ascertaining whether it is one of the treasure cities built by the Hebrews and whether it may give any clue to know the way of the Exodus'.[45] Within a month he was writing to Mr Poole: 'I have a good piece of news to begin with: Tell el-Maskhuta [*sic*] *is Pithom*. I can give it as certain from the inscription of a fragment of statue … I consider it as an important fact, to have been able to establish the site of one of the Biblical cities.'[46]

Stuart Poole was delighted at this exciting news, and in conveying it to Amelia asked her to write an announcement for the papers, which she did 'wonderfully well, with equal quickness and discretion'[47] taking care to emphasise their co-operation with Maspero. The discovery did not, however, go unchallenged.

An American, Cope Whitehouse, who had travelled in Egypt and had met the young Flinders Petrie there in the spring of 1882, published an anonymous article in January 1884 in America challenging the identification of Tell el-Maskhuta as Pithom.[48] He reprinted his original article as a pamphlet and distributed it widely. A correspondent in America, the Reverend William Copley Winslow, forwarded a copy to Amelia, writing on 8 April 1884 that

> Mr W. seems to have a strong personal animus against not only the whole Pithom & Zoan business, but against the EEF &c. If possible he had better not be gratified … He has wealth, nothing to do, & the libraries of N.Y. at his disposal.[49]

This indeed proved to be the case. Both Stuart Poole and Amelia were dismayed, fearing the effect on subscriptions. Stuart urged caution: 'He is anxious to draw you … I have grave doubts of the wisdom or dignity of our touching him', he advised Amelia.[50] Cope Whitehouse wrote to Amelia and to Naville, appearing to impugn Naville's good faith, and Amelia, angry and hurt, was all for writing a strong reply to him in a private capacity, but again Stuart urged her against it: 'I don't see how you as Secretary can write a letter of private feeling. He will quote you as speaking for us … Your beautiful woman's way of appealing to his

honour would only give a handle to a man without scruple.'[51] Cope
Whitehouse continued to write letters and articles highly critical of the
Fund throughout the decade, and was an ongoing source of irritation,
but Stuart's advice was heeded and Amelia resisted the temptation to
respond.

Amelia was often frustrated by Stuart's extreme caution. He had
asked her to 'write nothing on these subjects [the results of Naville's
campaign in the Delta] without my seeing it. Every line I have printed
has gone through the Sub-Committee.'[52] She depended on him heavily,
however, for the background notes without which she could not have
written her many articles on the work of the Fund. Amelia's own
knowledge of ancient Egypt was very considerable. She had taught
herself to read hieroglyphs and was familiar with a wide range of
Egyptological literature, but she did not have the long experience of the
subject, or the background knowledge of neighbouring races and
languages which her friend Stuart Poole had gained over a lifetime. He
provided the scholarship, she the style appropriate for the daily and
weekly press. Her constant requests for information put a considerable
strain on him. 'We must not drive Mr Poole too hard', Sir Erasmus
Wilson admonished her gently. 'He seems to have his hands more than
full. And you also have occupation enough to keep your pen from
getting rusty.'[53]

The chief vehicle for Amelia's writings on Egyptological subjects was
The Academy, edited by James Cotton, who became a member of the
committee of the Fund, and was always supportive. She had been
writing for *The Academy* at intervals since 1877 and between that year
and her last contribution in 1891, she submitted well over 100 signed
articles, as well as shorter unsigned notes which can be identified from
a scrapbook in the Sackler Library.[54] She also contributed seventy-four
articles to *The Times* during the 1880s, unsigned.[55] Between June 1882
and January 1883 she contributed sixteen papers to successive issues of
Knowledge on the theme: 'Was Rameses II the Pharaoh of the
Oppression' and on 2 March 1883 it was agreed that she should
contribute the article 'Mummy' to the new edition of the *Encyclopaedia
Britannica*, apparently at her own suggestion.[56] The labour which this
writing involved may well have been a cause of a series of periods of ill-
health during the 1880s, and they were the only source of her earned
income at that time.

Stuart Poole also regularly contributed articles, reviews and letters to
learned journals. Amelia did not hesitate to criticise his style, which did
not always please him, even when he thought her comments 'perfectly
just … It is very kind of you to offer to help me, but I like to do my own

work single-handed.'[57] Edouard Naville was genuinely appreciative of her translation of one of his reports, which 'looks much better in English than in French',[58] but even he would not always accept her suggestions, though demurring with diffidence: 'I do hope that Miss Edwards will not be offended at my not accepting all her corrections', he wrote to Poole on 31 July 1884,[59] and two years later he observed that 'Ladies are more sensitive to criticism than we are.'[60]

As a reviewer Amelia could be damning: 'When Mr McCoan talks of the "luxuriant vegetation" of Philae, which grows only a dozen or so of under-sized palms and a few straggling bushes, one is tempted to ask whether he has ever made the trip to the first cataract,' she wrote in *The Academy*,[61] and of a translation of Brugsch-Bey's *History of Egypt under the Pharaohs* she wrote: 'But of the translation of these volumes the less said the better. Frequently incorrect and always inelegant, it wearies and obstructs the reader from the first page to the last.'[62] On the other hand she could praise with an ardour much appreciated by her friends: 'That review was indeed a splendid New Year's gift … A most eloquent paper which for power and picturesqueness and grasp makes me feel very humble', Stuart wrote to her on reading her review of his *Cities of Egypt*.[63]

The joint honorary secretaries had been so preoccupied with the launch of the Fund that they had not fully prepared themselves for its consequences. Enquiries about subscriptions began to arrive almost at once. 'Read enclosed letters from praiseworthy Britons', Amelia had written to Stuart on 2 April 1882, 'Verily I scent gold. Subscription forms are urgently needed. I think 250 should be printed immediately … I scent a government grant in the possible distance.'[64] She signed herself 'Your affectionate Co Hony Secry' and illustrated her letter with a drawing of 'The Secretary-Bird'.

Sir Erasmus Wilson had been elected the first Honorary Treasurer of the Fund at the inaugural meeting on 27 March 1882, but when he was elected President on 8 January 1883, the office of Honorary Treasurer was taken by Canon Greenwell, a minor canon of Durham Cathedral. The labour of collecting, acknowledging and accounting for subscriptions, however, fell entirely on the joint honorary secretaries. Amelia took to this task readily, and was somewhat put out to learn from Stuart on 17 April 1883 that there was a third collector of subscriptions, a Mr Pope, a JP for Gloucestershire. She saw this as a threat to her own canvassing success, especially as he was a neighbour, living at Clifton. 'Anyone can receive subscriptions', replied Stuart, 'provided they are handed over', and he hoped that she would keep on good terms with Mr Pope, as he was 'a valuable man'.[65]

Keeping accounts did not come naturally to either Honorary Secretary. 'You are a capital woman of business' Stuart wrote on 1 September 1884, but he added that 'I must save my criticism recollecting your sufferings with the accounts.'[66] In the summer of 1883 when the first general meeting was called and a balance sheet was to be presented, problems of reconciling their accounts emerged. Stuart had repeatedly asked Amelia to pay in the cheques which she had received, and to 'compare cheque and receipt foils. That will settle the matter.'[67] She replied at last on 22 July: 'I have made a stupendous effort of bookkeeping & written you out a clean and clear account, added up, carried forward & all. I hope the auditor will find it correct.'[68]

In November 1884 Mr E. Gilbertson, a friend of Mr Poole's and a man 'of great taste and a collector' was elected Honorary Treasurer in succession to Canon Greenwell. He was prepared to play an active role in this capacity, and Stuart Poole suggested that he should sign all official receipts, 'to be uniform, and save all trouble with balancing', as he explained to Amelia. 'It would really save you a great deal of trouble – and us too – and no small responsibility of a kind you hate.'[69] Amelia, however, was reluctant to change her system, and proposed a modified plan, which Mr Gilbertson obligingly adopted; but it irked him increasingly as the years went by, to see what he regarded as inefficiency. On 4 February 1885 he wrote to Amelia: 'I think I have got to the bottom of the discrepancy in the accounts as far as your subscriptions are concerned.'[70] By April he was writing that he could not take on 'any more than the barest Treasury duties. I only volunteered to lift a little of the drudgery from your shoulders and Mr Poole's.'[71] Amelia liked the gentlemanly Mr Gilbertson, and remained on friendly terms with him. She was touched to discover that he was interested in her 'as an authoress' as he put it,[72] but she could never bring herself to relinquish completely her control of her subscribers' records. Amelia insisted on maintaining a list of 'her' subscribers, separate from that of Stuart Poole's. 'I am as you know', Mr Gilbertson wrote to her on 4 January 1887, 'quite incapable of understanding the advantage of separating sources of income … It looks rather unusual and out of place to me as a business man.'[73] Eventually, on 25 January 1887, he wrote that 'as I feared, the Treasury department does not work very well … so I am now anxious that a new Treasurer and member of Committee be found.'[74]

No subsequent Honorary Treasurer attempted to reform the account keeping, and problems continued to arise throughout the decade. Amelia never forgot what she regarded as Mr Gilbertson's 'curious mistakes … and I had repeatedly to correct him', she wrote in June 1889, and she referred, six years after the event, to the 'discrepancy of £14, I think (£14 or £11, I no longer remember which)' in the making up of the first balance sheet of 1883, adding: 'The muddles were simply awful.'[75]

'Delegation,' Stuart wrote to Amelia on 6 April 1883, 'is the hardest thing in the world.'[76] It was equally difficult for Amelia. She was extremely reluctant to relinquish control of any part of the administration of the Fund's affairs. Differences over the accounts, whether she was in the right or not, were matched by differences in other spheres: arrangements for the printing of publications, or for the publication of announcements in the press, or for the distribution of what they jokingly called 'plunder', those monuments and small objects which they were allowed to ship to Britain, were all spheres in which she wished to set her mark. This was understandable, for as she was to write to Flinders Petrie on 14 September 1887, 'the Fund is my own child',[77] but it did not make her an easy colleague. To a neighbour in Westbury who had invited her to dinner she wrote, as early as April 1883,

> I have scarcely time to snatch half a dinner at home; to go out and eat a real dinner just now is impossible. I am driven to the last verge of overwork … at it all day & half the night – & never leaving my desk till 2 A.M. Please don't imagine I am killing myself for 'filthy lucre' – the work that keeps me up does not bring me a penny. I am working [for] the Egypt Exploration Fund of which I have the honour in some degree of being the Founder. But it is like the old story of Frankenstein. I have created a monster & it is hunting me to death.[78]

If she was less than efficient in her account keeping – and she would have disputed such a suggestion – Amelia more than made up for it in her effectiveness in canvassing for support for the Fund. She was expert at coaxing contributions from all manner of people. By April 1883, a year after the launch of the Fund, she had recruited twenty-five subscribers, among whom friends and neighbours figured prominently: Mrs Braysher, Marianne Brocklehurst and Lucy Renshaw predictably appear in the list, along with her neighbours H. St. Vincent Ames, Mrs Cave and Miss Worrall. Her publishers Longmans, Macmillan and John Murray were included, and there were writers such as Arthur Rhoné and clerics such as the Reverend Henry Tomkins, who was, however, something of a mixed blessing and lived at Weston-Super-Mare, which she found rather too close for comfort. 'Oh yes, I know that Tomkins is in town', she wrote to Stuart on 7 May 1883. 'Blessed fact. Keep him there. If you love me, keep him. Lure him down into the basement & turn the key upon him … Do this & I will bless you & leave you something handsome in my will.'[79] What her reservations were about Mr Tomkins is not known, but they were shared by Stuart Poole, who wrote on 13 September 1883: 'Tomkins is going to the Church Congress. Between ourselves, I fear Mr T. will make a mess of it and our whole scheme will get mauled.'[80]

Not all her approaches were successful: 'I am always disinclined to give my name to undertakings of which I am unable to form a judgement,' wrote Benjamin Jowett on 18 April 1882, 'and I am afraid that the request of a distinguished lady is not a sufficient reason for departing from this rule.'[81]

By 31 July 1884 the number of subscribers whom she called her own had risen from twenty-five to ninety-two, and by December 1886 she claimed to have 'about 160' on her list.[82] This must have represented a very considerable effort. The list of 1884 includes more friends and neighbours: more of the Ames family, more Brocklehursts (including Mrs Dent, Marianne's sister, whom Amelia had visited at Sudeley Castle with Lucy Renshaw in the summer of 1882) and Marianne's companion, Mary Booth. Miss Du Bois, Amelia's childhood friend, also appears on the list. Amelia's subscribers developed a particular loyalty to her, which she undoubtedly enjoyed and of which she was jealously proud.

In a letter to Flinders Petrie written on 22 September 1887, Amelia amusingly describes how she recruited subscribers:

> It is true that any dunce can answer subscribers – but it needs a diplomatist to net them. If you but knew the wealth of diplomacy I have poured out on paper! I first of all select a *likely* person – being of course acquainted with that person's special leanings; then I write him a beautiful letter, pointing out to him how the aims of our society are precisely *his* aims; & how valuable our publications will be to him; & how, being who & what he is – his name & support will be peculiarly precious to us. Thus I took Lord Shaftesbury with *Pithom* and the Exodus, the Bishop of Durham (who was retiring after a donation & brought back & converted into an annual) with your early Greek papyri. Jews I attack not with the Oppression & Exodus (because they don't like it) but with Joseph & the 500 years of prosperity when the Hebrews were mighty in the land. Dilletanti I dazzle with the Greek art possibilities, clergy generally with the chances of a 1st or 2nd century New Testament. Quakers prefer the Old Testament I find; & thus I skim gracefully over the heads of the people. These special letters rarely fail, & I have got most of my good subscribers that way; but it takes a terrible amount of valuable time.[83]

By the end of 1883 the work of the Fund had already aroused interest overseas, and subscribers had been recruited, chiefly through Amelia's efforts, in the United States. On 7 May she had sent Stuart Poole a list of 'dearly beloved Yankees… with their good dollars & good sense (cents).'[84] There were nine on the list, from Boston, New York, Baltimore, Chicago and Maine. Some may have been known to her personally, but more probably she was known to them through her writings. Stuart was wary of the American influence: 'I should leave the Americans wholly alone if I were you', he wrote to her on 28 December 1883.[85] He was 'averse to an American Fund which means a Dual Control even in a modified form … And have you seriously thought', he added on 18 January, 'of the trouble and cost of sending voting forms and proxies in the same way as to every English donor?'[86] Amelia was not prepared to leave the Americans alone: she had been well-disposed to Americans ever since she had enjoyed American friendships in Rome in the winter of 1871, and she relished her contacts with the New World. She delighted in the American interest in Egyptology: 'It is impossible not to watch with interest', she wrote in an article in *The Academy* in 1884,

> the growing earnestness with which the study of Egyptology is being taken up by learned Americans. It was to be expected that the Biblical, rather than the archaeological or philological, aspect of the science would earliest attract Transatlantic students.[87]

Foremost among the early American subscribers was the Episcopalian clergyman of Boston, the Reverend William Copley Winslow, who was to play a major role in the Fund. He was exceptionally energetic and successful in raising funds for the cause in America. One of his initiatives was to appeal for subscriptions as 'Spades for Zoan', the site (Tanis) identified as the next to be excavated. This brought a good response, including one from Oliver Wendell Holmes, whose amusing letter he forwarded to Amelia with glee.[88] As his subscribers rose above the 100 mark Amelia suggested to Stuart Poole that the committee should consider rewarding him with an official position in the Society. Mr Poole replied on 9 February 1884 that 'the discussion of "the Winslow question" has been postponed. The Americans would claim a share of finds, & Sydney, the West & North of England have a stronger claim'.[89] He wrote to Amelia again on 5 July, warning: 'You are getting too large a body of American subscribers, more numerous and paying more than the English, and if our donors don't convert themselves into subscribers it will be most serious.'[90] Sure enough within two weeks Mr Winslow was writing to Amelia that he would be 'very grateful if some amphorae, etc.' were to reach him 'for the Art Museum in Boston'.[91]

However, Mr Poole's reservations about American subscribers were short-lived. He was very much a creature of moods and fluctuating attitudes, and as Mr Gilbertson wrote to Amelia on 21 October 1886, a man 'of nervous temperament'.[92] On 26 June he was writing to Mr Winslow to express the sincere thanks of the committee,

> for your efforts in the cause of the Fund. They are gratified by the support of an intelligent body of American subscribers … Should any future gift from the Egyptian Government contain duplicates, it will be matter of consideration to the committee how they may be most fairly and beneficially distributed.[93]

He was happy for Mr Winslow to be elected Honorary Treasurer for America in 1883 and in October 1885 he conceded in a letter to Amelia that 'Winslow deserves to be a V.P.'[94]

As the decade progressed Mr Winslow's letters to Amelia became more frequent and more intimate: 'How we are getting bound to each other in these official ties!' he wrote on 17 November 1884.[95] 'What a naughty, sly but dear puss you are, my dear friend', he teased in a letter of 24 December 1884, on discovering that she had recruited one of the Ames family who was resident in America to her list, 'to go mousing within half a mile of here. But it's all the same. Mr Fred Ames, of great wealth, *I* had in special view to aid us.'[96] He expressed his admiration for her in increasingly extravagant terms. He asked her for her photograph, and when it arrived, wrote:

> Is it you? You, one of the truest of all women since Eve began? It is less than two feet from my pen & I look on it just as I say this. Are those eyes chestnut or hazel? They are gazing on, on, on, like those of the Sphinx. Tell me … of thy eyes, complexion, hair & *smile* …[97]

What Amelia thought of such outbursts is difficult to imagine. Was he teasing her again? Her own letters, even to such as Dr Birch, were often witty and humorous, but she would never have written thus to someone whom she had never met. On 11 June 1887 he poured out his domestic troubles to her in a long letter: 'I am LLD, bootblack, nurse, steward, preacher, lecturer, factotum, waiter, runner, repairer of everything broken … buy every ounce of food used in the house; have a wife much run down, nervous & what not.'[98]

On 3 May 1886 Mr Winslow raised the question of honorary degrees. He would like one from a British university, preferably Oxford or Cambridge. He offered to seek honorary degrees for Amelia, and asked if she would do likewise for him:

> Not for worlds would I have it leak out here that I was cognisant, in the least, of any efforts to secure me a degree. I am sensitive on the above point & the feeling here is different from that in England. Here a man is supposed never to seek an honorary degree. Please do not allude to this topic on postcards.[99]

All three honorary degrees which Amelia received – an LLD from Smith College, Northampton, Mass., a PhD Diploma from the College of the Sisters of Bethany, at Topeka, KS, both in June 1886, and an LLD from Columbia University in 1887 – were prompted by overtures on Mr Winslow's part. ('We cannot imagine you belonging to a sisterhood of any kind – there is none big enough to hold you', wrote Mr Gilbertson on 4 August 1886.)[100] Amelia agreed to enquire about an honorary degree for him and met with a favourable response from St Andrews University.[101] He continued to seek academic honours, degrees and membership of learned societies and academies, both for himself and for others – he claimed that a Doctorate from Dartmouth College for Mr Poole was 'all my doing'.[102] Amassing qualifications seems to have been an obsession for him.

As early as February 1887 Mr Winslow was suggesting that Amelia should go over to receive her honorary degree from Columbia in person that June, and give one or two lectures at the same time. 'It is my dream', he added, 'to have you in the U.S. two months at least, & to prearrange lectures for you.'[103] The tour which she eventually made in the winter of 1889–90 was largely due to his planning, and she always appreciated his help; yet during her tour she had very little contact with him and one might almost suspect that she shunned him. Certainly he was disappointed: 'Miss Edwards has closed a wonderfully successful course of lectures here [in Boston]', he wrote to her secretary in Westbury on 2 December 1889. 'I deplore that I have seen, & shall see, her so little. It is cruelly hard for me to bear, & I feel she does not realise it.'[104]

Naville returned to his home in Switzerland in late March 1883. The season for excavations in Egypt was short, determined by the summer heat and the flooding of the Nile. His first campaign on behalf of the Fund had pleased not only Stuart and Amelia but also Gaston Maspero. Maspero wrote to Amelia on 16 March from Luxor, where he had just completed his own highly successful campaign in Upper Egypt:

Naville's success is a very happy one. What he has found is no
great thing in itself, but is such as to stimulate the zeal of the
English public. A Biblical name such as that of Pithom is the best
thing one could wish for. I believe that now is the time to press the
business forward and give it as much publicity as possible.[105]

On 26 June he wrote to her again with welcome news: 'I have obtained
two monuments from Tell el-Maskhuta for your Society and have
advised Mr Poole of it. I hope this will encourage subscriptions.'[106] He
had been as good as his word, and had arranged permission for two
statues, a figure of a hawk and one of a seated scribe, to be transported
to Britain. 'This is splendid news', wrote Stuart Poole,[107] and indeed it
was in one sense a turning point for the Fund. They began to falter in
their claims that their object was purely scientific, now that they had the
prospect of tangible results.

On 3 July Amelia was in London for the first Annual General Meeting
of the Fund, held in the theatre of the Royal Institution. Sir Erasmus
Wilson also came up to London for the meeting, and took the chair as
President. Amelia followed his opening remarks with a summary of the
work achieved, 'showing the great value of the discovery of Pithom-
Succoth, and its bearing on Egyptian and Biblical history'. It was Stuart
Poole's idea that she should take the floor so early in the meeting: 'The
Royal Institution must be sick of me by that time [he had been lecturing
there during the spring], but you would be novel and have fire enough
for the three of us.' He had hoped that Lord Dufferin would be present
although in the event he sent his apologies. 'You see I could not put
myself before Lord D. ... but you would, as a lady, take preference.'[108]
The meeting was a great success, especially as the President was able to
announce the 'don gracieux'. A vote of thanks was recorded to the
Egyptian government, and it was resolved to present the two statues to
the British Museum.

It was some time before the minutes were printed, together with the
balance sheet. All receipts to 10 September were included, amounting to
£1531.1s.4d. At the meeting Sir Erasmus Wilson had announced that he
would make a further donation of £1000. The joint honorary secretaries
had good reason to be satisfied with the first year's work.

Amelia was at home for much of the summer, writing reviews and
articles. Maspero wrote to her on 23 August expressing his pleasure at
the society's success, but asking her to remind subscribers that
'permission to excavate is a courtesy of the Egyptian government. Praise
of the Khedive on this subject would be useful.'[109] In September she

travelled to Leiden to attend the International Congress of Orientalists, and delivered two papers on Egyptian antiquities.[110] Stuart had had a difficult summer. His daughter Sophy had become engaged to a French Egyptologist but had broken it off on his insistence. Then he had had a disagreement with his colleague Charles Newton, an 'official worry' which he revealed to Amelia 'because of your deep interest in all that concerns us and because of its possible bearing on the Fund'.[111] She replied warmly and sympathetically in what he called a 'beautiful letter'.[112] The quarrel was soon healed, but upset him badly at the time. He was desperately overworked, and when she wrote to him with a number of critical comments he replied sharply from holiday in Devon: 'Your 16 pages of blame make a bad beginning to my holiday. If I am to do any work for the Fund during my six weeks' holiday I must leave it.'[113] It was a threat which he was to repeat several times over the next two years.

Back in London, refreshed by his holiday, Stuart Poole began to look for a new man who could work for the Fund in Egypt, as Edouard Naville was anxious to complete his edition of the *Book of the Dead* and to delay his return to Egypt. He had not long been back at his desk when he met a relatively young man, W.M. Flinders Petrie, a surveyor by training, forty years old, who had spent three years independently measuring and exploring the pyramids of Giza. He had come to the British Museum to bring copies of his newly published book on this work for Dr Samuel Birch and Mr Poole. Stuart was impressed. He wrote to Amelia on 13 September 1883 that Flinders Petrie 'has written a most capable book on the Pyramids ... He would be a most useful help and does his work for next to nothing',[114] and a few days later suggested that if Maspero would give him leave to work, 'why should we not utilize a scientific and very economical man?'[115] Amelia had initial reservations, having heard rumours that Petrie had overstepped the limit of the permission granted him by Maspero when exploring the pyramid of Pepe in 1881 and again at Maidum in 1882.[116] She too, however, was impressed by his book on the pyramids, which she reviewed in *The Academy*: 'One is scarcely more impressed', she wrote, 'by the magnitude of the achievement than by the modesty of the record ... The book is a monument of industry, accuracy and endurance',[117] and when Stuart Poole reported that he had discussed the prospect with Petrie himself and had found him 'interesting, highly intelligent and in earnest',[118] and she learned that neither Naville nor Maspero had any objection to Petrie's involvement, she had no further qualms. it was agreed that Petrie should go out ahead of him and make a reconnaissance which might reveal the Greek city of Naucratis, and on

Maspero's arrival begin excavating at Tanis. The publication of any inscriptions found would be entrusted to Naville.[119] This plan was agreed at a meeting of the sub-committee, at which Petrie had presented a 'most businesslike financial statement'.[120] Stuart wrote afterwards to Amelia, disarmingly – perhaps embarrassed that they were sending out someone whom she had never met and did not know:

> I hope much of Petrie, tho' I don't think him A.B.E.ish. Yet these cold men have a great admiration for heroical women. Nothing can exceed Gardner's admiration of your dash, your style, your calm indifference to the bullfinches of life (how odd it sounds in so ornithophilous a person) and your splendid way of getting over them.[121]

On 2 November 1883 Stuart Poole wrote to tell Amelia that 'Petrie has raised a very important question. He says and truly that it is a sin to dig up a mound and not save all small objects of interest by a small payment to workmen who find them ... Here we touch on the delicate ground of purchasing.'[122] Petrie's conviction that small finds were potentially of more historical significance than that of great monuments was the distinguishing mark of his scientific method, and revealed his innovative approach to excavation; as Mr Poole said, 'Nothing portable came out of Pithom', and he probably knew that Petrie blamed Naville for this. Poole's delicate negotiations with Maspero resulted in an agreement that while all large objects should go to Bulaq, a purchase fund should be established for the acquisition of smaller objects, half of which should be handed over to Maspero for the Bulaq Museum and the other half retained by the Fund. Maspero was even prepared to allow duplicates of larger objects to be given to the Fund provided the Fund met the cost of transport.[123] Sir Erasmus Wilson agreed to pay the cost of transport on the understanding that the duplicates would be presented to him. 'This is simply a private arrangement and does not in any way involve the subscribers in costs.' Amelia had initial reservations about removing monuments from Egypt, but Stuart argued: 'I don't agree with you as to the little use of removal. The statues are perishing in the damp air [of the Delta] and they are historically and artistically of high importance. And it is of the utmost consequence that we should obtain some large objects.'[124] Amelia could see the sense of this, and over the next eight years was to play an eager and active role in the distribution of antiquities acquired by the Fund to museums in Britain and the United States, and later to museums elsewhere in Europe. The receipt and distribution of antiquities found by the Fund's explorers was indeed already very much part of Amelia's vision. By this time Petrie had begun digging at Tanis, the desolate area where Naville had worked, and Amelia suggested that some of Petrie's finds at Tanis should go to Bristol, where the supporters in her own locality could see them. Poole agreed: 'I believe the order of claim could be: 1. London, 2. America, 3. Bristol, 4. Sydney, 5. Lancashire.'[125] They had one major Australian subscriber, and Poole's own lectures in Oldham and its neighbourhood the previous year had encouraged enthusiastic northerners, especially non-conformists, to join the Fund. 'Of course,' he adds revealingly, 'you shall have your share and mine. I am forbidden to collect.' The original claim of the Fund, to dig purely for the advancement of knowledge, was soon lost, and it appears that Amelia was ready enough to add to her own private collection from the minor finds.

Amelia was also concerned about the publication of results. She was anxious to have an agreement with *The Times* for the rapid transmission of news, giving them priority over other newspapers. 'I detest the paper and despise the editor', wrote Stuart, 'but if the Fund will profit I suppose we must, provided Petrie's journal, if good for publishing as I predict, is taken and paid for handsomely to him.'[126]

Petrie kept careful journals of his progress and sent them regularly to London, where they were circulated round his friends. Mr Poole normally saw them first, and passed them to Petrie's mother, who was living in Bromley, Kent. Amelia was soon on the circuit and normally received them from his mother, and by agreement with him she used them as the basis for her articles in *The Times*. This arrangement was devised by Stuart Poole who was concerned that Amelia should not overlook Petrie's rights in what she relayed from his journal letters: 'Nothing could be better than that you should work up Petrie's materials but you will have to allow him so much per article and I must when this is settled ask Mrs Petrie to send them on to you after she has read them.'[127] He repeated this injunction three days later:

> You cannot arrange to contribute till you tell me what you will give Petrie for his journal, which is his private property, written for publication … Remember Petrie is working for nothing, counting on remuneration from publication exactly like you, and made this condition.[128]

Amelia abided strictly by this arrangement, which suited both her and Petrie. *The Times* paid her their top rate, £5 per column, and this she shared with him. 'I know you so intimately now, through your journals', she wrote on 15 May 1884, that I feel we are old friends – at all events on *one* side; and I address you accordingly. I wish to tell you again with what deep interest I follow you in these records of your daily life & arduous work; and how heartily I appreciate your courage, your endurance, your wonderful pursuit of good humour under difficulties, and your thoroughgoing style of work in whatever you do or undertake. In adapting your material to journalistic purposes, I beg you to believe that I take a hearty pleasure & pride in the task of making your manner of work known to the public, and I feel that you are setting a splendid example of scientific excavation to all Europe ... I tell Mrs Petrie that there is but one W.F.P. and that I am his prophet.[129]

Amelia admired Petrie from the first, and as she came to know him better her respect developed into warm affection. If Sir Erasmus Wilson was almost a 'second father', Flinders Petrie was almost like a son. He became her protégé; she had a personal and pecuniary interest in his journals it is true, but she was also genuinely concerned for his career. When his friend Flaxman Spurrell once reproached him with leaving all the publicity for his work to Miss Edwards he replied on 23 October 1885:

Fig. 30: Flinders Petrie at Giza.

As to ABE's letters I am only too glad if anyone will relieve me of making anything public. I can turn up at least three times as much as I can publish in the year, and as long as it is done, that is all I care for. Finding, no-one else will do, or scarcely anyone; publishing, many will do.[130]

Amelia was unable to attend the meeting of the sub-committee on 30 October, at which the employment of Petrie was formally agreed. Mrs Braysher was ill with bronchitis,[131] and she herself 'out of sorts and tired'.[132] On 28 October, accompanied by her elderly friend, she went to Weston-Super-Mare for a brief rest; by the 1880s Mrs Braysher's health was becoming a real concern. Amelia felt tied to Westbury, and when Maspero invited her in 1884 to join him and his wife on his dahabiyah on the Nile,[133] there was nothing she would have liked better. But she knew the force of Stuart Poole's comment when she relayed the idea to him: 'Surely it would be risky on the ground of health to Mrs Braysher?'[134] They did, however, spend some time each year away in Weston-Super-Mare. One such occasion was in November 1883, at 11 Park Place, about the time that Petrie was leaving for Egypt. She could maintain her correspondence with Stuart Poole and Flinders Petrie from Weston, although she missed having her growing library to hand. She describes life in Park Place to her neighbour Miss Worrall in a letter of 1 December 1883:

It is the choice situation of the place – away from the noisy road, yet separated only by a pretty public (or rather private) garden, with a full view of the bay, & the carriages & the passers by. Far enough off, though, as not to hear the noise of the wheels. The house is a private house belonging to a lady who is a friend of some of our friends here. It is a remarkably comfortable, pretty house – with good-sized dining & drawing rooms, two large best bedrooms & three maids' rooms. There are two excellent servants, who sleep in their own room. The cook is a very nice cook indeed … We have brought only Mrs Braysher's maid with us. We pay £3.3.0 a week, & keep the servants, & find of course everything.[135]

The house in Weston was to become a frequent retreat in the 1880s, especially when either Mrs Braysher or Amelia needed to recover from illness.

Weston was, however, not always a welcome change for Amelia. On 4 May 1884 she wrote to Stuart Poole:

I dread Weston. Here I can shut out the world & get enough air & exercise in our own bit of ground, but there everyone pounces on me, & the terrible Tomkins comes at all hours, insisting on seeing me 'for five minutes' and talking for an hour. But the change is necessary for Mrs Braysher, & that of course is paramount. I am so very grieved to hear of Mrs Poole's [his mother's] illness ... Old ladies and babies are bound to be vegetables. My old lady is a most rampaging, vehement, political, belligerent, Gladstone-hating, boiling-over vegetable – quite uncontrollable [*sic*] & unmanageable.[136]

Amelia and Mrs Braysher were back at The Larches early in December, shortly before the publication of a full-page profile of Amelia in *The Queen*[137] with two engravings: a portrait, and a picture of her library. It paid tribute to her work for the Fund and to her writings on Egyptological matters as well as to her novels. 'It is very good and the portrait charming', wrote Stuart Poole.[138] In the same issue, however, Amelia's article on Marianne North and her travels abroad appeared,[139] and it seems to have sparked off an objection from Marianne's childhood friend, Mary Ewart. Marianne herself was happy enough with it, when it reached her in the Seychelles late in January 1884, writing in response, 'What a grand story you have made of me!'[140] In the absence of other correspondence it is impossible to recover the circumstances, but Amelia appealed to Stuart to mediate. He was not going to be drawn: 'I am very anxious not to enter into the question of Miss North's life', he wrote to her on 28 December. 'All three are old friends of mine and tho' you are the most intimate by far, I should be sorry to lose the other two, or all three when you make it up!'[141] Make it up they did, for three weeks later he was writing: 'So glad your storm has blown over.'[142]

The second season of the Egypt Exploration Fund was as successful as the first. Early in his stay in Egypt Petrie discovered the remains of the city of Tanis spanning Greek and Roman times, and an earlier city, then believed to be the capital of the Hyksos and the site of 'Raamses'. He had reached Cairo on 23 November 1883. He first made a short excursion to Nebireh, where he found the remains of a Greek city (Naucratis), which excited him, but he did not have time to excavate there. Then he moved on to begin digging at Tanis, where he made important discoveries of pottery and papyrus in one of the houses. Passing on one of Petrie's journals to his mother on 30 June 1884, Amelia wrote: 'May I ask you not to tell anyone about the gold ornaments found on the mummy described on page 1 ... and to pass on the caution ... Things whispered in England are echoed in Egypt.'[143] Petrie bore the heat late into the year, and did not leave Egypt until mid-June. He submitted his many finds to Maspero and was allowed to ship some of them, including papyri, to Britain. Back in London, he prepared them for display in the Royal Archaeological Institute. 'I think the exhibition shows that we have got our money's worth this time, and that is encouraging', wrote Poole. 'There is plenty for the BM, Boston, Sydney, Bristol and Liverpool, as Petrie specially brought out duplicates. The necklace beats anything we have.'[144]

The great blow of the summer for Amelia was the death of Sir Erasmus Wilson on 7 August. One of his last letters to her shows his shrewdness in assessing personalities. After Naville had spent a day with him at Westgate on 30 June Sir Erasmus wrote:

> I have discovered that his relations with Flinders Petrie are not perfectly harmonious and I am afraid that Petrie has not used all the discretion he might have used towards so learned a collaborator … Now although magnificent as an excavator, enquirer, photographer & so forth, Petrie is not an interpreter of hieroglyphs … I hope that Petrie has not shunted M. Naville … our friend Naville must not be set aside. You see I have breathed my suspicions.[145]

Naville was in London in June and visited Mr Poole, who subsequently reported to Amelia:

> We have had a long talk about plans and he agrees to my scheme, which is (if you and all approve) for N. to take the outlying mounds of San, and P. the Greek mound near Naucratis, then to join at San and decide. P. to remain I think at the centre, N. to move ahead and examine … the probable sites of Rameses.[146]

With the growing complexity of the Fund's activities, the workload of the joint honorary secretaries increased. The publication of annual memoirs reporting the explorers' results brought the work of obtaining estimates for printing, preparing the texts for the press, proofreading and later packing and labelling the books, while with cases of antiquities for distribution to museums at home and abroad came the need for arranging, examination and sorting, and onward shipment to the selected destinations. Stuart Poole's son, Reggie, then an undergraduate at Oxford, helped with the more routine tasks of labelling and packing in his vacations for a small honorarium. Amelia urged the rival claims of a 'poor pensioner' in Peckham whom she hoped to help by finding small jobs for him. Stuart was clearly hurt when Amelia expressed her 'dissatisfaction with Reggie and consequently with me in the very tender subject of spending money'.[147] Differences over trivial matters tended to spring up with increasing frequency. 'A difference of opinion is not necessarily a misfortune', Stuart wrote to Amelia on 13 February 1884, adding: 'You and I almost always differ, not as to what should be done but as to how to do it … so we must find a *modus vivendi*.' But his patience was again near to breaking:

> You have one object of interest instead of my many … You can control your time, being unmarried and in the country, and I suppose are not subjected to disturbances from friends from 9AM to 11PM. You sacrifice money and time but you *can* sacrifice them … I have had the utmost difficulty getting time for this note.[148]

There is some evidence that Amelia was planning a visit to Switzerland in the autumn of 1884. Writing to her on 22 July about an early October date for the second Annual General Meeting, Stuart Poole writes: 'Surely you will be back from Switzerland by that time and thus able to come and bring Naville with you',[149] but there is no evidence that the visit took place. She was at The Larches in the first week of October.[150] She had spent the summer there, it seems; on 29 July she wrote: 'I have an awful cold on the chest, and am crippled up with aches & pains – from gathering flowers in the rain.'[151] The death of Sir Erasmus may well have put thoughts of foreign travel out of her mind. 'For your own sake and Mrs Braysher's it is best you are at home', wrote Stuart on 13 August. 'God bless you. I will do all I can to help you in all ways and so will dear Lizzie.'[152] Both Amelia and Stuart were surprised and a little disappointed to learn that Sir Erasmus had not left anything in his will to the Fund. Hitherto it had been his large donations which had made the excavations possible. In April Stuart had been asking Amelia to 'keep back the American subscribers' as they were becoming too numerous and the funds were in good shape.[153] Now they would need every pound and dollar they could attract, in order to maintain the excavations and publications.

Amelia went up to London for the Annual General Meeting on 29 October and for related committee meetings. The Pooles had invited her to stay with them, but she preferred to stay at the Langham Hotel again.[154] 'You are quite right about the Hotel', Stuart wrote, without taking offence, 'you ought to be free. We sympathise while we regret. I especially sympathise, for staying at a house is a complete loss of freedom.'[155]

Petrie had asked for an assistant for his next expedition on behalf of the Fund. It was agreed that it would be good to send out a student who could learn his innovative methods. A young man of twenty-two, Francis Llewellyn Griffith, had offered himself, and Stuart and Amelia approached potential sponsors for a 'Student Fund'. They raised enough, supplemented by help from his family, to engage him for three years. Petrie was delighted. 'Please tell Mr Griffith that I have half a cwt of ship biscuits over, which I will send wherever he wishes', he wrote, with typical frugality, 'This will save his ordering more than 1 cwt.'[156]

On 7 December 1884 Petrie sent a telegram to Stuart Poole indicating that he had found Naucratis. This was excellent news, but Poole was not sure whether it was intended for publication. He was always anxious not to announce results before they were fully authenticated. The New Year brought further news both from Naville and from Petrie. Naville had made 'an important discovery bearing on Biblical geography' but Petrie's letter 'is one string of complaints against me about Naucratis pages. It really is too bad … You know the trouble I took over Naucratis … My fate is ingratitude.'[157] He was near to losing patience with Amelia too at times. 'You have a right to know everything and I am killed by telling you half … What I feel is that three fourths of our correspondence is mere waste of time.'

The strain of overwork was telling both on Stuart and on Amelia by 1885. In January Amelia complained that Naville's memoir on Pithom was too expensive and that the committee had not obtained proper estimates.[158] In February she complained about the delay in the distribution of the memoir.[159] Relations between Stuart Poole and Flinders Petrie were also becoming precarious: 'Petrie's today's letter … to me … was very ill-humoured. He answers my style "Dear Petrie" [with] "My dear Sir".'[160] Sometimes Amelia's imaginative enthusiasm got the better of her reason. In May she suggested to Petrie, then working at Naucratis, that he send 1,000 bricks, made without straw as recorded in Exodus, from Tell el-Maskhuta (Pithom) to be distributed to subscribers to the Fund, mementos that they could treasure. Petrie let Poole know in no uncertain terms that this would be time-wasting and pointless; all Egyptian bricks looked much alike and most were made without straw. Packing 1,000 of them would take a week off their excavation time.[161]

At the same time, Mr Gilbertson was gloomy about the Fund's finances: 'If in spite of the distribution of [Naville's book on] Pithom, and of the articles from Tanis, our subscriptions are, as you say, already on the decline, the collapse of the Society seems to me to be … not very far distant.'[162] Stuart's gloom was temporarily relieved by the news that

Maspero was allowing all the finds from a Ptolemaic shrine to be removed to Britain, together with a selection of pottery from Naucratis, and he expected the memoir on Naucratis to be a great success; but when further critical comments appeared in the press querying Naville's identification of Pithom he was again plunged into despair: 'All I have to thank the Fund for is this exposure to mud-throwing … I am heartily sick of the whole affair,' he wrote on 9 May.[163]

Petrie and Griffith were delayed at Alexandria because of Griffith's ill health. 'Poor Griffith has at last knocked under the supremely ridiculous Petrie dietary', wrote Poole. Petrie's extreme frugality had been a matter for congratulation when he was first employed, as it made him an economical choice, but now it seemed a foolish risk. Petrie arrived back in London on 30 June 1885, but the Annual General Meeting could not be arranged until his fifty-six cases of antiquities, and Naville's two, had arrived and been opened and sorted.[164] Amelia wrote soothingly to him on 1 July:

> The season's work will greatly enhance the fame of our Society –
> to say nothing of your own as an explorer. I think it is an important
> achievement to have interested the world of classical scholars – it
> doubles our friends all over the world … I am sure that we are all
> immensely indebted to you for your immense labours. I wish
> however that you gave yourself more comforts.[165]

In April Mrs Braysher had been ill with gout, and was still making a slow recovery in June.[166] By then Amelia herself was having trouble with her eyes.[167] They went to Weston again on 17 June, where Mrs Braysher was well enough to drive out.[168] Amelia had a personal interest in the arrival of Petrie's boxes, as she had asked him to purchase some objects for her own collection. 'He will no doubt give you a good set of things but is bound to offer all he buys to the Trustees [of the British Museum] and to Birch', wrote Poole. 'I thought if I gave you the money, it was understood that you wd buy objects expressly for *me*',[169] wrote Amelia to Petrie somewhat aggrieved, but Petrie was intractable. 'My domestic troubles and anxieties have been so heavy & so distressing for months past', she told him in the same letter, 'that all my work is in arrears.'

She had other worries too. She believed that the cost of printing the Fund memoirs was too high, and suspected that the committee did not obtain competitive estimates, and wrote to Stuart:

> I am confident if you would entrust me with this part of the work,
> I should get the printing, revising & issuing done more promptly

> & cheaply than before. I do not mind the trouble – & I am a real
> woman of business. The Society must collapse & end in nothing, if
> we spend lavishly on publications, send out more explorers than
> we have time to report or means of publishing for – & have no
> princely President to help us out of our difficulties.[170]

She was also 'very much worried about Cope Whitehouse. He is
dragging me in now, & says I accepted his Pyramid theory in *The
Academy*. I did not', she complained. Again Stuart Poole persuaded her
not to reply.

He was himself at the end of his tether, and on 3 August told Amelia
that he had decided to give notice of his resignation as Honorary
Secretary. 'I do want to devote the small remainder of my days to higher
and larger pursuits than this clerk's work.'[171] On this occasion he was
persuaded to remain in office, with his son Reggie employed as an
under-secretary at £1 a week, but within three weeks he was writing that
'I now very much regret I did not retire when I wished.'[172]

Petrie spent the summer arranging another display of his latest finds
from Naucratis. 'Oh dear!', wrote Amelia on 11 August, 'How I shd like
to see the Exhibition!'[173] She was ill again in September, and when she
went to London to visit the exhibition at the beginning of October, Mr
Gilbertson commented that 'we were all much grieved to see how much
thinner you had become, and how evidently your strength had been
overtaxed during the past year.'[174] She travelled to London again for the
third Annual General Meeting on 28 October, and found time to visit the
Gilbertsons and to go to the theatre. By the time Petrie sailed again for
Egypt on 22 November to excavate at Defenneh, Amelia was back at The
Larches trapped in her domestic routine. At the end of the month she
had influenza, but on 10 December a five-day visit from Marianne
Brocklehurst and Mary Booth made a pleasant interlude.

With the arrival of 1886, difficulties between Stuart Poole and
Flinders Petrie came to a head. Stuart had been grumbling to Amelia on
1 December that Petrie 'has failed in his duty in many ways, not
rendered his accounts, and crowded the really important work into a
corner to satisfy his vanity which exceeds that of Ramses.'[175] Annoyance
was mutual, and even Mrs Poole confessed to Amelia: 'Oh dear friend!
he *is* trying to work with – most painfully obstructive & dilatory. It is the
nature of the man & he can't help it.'[176] Her husband was suffering from
writer's cramp; the nerves of his hand were badly affected and she had
to write all his letters for him.

Petrie for his part complained about the high cost which the committee
had incurred for printing the plates for his memoir on Tanis. In the same

letter he congratulated Amelia on her LLD from Smith College, just
announced in June 1886. 'But what LL does the D. refer to? Laws of
History? of Fiction? of travelling? or not rather the laws of promoting the
general stock of human interests & ideas.'[177] On 30 July he wrote to her
that 'there seems a desire (at least from the committee) to negative
whatever I propose, or else to make a mess of it'.[178] Another matter of
annoyance to him was the discovery that the finds from Naucratis
awaiting despatch to provincial museums had been left at Oxford
Mansion for weeks, and a workman had fallen through the skylight and
broken the pottery destined for the Ashmolean Museum.[179] The final
straw, however, was a difference over whether or not he had a right to use
as he wished any of his allowance which he had not spent in the field.

Amelia was annoyed to discover that Stuart had 'pledged the word of
the Fund to M. Naville' that he should go out for them next season. 'I
think I might have been taken into the Council ... If M. Naville goes out
unaccompanied by Mr Griffith, we shall get no small objects at all, & be
unable to distribute to Boston & English provl. museums ... Not to send
out Mr Petrie would be very unjust. He has worked harder than Naville
ever worked & brought home richer results.'[180]

Petrie was equally angry at what he saw as the incompetence of the
committee. Writing to Amelia on 13 August he outlined three courses of
action: he should resign; the committee should be re-organised; or he
should 'openly call attention to the waste and mismanagement' so that
the executive would be shamed into resigning and a new organisation
would be formed.[181]

Amelia did not reply at once, and when she wrote on 23 August it was
from Weston-Super-Mare, where she had been 'working like a slave to
raise funds for the coming season':[182]

> Your quitting the Fund wd. be a grievous loss to the Society. It
> would mean the loss of the finest expert in the world, and of the
> greater part of the portable objects ... Mr Poole ... has made great
> sacrifices ... worked very hard ... given up his daily exercise,
> turned his house into an office, & done more than any of us have
> perhaps fully appreciated ... He feels he cannot go on – & his
> family are alarmed at his late illness ... But where should we find
> his successor? ... Your third course, of openly calling attention &c
> &c would never do! It would certainly clear the air – but it would
> also clear the ground – of the Egypt Expln. Fund!

She ended her long letter with a reminder of all she had done for the
Fund:

I have given the best part of 7 years to it. My time, I admit, is not scientifically so valuable as yours. I have written nothing in my whole life so important as your book on the second pyramid – and I have discovered no Naucratis. But *in the market* my time is worth a great deal more than yours. A novel is worth £1500 to me. I was making from £500 to £700 a year. Since I have been Hon. Sec: of the Fund I have not earned £75 in any one year. I could have written two novels in the time; and I have actually refused to write two – one for the Ill. News & the other for the Graphic. For those in serial form I should have recd £600 each; for the 3 vol form, the same – or perhaps more – & from U.S.A., France, Germany & the Colonies at least £300 each besides. The demolition of the Fund would be for me a return to comparative riches, to real liberty – to that literary position which I am fast losing before the eyes of the public … It is madness perhaps on my part to desire to preserve my chains unbroken – & yet I wd fain see the work go on; that work wh. is glory to you & M. Naville – & poverty & drudgery & obscurity for me.[183]

Petrie was not moved. 'In short to me personally the Fund is a failure … I do not see that I dishonour it simply by leaving it after giving it 3 years work … It is not my business to keep the Fund going.'[184]

On 4 September Stuart Poole formally resigned. Amelia wrote to his colleague, Barclay Head, urging that he and the other British Museum members would stay loyal, and that they should seek a good paid clerk, who would 'not only do routine work, but make it part of his duty to get new subscribers, his industry being stimulated by a capitation fee'.[185] She confessed that she was 'very unwell & quite worn out… It is imperative that I now take some short vacation – & I am hoping to go to the Congress at Vienna.' She left on 18 September for the International Congress of Orientalists. Four days earlier she had not even begun the paper which she was to present on *The Dispersion of Antiquities*. Petrie had drafted a scheme for the re-organisation of the Fund to produce the business-like arrangement without which he felt he could not work. Amelia wrote to Mr Head from Vienna, supporting his proposed 'new rules' in principle on 27 September:

To have no rules, & to conduct the business of a Society wh. is built up with public money in a perfectly irresponsible manner, seems to me actually wrong … And I do not think it ought to be in the power of 3 members to dispose of large sums of public money without reference to the General Committee.[186]

Petrie's 'rules' were printed for the committee, but the President, Charles Newton, would not allow them to be circulated. Petrie naturally enough regarded this as a 'declaration of war ... This clinches my determination not to co-operate in any way with Mr Newton in future.'[187] On 11 October he formally tendered his resignation. Amelia was in Amsterdam on her way back from the Congress, and arranged for a Committee meeting on the 16th. Writing to Petrie from the Langham Hotel after the meeting, she reported:

> Mr Newton stays. Mr Poole ... remains only as member of Committee. I found myself quite powerless. Mr Newton staying, I had no resource but to obey your instructions, which I did with great reluctance ... They were all horribly confounded & shocked by your resignation ... & refused to believe you wd not be induced to reconsider it. Mr Poole scarcely looked at me, or spoke to me, till just at the last, when he seemed more like himself.[188]

In the last weeks of 1886 Amelia had another worry, small in comparison with what she saw as the threat to the very survival of the Fund, yet one which troubled her deeply. 'I had given Mr Winslow to understand that the Rameses colossus [destined for the Museum of Fine Arts, Boston] was 13 ft high', she wrote to Frank Griffith:

> My eyes have suffered very much this year from overwork ... Anyhow I committed a deplorable error in the copying, & then when the time came that I had to announce the donation of the colossus, I gave it precisely double its actual dimensions. I do not know that I have ever before committed a serious blunder. I am inexpressibly grieved & mortified. Mr Winslow meanwhile has published false dimensions in some 25 American newspapers.[189]

Her extreme concern over this is some indication of the state of her health at this time, but there is no doubt that she cared deeply for the American museums, and she asked Griffith to ensure that the Boston Museum received something particularly fine in compensation.

Amelia had one last hope of retaining Petrie for the Fund. She would propose that he be made 'Director'. But Petrie had antagonised most of the committee – even Mr Gilbertson – by proposing rules for their better management, when he was not even a member of the committee.[190] Having lost Stuart Poole, it was agreed to appoint a paid secretary, Helier Gosselin, and to hire a room for meetings and a storeroom at Oxford Mansion, but that was all. 'Petrie flinging an ultimatum in the face of men who have after all a higher standing than he has in the public eye, is not the way to arrive at a satisfactory, or even a rational, decision', wrote Mr Gilbertson to Amelia, and he was no doubt expressing the majority view.

Petrie had no intention of withdrawing his resignation, and he sailed for Egypt with a private commission to photograph sculptures on 28 November, without waiting for the Annual General Meeting of the Fund on 8 December, '& to my thinking', wrote Amelia to Mr Gosselin, 'the glory of the Fund goes with him. I am deeply grieved – his loss is irreparable to us.'[191] On 2 December 1886 she wrote to Petrie, saying that she had received his report and would read it for him at the meeting. 'Goodbye, good speed to you', she ended, 'good luck, God bless you. Ever your faithful friend, A.B. Edwards.'[192]

Notes

[1] SCO Edwards 565, no. 13. See p. 306.

[2] EES IV.e.1. 'Il m'a toujours dit qu'il comptait abandonner le Delta aux Anglais ... Ce que M. Maspero ne veut pas, c'est qu'on fouille dans un but mercantile pour trouver des objets et les vendre ...'

[3] EES IV.e.2.

[4] SCO Edwards 165: 'L'intervention de M. Schliemann me parait être malheureuse à tous égards ... M. Schliemann entre autres vertus n'a pas celle de la discretion. Il aime le bruit, les articles de journaux à fracas.'

[5] EES IV.b.18

[6] SCO Edwards 164: 'En principe ... tout monument trouvé appartient à l'Egypte. Maintenant j'espère bien que le gouvernement égyptien, pour reconnaitre la générosité des souscripteurs, leur offrira, en don gracieux, quelques monuments de choix: je le demanderai dès que je pourrai. Mais c'est un don, et on ne peut guère exiger autre chose qu'un don.'

[7] EES IV.b.19.

[8] EES IV.e.1. '[U]ne scène de désolation plus frappante. Il y a, j'en suis convaincu, beaucoup à faire à San'.

[9] EES V.a.2.

[10] EES IV.b.26.

[11] BM WA 1883.138, 27 April 1883.

[12] EES IV.c.90, 4 May 1882.

[13] EES IV.b.40.

[14] SCO Edwards 166: 'La position devenait intenable ... Je pense que je retournerai en Egypte ... Si le gouvernement anglais n'a aucune objection à me laisser à la tête des fouilleurs, le gouvernement français ne s'opposera pas à ce que je reste au service égyptien quelques années encore ... Incertain comme je suis de ce qui se passera, je n'ose pas reprendre l'affaire de la société nouvelle et écrire à ce sujet à M. Stuart Poole. Vous pouvez me conseiller à cet égard.'

15 EES XVII.b.3, 11 September 1882.

16 EES IV.b.32, 16 September 1882.

17 EES IV.b.33, 18 September 1882.

18 EES IV.b.35, 30 September 1882.

19 EES XVII.b.4.

20 EES XVII.b.5, 27 October 1882.

21 EES IV.b.41, 2 November 1882.

22 EES IV.e.5, 13 November [1882].

23 EES IV.b.41, 2 November 1882.

24 EES IV.b.43, 6 November 1882.

25 SCO 167.

26 EES IV.b.45.

27 EES IV.b.44.

28 UCL Ms Add. Mss 181.3.

29 BM Ms Add. 41496 f.87.

30 SCO 23.

31 SCO 258.

32 EES IV.b.58, 29 December 1882.

33 SCO Edwards 608.

34 Sir W.J. Erasmus Wilson, *Egypt of the Past* (London: Kegan Paul, Trench & Co., 1881).

35 *The Academy*, Vol. 20, No. 498 (19 November 1881), pp. 375–76.

36 SCO Edwards 326, 20 December 1880.

37 EES XVII.b.18.

38 *The Times* (London), 5 February 1883, p. 9.

39 EES XVII.b.7.

40 EES XVII.b.8.

41 EES XVII.b.17, 6 May 1882.

42 PP 9.iv.2

43 UCL Ms Add. 184, No. 1.

44 EES IV.e.12, 21 January 1883.

45 EES IV.f.1, 5 February 1883.

46 EES IV.f.2, 12 February 1883.

47 EES IV.d.11, 16 February 1883.

48 *The Churchman* (New York), 26 January 1884.

49 EES II.d.4.

50 EES III.f.34, 14 April [1884].

51 EES III.f.37, 22 April 1884.

52 EES IV.d.15, 22 February 1883.

53 EES XVII.b.13, 25 March 1883.

54 SAC fol. 333 Edw. [2].

55 SAC fol. 333 Edw. [1].

56 SCO Edwards 302.

57 EES IV.b.30, 10 May 1882.

58 GI E/N1, 30 June 1882.

[59] EES V.b.7.

[60] EES V.b.10.

[61] *The Academy*, Vol. 12, No. 291 (1 December 1877), p. 506, reviewing J.C. McCoan, *Egypt as it is* (London: Cassell, Petteer & Galpin, [1877]).

[62] *The Academy*, Vol. 15 (28 June 1879), p. 559, reviewing H. Brugsch, *A History of Egypt under the Pharaohs…* (London: John Murray, 1879).

[63] EES IV.d.1, 1 January 1883; her review of R.S. Poole, *Cities of Egypt* (London: Smith, Elder, 1882) appeared in *The Academy*, Vol. 22, No. 552 (2 December 1882), pp. 389–90.

[64] EES V.a.1.

[65] EES IV.d.80, 18 July 1883.

[66] EES III.f.98.

[67] EES IV.d.35, 17 March 1883.

[68] EES III.a.2.

[69] EES.III.f.167, 27 December 1884.

[70] EES III.c.9.

[71] EES III.c.32, 13 April 1885.

[72] EES III.c.101, 7 October 1885.

[73] EES IX.a.68.

[74] EES IX.a.68, 4 January 1887.

[75] EES X.f.32.

[76] EES IV.d.41.

[77] PP 9.iv.31.

[78] UCL Mss Add 181/4, 4 April 1883.

[79] EES III.a.4.

[80] EES IV.d.93.

[81] SCO Edwards 90.

[82] EES III.b.74.

[83] PP 9.iv.33.

[84] EES III.a.4.

[85] EES IV.d.121.

[86] EES III.f.2.

[87] *The Academy*, Vol. 25, No. 615 (16 February 1884), pp. 107–8.

[88] EES XVII.d.26, 11 May 1884.

[89] EES III.f.7.

[90] EES III.f.69.

[91] EES II.d.12.

[92] EES IX.a.50.

[93] EES III.f.64.

[94] EES III.g.131.

[95] EES II.d.25.

[96] EES II.d.35.

[97] EES II.d.95, 20 April 1886.

[98] EES II.d.159.

[99] EES II.d.103.

[100] EES IX.a.25.

[101] EES II.d.138, 17 January 1887.

[102] EES II.d.107, 30 June 1886.

[103] EES II.d.143.

[104] EES II.e.25.

[105] SCO Edwards 168: 'Le succès de Naville est fort heureux. Ce qu'il a trouvé n'est pas grand chose en soi, mais est de nature a stimuler le zèle du publique anglais. Un nom biblique, comme celle de Pithom, est ce que l'on pouvait souhaiter de mieux. Je croix que maintenant est le temps de lancer l'affaire et de lui donner le plus publicité possible.'

[106] SCO Edwards 169: 'J'ai obtenu deux des monuments de Tell el Maskhuta pour votre société, et j'en ai donné avis a M. Poole… J'espère que cela encouragera les souscriptions.'

[107] EES IV.d.75, 27 June 1883.

[108] EES IV.d.74, 25 June 1883.

[109] SCO Edwards 170: '[L]a permission de fouiller est un gracieusété du gouvernement Egyptien: un éloge du Khedive à ce sujet serait utile.'

[110] EES IV.d.98, 21 September 1883.

[111] EES IV.d.49, 24 April 1883.

[112] EES IV.d.50, 26 April 1883.

[113] EES IV.d.87, 17 August 1883.

[114] EES IV.d.19.

[115] EES IV.d.94, 15 September 1883.

[116] EES III.a.1, 6 April 1883.

[117] *The Academy*, Vol. 21, No. 601 (10 November 1883), pp. 308–9.

[118] EES IV.d.99, 22 September 1883.

[119] EES IV.d.106, 23 October 1883.

[120] EES IV.d.107, 27 October 1883

[121] EES IV.d.108, 30 October 1883.

[122] EES IV.d.110.

[123] EES IV.d.112, 8 November 1883.

[124] EES IV.d.114, 13 November 1883.

[125] EES III.f.71, 16 July 1884.

[126] EES IV.d.115, 13 November 1883.

[127] EES III.f.16, 22 February 1884.

[128] EES III.f.18, 25 February 1884.

[129] PP 9.iv.i.

[130] W.M.F. Petrie, letter to Flaxman Spurrell, *Seventy Years in Archaeology* (London: Kegan Paul, 1931).

[131] UCL MS Add. 183/4, 18 October 1883.

[132] EES IV.d.104, 29 September 1883.

[133] SCO Edwards 173, 19 November 1883.

[134] EES IV.d.118, 1 December 1883

[135] UCL Ms Add. 181.7, 1 December 1883.

[136] EES III.a.3, 4 May 1884.

[137] *The Queen, The Lady's Newspaper* (London), 15 December 1883, pp. 605–6.
[138] EES IV.d.122, 19 December 1883.
[139] *The Queen*, 15 December 1883, pp. 603–4.
[140] SCO 262, 30 January 1884.
[141] EES IV.d.121.
[142] EES III.f.2, 18 January 1884.
[143] GI Petrie III.2.
[144] EES III.f.100.
[145] EES XVII.b.25, 2 July 1884.
[146] EES III.f.63, 26 June 1884.
[147] EES III.f.162, 18 December 1884.
[148] EES III.f.11, 13 February 1884.
[149] EES III.f.73.
[150] EES III.a.6.
[151] EES III.a.5.
[152] EES III.f.92.
[153] EES III.f.38, 23 April 1884.
[154] EES III.f.133, 25 October 1884.
[155] EES III.f.104, 22 September 1884.
[156] EES II.d.23, 4 November 1884.
[157] EES III.g.7, 12 January 1885.
[158] EES III.g.18, 2 February 1885.
[159] EES III.g.26, 16 February 1885.
[160] EES III.g.32, 3 March 1885.
[161] EES XVI.f.83, 25 May 1885.
[162] EES III.c.16, 4 March 1885.
[163] EES III.g.70.
[164] EES III.g.84, 26 June 1885.
[165] PP 9.iv.4, 1 July 1885.
[166] EES III.g.58 & EES III.c.46.
[167] EES III.c.48.
[168] SCO Edwards 45, 18 June 1885.
[169] PP 9.iv.4, 1 July 1885. 9.4.
[170] EES III.a.8, 1 July 1885.
[171] EES III.g.96.
[172] EES III.g.106.
[173] PP 9.iv.5.
[174] EES III.c.100, 4 October 1885.
[175] EES III.g.140.
[176] EES III.e.21 [15 December 1885].
[177] EES XVII.c.5, 20 July 1886.
[178] EES XVII.c.6.
[179] EES Executive Committee Minutes, 7 August 1886.
[180] EES XIX.b.28, 9 August 1886.
[181] EES XVII.c.7.

[182] EES III.a.32.
[183] PP 9.iv.6.
[184] EES XVII.c.10, 26 August 1886.
[185] EES III.a.32.
[186] EES III.a.42.
[187] EES XVII.c.23, 7 October 1886.
[188] PP 9.iv.12.
[189] EES III.a.43, 19 October 1886.
[190] EES IX.a.50, 21 October 1886.
[191] EES III.b.65, 27 November 1886.
[192] PP. 9.iv.16.

❖ 12 ❖

'The Fund is my own child'

The New Year 1887 marked a turning point in Amelia's life. The three people with whom she had worked most closely in the early years of the Fund were now less involved. Gaston Maspero had resigned his post as curator of the Bulaq Museum in June 1886 and was lecturing in Paris, Stuart Poole had resigned as joint Honorary Secretary, and now Flinders Petrie had resigned from any association with the Fund. Petrie repeatedly suggested that Amelia break with the Fund too, but this she was not prepared to do. She spelled out her position to him in a letter of 26 September 1887:

> If Mr Poole were not really a dear friend & if I was not sincerely attached to Mrs Poole & the children, I should do all you point out without hesitation – namely write round to the Committee & expose all the shortcomings of the Executive. But I confess I cannot bring myself to this heroic sacrifice of the friendship of a family with whom I enjoy such close & delightful intercourse whenever I am in London. Mr Poole would become my enemy – Mrs Poole would see with his eyes – & life would lose one of the few charms it has left for me. I make very few new acquaintances & really no new friends. You are the last I have made & I do not suppose I shall make another. And you were the first since 12 or 14 years. I am getting on towards the evening of life – I cannot take new people into my heart – & I cling to the few – the very few – friends I have. This is a very selfish way of putting it – but it is the truth.[1]

'The Fund is my own child', she wrote to him on 14 September, '& I have sacrificed so much for it that I do wish it to achieve success. My feeling for the Fund – the impersonal entity – is entirely separate from my feelings with regard to the Committee or its ways. I bear all I do bear – for the Fund's own sake.'[2]

She was still fully committed to the Fund, and in some ways she now had more control over it, as sole Honorary Secretary. Working with Hellier Gosselin, a paid official, was less exhausting than working with

Stuart Poole. The work involved in the publications of the Fund, which
Stuart had been so loathe to leave to her, she now took wholly under her
wing. She worked as hard as ever in corresponding with her subscribers
and in writing for the press; in addition she was engaged in translating
Maspero's *L'Archéologie égyptienne* into English; she was correcting the
proofs in October 1886.[3] Both French and English versions appeared in
1887.[4]

Amelia took a continuing interest in the dispersal of finds brought
back to Britain; in spite of her fear that with Petrie's resignation there
would be no finds to distribute, between 1887 and 1892 donations were
made to the British Museum and thirty provincial museums, to five in
the United States, to one in Canada, two in Australia, one in France and
two in Germany. Small museums in areas where there were loyal
subscribers, such as Bolton, Macclesfield and Tamworth, were not
forgotten, but her special concern was that the Boston Museum of Fine
Arts should be well served.

While she was still, as she wished to be, fully involved with the Fund,
she was also as regular a correspondent as ever with Petrie. She
managed this dual role with remarkable diplomacy, fully aware of the
need for discretion when speaking to the one of the other. One service
which Petrie had performed for her was to bring back small objects for
her own collection, purchased within the budget which she had named.
While he was purchasing for the Fund, those objects which he brought
back had to be offered first to the British Museum, but now that he was
no longer an agent of the Fund he could buy for her more freely. 'I hope
you got your basket at the Langham', he wrote on 22 October 1886, 'with
several of the things you wanted, which I thought had gone to the B.M.'[5]
'I did get the little hamper', she replied the next day, '& I have been an
ungrateful monster not to thank you for yr. kindness in putting in the
addl. objects &c – very glad to have these – & will only return the Sekhet
– of whom I have already two or three good specimens.'[6]

Amelia described her collection in an article in *Arena* in 1891:

> Dearer to me than all the rest of my curios are my Egyptian
> antiquities; and of these ... I have enough to stock a modest little
> museum. Stowed away in all kinds of nooks and corners ... are
> hundreds, nay, thousands, of those fascinating objects in bronze
> and glazed ware, in carved wood and ivory, in glass and pottery
> and sculpted stone, which are the delight of archaeologists and
> collectors. And there are stranger things than these – fragments of
> spiced and bituminized humanity to be shown to visitors who are
> not nervous nor given to midnight terrors.[7]

Amelia was careful to co-ordinate what she purchased for her own collection and the purchases for the Fund which were destined for University College London. 'I will return you', she wrote to Hellier Gosselin on 14 November 1886, 'some of the amulets allotted by Mr Griffith for University College & brought away by me last Wednesday. There are several duplicate objects & some of which I already possess specimens in my own collection; they will do for other museums.'[8]

She corresponded with other collectors and it is in this connection that the name of Aquila Dodgson of Limehurst, Ashton-under-Lyne, first arises. Mr Dodgson had recently joined the Society and wrote to Amelia about his own collection 'which is very modest, but I shall be happy to forward you a list of what I have & also to obtain for you particulars of others which have come under my notice. I will also make enquiries respecting any wh. may be in the hands of private gentlemen in this district.'[9] This may have been Amelia's first introduction to the enthusiasm for ancient Egypt alive in a part of northern England which was to hold a large place in her affection in her final years.

Amelia now began to think of the ultimate destiny of her collection and her savings. The indifference of Dr Samuel Birch, and now his successor, M. Renouf, to the work of the Fund had predisposed her against leaving anything in her will to the British Museum. Now the hostility of Charles Newton towards Petrie reinforced her resolve. She wanted to help Petrie financially and to secure his future in archaeology, and she decided on endowing a lectureship (in the event she endowed a professorship) in Egyptology at University College London, an institution with a liberal policy with regard to women students, with the hope that he should be the first holder. She discussed her plan with Petrie, including her intention (to which she adhered) of limiting it to candidates other than members of the British Museum staff. He wrote on 26 November, two days before sailing for Egypt:

> Now you ask me about your own Egyptological affairs. But if you saw the many risks I have & the near shaves of being smashed, you would not think of me as a permanency … However if it ever should fall to me to arrange your collections be assured that I will do my very best. As to the lectureship that is another affair altogether. Pray do not limit it to outside B.M. for there may then be no competent person.[10]

A more immediate concern was to ensure that Petrie's current resources were adequate. She wrote to him on 14 November 1886 with regard to the balance in his 'travelling allowance':

> I wish … that you … would take the money out to Egypt & spend
> it in one excavation for the Fund … as an independent agent … If
> not, pray be persuaded to take the money into your banking
> account & spend it in Egypt as you think fit … Remember, M.
> Naville ate & drank & cooked all his allowance … I am fully
> sensible of the delicate sense of honour by which you are activated
> … But whatever you do, don't hand it over … Let me rather
> suggest that if you never use it, you will arrange that your
> informal trustee may bequeath it in your name to University
> College London to swell the modest endowment I have promised
> them.[11]

Petrie chose the last course.

The work of the Fund continued for a sixth season. Naville went out to
Cairo with his family in December, intending to winter there and not to
begin work for the Fund until February, because of what he believed to
be the low state of the Fund's finances.[12] Amelia persuaded Griffith to
join Petrie first, since Petrie was going to Upper Egypt. 'You wd. have
plenty of time to see the glories of Thebes, Dendera, Abydos, &c &c …
Take it while you can get it.'[13] She must also have thought that it would
be useful for the Fund if Griffith had the benefit of working with Petrie
and learning his methods.

  After Petrie's departure, Amelia began to take stock of the new
situation. The organisation of the Fund seemed to be working better than
it had done for some time. 'I must say', she wrote to Stuart Poole on
23 December 1886, 'that the businesslike way in wh. the C. is working, &
the promptitude with which things seem to be getting pushed forward,
is most refreshing. All you tell me is gratifying & I am much cheered.'[14]
She admitted, however, that she was 'fagged out – dead beat', and in a
letter to Petrie on 30 December she wrote that she pined for the Nile: 'I
am heartsick – literally heartsick, sometimes, with the infinite yearning
one has for the palms & the sands & the wide rushing river.'[15]

In 1887 Amelia began to develop a scheme for sharing the burden of
soliciting and maintaining subscriptions and generally fostering
enthusiasm for the cause throughout the country. She used the goodwill
of her more loyal subscribers to establish a network of 'Local Honorary
Secretaries'. She involved Stuart Poole in the plan, drawing also on the
subscribers whom he had attracted, and found him most co-operative. 'I
have got a first rate Loc. Hon. Sec. for Durham,' he wrote on 9 February,
'the Librarian, young and enthusiastic'.[16] In January 1888 she proposed

that the Fund should set up a circulating library for the use of the Local Honorary Secretaries, and in collaboration with Stuart she drew up a book list[17] and obtained the books at a discount from a friendly bookseller.

She had a personal interest in developing the scheme. 'My life & time have been, as usual, consumed by letter writing since my return home', she wrote to Petrie on 5 January 1888.

> I am hoping to shake myself free of this weary correspondence in the course of a few months, by the working of my scheme of Local Hon. Secs. I now have 4 for London, & want one (or two) in every postal district – & I have a good many in the North. I am going to hand over the subs. in his or her district to each local Hon. S. ... It is not reasonable that my whole life should be squandered on business & begging-letter-writing. I *must* have more time in future for my private studies & pursuits – & I *mean* to have it.[18]

The scheme was soon off to a good start. 'Already the L.H. Secretaries are buckling heartily to their work & beginning to win local support for themselves', she wrote to Mr Gosselin at the end of January.[19] In April it was agreed that the Secretaries should be able to buy sets of slides at cost price, to assist them in their studies.[20] The scheme did much for the promotion of the Fund in the provinces. 'I am sure that the idea of the L.H.S.s was a very bright one and will save you a world of trouble', Stuart commented.[21]

On 19 January 1887 Amelia wrote to Petrie about 'a very wealthy & intelligent man (merchant class) who has travelled in Egypt & is enthusiastically fond of Egyptian antiquities':

> The acquaintance is quite recent – since you left England – but I think from what I have learned of him in this short time that he is a sort of Erasmus Wilson. Now it has occurred to me that he is just the man who might be got to undertake the excavation of the Labyrinth [at Hawara, which attracted Petrie], & if I go on improving the acquaintance I do not see why I should not succeed in gaining enough influence over him to get him to do it ... Do not think this is mere moonshine. I am used to working a scheme of this sort ... It is all a question of patience, management & cussedness.[22]

By 7 March she had revealed the name of the rich man, who wished, however, to remain anonymous. He was Mr Jesse Haworth, a manufacturer and 'a religious man' as Amelia put it, who was to prove a major benefactor to museums, and to the Fund, as well as to Petrie. Maybe he was one of the 'private gentlemen in this district' to whom Mr Dodgson had referred. Amelia was sufficiently confident to tell Petrie: 'I will get all smoothed for you in whichever direction you prefer',[23] and indeed she did, with no strings attached. Mr Haworth provided the money for Petrie's excavation, unconditionally.

Petrie greatly appreciated Amelia's continuing support. In a letter to his friend Flaxman Spurrell he wrote on 1 February 1887:

> As to Miss E. I feel the difficulties of her position … I am (believing the honesty of her intentions throughout) quite willing to take her under these trying circumstances on her own shewing … Further she has offered to do all she can in putting any news I send of my doings in Egypt into [*The*] *Times* or other papers, though that will of course tell against [the] Fund… Now that is as much (and rather more) than could be expected under the circumstances.[24]

With the success of her paper at the Vienna Congress behind her, Amelia was ready to accept invitations to lecture locally and elsewhere in Britain. 'I am glad you have made a beginning as it will doubtless lead to more', wrote Petrie on 9 April 1887, hearing that she had been giving a lecture locally. 'I believe your true function is most of all as *social* leader in the Egyptological interest of England, keeping up a bond of union between private collectors & others throughout the country & working on their feelings by letters & lectures.'[25] He was to be proved right. She no doubt realised that the success of the Local Honorary Secretaries scheme would be aided by her presence in the provinces from time to time. 'Don't be nervous about your lecture', wrote Stuart Poole on 19 April,

> All you have to do is not to learn it by heart and not to put in too much. Don't lecture too soon after a meal and don't lecture faint. I find a cup of coffee the best preparation, failing that, a cup of tea. The anticipation of lecturing is always dreadful, the reality nothing.[26]

In the event her lecture the next day was highly successful.[27]

Amelia had been drawn into the campaign for votes for women by her election as Vice-President of the Society for Promoting Women's Suffrage, but she did not have time to give it much more than her name. She did, however, circulate a petition among her friends in May 1887, with small response from the Pooles: 'Everyone is profoundly indifferent to women's suffrage,' Stuart wrote,[28] and later: 'I am sorry to say all my household of the female persuasion decline to sign.'[29] He returned it on 21 May with the note: 'I don't think there will be one signature beyond Reggie's. I am changed by the last utterances of the party, which are wild.'[30] She had slightly more success with the Petries.

> Will you, & your father & Mrs Petrie sign the enclosed petition for me? Mrs Petrie signed one paper on the subject for me a month or so ago. I consider the vote of immense importance now, as women need protection & are on the side of conservatism, law & order, as a rule – & this measure would add about 200,000 votes to the safe side.[31]

In May 1887 Amelia and Mrs Braysher went to Weston for the summer,[32] but by the middle of June Mrs Braysher was 'very poorly',[33] and in August Amelia herself was ill. 'I am very nearly done for', she wrote to Petrie. She was still 'unwell' when they returned to The Larches in September.[34] The following month Petrie, who had been to Manchester for the meeting of the British Association, and had visited Macclesfield and Liverpool, returning through Shropshire, came to visit Amelia at Westbury. 'I am delighted that there is yet a prospect of seeing you,' she wrote on 30 September. 'I will get you a bed close by as we now have no spare room, & you will have no more hearty welcome.'[35] He took her a basket of antiquities for her collection.[36] In a later letter he wrote affectionately: 'My best remembrances to Mrs Braysher … Three extra strokes to Polly [Amelia's cockatoo] tonight on my account please. She will understand that.'[37]

Amelia travelled north in the autumn to give a series of lectures. She was busy preparing them early in October.[38] One of her first lectures was on 8 November 1887 at the Royal Institution, Manchester. Her script, in an exercise book, survives,[39] and with its variants such as 'British Museum' or 'Peel Park Museum', was clearly used on several occasions and adapted for each. There are indications of where the lights were to be dimmed ('Gas out') and where each slide was to come, of where a cutting from *The Times* was to be read, and where certain artifacts which she had brought with her were to be shown. The lecture had been meticulously prepared. 'I am very glad your lectures are so successful', Stuart wrote to her on 8 November, but added: 'In future I would suggest your limiting yourself to an hour.'[40] On 30 November Petrie promised to send her a figurine which she could use to illustrate her lectures. 'You shall have a dolly if you want one … I admire the notion of carrying it all over the country unbeknown, safe in the bottom of the box.'[41]

The title of Amelia's first lecture in the north, 'The Social and Political Position of Women in Ancient Egypt', is known only from the manuscript in the Egypt Exploration Society archive;[42] the lecture was not one that was used on her American lecture tour eighteen months later, nor published with those in *Pharaohs, Fellahs and Explorers* in 1891.[43] While she gives a historical account of the subject, Amelia includes comments which would be of particular interest to her late nineteenth-century audience. She cites, for example, 'a private lady renowned for wisdom ... and on that account ... the chosen friend & counsellor of her sovereign ... owing it not to her beauty or her fascination, but to her intellect'. Commenting on one of the slides, she says: 'We see Queen Hatasu in male attire, wearing the short kilt & sandals of a king.' The lecture has moments of humour, as when she speaks of Queen Hatasu as a canal-builder: 'For my own part, I have not the slightest doubt that Queen Hatasu was the scientific ancestress of M. de Lesseps', the engineer of the Suez Canal. She draws contemporary parallels, as when she explains her masculine title of Pharaoh: 'If it had pleased her Majesty's Ministers to appoint a lady as next successor to Lord Dufferin, for instance, they could scarcely have given her the rank of Governess General – or Governor Generaless of India.' The lecture gives a balanced picture: 'The excessive rights of women led to many abuses, & the marriage & property laws concerning women underwent a sweeping reform during the reign of Ptolemy Philadelphus,' but she ended: 'I only hope that the picture I have drawn may not have excited a sentiment of retrospective envy in the ladies here present.' She may never have used one paragraph, later deleted, perhaps nervous of its daring:

> Descent & inheritance through the female line is essentially a charac-teristic of savage society. It points to a period when the wars of tribes & the absence of legal safeguards compelled men to date what, for want of a better term, we must call their legitimate status, from the one parent of whose identity they could be absolutely certain.

On December 5 Amelia was lecturing in Tamworth. 'My new trade is increasing', she wrote to Mrs Petrie. It was a prelude to a further tour in the north in the new year. Petrie had visited the Dodgsons and the Haworths in Manchester during his travels, and gave Amelia useful background information on them before she travelled. 'What you tell me', she wrote, 'is just what I had imagined of both families; but it is a great comfort to find they are all so nice & so simple in their ways. Their letters all round, husbands' & wives', show a charming hospitality & great intelligence.'[44]

While she was in the north, Amelia was introduced to a younger woman, Kate Bradbury, who lived at Riversvale Hall, Ashton under Lyne. Kate was thirty-four, the daughter of Mr Charles T. Bradbury, JP, a wealthy cotton manufacturer and a pillar of the influential Albion Congregational Church in Ashton. Amelia mentioned Kate to Stuart Poole in a letter, enclosing a poem of Heine's in Kate's translation. 'The work is wonderfully well done,' he replied, 'I should like to see something original.'[45] In February 1888 Kate was apparently staying with Amelia in London, and visited the Pooles with her. 'We shall be delighted to see you on Sunday,' Stuart wrote on the 14th. 'We hope that Miss Bradbury will come too. She interests me awfully. Your picture of the Vale is pathetic.'[46] It would seem that Kate had recently been disappointed in love. 'There is very much inside the shy outside of Miss Bradbury,' Stuart wrote again, on 20 April,

> It is not hard to feel a deep interest in her after all you have told me and written me. Of course I have carefully burnt the private pages of your letter. What more you have told me makes me really admire her … But he is a poor thing … He had the heroic part to play and he left it to her … Men in love are wonderfully selfish.[47]

Kate spent a fortnight at The Larches in May 1888 and helped Amelia with the addressing of envelopes for the Fund,[48] and would thus have had an opportunity to learn Amelia's manner of work and way of life.

In Kate, Amelia found companionship such as she had not known since Marianne North departed on the first of her travels in 1871, and this new friendship was to transform the last years of Amelia's life; but the intimacy of Amelia and Kate was that of an older and a younger woman, not of contemporaries. A few fragments of letters from Amelia in the Griffith Institute, Oxford, among papers which belonged to Kate, provide a glimpse of their relationship. That they have been preserved in an album there is probably due not to their textual content but to the small sketches by Amelia which they contain. One, dated 11 April 1888, is addressed to 'My own love', with a sketch of an owl holding a harp on one wing and a quill pen on the other: 'I have just been writing to Mrs Haworth & have made her an elaborate Syrian sketch … When you go to see her again, ask her if she has any pen and ink of mine.'[49] Another fragment shows a playful imagery already established:

> Tell thy Owl what G. Chester charges thee for the amulets. I cannot find the string of scarabs which came to me with Sir E.

Wilson's little collection. I should be sorry if they were mislaid or lost, like Petrie's things. My sweet own darling Baby love-bird, goodbye ...[50]

Meanwhile Stuart Poole was urging Amelia to engage an assistant secretary who could be trained to become an Honorary Secretary in due course, and relieve her of that role; but he insisted that she should be engaged for sufficient hours to make it worth her while and encourage her to 'enter heart and soul into the business'.[51] This appointment was to be at the expense of the Fund and was 'most readily agreed' by the committee in March 1888. Various names were suggested, but it was on Stuart Poole's recommendation that Miss Emily Paterson was engaged, initially on a trial basis. Amelia had resisted at first, but in the event was quite delighted with Miss Paterson. 'I am carefully training Miss Paterson', she wrote to the Committee, 'in the work of the Fund. I find her exceedingly apt, businesslike and methodical. Already she is interested in

Fig. 31: Kate Bradbury, from a photograph hanging in the Griffith Institute, Oxford.

the objects and aims of the Society… She gets through a large amount of correspondence daily.'[52] Her testimonial listed numerous other good attributes. 'When I suggested you to Miss Edwards I knew that you would work with conscientiousness', Mr Poole wrote to her, delighted, 'and I am very glad that you have succeeded so well.'[53] It was a happy relationship that would last for the rest of Amelia's life.

Amelia had, in her own way and indeed in her own interest, re-organised the working of the Fund. With a paid assistant secretary at The Larches, a paid assistant secretary in London, and a country-wide network of supporters, she could seriously contemplate the possibility of the American lecture tour which Mr Winslow had been urging upon her, and in Kate, a new friend when she had thought she would make no more friends, she had found the travelling companion whom she knew she desperately needed. It was time to tell her friends of her plan. She wrote to Flinders Petrie on 19 April 1888:

> Now I am going to tell you a thing that I have told only two or three people & that I don't mean to tell people generally for some months to come. When I last wrote to you it was not sufficiently matured or decided to be worth mentioning; but now that my mind is made up, finally, I hasten to take you into my confidence: I am going to America next Sept. on a lecturing tour. For the last two years I have been over & over again urged to do so – by Winslow, the Presidents of Columbia, Northampton & other colleges, & at last I have settled to do it.
>
> I had a long & anxious consultation with Mrs Braysher's doctor about it (in her presence) & he said I should be very foolish not to go & make 'a hatful of dollars' while I yet have the elasticity & strength to do it – & he says that with Mrs Braysher's marvellous constitution, she may live for 10 or 15 years longer – so that if I waited till then I should be too old myself to knock about the world, or address audiences.
>
> The truth is that I want the money very much. This house wants repairing, much renewal of furniture, &c. – & I want to build out a little snug room wh. shall serve as a museum, & be warm for me to write in winter… Mr Winslow prophesies that I shall make from £200 to £600. My expenses will be *great* – so I hope it may be the last. And I think a very clever, energetic, capable friend will be willing to go with me – one who would really look after me, & take care of me if I were ill – & who wd. even be capable of herself reading a lecture for me, if I fell ill, or lost my voice from cold, & had an engagement to fulfil.[54]

In a letter of 21 February 1888 Winslow gave Amelia one of many notes of advice on the tour. He was confident that she would succeed '& financially too ... Could you stand 30 lectures in 60 days?'[55] He recommended her to have

> 4 to 6 lectures of a popular sort, yet suited for cultured people as well. Those for Boston (perhaps Cambridge), N.Y., Phila., Baltimore. And one lecture for other places which is a *multum in parvo* in your bright way – I mean a lecture of 1 ¼ to 1 ½ hours that covers much ground and gives a good idea of the history, digging, results to the ordinary reader.[56]

The American tour was originally planned for the winter of 1888–89, but it was postponed for a year on the advice of the agent, because of impending elections in America which he thought could distract potential audiences and affect the success of the tour. The delay proved fortuitous, for in June 1888 Amelia fell quite seriously ill with typhoid fever. She wrote to Petrie in pencil from Weston on 21 June:

> I am wonderfully well considering what I ail and my doctor is never weary of wondering at my freedom from all sorts of canonical aches & pains belonging to typhoid – but he keeps me in bed, & this is the 7th day of it. He says I need not expect to be well under 21 days from that on which I fell ill. This is despair – and my *Harper's* article, *Century* article, *Ill. News article* & lectures all to write! Meanwhile I am allowed to swallow no crumb of anything – only milk, Brand's essence, & beaten up eggs. I shall be too weak to work when it is over.[57]

In July Kate went to Weston to be with her. On 7 July Amelia wrote,

> Miss Bradbury is coming today & I hope I may be allowed to go downstairs on Sunday & out for a drive on Monday. It is so good of her to come now, for Mrs B. is not up early enough of a day to go out at the hours when I shall be ordered out – & I should have had no one to help, or look after me, but servants. I shall get on twice as fast now.[58]

When she was well enough, Amelia went to Ashton to stay with the Bradburys,[59] then rejoined Mrs Braysher at Weston for the rest of the summer.[60] It was not until mid-September that they returned to The Larches.

The lectures about which she had been so concerned when she was ill were a second series in the north of England and in Scotland in the autumn and spring. She had nine engagements booked as early as June 1888.[61] She left home on 25 October, lectured at Burton on Trent on the 27th,[62] travelled north to stay with the Bradburys again and lectured at Bowdon on the 30th.[63] She may have given a lecture at Dundee in the first week of December, when a Dundee Group of the Fund was formed, and at Ayr on 9 December when the Ayr Group was formed,[64] but the details of the tour have not been precisely established. She returned home for Christmas, but was back in the north in February 1889, lecturing at Liverpool on the 7th,[65] Alderley Edge on the 11th, and Manchester Town Hall on the 13th. She was once more staying with the Bradburys, and did not return to Westbury until late March, although she was in London for the Annual General Meeting of the Fund on 12 March.[66] This was a demanding schedule, yet it was probably a great relief to Amelia to escape for a time from the company of Mrs Braysher, and to stay with friends with whom she could feel very much at home.

In April 1889 she spent some time in London, giving her lecture on 'women in ancient Egypt' at South Kensington,[67] visiting the Pooles, going to the theatre[68] and attending a meeting of the Fund.[69] After years of confinement to Westbury, tied by Mrs Braysher's health and by the demanding routines of the Fund, it seems that Amelia had to escape. She could now leave the secretarial work to Miss Paterson. As for Mrs Braysher, it would be a foretaste of a longer absence in America. When Mrs Braysher left for the usual summer residence in Weston on 13 June, Amelia did not go with her. 'Don't smile', she wrote to Petrie on 26 June, 'when I tell you why I am staying behind. My dear cockatoo … had a frightful fall & broke a wing & seriously injured a leg. I have nursed him day & night ever since & have saved his life.'[70] There was more to her delay, however, than an injured cockatoo: 'Meanwhile I have … "Century" article not yet finished, & America drawing nearer every day. I get very frightened & nervous about it all.'

Amelia and Kate Bradbury embarked on the *Etruria* at Liverpool on 26 October 1889. The details of the tour are unusually well documented, because Kate's letters home written during the tour but later abridged and typed in the form of a journal, survive in the Griffith Institute, Oxford.[71] From the start the two women received favoured treatment. The Captain gave them the use of a deck cabin, and had the ship's carpenter fit it out with a firm table, so that Amelia could copy out her lectures 'in a round, black hand, which she would be able to read at a glance when speaking'. They reached New York on 1 November.

Coming up on deck, Kate recognised the Statue of Liberty. She called Amelia, whose comment, typically forthright, was 'Well, she's a brute'.

Mr Bowker, with whom Amelia had frequently corresponded, met them through the customs. Mr Winslow had done his advance publicity well, and they were quickly approached by several 'lady reporters'. The long wait on the cold quay took its toll, and by the time they reached the George Hotel, Brooklyn, Amelia was suffering from a bad attack of laryngitis. The doctor was called and ordered her to bed. It was an inauspicious beginning to the tour, but by 5 November she was recovering. 'There are constant letters to answer – letters which I answer, for Miss E. *must* work at the lecture-copying every spare minute', wrote Kate. 'The interest in Miss E. is very great, there are piles of newspaper notices sent in to us, few of which we have time to read.'

The programme began with a series of lectures in the Academy of Music, which seated 2,400. Over 2,000 attended the first lecture on 7 November, on 'The buried cities of ancient Egypt'. It must have been something of an ordeal for Amelia as she was still suffering from her cold. When Stuart Poole heard of this from Miss Paterson in Westbury, he commented wryly: 'I should think Miss Edwards' elasticity with the support of Miss Bradbury would carry her thro' well, and she likes popularity', adding more kindly, 'Who does not?'[72] A woman scholar was something of a phenomenon, and one who could lecture amusingly and combine showmanship with scholarship as Amelia could was an instant success.

On 8 November they travelled to Poughkeepsie, an hour's journey by train, visiting Vassar College, where Amelia gave her first lecture, and returning the next morning to Brooklyn for the weekend, enjoying Sunday lunch with Richard Bowker, the publisher, and his wife.

On Monday 11 November the tour began in earnest. This was the first day of their contract with George Hathaway of the Redpath Lyceum Bureau and Mr Whittredge, the business manager, joined them. He had 'managed Farrer and Justin McCarthy and Mr [Matthew] Arnold.' Amelia was contracted to give six lectures a week for a period of twenty weeks. She was to receive a weekly fee of $500, and expenses of up to $125 per week. A stereopticon lantern would be provided, and a competent man to operate it. The stereopticon operator, Mr Magee, also joined them at Newhaven. The press reports frequently made reference to the lantern slides, 'not artists' impressions, but specially taken photographs'.[73]

At the lecture at the Hyperion Theatre that day, Mr Bowker made an appeal for an international copyright agreement. Amelia, who had equally strong feelings on the question of copyright, rose to the occasion at once.

> [She] threw off the gorgeous Japanese cloak and addressed the
> audience: 'I do begrudge the publication of my books in Australia
> and in ... other of the colonial possessions of my beloved England;
> but never have I begrudged their publication in America, where I
> have received so much kindness.'[74]

'Miss E's voice is nearly right again', wrote Kate. 'After the lecture we
crossed the street to the Library – at least I stayed behind to look after
one or two things, while Miss E. went on first', but they could not make
their way through the crowds. 'Doors, passages and staircases were
jammed, so we turned, and [Mr Bowker] got me in through subterrane-
ous and devious ways, and I found Miss E. in a bower of flowers and
plants, a regular arbour, receiving some 1000 people.' The spectacular
success of the tour had begun.

On 13 November they made the six-hour train journey from New
York to Boston for the first of six lectures at the Chickering Hall. As they
both had a good deal of writing to do they took a stateroom, paying the
Pullman price for all six seats. Boston was to be their centre for the rest
of the month, and they stayed with Mrs Annie Fields. They could hardly
have found a more congenial base from which to be launched into the
intellectual society of Boston.

Saturday 16 November was a highlight of the tour, because Oliver
Wendell Holmes and James Russell Lowell came to breakfast at noon,
and they were joined by Mrs Jewitt, an authoress who had been living
with the Fields since her husband died. It was not so much the elegant
repast which pleased them as the conversation. Hearing that he had just
celebrated his eighty-first birthday, Amelia said to Dr Holmes: 'I think
you are still young enough to ask the schoolmistress to take the long
walk with you!' When conversation turned to the question of drink, and
she learnt that in Massachussetts a habitual drunkard could be confined
to an insane or inebriate asylum, she 'was horrified at such interference
with the liberty of the subject'.

Sundays were the only days on the tour when there were no lectures
to be given. They enjoyed the quiet Sundays in Boston. There was
always literary gossip to be had, and William, the black servant, would
often come up to pass the time of day with them by the wood fire in
Amelia's bedroom when they were writing.

From Boston they visited Lowell, where Amelia lectured in the new
opera house. She was by now completely at ease, passing jokes with the
audience, remarking that the unwieldy pointer was 'as hard to manage as
a boa constrictor'. The next excursion was to Northampton for a lecture
at Smith College, which had awarded her an honorary degree in 1886.

On 23 November they travelled to Hartford, accompanied now by Mr Magee, the projectionist. Unfortunately Amelia's travelling box, containing all she needed for the evening's lecture, was sent on to New York by mistake. Kate's description of Amelia's reaction is revealing:

> Miss Edwards was horrified to think that she must lecture in her travelling dress; I was horrified because I knew that she had for the first time put her lecture in the box … As I was doing her hair … it flashed upon her, and to my great relief the enormity of the whole thing made the tragic overbalance itself and fall into the comic. I knew quite well that if only she did not feel upset she would do the whole thing beautifully without her manuscript, and that probably she would once and for all acquire a golden possession of faith in her own power to speak without it too.

Few ever appreciated as Kate did Amelia's vulnerability and lack of self-confidence, even at the height of her success.

Back in Boston on Sunday 24 November, they enjoyed dinner at the Fields' with Samuel Clemens as a guest. Afterwards Amelia teased Kate about her 'expression of mingled agony and rapture' as she listened to the stories told. The new week's busy schedule came round all too soon. 'Egyptology has become the very latest Boston fad and attendance on these lectures is one of the most popular social events of the season', wrote Jean Kincaid in the *Boston Daily Globe*.[75]

Friday 29 November was 'a most fatiguing day:

> The New England Women's Press Association gave Miss E. a breakfast. She might have a reception every day if she would, but this Mr Hathaway advised her not to refuse … Poor Miss E. had the place of honour, and that was all. Mrs Sallie Joy White, President of the Club, was on one side, and Dr Winslow was placed on the other. The President is a loud assertive woman … The breakfast was gorgeous but bad, and there was no wine. Our menus were wonderful, of various coloured silks, and with Miss E's photograph upon them.' [Amelia's menu, now in the Edwards archive at Somerville College, was embellished with a dainty painting of pyramids.][76] 'Remarkable women spoke, and tame poets spouted verses in honour of the occasion, and yesterday's papers are all full of it. Miss Edwards and I dare not look at each other often.'

One of the tributes in verse, in ten stanzas, has survived:[77]

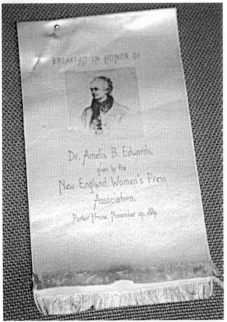

*Fig. 32: Menu on satin from the New England Women's Press Association breakfast,
29 November 1889; the upper menu was painted for Amelia herself; the lower
one was printed for all guests.*

From the land that has queened it for ages
With ever-extending sway,
By the spell of her seers and sages
Writ large on History's pages
From the land that has queened it for ages
We welcome a queen today …

For not content with the pleasure
Which her graceful novels lend
To gather up Learning's treasure
By a sacrifice of leisure
She hath reckoned a sweeter pleasure
Since it serveth a nobler end …

Yea, by such lives laborious
Is quicker shapen the plan
Of the day when woman glorious
Shall arise, arise victorious
No longer the slave laborious
or the tempting toy of man …

And so from the land that for ages
Has queened it, we welcome here
For the Past lit up by her pages
For the Future her life presages
From the land that has queened it for ages
A queen and a pioneer.

On 2 December they went to Philadephia, which was to be their
base for much of the week. Amelia lectured at Bryn Mawr, and later at
the Peabody Institute, where she was the first woman admitted to
lecture. She was dismayed to find that 'she had not brought the
boddice [sic] of her dress, and she meant to look very nice tonight. She
does look very nice, but no matter how hot it is, she cannot throw off
her wrap and show her motley attire.' The Peabody Institute was
crowded, with over a thousand people in the audience. It was quite a
relief to them to be staying in a hotel that night. 'One is so much more
independent, gets so much more bed in hotels than in private houses
as a rule.'

On 7 December the lecture on 'Egypt as the birthplace of Greek art'
was again well received. According to Kate,

All Miss E's lectures go well now and her voice shows no signs of wear at all. Very early she ceased to feel 'woodenness' such as compelled her to gather herself together to keep in touch with her audience. She now feels just in easy and pleasant mastery of the situation.

The Provost of the University of Philadelphia escorted them over the University buildings one afternoon, and they visited the museum.

What the Provost had really got Miss Edwards there for came out at the end of the show. He is ambitious for the University, and money seems to come to them whenever they ask for it. They want to become a separate American branch of the Egypt Exploration Fund and get Egyptian things for their Museum, not to be mere subscribers to Dr Winslow.

From Philadelphia they returned to Boston, and then on to New York, and on 10 December to Baltimore, a journey of 182 miles. At Baltimore there was

a very grand reception indeed – some 1500 people there, and all in evening dress ... These receptions are a very national device to secure the greatest contact of the greatest number with any important celebrity ... You get no real conversation of course. Miss E. says it amuses her to try and say something different to everyone ...

They returned on 21 December to Philadelphia for the final lecture in the series. This was the thirty-seventh lecture in forty-four days.

They were to spend Christmas with Frederick Church, the artist, and his wife, old friends of Amelia from her travels in Rome.

As we came along up the Hudson in the early evening, the hills ... were all amethistine against the pale green sky. Then they were the colour of damson, then the deepest indigo, then little scarlet clouds ... floated up over them. On the opposite side a blue like a spring rain-cloud crept up, like the shadow of the earth, into the rosy glow. Miss E. said she had seen it in Egypt, and it *is* the shadow of the world. (23 December 1889)

At Catskill station they found the Churchs' sledge waiting for them. 'Miss E's horror at the sight of an open carriage and the "pair of panthers" … was comic.' On Christmas Day the sunset was marvellous:

> The sky was full of colour, scarlet, orange, yellow, primrose, pale green, pale blue – up into deep blue – the sharp young moon came out, and the Hudson reflected it & the pale green and blue of the sky. Then there were no more buildings to be seen, it all belonged to the Indian again. Miss Edwards came for me to my room, and found me doing just what she had been doing, sitting spell-bound at the window. She said: 'It might be the end of the world. This sunset looks as though there would never be another.' And so it did.

On 27 December they returned to Boston to resume the lecturing commitments, both in Boston itself and in neighbouring towns – Malden, Portland, Concord, Springfield, and others, involving much travelling. Then on 6 January they went on to New York, for a lecture at Columbia University. 'With a wild scramble we were ready, slides and all, for dinner and lecture. In the morning 'Miss E. copied her last uncopied lecture' and in the afternoon they went to see the Egyptian collection in the Central Park Museum. While based in New York they travelled to Princeton, and on 16 January they went on to Albany then Auburn, Genesco, Elmira and Farmington, with lecturing engagements everywhere, and then back to Hartford on 25 January to stay with the Charles Dudley Warners, delighted to have an evening visit from Mr Clemens again. 'He was more than ever master of everybody. He strolled into the further drawing room and began to play and sing old negro hymns, sang them like the old negroes, who as he said, "expected to go from slavery up into glory".'

On 27 January they left for Worcester, and from there went to Mount Holyoak, Syracuse and Buffalo, which they reached on 31 January. Having a free weekend, they went to see Niagara. 'The very thought of it is emotion.' Then remorselessly on to Cleveland on the Monday, then Toledo, then Cincinnati. Amelia passed the journey reading *The Virginians*, 'and from time to time exclaimed that Thackeray is the greatest of English novelists. She says that she has not done so much reading for years as since we came to America. She cannot write in the cars.' They travelled overnight from Cincinnati to Milwaukee, reaching it by lunchtime. 'Mr Whitredge has managed that no one shall know that Miss E. is here. She is supposed to arrive tomorrow from Chicago at noon.' Amelia lectured in Wisconsin on 10 February, then on to St Paul's and Fairbault and to Minneapolis by 14 February. 'We are altogether sorry not to be still going westward. It is so much more foreign, so much more interesting for every hour in the cars, and we are nearly half way across.'

Back at St Paul's on 15 February, they went to see

> a few remaining Indians some four miles off… The drive was all along the banks of the Mississippi, and we found our Indians at last in two 'Tepees', not close together, on drier ground in the swamp by the river. But after we left the road, the drive to these 'Tepees' was an amazing one. It was literally across a frozen swamp, full of stumps of felled trees.

On Sunday 16 February they arrived in Chicago and found themselves comfortably quartered with the Dexters. In the evening 'Miss Hatty Hosmer, the sculptress, whom she had known in Rome 30 years ago, came to see Miss E. …. The Prominent Ladies of Chicago think a great deal of Miss Hosmer.'

They left Chicago on 18 February for Aurora. The constant travelling and late nights were beginning to tell on Kate. She had none of the glory which no doubt buoyed up Amelia. Another six-hour journey the next day took them to Albion, then back to Chicago on the 21st for the last of the lectures there at the Central Music Hall. From there they made an excursion to Ann Arbor, and on to Detroit. 'Coming to Detroit this morning', wrote Kate on 24 February, 'a young woman interviewer boarded the train and talked to Miss E. In fact Miss E. has had 5 interviewers, a reception, 2 poems and wheelbarrow fulls of flowers fom her ardent admirers here today.' Not all the press notices pleased them. 'Some of the notices are so personal as to be impudent', Kate wrote, 'speaking of her dress as "seeming to be hers by accident" and her bonnet as "recalling to one's mind the fact that in England … ladies make their own bonnets".'

On 27 February they left for Springfield, and the next day reached Oberlin, 'very tired', then to Cleveland, and on the lecture-free Sunday to Columbus. It was there that 'a serious mishap' occurred at 5.30 p.m on Monday 3 March:

> Miss E. fell and broke her left arm, an inch and a half above the wrist. I was in her bedroom just at the head of the stairs and heard a fall and a cry. I ran out and found her all in a heap at the bottom of a little flight of seven stairs. We got the best surgeon in the place within half an hour, and he set it at once, as it had not swollen too much. She was fortunately dressed. I fed her and she slept a little, and was able to lecture at night. It was an effort, and felt more

afterwards than at the time. I stayed just behind the scene close to her, getting a sleeve out of her dress and opening it, so that it is tied on and up with 14 ribands.

Amelia's courage in lecturing at Columbus just two and a half hours after breaking her arm, endeared her more than ever to her audiences and to the press. Subsequent lectures were reported under banners such as 'A woman of bravery' and 'A plucky lecturer'. The rest of the tour was something of a trial for both of them.

On 5 March they went on to Philadalphia, on the 7 to Haverhill, and on the 8th with relief to the Warners at Hartford. On the Sunday 'Mr Clemens came in, but he would not peril his soul's honour by stopping. "My sailing orders are plain."… "But you will do me good", said Miss E. "I know I should, but Mrs Clemens would not believe it".' The next day the lectures resumed, with journeys to Wilkes Barre and Wilmington and on Friday to Washington, where Amelia gave two lectures in the Lincoln Hall.

> We had hoped to be received by the President at the White House on our way back from the Saturday evening lecture, but the President, who was very anxious to see Miss E., was not there … 'A cheap kind of president, anyway', as Mr Whittredge (a democrat) says.

In spite of some adverse reviews, Amelia still generally met with a rapturous reception, and the reception by Sorosis in New York on 18 March was no exception:

> a long fatiguing day. The Sorosis, the great new York women's club, made Amelia their principal guest at their annual luncheon at Delmonico's … The luncheon was good, but wine-less, only I had asked Mrs Clymer beforehand to secure some wine for Miss E., and, not to shock and hurt some strongly teetotal members of the Club, claret, sent by the doctor husband of one member, was put before Miss E. in a plated jug, and drunk by her out of a coffee cup, to match the rest of us.

The following day was a day of interviewers and publishers, and in the afternoon a grand reception at the Deanery. Amelia went out of her way to put the record straight with regard to Kate:

> Miss Bradbury is my very dear friend, not my maid or companion or nurse or secretary, or any of the other things the reporters have

called her, who is travelling with our party to see the country, but more because her parents, also dear friends of mine, didn't wish me to come so far alone.[78]

Dear friend as she was, Kate certainly acted as companion, maid and, after Amelia's accident, nurse, and the success of the tour could scarcely have been so great if Kate had not been at her side.

Kate and Amelia embarked on 29 March for what they must have hoped would be a restful voyage, but it proved otherwise. Writing before 12 April to one of their hostesses shortly after their return home, Amelia describes how

> my good fortune deserted me when I left your dear shores. A big gale … overtook us and lasted till Thursday morning; and I was unlucky enough to be flung quite across the state-room, coming with all the force of the blow upon my crippled arm against the opposite berth.[79]

Nevertheless, at a gala concert on the last evening abord the *Etruria* Amelia spoke, and Kate sang. Three days after landing Amelia had a third heavy fall.

> These supplementary accidents … have thrown me back greatly … Anyhow I *did* reach home in time for my beloved and aged friend's eighty-sixth birthday, and so triumphantly kept the promise made before I left England, and fulfilled the *last* engagement on my list.[80]

Unfortunately the summer brought Amelia not the rest that she so badly needed, but further troubles. Writing to Petrie on 1 May she describes the accident during the gale, and adds:

> & since landing (while at Riversvale on my homeward way) I had a heavy fall wh. caused a splinter of bone to pierce the main artery & a vein close to it. This is rather a bad job, & promises to be a long one. I can do nothing for myself – a miserable, helpless, one-handed cripple; & I suffer great discomfort. The worst of it is, it stops my work.[81]

Amelia had a further, more serious health worry on her mind, which she did not reveal other than to her closest friends, although the Pooles apparently knew of it. 'We were very grieved to hear of the cause of your coming to Town', Stuart wrote on 8 May, 'and hope there will be no need for an operation ... Have you fixed on your rooms?' and he recommended a 'House for Ladies' in Harley Street.[82] The details have only become known with the discovery and publication by John W. Pye in 1994 of letters to Alice and Edith Kingsbury, two of their American hostesses. One of the letters was written by Kate Bradbury to Edith Kingsbury on 17 January 1893, two and a half years later; she writes:

> In July 1890 Miss Edwards became aware of trouble in the left breast, against wh. her wrist had been broken. We saw Sir James Paget. I met her in town for that purpose & for some Egyptological work. We saw him on that Friday. He said 'There is that here which will become cancerous unless it is at once removed.' We went into private hospital & the operation took place that Sunday morning. It was successful – the dreaded evil never returned; but the loss of blood, & the nervous exhaustion, & the shock, she never recovered from.[83]

Amelia spent the summer in Weston-Super-Mare as was her custom, both before and after her operation, which she apparently underwent in London. She was staying at Saville Villa, Park Place, on 29 June,[84] writing on Fund business, writing again from there on 2 July to Petrie, who was home from his excavation at Hawara under the aegis of Mr Haworth:

> I am anxious to know when your cases will be opened & the contents visible, that I may go up. I ought to see Mr Willett (the surgeon) soon, & I only await your orders. The hand & arm are getting *very* slowly better; but the hand is fixed at a wrong angle to the arm & I fear I shall never regain the full use of either.[85]

She writes to Petrie again from Saville Villa in an undated letter, telling him that she will be leaving in a week's time, and expressing pleasure that he has been invited to Bowdon, Mr Haworth's home: 'I hope they will ask me at the same time ... If they don't, & I am not away in some health place, I will invite myself.'[86] It is not certain when the operation on her left breast took place; John Pye suggests 6 July, but this seems unlikely since she was writing and signing letters on the 8th.[87] It was over, at any rate, by late August, for Stuart Poole writes on 23 August to Miss Paterson, who had been staying at Saville Villa: 'We were greatly relieved to receive the good news of your letter. Pray don't let Miss Edwards write to me. You can do that for her perfectly.'[88] Amelia herself wrote on 4 September from Saville Villa to say:

> I wish I *could* have stayed a week longer in London, for I am
> persuaded that I travelled at least a week too soon; but my doctor
> was most anxious to bid me goodbye that he might have his own
> holiday. I have now been nearly a week in bed from inflammation
> with a touch of erysipilitis, both now subdued I am glad to say, and
> I begin to fear that by the time I am able to go northwards, the
> weather will be getting too cold for me ... PS I have the quietest
> bedroom in the house, & a large & comfortable dressing room,
> where I have a second bed for day, and can see the trees and the
> sky. Miss Bradbury arranges everything to suit my requirements.[89]

Amelia's health was clearly giving cause for concern. On 11 October Kate
writes from Grange over Sands to Frank Griffith: 'Miss Edwards was just
able to come north with me a fortnight ago. Since then we have tried
another change and have now come here, where I hope she will gain
strength more rapidly than she has hitherto done.'[90]

Amelia had, however, by no means abandoned her work for the Fund.
She was back at Riversvale by mid-October and prepared the necessary
papers for the committee urging the employment of Mr Newberry and
Mr Fraser for the Archaeological Survey, 'a work which cannot but
redound to the honour of the Society & add largely to its scientific
reputation'. On 18 October she wrote to Villiers Stuart, chiding him for
supporting the Society for the Preservation of the Monuments of Ancient
Egypt rather than the Fund:

> Is it possible that you have never read our last Annual Report?
> Had you read it, you would surely have communicated with your
> own society before initiating a rival scheme ... Is it not yet possible
> for you to tell Mr Poynter that you propose to support the Society
> which you have helped to build up from its earliest beginnings?
> Pray think of it. After all, ours is the official society, ours are the
> best men, the trained men, the whole machinery of publication
> and organisation.[91]

On 24 November she left for a third lecturing tour in the north.[92] Little
is known of this tour, except that she was in Edinburgh on 15 December,
and she referred to the tour as 'an arctic experience'.[93] In her letter to
Edith Kingsbury, Kate explains:

> Miss E. went on lecturing; she liked it, it brought her change, and
> absence from The Larches which Mrs B. did not resent. I always

went with her, & though I knew that she ought to rest, I knew too her constitutional tendency to melancholia, & could only make all as easy & safe to her as possible.[94]

They stayed in the north of England until Christmas Eve. On Christmas Day 1890 Kate wrote to Petrie,

> Yesterday I took my dear Miss Edwards as far as Birmingham on her way to Bristol that she might do her Xmas duty to Mrs Braysher's threadbare & exacting life. And now she is away from me for the first time since I joined her in London last July. I shall go to her in a week. She is very weak, & entirely helpless, & the weight of my heart about her wakes me at nights. She has been here a good deal, & lastly for a month, making this the centre of a Northern lecturing tour whereby she has repaid herself for the operating surgeon's fee. Could she have remained here for a long rest, unharassed by domestic worry, the lecturing would have done her no harm, but actually good. Travel always pleases her, & to be doing something, one among the living again. The local mischief is not the only one that I dread now, & she does not like me out of her sight for 5 minutes. But it was right that she should spend Xmas Day with Mrs Braysher, & right that I should spend it here.[95]

By 4 January 1891 Kate was with Amelia again at The Larches, and it was on that day that Amelia learnt that she had been awarded a State Pension. Writing to her friend Agnes Strickland, who had had a hand in the recommendation, Kate reported that Amelia had learnt it from Mr Romanes. He had enclosed the official letter from Mr Balfour in a kind note of his own.

> Amy had had a bad night, & had been fighting paroxysms of coughing for hours of it, & when the letters came & the breakfast & she was smoothed over & washed, I gave her all the letters to look at. One was from Oxford, & we neither of us knew the writing. It lay at the top of the pile, & she opened that first. I gave my attention to her tea, but suddenly looking up I saw her holding a half sheet in her hand, & crying, with a very white face … So I took the sheet out of her hands – & then – we both cried.[96]

By the end of January Amelia was planning to travel again. Writing to Petrie, she announced that,

> On the 9th of Feby. I go to Woodside to spend a few days with the Haworths & some time in March I am to go to a warm climate for a couple of months – such are my doctor's orders. He says I cannot get well without a radical change, so, if Mr & Mrs Bradbury consent, Miss B. will go with me to Italy & Sicily.[97]

She was still vigorously occupied with the Fund; Percy Newberry, writing from Beni Hasan, had to apologise on one occasion for not keeping her fully informed.[98] She was still writing to the press, correcting proofs, and challenging any committee proposals with which she did not agree.

Amelia had been preparing her American lectures for publication, with much help from Kate, who wrote later to Edith Kingsbury that 'I could not bear that those lectures should not have the permanence of literary form.'[99] In her preface dated March 1891 Amelia writes: 'While necessarily recasting the form of these lectures, I have to some extent preserved the colloquial style – in the hope, I confess, of being the better remembered by those who have heard them.' The book was published by the end of the year with the title *Pharaohs, Fellahs and Explorers*,[100] and received good reviews. According to *The Athenaeum*,

> There is an impression abroad that we are having too many books about Egypt; but the reader has only to turn to Miss Edwards's pages to see how much there is still to be said about that Egypt which is supposed to be overwritten … and no English Egyptologist possesses in greater perfection the art of lucid exposition and the analogical grasp which are essential to the popular treatment of a complicated subject.[101]

In March Amelia and Kate set out on the journey which they hoped would bring new strength and health to Amelia. 'This time next week we hope to be in Monte Carlo', wrote Kate to Petrie on 13 March.

> The doctors all agree there is not even return of the mischief, which was *not* fully established before the operation. The case was a peculiar one, it seems, & by its very peculiarities made hopeful. But she is very aged & weakened, & very helpless. Yet I am thankful to say, that the depression is less. That I dreaded, considering her hereditary tendencies, & her ways of looking at things.[102]

Her mention of depression reminds one of Amelia's reference to 'brain-fever' in her youth, but there is no other indication in the archives of a hereditary problem of this kind. They travelled from Bristol on 17 March, reaching Paris on the 18th and Monte Carlo on the 20th. The journey was trying, and 'it has been very bleak & comfortless', Amelia wrote to Stuart Poole on 27 March, 'despite palm trees & groves of oranges & lemons. We shall probably go on to Genoa… creeping slowly towards Sicily. K.B. has been very bad with severe rheumatism, but is mending.'[103] An album headed 'Sketchbook in Italy, 1891' survives in the Somerville archive,[104] but it contains only three sketches, one of Vesuvius from Castelnuovo, and two heads of women; the draughtsmanship is unimpaired. Amelia was 'laid up at Naples, depressed & very unwell'.[105] 'I was just able', Amelia wrote, 'in my lucid intervals, to go about Pompeii in a *portantina*, looking & feeling like a Guy Fawkes.'[106] They turned north to Rome, where she was much happier, and her health improved as they progressed through Switzerland in July on their homeward journey. Emily Paterson forwarded letters and conveyed news and messages between the travellers and the officers of the Fund. A witty letter from Amelia to Edith Kingsbury written on 27 November 1891 describing the tour, has recently been discovered and published by John W. Pye:

> I was much too ill while in Rome, both in April and again in June, to go into any society – & in May I lay at the point of death in our hotel in Posilippo … How [Miss Bradbury] got me back to North Italy is a miracle – but she did it, & at Florence & Venice I gradually began to get better. At last we reached Switzerland, & three weeks on the Rigi Scheideck in polar weather … did me miraculous good! Ordered to a warm climate, I almost died in it – escaping to a frozen region, I recovered. So much for the doctors![107]

By 20 August Amelia was back in England, staying at Saville Villa in Weston again. On that day she was complaining to Mr Renouf of the rumour which she had heard that the Orientalist Congress in Florence was intending not to admit women.[108] It was from Saville Villa that she wrote to Kate on 25 August in a manner that reveals more than any other their intimacy:

> My own darling one, tomorrow will be thy birthday, & a little sketch is all a poo' owl has to send thee, but Owl thinks that perhaps a wee little sketch from Pompeii, done from the one made when Owl was such a very poo Owl, will please thee more than a more valuable gift … God bless you my own one & I hope thou wilt have many, many birthdays, & happy years between each, & that thy owl may live to give thee less anxiety & more happiness for the future.[109]

She goes on to comment on 'a very satisfactory letter from Petrie'; she had

> tried by writing to him to let him see by a sort of sidelight that I deemed it of real importance – yet not to make too much of it. I did not want to make him feel the painful weight of obligation … He is so very sharp, that I fancy he wd not fail to see a shade of meaning, however slight.

The context here is obscure, but it may possibly relate to the desirability (as she saw it) of his visiting and maybe staying with the Haworths.

Reverting to Kate, she adds: 'Baby's little drawing of the tablet is very good – very good indeed. I am sure that thou could draw well, with a little teaching & appreciation' and in another fragment, probably part of the same letter, she writes: 'I wish I was with thee on thy birthday … I get so moped & out of spirits, owing to dull weather, rain & no Baby,' and signs herself 'Thine own Owl'.

In mid-October she was at home in Westbury campaigning against the 'great scandal' of the proposed submersion of Philae.[110] On 3 December she wrote that she was 'much driven … wretched, more or less, since I caught that bad bronchial attack at Millwall Docks [where she had been checking a consignment on behalf of the Fund] & superadded a severe influenza'.[111] Yet once again she planned to undertake a programme of winter lectures in the north. 'The kind Haworths invited K.B. & myself for a week to the Palace Hotel Southport (I had a lecture in Southport) & I hoped to lose all cold & cough there … I tremble for my lectures in January & February.'

Those lectures were never given. Just before Christmas Amelia was ill again with acute bronchitis and congestion of the lung, and Emily Paterson telegraphed for Kate Bradbury to come. On reaching The Larches, Kate noticed a restlessness and a change in Mrs Braysher, and wrote to her parents:

> You may judge that Miss Edwards was utterly unfit to be allowed to go near Mrs Braysher. Indeed our doctor forbad it. But I told the doctor who knew as I did that Mrs Braysher was going away, that Amy must and should go in to see her dear old friend & companion of 35 years. One can easily run worse risks than that of death. So … she was daily wrapped up & went through … & said 'goodnight'. Amy could not realise that the time of parting was at hand … & she hoped against hope, even to the end. When Mrs

Braysher saw her, it was beautiful to see the strong faithful love of years rise to dominate all that weakness & unrest … Considering the long preceding brain failure it was a blessed thing that she went away from us herself, & her best self.[112]

Kate hoped that Amelia, freed from the worry and distress of her friend's illness, would improve in health, albeit full of grief; but an initial improvement was soon reversed. Kate wrote on 9 February to tell Petrie 'how things have gone here for the last 2 or 3 weeks. Amy's doctors have been … almost hopeless … Suddenly she opened her eyes & said: "I think I have turned the corner. Don't tell anyone – I may be mistaken – but I *think* I have turned the corner". Once again there is hope.' Kate goes on to confide in Petrie:

knowing … that Amy has for you a positive affection, & she does not love many people for all her seeming geniality. She once enumerated to me 2 or 3 people for whom she 'cared' – & of you she said 'And I am fond of Petrie, – though I might as well be fond of a young obelisk.' Her love for me, & her seizure of me – unwilling – almost at first sight, has always been to me one of the strangest things I have known – so strange that I dared not refuse it either, or its consequences … Of course I have grown to love her with a love as great as hers has always been for me, I think.[113]

Amelia died at Weston-super-Mare on 15 April 1892. She was buried at Henbury, near Westbury-on-Trym, and her funeral was attended by her cousins Matilda Betham-Edwards and Captain Fitzgerald of the Royal Scots, and by numerous friends and neighbours, the mourners in five carriages. The Egypt Exploration Fund was represented by Percy Newberry, one of its 'explorers' and by Miss Paterson; the Haworths and the Bradburys travelled from Lancashire. Obituaries soon appeared in papers and journals on both sides of the Atlantic; Kate pasted over 200 of them in a scrapbook now in the Sackler Library, Oxford. A tombstone in the form of an obelisk in Henbury churchyard commemorates Amelia 'who by her writings and her labours enriched the thought and interests of her time'. It had first been erected by Mrs Braysher in memory of her daughter Sarah Harriet who died in 1864, and also commemorates Mrs Braysher herself.

Amelia's will provided for the establishment of a Chair at University College, London and the Edwards Chair in Egyptology was accordingly created; the first holder was, as she had wished, Flinders Petrie. Her collection of Egyptian antiquities was bequeathed to the College, and forms the basis of the Petrie Museum there, as were her Egyptological books; other books went to Somerville College Oxford. Kate as her executor carried out her wishes with meticulous and generous attention to detail. She wrote from The Larches to Petrie on 24 October:

> It is so cold that I cannot sit at the desk in this vault of a room and write legibly at all, I shiver and shake … I have been packing ever since I came here. The house was so crammed that it has been like digging things out all along. I am packing all Amy's books myself – wrapping each one separately of course, and making small cases.[114]

Of Amelia's three close women friends Marianne North had died on 30 August 1890, at the age of sixty, at Alderley in Gloucestershire, where she had spent the last five years of her life quietly at home, writing her *Recollections of a Happy Life* and enjoying her garden. Lucy Renshaw lived longest, but in increasing ill health, and died in 'Pekes', a mental hospital, at Hellingly, Sussex, on 28 September 1913 at the age of eighty. Kate Bradbury, the closest of the three, married the Egyptologist Francis ('Frank') Llewellyn Griffith in 1896 but died before him in 1902 at Silverdale, Grange over Sands, at the age of forty-six. A settlement from her father at her marriage enabled her husband to devote himself to Egyptology; he became Professor of Egyptology in the University of Oxford, and an endowment from Kate formed the basis of his bequest which provided for the foundation of the Griffith Institute at the University.

The Egypt Exploration Fund, now called The Egypt Exploration Society, has gone from strength to strength, and now has around 3,000 members. Many notable archaeologists have been trained and have worked under its auspices, many museums have been enriched through their labours, many discoveries recorded in the Society's publications.

On 26 October Kate received from Petrie an archaeological report in draft which was critical of Amelia and especially of her tendency to exaggerate and dramatise. She replied:

> As for exaggeration, I know it all too well, and you cannot dislike it more than I do. But she to whose imaginative mind and unbalanced, unsubmitted nature it was due, is gone, as some believe, to face the 'eternal veracities'. There is no one left who can err in this way. Let it alone. In blaming this you blame her. I know now – from many papers not relating to Fund matters – what a

heavy weight of herself she had to carry, and how near insanity, with its many miserable connotations, she often was … Exaggerated admirations, and appreciations of her interest &c alone made life bearable. But she made the Fund. It is a good tool, say what you will, an organisation to be used, not broken and thrown away.

But ah! how loveable she was after all is said and done, all that I now know. She was always worrying me with – 'if there *is* a next world, will you stand by me in it?' and trying to secure this from me. I will, and said so. But it was all so strange and intense. One will have a good deal to do in the next world in the way of standing by others. Well, it was possible here, and somehow it will be possible there – *how*, one cannot see.[115]

Notes

[1] PP 9.iv.34.
[2] PP 9.iv.31.
[3] SCO Edwards 187.
[4] Gaston Maspero, *Egyptian Archaeology*, trans. Amelia B. Edwards (London & New York: Putnam, 1887).
[5] EES XVII.c.26.
[6] PP 9.iv.14.
[7] Amelia B. Edwards, 'My Home life', *Arena*, 4 (1891), pp. 299–310.
[8] EES III.b.30.
[9] EES XVI.e.36, 4 November 1886.
[10] EES XVII.a.44.
[11] PP 9.iv.15.
[12] EES V.d.17, 30 October 1886.
[13] EES III.a.53, 18 November 1886.
[14] EES III.a.54.
[15] PP 9.iv.18.
[16] EES IX.b.19.
[17] EES IX.g.4.
[18] PP 9.iv.36.
[19] EES III.j.53, 31 January 1888.
[20] EES IX.g.36.
[21] EES IX.g.20, 14 February 1888.
[22] PP 9.iv.19.
[23] PP 9.iv.21.
[24] Petrie Letters 1887.1.
[25] EES XVII.c.54.
[26] EES IX.c.6.

27 EES IX.c.8, 22 April 1888.

28 EES IX.c.17.

29 EES IX.c.22.

30 EES IX.c.21.

31 PP 9.iv.27.

32 PP 9.iv.25, 12 May 1887.

33 PP 9.iv.20, 16 June 1887.

34 EES IX.d.7, 13 September 1887.

35 PP 9.iv.35.

36 EES XVII.c.76, 21 October.

37 EES XVII.c.85, 11 February 1888.

38 EES XVII.c.73.

39 EES III.m; it has recently been published with an introduction by Patricia O'Neill, 'The Social and Political Position of Women in Ancient Egypt', in PMLA 120, 3 (May 2005), pp. 843–57.

40 EES IX.d.34.

41 EES XVII.c.80.

42 EES III.m; see O'Neill, 'The Social and Political Position of Women in Ancient Egypt'.

43 Amelia B. Edwards, *Pharaohs, Fellahs and Explorers* (London: Osgood, McIlvaine, 1891).

44 PP 9.iv.31.

45 EES IX.g.11.

46 EES IX.g.20.

47 EES IX.g.42.

48 EES III.d.19.

49 GI II.3/39.

50 GI II.3/25.

51 EES IX.g.25, 13 March 1888.

52 EES VIII.25, 11 July 1888.

53 EES IX.g.60, 13 July 1888.

54 PP 9.iv.38.

55 EES II.d.179.

56 Ibid.

57 PP 9.iv.39.

58 PP 9.iv.41.

59 UCL Ms Add.184.3.

60 EES III.d.19, 2 August 1888.

61 PP 9.iv.39.

62 SAC fol. 318 Edw. SAC C RBR, no. 183.

63 EES X.b.12.

64 EES XV.47.

65 PP 9.iv.43.

66 SAC fol. 318 Edw. SAC C RBR, no. 168.

67 EES X.a.18.

[68] EES X.n.1.

[69] BM EAA 1889.43.

[70] PP 9.iv.46.

[71] GI Bradbury Mss.i 1–2; all quotations from Kate Bradbury relating to the American tour are from this journal.

[72] EES X.o.50, 15 November 1889.

[73] *The Brooklyn Eagle*, 13 November 1889.

[74] Ibid.

[75] *Boston Daily Globe*, 21 November 1889.

[76] SCO Edwards 350.

[77] SCO 528; the verse, by Henry Austin, was printed in a brochure advertising her 'Farewell Course of Lectures … under the auspices of the New England Women's Press Association, Music Hall, Boston, March … 1890' (Boston, MA: Mudge, 1890). Other copies survive on both sides of the Atlantic.

[78] *New York Sun*, 23 March 1990.

[79] SCO Edwards 528, p. 35; letter to Mrs Croly, quoted in the *Galignani Messenger*, 12 April 1890.

[80] Ibid.

[81] PP 9.iv.52.

[82] EES XII.c.28.

[83] J.W. Pye: 'The last days of the Queen of Egyptology', *KMT* (Sebastopol, CA: KMT, Winter 1994–95), pp. 77–81.

[84] EES VIII.b.31.

[85] PP 9.iv.53.

[86] PP 9.iv.54.

[87] EES III.j.95.

[88] EES XII.c.40.

[89] PP 9.iv.55.

[90] EES XVII.d.7.

[91] EES XII.e.2.

[92] EES III.d.26.

[93] PP 9.iv.56.

[94] Pye, 'The last days of the Queen of Egyptology', p. 80.

[95] PP 9.iv.1.

[96] SCO 459.

[97] PP 9.iv.56.

[98] EES XII.d.31.

[99] Pye, 'The last days of the Queen of Egyptology', p. 80.

[100] Edwards, *Pharaohs, Fellahs and Explorers*.

[101] *The Athenaeum*, No. 3357 (27 February 1892), pp. 274–75.

[102] PP 10.iv.2.

[103] EES XII.c.14.

[104] SCO Edwards 536.

[105] EES XII.e.17.

[106] PP 9.iv.58.

[107] Pye, 'The last days of the Queen of Egyptology', p. 80.
[108] BM EAA 1890-92, no. 59.
[109] GI II.3/35 and II.3/28.
[110] EES I.b.2, 14 October 1891.
[111] PP 9.iv.63, 3 December 1891.
[112] PP 10.iv.3, 10 January 1892.
[113] PP 10.iv.6.
[114] PP 10.iv.13.
[115] PP 10.iv.8.

❖ Appendix 1 ❖

Chronological summary of Amelia Edwards' life

1831   born 7 June

1841   visits Ireland with her mother

1845   begins music lessons under Miss Mounsey
        writes and illustrates *Patrick Murphy*

1848   begins organ and guitar lessons
        writes and illustrates *The Travelling Adventures of Mrs Roliston*

1849–50 ill with typhus fever

1850   employed as an organist at St Michael's, Wood Green

1851   January: engaged to Mr Bacon
        summer, ill
        September: resigns post as organist; gives music lessons
        December: breaks off her engagement

1853   ill; visits Paris with a cousin
        October: *Annette* published in *Chambers's Journal*

1854   Writing in *Chambers's Journal*, *Household Words*, &c.

1855   June: visits Paris with her father; continues to Burgundy with a
        friend
        My Brother's Wife published (imprint 1857)

1856   *A Summary of English History* published
        December: *Home and Foreign Lyrics*, a revue, performed in the
        provinces
        December: *The Ladder of Life* published

1857   15 January: leaves for tour of France, Switzerland and Italy
        5 February: reaches Rome
        March: *The Young Marquis* published
        25 April: returns to Dover by Austria and Germany

1858   *Hand and Glove* published
        A History of France published
        Her translation of the *Adventures of Fanny Loviot* published

1859	2 October: travels to Switzerland returns via Paris, where she stays with the Stégers 1 November: returns to London
1860	April: her parents both die She goes to live with Mr and Mrs Braysher in Kensington
1861	Visits the Wye Valley
1862	Travels to Switzerland and the Rhine, probably with Mr and Mrs Braysher *Sights and Stories* published
1863	*The Story of Cervantes* published Mr Braysher dies November: *Barbara's History* published (imprint 1864)
1864	November: *Ballads* published (imprint 1865) about this time moves to Westbury-on-Trym with Mrs Braysher
1865	*Miss Carew* published *Half a Million of Money* published in serial form; 1866 in 3 vols.
1869	*Debenham's Vow* published
1870	Meets Marianne North in London
1871	winter: prolonged illness 16 September: leaves for Bavaria 23 September: attends the Passion Play at Oberammergau winter: in Rome
1872	April: reaches Naples, and witnesses an eruption of Vesuvius June: meets Lucy Renshaw, and travels in the Dolomites with her
1873	*In the Days of My Youth* published *Untrodden Peaks and Unfrequented Valleys* published *Monsieur Maurice* published autumn: travels in France with Lucy Renshaw, then through Italy, and sails for Alexandria December: boards a dahabiyah for a trip up the Nile
1874	31 January: reaches Abu Simbel April: returns to Cairo; travels to Syria, Lebanon and the Greek islands June: reaches Athens; meets Heinrich Schliemann

1876   *A Thousand Miles up the Nile* published (imprint 1877)
        irregular correspondence with Gaston Maspero

1878   *A Poetry Book of Modern Poets* published (imprint 1879)
        A Poetry Book of Elder Poets published (imprint 1879)

1880   16 June: first meeting about the need to save Egyptian
        antiquities held at University College, London
        Lord Brackenbury published in serial form and in 3 vols.

1882   27 March: the Egypt Exploration Fund is founded
        December: first of many contributions to journals on
        Egyptological subjects

1882–89 Working as Joint (later sole) Honorary Secretary for the Fund,
        living at Westbury, visiting Weston-super-Mare in the summer
        with the ageing Mrs Braysher, and visiting London frequently
        for meetings, theatre and entertaining

1887   Begins lecturing in the provinces; meets Kate Bradbury

1888   July: living at Westbury
        Emily Paterson is appointed as her assistant secretary

1889   26 October: sails for a lecturing tour in America with Kate
        Bradbury

1890   3 March: breaks her arm while lecturing at Columbus, Ohio
        29 March: sails for home
        July: operation for breast cancer; Kate Bradbury comes to stay
        with her; convalescence in Weston-Super-Mare
        November: to Kate's home in Lancashire

1891   March–August: to the South of France and Italy to recuperate
        October: visits Millwall Docks to check a consignment from
        Egypt; catches influenza; returns to Westbury with Kate, but
        her condition deteriorates;
        Pharaohs, Fellahs and Explorers published

1892   9 January: Mrs Braysher dies
        15 April: Amelia Edwards dies

❖ Appendix 2 ❖

List of Amelia Edwards' published works

In this list, Amelia Edwards' published works are arranged in order of date of first publication. Within each year, books are listed first, then contributions to journals, collections and newspapers, in date order.

Many of Amelia Edwards' contributions to journals and newspapers were published anonymously. Identification in these cases is dependent on cuttings, references, etc., in the relevant archives. If the date of first publication has not been traced but the date of a reprint is known, these articles are entered under the date of the reprint. Where no date can be established they are listed immediately below, with a reference to the source of information.

Dates not traced:

'Bertha's Choice: a Story of the Rhine' [source not traced, c.1853], pp. 39a–53b (see SCO Edwards 525, No. 129).

'Eric's Wedding Day: a tale of the great copper mountain' [source not traced], pp. 147a–52a (see SCO Edwards 525, No. 117).

'Fruit: an essay,' [source not traced], pp. 79a–83b (see SCO Edwards 525, No. 123).

'A Happy Dilemma' [source not traced], pp. 250a–52 (see SCO Edwards 526, No. 70).

'The House of Hazelwood: tale' [source not traced] (see SCO Edwards 565, No. 263).

'July' [ballad]: *Gems of British Ballads*, [publisher and date not traced], p. 343 (see SCO Edwards 565, p. 2).

'Migrations of Birds', *Knowledge*, Vol. 5, No. 114 (18 January 1884), pp. 41–2.

'The Mulatto painter' [source not traced], pp. 244a–46b (see SCO Edwards 525, p. 38).

'On the Madonna Pia of Dante', *Illustrated Magazine of Art* [date not traced], pp. 150a–51b (see SCO Edwards 525, p. 13).

'The Progress of Properties' [source not traced], pp. 236a–41b (see SCO Edwards 525, p. 204).

1838/39

'The Knights of Old' [published in 'a penny paper'; source not traced] (see SCO
    Edwards 351).

1850

Vocal Pieces: A Persian Love Song; The Home Polka (London: Ewer & Co., 1850).

1851

'The Snowdrop Schottische', *Illustrated London News* (22 February 1851), p. 152.
'The Snowdrop Schottische', Snow Drop Schottische, composed for the Piano
    forte by A. Edwards, arranged by W.J. Wetmore (New York: [publisher not
    traced], 1852).
Vision of the Heart: [song], c.1851 (see SCO Edwards 526, No. 170).
'Love and Money: a tale', *Eliza Cook's Journal,* Vol. 5, No. 123 (6 September 1851),
    pp. 291b–95a.
'Love and Money: a tale', reprinted in *Miss Carew* (1865), q.v., Vol. 1, pp. 250–77.

1853

'The Painter of Pisa', *Illustrated Magazine of Art,* Vol. 1 (1853), pp. 330a–31b,
    350a–51b.
'The Rainbow', *Eliza Cook's Journal,* Vol. 8, No. 204 (26 March 1853),
    pp. 339a–41a.
'The Château Regnier', *Eliza Cook's Journal,* Vol. 8, No. 207 (16 April 1853),
    pp. 387a–90b.
'Annette', *Chambers's Edinburgh Journal,* New Series, Vol. 20, No. 511 (15 October
    1853), pp. 246a–50b, and New Series, Vol. 21, No. 512 (22 October 1853),
    pp. 261b–66b.

1854

'Alice Hoffman: an autobiography', *Chambers's Repository of Instructive and
    Amusing Tracts,* Vol. 9, No. 67 (Edinburgh: Chambers, 1854), 32pp.
'Alice Hoffman: an autobiography', reprinted as 'The Autobiography of Alice
    Hoffman', in *Miss Carew* (1865), q.v., Vol. 3, pp. 103–96.

'Curiosities of Burial', *Chambers's Repository of Instructive and Amusing Tracts*, Vol. 10, No. 79 (Edinburgh: Chambers, 1854), 32pp.

'A Glance at my Inner Life, by a Musician on the Continent', *Chambers's Journal*, Vol. 1, No. 8 (25 February 1854), pp. 113a–17b.

'Music of Barbarous Nations, by a Musician on the Continent', *Eliza Cook's Journal*, Vol. 10, No. 259 (22 April 1854), pp. 405b–8a.

'The Last Moments of Beethoven', *Eliza Cook's Journal*, Vol. 10, No. 260 (29 April 1854), pp. 15a–16a.

'Bertrand Woodhall', *The Ladies' Companion*, Vol. 5 (May 1854), pp. 239a–47b.

'Pierre Dupont and his Poetry', *Chambers's Journal*, Vol. 1, No. 18 (6 May 1854), pp. 280b–83a.

'A Page of Paris Gossip', *Eliza Cook's Journal*, Vol. 11 (3 June 1854; 16 July 1854), pp. 88a–90a, 182b–84b.

'Nine Months at Vallonvert, by an Organist', *Chambers's Journal*, Vol. 1, No. 25 (24 June 1854), pp. 394b–98b.

'The Cabaret at the Break of Day', *Chambers's Journal*, Vol. 2, No. 28 (16 July 1854), pp. 46a–48b.

'The Cabaret at the Break of Day', reprinted in *Monsieur Maurice* (1873), q.v., Vol. 1, pp. 281–303.

'The First Poor Traveller', *Household Words* (Christmas 1854), pp. 1a–10b.

1855

Etiquette for Ladies in Public and Private, new and revised edition (London: Warne, [1855]).

My Brother's Wife: a life-history (London: Hurst & Blackett, 1855).

My Brother's Wife: a life-history (New York: Harper, 1865).

My Brother's Wife: a life-history (New York: Munro, 1877), extracts only.

My Brother's Wife: a life-history (New York: Lovell, 1889).

'Two New Year's Days' [c.1855, original publication not traced].

'Two New Year's Days', reprinted in *Miss Carew* (1865), q.v., Vol. 1, pp. 199–221.

'A First Appearance upon any Stage', *Chambers's Journal*, Vol. 3, No. 61 (3 March 1855), pp. 129–32a.

'Flaws in Diamonds', *Chambers's Journal*, Vol. 3, No. 70 (5 May 1855), pp. 286b–88a.

'Celeste Bertin: a Few Leaves from the Notebook of a Physician', *Eliza Cook's Journal*, Vol. 9, No. 219 (9 July 1855), pp. 171a–74b.

'A Chapter on Bells', *Chambers's Journal*, Vol. 4, No. 84 (11 August 1855), pp. 87b–89b.

'Shadow and Sunlight', *Sharpe's London Magazine* [1855], pp. 36a–53b.

'The Story of a Familiar Friend', *Chambers' Journal*, Vol. 4, No. 95 (27 October 1855), pp. 257a–60a.
'The Boots', *Household Words* (15 December 1855), pp. 18b–22b.

1856

Home and Foreign Lyrics [libretto by Amelia B. Edwards] (publisher not named, 1856).
A Summary of English History from the Norman Conquest to the Present Time: with observations on the progress of art, science and civilisation ... for the use of schools (London: Routledge, 1856).
'The Painter and his Pupil: a Flemish Story', *Chambers's Journal*, 3rd series, Vol. 5, No. 125 (24 May 1856), pp. 326a–29a.
'Superstitions connected with Storms', *Chambers's Journal*, Vol. 5, No. 106 (12 January 1856), pp. 30a–32b.
'The Museum of Arts and Trades at Paris', *Chambers's Journal*, Vol. 5, No. 108 (2 February 1856), pp. 76a–78a.
'Conjectural Astronomy', *Chambers's Journal*, Vol. 5, No. 111 (16 February 1856), pp. 100a–2b.
'A New View of an Old Subject', *Chambers's Journal*, Vol. 5, No. 115 (15 March 1856), pp. 163b–66a.
'A Titled Family', *Chambers's Journal*, Vol. 5, No. 121 (26 April 1856), pp. 259a–61a.
'The Reliquary of St Ursula: a Story of Bruges in the Fifteenth Century', *The Ladies' Companion*, Vol. 9 (May 1856), pp. 231a–32b.
'The Doppelgänger', *Chambers's Journal*, Vol. 5, No. 107 (19 January 1856), pp. 37a–40b.
'A Sketch in Chalks', *Chambers's Journal*, Vol. 6, No. 143 (27 September 1856), pp. 202b–5a.

1857

Etiquette for Gentlemen: being a manual of minor social ethics and customary observances, [with] *The Ballroom Guide* (London: Knight, 1857).
The Ladder of Life: a heart history (London: Routledge [1856] 1857).
The Ladder of Life: a heart history (New York: Harper, 1864).
The Ladder of Life: a heart history (New York: Beadle & Adams, 1882).
The Young Marquis: or, scenes from a reign (London: J. & C. Brown [1857]).
'Béranger and his Poetry' [source not traced] (27 July 1857), 119a–22b (see SCO Edwards 525, p. 255).

'At the Hotel Dessin', *Chambers's Journal*, Vol. 7, No. 163 (14 February 1857), pp. 103a–6a.
'Wanderings and Ponderings of a Man about Town' [*weekly, source not traced*], 21 June 1857–10 October 1858).
'Pictures in Stone', *Chambers's Journal*, Vol. 8, No. 194 (19 September 1857), pp. 177a–80a.

1858

A History of France from the Conquest of Gaul by the Romans to the Peace of 1856 (London: Routledge, 1858).
A History of France from the Conquest of Gaul by the Romans to the Peace of 1856, new edition, continued to the death of the Prince Imperial by Thomas Archer (London: Routledge, 1880).
Hand and Glove (London: J. & C. Brown [1858] 1859).
Hand and Glove (London: Parlour Library [1859] 1860).
Hand and Glove, new edition (London: J. & C. Brown, 1865).
Hand and Glove (Leipzig: Tauchnitz, 1865).
Hand and Glove (New York: Harper, 1866).
Hand and Glove (New York: Munro, 1877).
Hand and Glove (London: Rubicon Press, 2000).
Hand and Glove, Il Guanto Fatale, 2 vols (Milan: Emilio Croce, 1872).
A Lady's Captivity among Chinese pirates in the Chinese seas, translated from the French of Mademoiselle Fanny Loviot by Amelia B. Edwards (London: Routledge [1858]).
A Lady's Captivity among Chinese pirates in the Chinese seas, reprinted in *Magazine of History*, Extra No. 156 (Tarrytown, NY: William Abbott, 1980).
'The Patagonian Brothers', *Household Words*, Vol. 17, No. 494 (23 January 1858), pp. 126b–31b.
'The Patagonian Brothers', reprinted in *Miss Carew* (1865), q.v., Vol. 2, pp. 1–31.
'The Brilliant Ring', *Illustrated Magazine of Art* (1858?), pp. 49a–111b.
'Bradshaw the Betrayer', *Englishwoman's Journal* (April 1858).
'Bradshaw the Betrayer', reprinted in *Miss Carew* (1865), q.v., Vol. 1, pp. 138–98.

1860

Photographic Historical Portrait Gallery … the illustrative letterpress by Amelia B.Edwards, photography by L. Caldesi (London: Colnaghi, 1860).
'Lonely' [poem], *All the Year Round* (25 February 1860), p. 416b.
'Lonely' [poem], reprinted in *Ballads*, q.v (1865).

'My Brother's Ghost Story', *All the Year Round* (Christmas number 1860), pp. 25–30.

'My Brother's Ghost Story', reprinted in *Miss Carew* (1865), q.v., Vol. 3, pp. 1–32.

'My Brother's Ghost Story', reprinted in *Supernatural Omnibus: being a collection of stories of apparitions, witchcraft ... ed. with an introduction by Montague Summers* (New York: Doubleday, 1932), pp. 435–46.

'My Brother's Ghost Story', reprinted in *A Circle of Witches: an anthology of Victorian witchcraft stories, selected and introduced by Peter Haining* (London: Robert Hale, 1971), pp. 134–46.

1861

'Picking up Terrible Company', *All the Year Round* (Christmas number 1861), pp. 14–20.

'Picking up Terrible Company', reprinted as 'Terrible Company', in *Miss Carew* (1865), q.v., Vol. 1, pp. 59–97.

1862

Sights and Stories: being some account of a holiday tour through the north of Belgium (London: Victoria Press, 1862).

'The Professor's Adventure', *All the Year Round* (10 December 1862), pp. 333–36.

'The Professor's Adventure', reprinted as 'The Professor's Story' in *Miss Carew* (1865), q.v., Vol. 1, pp. 118–37.

'Reliques' [poem], *All the Year Round* (7 June 1862), p. 301.

'Reliques' [poem], reprinted in *Ballads*, q.v (1865), pp. 10–12.

1863

The Story of Cervantes, who was a Scholar, a Poet, a Soldier, a Slave among the Moors and the Author of Don Quixote, serialised in *Routledge's Every Boy's Annual* (1863), pp. 225–35, &c.

The Story of Cervantes (London: Routledge [1862] 1863).

'The Eleventh of March', *A Welcome: original contributions in poetry and prose* (London: Emily Faithfull, March 1863), pp. 130–46.

'The Eleventh of March', reprinted in *Miss Carew* (1865), q.v., Vol. 1, pp. 98–117.

'How the Third Floor Knew the Potteries', *All the Year Round* (Christmas number 1863), pp. 35–40.

'How the Third Floor Knew the Potteries', reprinted as 'Number Three', in *Miss Carew* (1865), q.v., Vol. 1, pp. 278–311.

'How the Third Floor Knew the Potteries', reprinted in *All the Year Round Christmas Numbers* (London: Chapman & Hall [1898]).

'How the Third Floor Knew the Potteries', reprinted in *Supernatural Omnibus: being a collection of stories of apparitions, witchcraft … ed. with an introduction by Montague Summers* (New York: Doubleday, 1932), pp. 154–56.

'Our First Great Sea-fight: an incident in the boyhood of Admiral Blake', *Routledge's Every Boy's Annual* (1863), pp. 26–36.

1864

Barbara's History, 3 vols (London: Hurst & Blackett [1863] 1864).

Barbara's History, 2 vols (Leipzig: Tauchnitz, 1864).

Barbara's History (New York: Harper, 1864).

Barbara's History (New York: Munro, 1877).

Barbara's History, new edition (London: Hurst & Blackett [1897]).

Barbara's History (London: Rubicon Press, 2000).

Ballads (London: Tinsley [1864] 1865).

Ballads (New York: Carleton, 1865).

'Cain' [c.1864, original publication not traced].

'Cain', reprinted in *Miss Carew* (1865), q.v., Vol. 2, pp. 167–87.

'The Guardship at the Aire', *Routledge's Every Boy's Annual: an original miscellany of entertaining literature* (London: Routledge, Warne & Routledge, 1864), pp. 42–55.

'The Guardship at the Aire', reprinted in *Miss Carew* (1865), q.v., Vol. 2, pp. 80–115.

'The Guardship at the Aire', reprinted in *Every Boy's Stories* (1896), pp. 150–65.

'The Six Boys of Guilton', *Routledge's Every Boy's Annual* (1864), pp. 57–64.

'The Six Boys of Guilton', reprinted in *Every Boy's Stories* (1896), pp. 166–77.

'[The Phantom Coach] Another Past Lodger relates his own Ghost Story', *All the Year Round* (Christmas number 1864), pp. 35–40.

'[The Phantom Coach] Another Past Lodger relates his own Ghost Story', reprinted in *All the Year Round Christmas Numbers* (London: Chapman & Hall [1898]).

'[The Phantom Coach] Another Past Lodger relates his own Ghost Story', reprinted in *Supernatural Omnibus; being a collection of stories of apparitions, witchcraft … ed. with an introduction by Montague Summers* (New York: Doubleday, 1932), pp. 122–35.

'[The Phantom Coach] Another Past Lodger relates his own Ghost Story', reprinted in *Great Ghost Stories: ed. by H. Van Thal* (London: Weidenfeld & Nicolson, 1960), pp. 207–23.

'[The Phantom Coach] Another Past Lodger relates his own Ghost Story',
   reprinted in *The Gentlewomen of Evil: an anthology of rare supernatural stories
   from the pens of Victorian ladies, selected and introduced by Peter Haining*
   (London: Taplinger, 1967), pp. 122–135.

'[The Phantom Coach] Another Past Lodger relates his own Ghost Story',
   reprinted in *Classic Ghost Stories, by Charles Dickens and others* (New York:
   Dover, 1975).

'[The Phantom Coach] Another Past Lodger relates his own Ghost Story',
   reprinted in *Masters of the Macabre: an anthology of mystery, horror and detection;
   ed. by Sean Manley and Gogo Lewis* (New York: Doubleday, 1975).

'[The Phantom Coach] Another Past Lodger relates his own Ghost Story',
   reprinted in *Spine-chillers: unforgettable tales of terror, by Algernon Blackwood
   [and others]* (New York: Doubleday, 1978).

'[The Phantom Coach] Another Past Lodger relates his own Ghost Story',
   reprinted as 'The North Mail', in *Camp Fire Chillers; ed. by E.M. Freeman* (East
   Woods Press, 1980).

'[The Phantom Coach] Another Past Lodger relates his own Ghost Story',
   reprinted in *The Oxford Book of English Ghost Stories, chosen by Michael Cox and
   R.A. Gilbert* (London: Oxford University Press, 1986), pp. 13–24.

'[The Phantom Coach] Another Past Lodger relates his own Ghost Story',
   reprinted in *The Lifted Veil: the book of fantastic literature by women, 1800 –
   World War II; ed. and introduced by A. Susan Williams* (London: Xanadu
   Publications, 1992), pp. 110–22.

'[The Phantom Coach] Another Past Lodger relates his own Ghost Story',
   reprinted in *The Phantom Coach: collected ghost stories; edited with an introduction by Richard Dalby* (Ashcroft, BC: Ash-Tree Press, 1999).

1865

Miss Carew, 3 vols (London: Hurst & Blackett, 1865).

Miss Carew, 2 vols (Leipzig: Tauchnitz, 1865).

Miss Carew (New York: Harper, 1865).

Miss Carew, new edition (London: Chapman & Hall, 1876).

Miss Carew, new edition (London: Ward, Lock [1890?]).

Half a Million of Money, serialised in *All the Year Round*, No. 313 (22 April 1865)
   &c.

Half a Million of Money, serialised in *Harper's Weekly* (New York: Harper, 1865).

Half a Million of Money (Leipzig: Tauchnitz, 1865).

Half a Million of Money, 3 vols (London: Tinsley Brothers, 1866).

Half a Million of Money (New York: Harper, 1866).

Half a Million of Money, Railway Library (London: Bradbury, Evans [1868]).

Half a Million of Money, 4th edition (London: Routledge, 1892).

Half a Million of Money, *L'Héritage de Jacob Trefelden* (Paris: Hachette, 1881).

'My Diamond Studs' [original publication not traced].

'My Diamond Studs', reprinted in *Miss Carew* (1865), q.v., Vol. 2, pp. 32–79.

'The Discovery of the Treasure Isles', serialised in *Routledge's Every Boy's Annual* (1865) &c.

'The Discovery of the Treasure Isles', reprinted in *Miss Carew* (1865), q.v., Vol. 2, pp. 188–285.

'The Painter of Rotterdam' [original publication not traced].

'The Painter of Rotterdam', reprinted in *Miss Carew* (1865), q.v., Vol. 1, pp. 222–49.

'A Railway Panic' [original publication not traced] (see SCO Edwards 525, No. 263).

'A Railway Panic', reprinted in *Miss Carew* (1865), q.v., Vol. 2, pp. 116–36.

'The Recollections of Professor Henneberg' [original publication not traced].

'The Recollections of Professor Henneberg', reprinted in *Miss Carew* (1865), q.v., Vol. 3, pp. 33–102.

'The Pleasures and Pains of Childhood', *Home Thoughts and Home Scenes: original poems* (London: Routledge, Warne & Routledge, 1865), p. 29.

'The Scramble for Sugarplums' [poem], *Home Thoughts and Home Scenes: original poems* (London: Routledge, Warne & Routledge, 1865), p. 21.

'The Staffordshire Renaissance', *All the Year Round* (24 June 1865), pp. 518–21 (see revised proof: SCO Edwards 568, No. 88).

1866

'All Saints' Eve' [c.1866, original publication not traced].

'All Saints' Eve', reprinted in *Monsieur Maurice* (1873), q.v., Vol. 3, pp. 171–310.

'The Engineer', *All the Year Round* (Christmas number 1866), pp. 42–48.

'The Engineer', reprinted as 'The Engineer's Story', in *Monsieur Maurice*, q.v., Vol. 1, pp. 231–79.

'The Engineer', reprinted as 'Branch Line: the Engineer', in *All the Year Round Christmas Numbers* (London: Chapman & Hall [1898]).

'The Engineer', reprinted in: *The Supernatural Omnibus: being a collection of stories of apparitions, witchcraft ... ed. with an introduction by Montague Summers* (New York: Doubleday, 1932), pp. 217–34.

'The Four-Fifteen Express', *Routledge's Christmas Annual for 1867* (December 1866), pp. 114–34.

'The Four-Fifteen Express', reprinted in *Mixed Sweets from Routledge's Annual* (London: Routledge, 1867), pp. 114–34.

'The Four-Fifteen Express', reprinted in *Monsieur Maurice* (1873), q.v., Vol. 3, pp. 65–133.

'The Four-Fifteen Express', reprinted in *Ghost Story Omnibus: complete stories by Bulwer Lytton… and others, ed. by J.L. French* (n.p.).

'The Four-Fifteen Express', reprinted in *Great Ghost Stories; ed. by J.L. French, with a foreword by James H. Hyslop* (Dodd, 1926).

'The Four-Fifteen Express', reprinted as 'The Signalman, by Charles Dickens', in *Great Ghost Stories, ed. by Herbert Van Thal* (London: Weidenfeld & Nicholson, 1960).

'The Four-Fifteen Express', reprinted in *Victorian Ghost Stories, selected and retold by Mike Stocks … edited by Felicity Brooks* (London: Usborne Publishing, 1996), pp. 54–69.

1867

'Titian's St Peter Martyr' [letter], *The Athenaeum*, no. 2091 (23 November 1867), p. 687.

'The Story of Salome', *Tinsley's Magazine, Christmas Number* (1867), pp. 39–52.

'The Story of Salome', reprinted in *Monsieur Maurice* (1873), q.v., Vol. 2, pp. 202–56.

'The Story of Salome', reprinted in: *Victorian Ghost Stories by Eminent Women Writers; ed. by Richard Dalby* (London: Carrol & Graf, 1990).

1868

'The Tragedy in the Palazzo Bardello', *The New Eclectic* (1868).

'The Tragedy in the Palazzo Bardello', reprinted in *Monsieur Maurice* (1873), q.v., Vol. 3, pp. 1–64.

'Mr Bierstadt's paintings of the Rocky Mountains', *Morning Post* (16 January 1868).

[Untitled, on education], *Morning Post* (16 January 1868).

[Untitled, on education], *Morning Post* (30 January 1868).

'The New Royalty Theatre', *Morning Post* (3 February 1868).

[Untitled, on education], *Morning Post* (3 February 1868).

[Untitled, on compulsory education], *Morning Post* (6 February 1868).

[Untitled, on the education rate], *Morning Post* (12 February 1868).

[Untitled, on education], *Morning Post* (21 February 1868).

'Exhibition of the Society of Female Artists', *Morning Post* (21 February 1868).

'Mr Church's "Falls of Niagara"', *Morning Post* (27 February 1868).

'Literature: "Children of the State"' [review of a book by Florence Hill], *Morning Post* (2 April 1868).

'Mr Bierstadt's "Domes of the Yosemite"', *Morning Post* (15 April 1868).

'The Exhibition of the Society of Painters in Watercolours', *Morning Post* (30 April 1868).

'Institute of Painters in Watercolours', *Morning Post* (8 May 1868).

'Mr Holman Hunt's "Isabella and the Pot of Basil"', *Morning Post* (27 May 1868).

'Exhibition of Drawings and Paintings by Members of the Royal Artillery', *Morning Post* (15 June 1868).

'Mr Gustave Doré's paintings at the German Gallery', *Morning Post* (29 June 1868).

'Doré's Dante: the "Purgatorio" and "Paradiso"', *Morning Post* (24 December 1868).

1869

Debenham's Vow, serialised in *Good Words* (1 January–1 December 1869).

Debenham's Vow, 3 vols (London: Hurst & Blackett, 1870).

Debenham's Vow, 2 vols (Leipzig: Tauchnitz, 1879).

Debenham's Vow (New York: Harper, 1870).

Debenham's Vow, Debenham's Gelübte ... aus den Englischen von Anna Wünn (Leipzig: Gunther, 1873).

'The Doré Gallery', *Morning Post* (4 May 1869).

[Letter, on *Hand and Glove*], *The Spectator* (8 May 1869).

'Mr Church's Damascus', *Morning Post* (24 June 1869).

'A Service of Danger', in *Routledge's Christmas Annual* (London: Routledge, 1869), pp. 112–14.

'A Service of Danger', reprinted in *Monsieur Maurice* (1873), q.v., Vol. 2, pp. 103–44.

1871

'The Castellani Collection at the British Museum', *Morning Post* (31 May 1871).

'The Castellani Collection at the British Museum. Concluding notice', *Morning Post* (1 June 1871).

'Engravings from M. Gustave Doré's Pictures', *Morning Post* (24 July 1871).

'In the Confessional', *All the Year Round* (Christmas number 1871), pp. 7–14.

'In the Confessional', reprinted in *Monsieur Maurice* (1873), q.v., Vol. 2, pp. 257–97.

'In the Confessional', reprinted in *The Mammoth Book of Ghost Stories; ed. by Richard Dalby* (London: Robinson Publishing, 1990), pp. 229–43.

1872

The Life Chase: song for baritone voice (London: Weippert [1872]).

'A New Story retold', *Ours* (May 1872).

'Sister Johanna's Story', *All the Year Round* (Christmas number 1872), pp. 21–27.

'Sister Johanna's Story', reprinted in *Monsieur Maurice* (1873), q.v., Vol. 3, pp. 135–70.

'A Night on the Borders of the Black Forest', *Routledge's Christmas Annual*, Vol. 6 (1872), pp. 83–89.

'A Night on the Borders of the Black Forest', reprinted in *Monsieur Maurice* (1873), q.v., Vol. 2, pp. 145–202.

'A Night on the Borders of the Black Forest', reprinted in *An Omnibus of British Mysteries, condensed; [ed. by George Bisserov]* (Juniper Press, 1959).

'A Night on the Borders of the Black Forest', reprinted in *Murder by Gaslight: Victorian tales; ed. by E.C. Wagenknecht* (New York: 1949, reprinted 1994).

1873

In the Days of my Youth, 3 vols (London: Hurst & Blackett, 1873).

In the Days of my Youth, 2 vols (Leipzig: Tauchnitz, 1876).

In the Days of my Youth, In meiner Jugend ... Frei nach dem Englischen von Elise Mirus, 4 vols (Leipzig: Gunther, 1876).

Monsieur Maurice: a new novelette, and other tales, 3 vols (London: Hurst & Blackett, 1873).

Monsieur Maurice: a new novelette, and other tales (Leipzig: Tauchnitz, 1873).

Monsieur Maurice, reprinted in *Five Victorian Ghost Novels, ed. by E.F. Bleiler* (New York: Dover, 1971), pp. 245–96.

Monsieur Maurice: a new novelette, and other tales, Unheimliche Geschichten; in deutsche Bearbeitung nach Amelia B. Edwards von A. von Winterfield. [1879].

Untrodden Peaks and Unfrequented Valleys: a midsummer ramble in the Dolomites (London: Longmans, Green, 1873).

Untrodden Peaks and Unfrequented Valleys: a midsummer ramble in the Dolomites (Leipzig: Tauchnitz, 1873).

A Midsummer Ramble in the Dolomites, new edition (London: Longmans, Green, 1890).

A Midsummer Ramble in the Dolomites, 2nd edition (London: Routledge [1889] 1890).

Untrodden Peaks and Unfrequented Valleys: a midsummer ramble in the Dolomites, with a new introduction by Philippa Levine (London: Longmans, Green, 1873, repr. London: Virago, 1986).

La Strada delle Dolomiti – Dolomitenstrasse: imagini e racconti (Mantova: Corraini, 1994).

'The New Pass' [original publication not traced].

'The New Pass', reprinted in *Monsieur Maurice* (1873), q.v., Vol. 2, pp. 65–102.

'The New Pass', reprinted in *Classic Ghost Stories, by Wilkie Collins ... and others, edited by John Grafton* (Mineola, NY: Dover Publications, 1998), pp. 74–85.

'The Story of Ernst Christian Schoeffer' [original publication not traced].

'The Story of Ernst Christian Schoeffer', reprinted in *Monsieur Maurice* (1873), q.v., Vol. 2, pp. 1–63.

'Vendetta' [original publication not traced].

'Vendetta', reprinted in *Monsieur Maurice* (1873), q.v., Vol. 1, pp. 161–230.

1877

A Thousand Miles up the Nile (London: Longmans, Green [1976], 1877).

A Thousand Miles up the Nile (New York: Caldwell, 1877).

A Thousand Miles up the Nile, 2 vols (Leipzig: Tauchnitz, 1878).

Tysiac mil no Falach Nilu (Lwow: 1880).

A Thousand Miles up the Nile, 2nd edition, revised by the author (London: Routledge, 1889 [1888]).

A Thousand Miles up the Nile (New York: Burt, 1888).

A Thousand Miles up the Nile (Boston, MA: Knight [1888]).

A Thousand Miles up the Nile, reprinted with an introduction by Quentin Crewe (London: Century Publishing, 1982).

A Thousand Miles up the Nile (London: Parkway, 1992).

A Thousand Miles up the Nile (London: Darf, 2000).

'Together' [poem], *All the Year Round*, New Series 18 (12 May 1877), p. 253.

'Together' [poem], song: words composed by Miss Amelia B. Edwards, the music composed by Mrs Mounsey-Bartholomew (London: Novello, Ewer [1877]).

'Mr Caryl Coleman's new picture, "The Bronze Horses of St Mark's"', *Morning Post*, (16 July 1877).

'"Egypt as it is", by J.C. McCoan' [review], *Academy*, Vol. 12, No. 291 (1 December 1877), pp. 505–7.

1878

A Poetry Book of Elder Poets: consisting of songs and sonnets, odes and idylls, selected and arranged by Amelia B. Edwards (London: Longman [1878], 1879).

A Poetry Book of Songs and Sonnets, Odes and Idylls: first series, from the fourteenth to the eighteenth century, selected and arranged with notes from the works of the elder English poets, by Amelia B. Edwards (Leipzig: Tauchnitz, 1878).

[A Poetry Book of Modern Poets] A Poetry Book of Songs and Sonnets, Odes and Idylls: second series, from the end of the eighteenth century to the present time, selected and

arranged with notes from the works of the modern English and American poets, by
Amelia B. Edwards, copyright edition (Leipzig: Tauchnitz, 1878).

A Poetry Book of Modern Poets: consisting of songs and sonnets, odes and idylls,
selected and arranged with notes from the works of the modern English and
American poets ... by Amelia B. Edwards (London: Longman [1879]).

'Miss North's paintings at South Kensington', *Morning Post* (7 January 1878).

'"Cleopatra's Needle, with brief notes on Egypt and Egyptian Obelisks", by
Erasmus Wilson, FRS, London: Brain & Co., 1877' [review], *Academy*, Vol. 13,
No. 300 (2 February 1878), p. 89.

'An Old Story Re-told', *Ours* (May 1878), pp. 3–8.

'M. Allemant's Egyptian Collection', *Academy*, Vol. 13, No. 309 (6 April 1878),
pp. 308–9.

'The Monuments of Upper Egypt; a translation of the *Itinéraire de la Haute*
Egypte of Auguste Mariette-Bey', *Academy*, Vol. 13, No. 313 (4 May 1878),
pp. 385–86.

'The Treasures of Mycenae' [letter], *Academy*, Vol. 13, No. 320 (22 June 1878),
p. 558.

'L'Egypte à petites journées' [review], *Academy*, Vol. 14, No. 326 (3 August 1878),
pp. 108–9.

'An Oriental Zadkiel: Egyptian Calendar for the year 1295 A.H (1878 A.D.)',
Academy, Vol. 14, No. 380 (31 August 1878), pp. 207–8.

'Egypt: a handbook for travellers' [review], *Academy*, Vol. 14, No. 333
(21 September 1878), pp. 281–82.

'An Unpublished Letter by Charles Lamb', *Academy* Vol. 14, No. 334
(28 September 1878), p. 317.

1879

Unheimliche Geschichten, in deutscher Bearbeitung nach A.B. Edwards und E.A. Poe,
2 vols (Jena: Altenburg [1879]).

'Miss North's Indian Sketches', *The Graphic*, 20 (1879), p. 43.

'"The Manners and Customs of the Ancient Egyptians", by Sir J. Gardner
Wilkinson, revised and corrected by Samuel Birch. A new edition' [review],
Academy, Vol. 15, No. 359 (22 March 1879), pp. 251–52.

'"A History of Egypt under the Pharaohs" ... by H. Brugsch-Bey' [review],
Academy, Vol. 15, No. 373 (28 June 1879), pp. 557–59.

'"A Ride in Egypt, by W.J. Loftie"' [review], *Academy*, Vol. 16, No. 388
(11 October 1879), pp. 257–58.

'Future Explorations in Egypt', *Academy*, Vol. 16, No. 392 (8 November 1879),
pp. 338–39.

1880

Lord Brackenbury, serialised in *The Graphic* (London, February 1880 &c.).

Lord Brackenbury, 3 vols (London: Hurst & Blackett, 1880).

Lord Brackenbury (New York: Harper, 1880).

Lord Brackenbury (Leipzig: Tauchnitz, 1880).

Lord Brackenbury, new edition (London: Hurst & Blackett [1881?]).

'Future Excavations in Egypt' [letter], *Academy*, Vol. 17, No. 406 (14 February 1880), pp. 121–22.

'"Geschichte Aegyptens", by Emile Brugsch' [review], *Revue Egyptologique* (3 April 1880).

'The Site of Raamses', *Academy*, Vol. 17, No. 416 (24 April 1880) pp. 307–8.

'Nile Gleanings by Villiers Stuart MP' [review], *Academy*, Vol. 17, No. 421 (29 May 1880), pp. 397–98.

'Ancient Egyptian Romance', *Academy*, Vol. 18, No. 432 (14 August 1880), pp. 112–13.

'The Poor Birds' [letter], *The Times* (19 July 1880).

'Murray's Handbook for Egypt' [review], *Academy*, Vol. 18, No. 435 (4 September 1880), pp. 164–65.

'Revue égyptologique' [review], *Academy*, Vol. 18, No. 450 (18 December 1880), p. 445.

1881

'"Catalogue générale des monuments d'Abydos ...", par August Mariette' [review], *Academy*, Vol. 19, No. 454 (15 January 1881), pp. 48–49.

'Mariette-Pasha' [obituary], *Academy*, Vol. 19, No. 456 (29 January 1881), pp. 87–88.

'Inscriptions et notices ... à Edfoo' [review], *Academy*, Vol. 19, No. 457 (5 February 1881), p. 104.

'Essai sur la mythologie égyptienne' [review], *Academy*, Vol. 19, No. 462 (12 March 1881), pp. 191–92.

'Latest Excavations in Egypt', *Academy*, Vol. 19, No. 465 (2 April 1881), p. 248.

'Revue égyptologique No. IV' [review], *Academy*, Vol. 19, No. 467 (16 April 1881), p. 292.

'Congrès provincial des Orientalistes françaises', *Academy*, Vol. 19, No. 468 (23 April 1881), p. 297.

'Revue égyptologique II No. I' [review], *Academy*, Vol. 19, No. 476 (18 June 1861), pp. 448–49.

'"History of Ancient Egypt", by G. Rawlinson' [review], *Academy*, Vol. 20,

No. 483 (6 August 1881), pp. 99–100.
'The Discovery at Thebes', *Academy*, Vol. 20, No. 484 (13 August 1881), p. 127.
'The Archaeological Discovery at Thebes', *Academy*, Vol. 20, No. 486 (27 August 1881), pp. 167–68.
'Arabs, travellers and anteekahs', *Academy*, Vol. 20, No. 487 (3 September 1881), pp. 186–87.
'The Orientalist Congress at Berlin', *Academy*, Vol. 20, No. 489 (17 September 1881), p. 225.
'M.G. Maspero on the recent discoveries at Thebes', *The Times* (19 September 1881), p. 4.
'The Prince of Wales' papyrus in the British Museum', *Academy*, Vol. 20, No. 491 (1 October 1881), pp. 264–65.
'Notes on Egyptology', *Academy*, Vol. 20, No. 495 (29 October 1881), pp. 334–35.
'A New Royal Papyrus', *Academy*, Vol. 20, No. 496 (5 November 1881), p. 351.
'The Egypt of the Past' [review], *Academy*, Vol. 20, No. 498 (19 November 1881), pp. 375–76.
'Was it an Illusion? a parson's story', *Arrowsmith's Christmas Annual for 1881: Thirteen for dinner* (Bristol: Arrowsmith, 1881).
'Was it an Illusion? a parson's story', reprinted in *Victorian Ghost Stories: an Oxford Anthology, ed. by Michael Cox and R.A. Gilbert* (London: Oxford University Press, 1992), pp. 239–55.
'Buried Treasure', *The Times* (24 December 1881), pp. 3–4; (9 January 1882), p. 8.
'M. Maspero's official report upon the late discovery at Thebes', *The Times* (27 December 1881), p. 8.

1882

[Letter], *Morning Star* (2 January 1882).
'Royal Mummies found near Thebes', *Illustrated London News* (4 February 1882).
'Royal Mummies found near Thebes', reprinted in *The Great Archaeologists*, edited by Edward Bacon (London: Secker & Warburg, 1976), pp. 79–83.
'Literary Identity', *Morning Post* (6 February 1882).
'The Opening of the Pyramid of Meydoom', *Academy*, Vol. 21, No. 511 (18 February 1882), p. 121.
'The Land of Khemi' [review], *Academy*, Vol. 21, No. 513 (4 March 1882), pp. 149–50.
'Egyptian Antiquities', *The Times* (30 March 1882).
'Lying in State in Cairo', *Harper's New Monthly Magazine* (April 1882), pp. 185–204.
'Proposed Excavation in the Egyptian Delta. Society for the Promotion of Excavation in the delta of the Nile', *Academy*, Vol. 21, No. 517 (1 April 1882), p. 516.

'Egyptian Jottings', *Academy*, Vol. 21, No. 519 (15 April 1882), p. 273.

'Explorations in the Delta of the Nile', *Academy*, Vol. 21, No. 523 (13 May 1882) pp. 346–47.

'Was Rameses II the Pharaoh of the Oppression?', serialised in *Knowledge*, No. 31 (2 June 1882) – No. 64 (19 January 1883) pp. i–xvi.

'M. Naville's visit to the ruins of Tanis (Zoan)', *Academy*, Vol. 22, No. 530 (1 July 1882), p. 17.

'Les Contes populaires de l'Egypte ancienne, traduits et commentés par G. Maspero' [review], *Academy*, Vol. 22, No. 531 (8 July 1882), pp. 24–25.

'In Memorium François Joseph Chabas', *Academy*, Vol. 22, No. 535 (5 August 1882), p. 108.

'A Waif from Deir-el-Baharee', *Academy*, Vol. 22, No. 538 (26 August 1882), p. 157.

'The Seat of the War in Egypt' [letter], *The Times* (29 August 1882).

'Sir Erasmus Wilson and the Royal Sea-Bathing Infirmary at Margate', *Morning Post* (31 August 1882).

'Recent Egyptian Books' [reviews], *Academy*, Vol. 22, No. 539 (2 September 1992), pp. 159–60.

'The Boolak Museum', *Academy*, Vol. 22, No. 542 (23 September 1882), p. 230.

'Advice to Travellers in Egypt', *The Times* (1 October 1882).

'The Destruction of Cairo', *Academy*, Vol. 22, No. 546 (21 October 1882), pp. 301–2.

'The flower-wreaths of the Pharaohs' [letter], *Academy*, Vol. 22, No. 550 (18 November 1882), p. 369.

'Cities of Egypt by Reginald Stuart Poole' [review], *Academy*, Vol. 22, No. 552 (2 December 1882), pp. 389–90.

'The Great Pyramid by Richard A. Proctor' [review], *Academy*, Vol. 22, No. 555 (23 December 1882), pp. 443–44.

1883

'Literary Identity' [letter], *Academy*, Vol. 21, No. 510 (11 February 1883), p. 103.

'The Progress of Discovery in Egypt', *Academy*, Vol. 23, No. 567 (17 February 1883), pp. 198–99.

'Vandalism at Bologna [letter]', *Academy*, Vol. 23, No. 563 (17 February 1883), p. 122.

'Perrot and Chippiez's "History of Art in Ancient Egypt" in original and translation by Walter Armstrong' [review], *Academy*, Vol. 23, No. 567 (17 February 1883), pp. 107–8.

'Canopic vases of Nesikhonsu', *The Times* (27 February 1883).

'Notes from Upper Egypt', *Academy*, Vol. 23, No. 568 (24 March 1883), p. 210.

'Egypt and Egyptology' [reviews], *Academy*, Vol. 23, No. 569 (31 March 1883), pp. 218–19.

'The Ark' [letter], *Academy*, Vol. 23, No. 570 (7 April 1883), pp. 241–42.

'Pleyte's Supplementary Chapters to "The Book of the Dead", "Chapîtres supplémentaires du Livre des Morts: traduction et commentaire", par W. Pleyte' [review], *Academy*, Vol. 23, No. 581 (23 June 1883), pp. 440–42.

'Egyptological Jottings', *Academy*, Vol. 24, No. 585 (21 July 1883), p. 51.

'Ancient Egyptian Art', *The Portfolio* (July–September 1883), parts 1–3, pp. 130–37, 153–58, 175–83.

'Art Books' [reviews], *Academy*, Vol. 24, No. 587 (4 August 1883), p. 845.

'La Palestine' [review], *Academy*, Vol. 24, No. 595 (29 September 1883), pp. 218–19.

'The Pyramids and Temples of Gizeh', *Academy*, Vol. 24, No. 601 (10 November 1883), p. 308.

'"Herodotus I–III: the Ancient empires of the East, with notes, introduction and appendices", by A.H. Sayce (Macmillan)' [review], *Academy*, Vol. 24, No. 602 (17 January 1883), pp. 323–24.

'Egyptian Jottings', *Academy*, Vol. 24, No. 605 (8 December 1883), pp. 387–88.

'Miss Marianne North', *The Queen* (15 December 1883), pp. 603–4.

'Twice Saved: a story of today', *Illustrated London News* (Christmas Number 1883), pp. 19–26.

1884

'On the dispersion of Egyptian antiquities' [paper read at the International Congress of Orientalists, Leiden, 1884]; offprint from *Travaux de la 6e section du Congrès International des Orientalistes* (Leiden: CIO, 1884).

'On a fragment of a mummy case containing part of a royal cartouche' [paper read at the International Congress of Orientalists, Leiden, 1884]; offprint from *Travaux de la 6e section du Congrès International des Orientalistes* (Leiden: CIO, 1884).

'Egypt after the War' [review], *Academy*, Vol. 5, No. 609 (5 January 1884), pp. 2–3.

'Professor Maspero's New Catalogue of the Bulaq Museum', *The Times* (11, 22 January 1884).

'Maspero's Handbook to the Boolak Museum' [review], *Academy*, Vol. 25, No. 610 (12 January 1884), pp. 33–34.

'On the late Mr Thomas Pease's support for the Egypt Exploration Fund', *Western Daily Press* (25 January 1884).

'A Theban Tomb of the Eleventh Dynasty', *Academy*, Vol. 25, No. 612 (26 January 1884), p. 612.

'Some Books on Egypt and Egyptology' [review], *Academy*, Vol. 25, No. 615 (16 February 1884), pp. 107–8.

'The destruction and preservation of Egyptian monuments', *Academy*, Vol. 25, No. 616 (23 February 1884), p. 139.

'"An Essay on Scarabs", by W.J. Loftie' [review], *Academy*, Vol. 25, No. 620 (2 March 1884), pp. 209–10.

'English Excavations at San', *The Times* (7 March 1884), p. 4.

'English Excavations at San (Zoan)', *The Times* (22 April 1884), p. 4.

'Egyptian Exploration Fund. Discovery of the Necropolis of Tanis', *Academy*, Vol. 25, No. 626 (3 May 1884), pp. 320–21.

'English Excavations at San (Tanis-Zoan)', *The Times* (30 May 1884), p. 10.

'Egypt Exploration Fund. A Colossus of Colossi', *Academy*, Vol. 25, No. 630 (31 May 1884), p. 392.

'Egypt Exploration Fund. Excavations at San', *Academy*, Vol. 25, No. 633 (21 June 1884), p. 446.

'Egypt Exploration Fund. Excavations at San (Tanis)', *Academy*, Vol. 26, No. 638 (26 July 1884), pp. 66–67.

'In Memoriam: Sir Erasmus Wilson', *Academy*, Vol. 26, No. 641 (16 August 1884), pp. 108–9.

'Some Books on Egyptology' [review], *Academy*, Vol. 26, No. 648 (27 September 1884), pp. 206–8.

'The Fellah and the Workman in the Time of the Pharaohs', *The Times* (9 October 1884), p. 3.

'Professor Maspero's forthcoming works', *Academy*, Vol. 26, No. 650 (18 October 1884), pp. 259–60.

'"The Rubá'iyát of 'Omar Khayyám", rendered into English verse by Edward Fitzgerald, with an accompaniment of drawings by Elihu Vedder (Boston, MA: Houghton Mifflin & Co; London: Quaritch), Second Notice' [review], *Academy*, Vol. 26, No. 658 (13 December 1884), p. 399.

1885

'English Exploration in the Delta', *The Times* (3 January 1885).

'Review of "Travels in the East" by Crown Prince Rudolf', *Academy*, Vol. 27, No. 662 (10 January 1885), p. 222.

'Naville's Critical Edition of the Book of the Dead', *Academy*, Vol. 27, No. 667 (14 February 1885), p. 122.

'Maspero at Luxor', *Academy*, Vol. 27, No. 672 (21 March 1885), pp. 212–13.

'Some minor books about Egypt' [reviews], *Academy*, Vol. 27, No. 675 (11 April 1885), pp. 264–65.

'"Life and reminiscences of Gustave Doré", by Blanche Roosevelt (Sampson Low)' [review], *Academy*, Vol. 28, No. 690 (25 July 1885), pp. 64–65.

'Maspero in Egypt', *The Times* (27 July 1885), pp. 3–4.

'Cradle of Hellenic art at Naucratis', *The Times* (5 August 1885), p. 13.

'Some minor Egyptological literature', *Academy*, Vol. 28, No. 699 (26 September 1885), pp. 209–11.

'The Terracottas of Naukratis (First Notice)', *Academy*, Vol. 28, No. 702 (17 October 1885), pp. 261–62.

'The Terracottas of Naukratis (Second Notice)', *Academy*, Vol. 28, No. 703 (24 October 1885), pp. 278–79.

'"Revue égyptologique, 2e année, 1881–2, 3e année, 1883–4–5" (Paris: Leroux)' [review], *Academy*, Vol. 28, No. 709 (5 December 1885), pp. 381–82.

1886

'Egyptological Jottings', *Academy*, Vol. 29, No. 719 (13 February 1886), pp. 381–82.

'"The Literature of Egypt and the Sudan", by Prince Ibrahim-Hilmy, Vol. 1 (Trübner)', *Academy*, Vol. 29, No. 720 (20 February 1886) pp. 126–27.

'English Exploration in Egypt: Tanis and Naucratis', *The Times* (26 February 1886), p. 3.

'Pharaoh's House in Tahpanhes', *The Times* (18 June 1886), p. 13.

'The Remains at Tiryns', *The Times* (3 July 1886), p. 12.

'"Egypt and Syria", by Sir J.W. Dawson' [review], *Academy*, Vol. 30, No. 749 (11 September 1886), pp. 161–62.

'The Story of Tanis', *Harper's New Monthly Magazine*, Vol. 73, No. 437 (October 1886), pp. 711–38.

'Maspero's forthcoming work on Egyptian Archaeology', *Academy*, Vol. 30, No. 757 (6 November 1886), pp. 314–15.

1887

Sir Gaston C.C. Maspero, *Egyptian archaeology, translated from the French by Amelia B. Edwards* (London: Putnam, 1887; 2nd edition, 1892).

'The Excavation of the Great Sphinx', *The Times* (7 January 1887), p. 4.

'"The Sarcophagus of Anchnesranferab", [by] E. Wallis Budge' [review], *Academy*, Vol. 31, No. 771 (12 February 1887), pp. 117–18.

'The City of Onia and "The Mound of the Jews"', *The Times* (20 April 1887), p. 15.

'Professor Maspero's lectures at the Collège de France', *Academy*, Vol. 31, No. 784 (14 May 1887), p. 350.

'Ancient Royal Egyptian Relics at the Manchester Exhibition', *The Times* (21 June 1887), p. 3.

'Egypt Exploration Fund. Discovery of the Great Temple of Bubastis (from a correspondent)', *The Times* (1 July 1887), p. 3.

'"Court Life in Egypt", by Alfred J. Butler (Chapman & Hall)' [review], *Academy*, Vol. 31, No. 784 (14 May 1887), p. 350.

'Egypt Exploration Fund. Exhibition of minor antiquities at Oxford mansions', *The Times* (8 August 1887), p. 14.

'"Abraham, Joseph and Moses in Egypt", by the Rev. A.H. Kellogg (Randolph; Trübner)' [review], *Academy*, Vol. 32, No. 798 (20 August 1887), pp. 124–25.

'The Egyptian Hell', *The Times* (22 August 1887), p. 13.

'Naville's edition of the Book of the Dead: "Das Aegyptische Todtenbuch der XVIII.bis XX. Dynastie, von Edouard Naville" (Berlin: Asher)' [review], *Academy*, Vol. 32, No. 801 (8 October 1887), pp. 170–72.

'English Excavations in Egypt: the season's work in the Delta', *Illustrated London News* (17 September 1887), pp. 355–58.

'English Excavations in Egypt: the season's work in the Delta', reprinted in *The Great Archaeologists, edited by Edward Bacon* (London: Secker & Warburg, 1976), pp. 104–7.

Egyptian Archaeology, by G. Maspero, translated from the French by Amelia B. Edwards (London: H. Grevel, 1887; 2nd edition, revised, 1889; new edition 1893).

1888

'Explorations in the Fayum (From a correspondent)', *The Times* (4 February 1888), p. 6.

'To his Love (who is younger than he)' [poem], *Academy*, Vol. 33, No. 824 (18 February 1888), p. 115.

'The Egypt Exploration Fund. M. Naville's discoveries at Bubastis', *The Times* (6 April 1888), p. 4.

'Maspero on the Egyptian Hierarchy' [review], *Academy*, Vol. 33, No. 833 (21 April 1888), pp. 280–81.

'"A season in Egypt – 1887", by W.M. Flinders Petrie (Field & Tuer)' [review], *Academy*, Vol. 33, No. 835 (5 May 1888), pp. 312–14.

'Mr Petrie's Excavations in the Fayum (From a correspondent)', *The Times* (9 June 1888), p. 7.

'"The Literature of Egypt and the Sudan, Vol. II, M–Z, with appendix of additional works to May 1887", by H.H. Prince Ibrahim-Hilmy (Trübner)' [review], *Academy*, Vol. 34, No. 853 (8 September 1888), pp. 146–47.

'"Leaves from an Egyptian Note-book", by Isaac Taylor (Kegan Paul, Trench, & Co.)' [review], *Academy*, Vol. 34, No. 865 (1 December 1888), pp. 346–48.

'On the dispersion of antiquities in connection with certain recent discoveries of ancient cemeteries in Upper Egypt' [paper read at the International Congress of Orientalists, Vienna, 1888]; offprint from *Verhandlungen des VII Internationalen Orientalisten Congress, Ägypt–Africanische Section*, 1888 (Vienna: ICO, 1888).

'Provincial and Private Collections of Egyptian Antiquities in Great Britain', *Receuil des Travaux de la 6e Congrès International des Orientalistes Vienna 1888*,Vol. 10 (1888) pp. 121–33.

The Sir Francis Drake Mazurka for the Piano forte (London: Weekes [1888]).

1889

'The Nature of the Egyptian "Ka"', *Academy*, Vol. 35, No. 870 (5 January 1889), pp. 12–14.

'Mr Petrie in the Fayum. Clearance of the Pyramid of Amenemhat III (From a correspondent)', *The Times* (9 March 1889), p. 4.

'President Barnard' [obituary], *Academy*, Vol. 35, No. 889 (3 May 1889), p. 341.

'The Royal Mummies of Deir-el-Bahari', *Academy*, Vol. 35, No. 891 (1 June 1889), pp. 383–84.

'Mr Petrie in the Fayum', *The Times* (20 July 1889), p. 6.

'"Hawara, Bishmu and Arsinoe. With thirty plates. By W.M. Flinders Petrie" (Field & Tuer)' [review], *Academy*, Vol. 36, No. 902 (17 August 1889), pp. 108–9.

'Mr Petrie's Egyptian Antiquities at Oxford Mansion', *The Times* (16 September 1889), p. 13.

1890

'Recent Discoveries in Egypt', *Bulletin of the American Geographical Society*, Vol. 22, No. 4 (1890) pp. 555–65.

['The *Antigone* at Bradfield'], *Academy*, Vol. 38, No. 948 (5 July 1890), pp. 17–18.

'"Historical scarabs: a series of drawings from the principal collections. By W.M. Flinders Petrie" (David Nutt)' [review], *Academy*, Vol. 38, No. 950 (19 July 1890), pp. 54–56.

'Ancient Egypt at Oxford Mansion', *The Times* (15 September 1890), p. 3.

'Grébaut's forthcoming work on the National Egyptian Museum. "Le Musée égyptien: recueil de monuments choisis et de notices sur les Fouilles en Egypte … (Cairo)"' [review], *Academy*, Vol. 38, No. 960 (27 September 1890), pp. 277–78.

'"Kahun, Gurob and Hawara. By W.M. Flinders Petrie. With chapters by F. Ll. Griffith and Percy Gardner" (Kegan Paul & Co.)' [review], *Academy*, Vol. 38, No. 965 (1 November 1890), pp. 397–98.

'Historical Sketches of Ancient Egypt and Assyria: "Lectures historiques: Egypte, Assyrie. Par G. Maspéro" (Hachette)' [review], *Academy*, Vol. 38, No. 969 (29 November 1890), pp. 510–11.

'Recent Discoveries in Egypt', *Bulletin of the American Geographical Society* (New York, AGS, 1890), pp. 1–13.

1891

Pharaohs, Fellahs and Explorers (London: Osgood, McIlvaine, 1891).

Pharaohs, Fellahs and Explorers (New York: Harper, 1891, reprinted 1892, 1893).

Pharaohs, Fellahs and Explorers (London: Kegan Paul, 2003).

'The Great discovery of Amenide Mummies at Thebes (From an occasional correspondent)', *The Times* (2 March 1891), p. 13.

'The recent Discovery at Thebes. (M. Grébaut's report)', *The Times*, (6 March 1891), p. 13.

'My Home Life', *Arena*, Vol. 4 (4 August 1891), pp. 299–310.

'Egyptological Jottings', *Academy*, Vol. 40, No. 1025 (26 December 1891), p. 594.

'"Illahun, Kahun and Gurob. By W.M. Flinders Petrie ..." (David Nutt)' [review], *Academy*, Vol. 40, No. 1023 (12 December 1891), pp. 541–43.

1892

'With a Scarab to a Friend' [poem], *Academy*, Vol. 42, No. 1057 (6 August 1892), pp. 110–11.

1893

'The Story of a Clock' [original publication not traced, c.1843]

'The Story of a Clock', reprinted by Matilda Betham–Edwards in *New England Magazine* (January 1893), pp. 564–65.

Sir Erasmus Wilson, *Egypt of the Past*, 2nd edition, revised by Amelia B. Edwards (London: Harrison & Sons, 1893).

1894

'The Art of the Novelist', *Contemporary Review*, Vol. 66, No. 3440 (August 1894), pp. 225–42.

2005

'The Social and Political Position of Women in Ancient Egypt', [edited with] introduction by Patricia O'Neill, PMLA (New York: Modern Language Association of America) Vol. 120, No. 3 (May 2005), pp. 843–57.

❖ Appendix 3 ❖

The art of the novelist: Amelia Edwards' fiction

As we have seen, it was early on in her life that Amelia Edwards began to demonstrate a gift for both writing and sketching, pleasures which she was to enjoy throughout her life.

Most of the novels have been long out of print,[1] and are not easily obtainable, so a summary of the plot is given below in each case. We start, however, with her juvenile work, the cartoons that she drew to entertain family and friends while she still only a child, and then move on to her earliest novels, before summarising the more major works of fiction that she produced at intervals during her lifetime.

The early works, 1845–55

Patrick Murphy (cartoon, 1845)

This tells the story of Patrick Murphy, an Irish country lad who is 'going to Dublin, Father, to sake [sic] my fortune and be a great man. I'll come back a gentleman with lashins [sic] of gold and make you rich.' After an evening drinking with two well-dressed youths they fall into a stupor and Pat steals their fine clothes and their money, escapes through a window, evades a night watchman, and hitches a lift in a drey: 'I'm of your party (I don't know what that is)', he says; 'Are you? very well! Get up, sir.' 'Vote for O'Gallagher! Of course I do, give me some of your ribbons', and with that he becomes involved in an imminent election and attends an election ball, where he is much attracted to a certain Lady Emily Stanhope. He fights a duel for her, wounding his adversary in the little finger, and saves her from robbers. She introduces him to her maiden aunt, Mrs Margery Spindleshanks, and the three embark for England. A gale blows up, and 'my aunt' (the possessive appears by mistake in two of the captions) 'faints into the arms of – an arm chair'. The ship sinks and they take to the boats, are rescued and brought to London. There they stay at the Clarendon Hotel, and Lady Emily proposes that they go to the Opera. A certain Count Polianski calls on Lady Emily, 'takes a great fancy to our hero' and offers to take him to court. There follows presentation to the Queen. The next day Patrick rides in the park, stops a bolting horse and saves the life of the rider, Mr

Merriman Yardcloth, who in return, learning that Pat has by now reached a state of near penury, signs a deed allowing him £500 a year. 'He [Patrick] tells Lady Emily of his altered circumstances, makes a passionate avowal of his love, and is accepted.' They visit her town mansion, where 'Murphy is delighted with all he sees and is particularly pleased with a picture of Boadicea and her army'. He chances to see the two men from whom he stole money and clothes in Dublin entering a Regent Street hotel, and sends them the sums which he had taken 'and 50 pounds surplus'. Preparations are made for the wedding of Pat and Lady Emily, and Mr Merriman Yardcloth gives them a carriage and pair as a wedding present, at which Pat responds: 'Sir, your present has been my bride, my fortune, my life's happiness.' After the wedding 'it is Mr Murphy's intention to visit his poor old father in Ireland'. They reach his father's village on the day of his sister's wedding and a dance is in progress. 'When they look in at the doors a merry scene meets their eyes, which reminds our hero of his former life … Murphy and his bride dance a jig with the bride and bridegroom and all the peasants.' Murphy is reunited with his parents and takes them to see an ornate country cottage. 'My father, this Rural retreat has been built on purpose for you; take it my dear parents, and I trust you'l [sic] pass many many years of happiness within its walls.' The next and last cartoon has the caption: '6 years have elapsed – Reader behold, *Poor* Pat Murphy surrounded by his darling children,

Fig. 33: Pen and ink drawing by Amelia Edwards from Patrick Murphy, *1845.*

happy in his beloved wife, with his aged parents always with him. A type of the good which attends perseverance, an honour to the far-famed wit of Old Ireland!'

The Travelling Adventures of Mrs Roliston (*cartoon, 1848*)

A robust middle-aged lady, Mrs Roliston, determines 'to see life by going to sea. And makes up her mind to travel.' At Dover she purchases one of the cannons from the Castle, thinking 'that fire-arms would be a protection. She has a difficulty in carrying it to the wharf. But is assisted by a benevolent public.' She sails to Amsterdam, then travels by train to Danzig and Moscow. She 'is horrified at the ghastly appearances by the wayside on the road to Moscow' according to a caption accompanying a picture of her carriage crossing a field of skulls, skeletons and corpses being attacked by carrion. The following page illustrates further gruesome scenes: 'One of the horses freezes. The other does the same. The coachman also. Mrs R. is in despair. She does not even find consolation in her travelling stores.' Here she is clutching a bottle. She is rescued by a Russian gentleman in a sleigh and reaches Moscow, then St Petersburgh, where she is invited by the Emperor Nicholas to a ball. He pays her particular attention and entertains her by 'chopping off the head of a political writer to show Mrs R. the national amusements'. She travels to Stockholm where she is invited to the opera by Jenny Lind.

Fig. 34: Mrs Roliston sets out on her travels, pen and ink drawing by Amelia Edwards, from The Travelling Adventures of Mrs Roliston, *1848.*

Fig. 35: Mrs Roliston arrives in Moscow.

Fig. 36: 'General Summary', in picture language, of The Travelling Adventures of Mrs Roliston, *1848; pen and ink drawing by Amelia Edwards.*

From Sweden she sails to Iceland, surviving shipwreck on the back of a whale, and eventually reaching the North Pole, from the top of which she has a view embracing a quarter of the globe. She sails for London, where she is met by the major political figures of the day, by Prince Albert and the military, and by 'a Committee of Gentlemen at the Clarendon who arrange with [her] the procession to … the Semi-

Detached!!!' A French army invades this desirable residence in Peckham, and 'Mrs R. hoists the British flag as a symbol of distress!!!' Might conquers right, and 'the Semi' falls to the enemy, but the colonel is overcome by Mrs R. and offers her his hand and heart, 'and his share of England when it is taken'. He is '*Accepted* and all parties are made happy' in the last of thirty-eight cartoons.

Annette *(1853)*

Annette[2] was, as far as is known, the first tale which Amelia had attempted since *Mrs Roliston*, in 1848. It is a slight tale, but the style of her novels is already apparent. The story is prefaced by a quotation from Hood: 'Evil is wrought by want of thought, As well as want of heart', establishing at the outset a moral tone perhaps to give validity to the story. The action takes place in Paris and London, with evocative descriptions of the byways and boulevards of Paris, drawn no doubt from her diary of her five-week visit there. Annette is the daughter of a humble family. They run a laundry service in a building in which a sculptor, Hippolyte, also has a studio. Her doting sister and aged father wait for her to return home from a business errand. She returns late, acknowledging that she has been amusing herself with friends. 'Oh dearest', her sister mildly chides, 'was it the Englishman – the false Englishman?' It was indeed, Sir Henry Sutton, Earl of Thornbury, with whom she subsequently runs away to England, leaving her father distraught and perplexed. Some years later Hippolyte, visiting England for the Great Exhibition where some of his work is on display, receives a commission from the Earl to take the bust of a 'lady… a – a near relative. His lordship blushed and faltered, like a man who is speaking an untruth against his inclination.' Hippolyte, waiting in the Earl's luxurious residence to begin his commission, sees the lady, and recognises her as Annette. 'Every feature, taken separately, is Annette's, but the expression of the whole is utterly unlike her: Madame St Victor is dignified, haughty, pale and indifferent. Annette was lively, cordial, rosy and enthusiastic.' Hippolyte makes himself known, and reminds her of her father and sister in Paris. Though feigning indifference she is touched and, already ill, makes the journey to to see them, but is overcome by exhaustion. She lies dying by the time the Earl arrives from London crying 'It is I – it is Henry, come to make you my loved and honoured wife. It is Henry, who cannot live without you! Live, dearest, live for me!' But his repentance, and hers, have come too late: Annette is dead.

The story has the melodrama typical of Amelia's writing. Annette is somewhat less vividly drawn than is her indulgent elder sister. The scene in which Hippolyte makes himself known and reminds her of her family is such as can be imagined on the stage. Amelia's sense of the dramatic both there and in the final scene is evident. Her familiarity with art and artists, and her recent discovery of Paris, are used to good effect.

Sights and Stories *(1855, imprint 1862)*

Sights and Stories is written for the most part in conversational style. It opens with a dialogue between two boys, but its tone is unmistakably didactic. The history and legends which form the greater part of the book are set in the framework of a walking tour undertaken by five boys 'with the permission of their parents under the care and guidance of … the head usher of their school'. Their characters are differentiated from his by their language. Interspersed with the description of their travels are snatches of dialogue which reveal Amelia's attitudes and opinions:

> 'These monks and nuns have done a great deal of good in their time, sir, have they not?'
> 'Whatever may be the religious errors of the Roman Catholic Church', replied Mr Butler, 'we are unquestionably indebted to its institutions for many of our greatest intellectual advantages.'

Slight though the work is, it is of interest as Amelia's first book of travel, combining scenic description, historical fact, fiction, and the reactions of observers, a mixture which was to become typical of her travel writing.

The Young Marquis, or scenes from a reign *[1857]*

This book bears no date, but the British Museum Library received its copy on 26 March 1857. It was well produced, with illustrations by Birket Foster and Edmund Evans, two of the leading illustrators of the time. The story is of two boys in Paris at the time of the French Revolution. They are awakened one night to the sound of a crowd with flaming torches chanting:

> Crowns and thrones are useless things
> The people are the only kings.

The boys' father, the Marquis of St Valéry, and the elder boy, Charles, attempt to help the King and the Dauphin escape, but are betrayed by the Marquis's valet. In an interesting scene his treachery is likened to that of Judas: 'The marquis turned, and looked him earnestly in the face.' The Marquis is arrested, and the Marchioness waits anxiously at home with her children. To keep them amused she tells them a story of 'Fritz of the Forest: a tale of Odinwald', in which a boy seeks his father, a woodcutter, and finds that he is dead. She is arrested, and accused of bringing up her children with 'pernicious opinions', and Charles is questioned. They are cast into prison, but helped to escape, and are reunited in a farmhouse with – the Marquis, who has also escaped, and is recovering from an injury there. He has lost all but 'his happy conscience, his friend, his life and his family. But he was wise enough to be content with these blessings.'

The story is packed with adventure and mystery, and the virtues of courage and faithfulness to one's parents are duly extolled in a convincing way. Amelia uses her knowledge of the area in vivid pictures of Paris and the escape route. The story of the wood-cutter is not germane to the main plot and detracts from the flow of the story. The second boy, Gabrielle, disappears from the story after the first scene and the frontispiece, and it is puzzling to know why he was included.

The later works (1855–80)

It is interesting to note that although twenty-five years elapsed between the first and last novels, they all have much in common: a complex plot, often with several distinct groups of players impinging on each other, as in a Shakespearean play; seemingly trivial incidents proving in the end to be significant in the development of the plot, resolving the element of mystery which is present in all her novels; action spread over wide areas, over western Europe and the New World, giving ample scope for her skill in conveying visual experiences in words, be they images of rural landscape or of urban scenes; characters depicted with keen perception and often with humour, though rarely with a depth of sensitivity to move the reader to tears at their circumstances. There is melodrama and excitement, but Amelia seldom induces in the reader any sense of deep involvement in the fortunes and misfortunes that befall her characters: she always seems to be viewing them from a distance, as if she were writing of people who are little more than acquaintances, even when she is writing in the first person.

Amelia herself, however, claimed to be deeply involved in, or rather possessed by, her characters: 'The novelist is each character in turn', she writes to Richard Bowker,

and has all the consciousness of being good and wicked, young
and old, man and woman in turn. This is what is so tiring. I am
quite exhausted by the time I get to the end of a long story, and
need what I never need after other literary work – a complete rest.[3]

She made it clear that she very rarely depicted persons whom she knew:

> no matter how distantly ... Yet, in a way, I draw characters from
> life. I find that I can work better from glimpses of people than from
> intimate studies. The people I meet when travelling, on the deck of
> a steamer, at a *table d'hôte*, and so on, suggest better characters to
> me than those whom I meet frequently, or know well ... I make the
> acquaintance of my characters as I go on ... it does not seem to me
> for a moment that I am inventing them ... The characters literally
> do as they please, marry whom they please, and have their own
> way entirely ... I overhear the conversation of the characters, and
> write it down ... The people have their special and separate voices,
> which I hear ... If a character makes a smart repartee, I am as much
> taken by surprise as if I heard it as a dinner party.

One of the talks which Amelia included in her repertoire during her
lecture tour of America in 1889–90, was on 'The Art of the Novelist'. It
was not printed with the other lectures in *Pharaohs, Fellahs and Explorers*[4]
but it was published posthumously in *The Contemporary Review*.[5] She
there answers the question of how she invents the plot:

> It seems to me that I do not invent the plot. The plot comes of itself.
> It flashes upon me suddenly, unexpectedly, when I am walking,
> perhaps, or actively employed. Sometimes it but half reveals itself.
> That is to say, it lacks some essential motive. In this case it is useless
> to puzzle over it. I let it alone, and by and by, in the course of a few
> hours, or a few days, the solution flashes upon me in the same
> unexpected way.

The passage of time may have embroidered on memory, however, for
she wrote this over ten years after publishing her last novel.

My Brother's Wife (1855)
Amelia was later to dismiss *My Brother's Wife*, along with *The Ladder of
Life* and *Hand and Glove* as 'three juvenile efforts',[6] but she was happy
enough with her first success at the age of twenty-four. *My Brother's Wife*

is written in the person of Paul Latour, a studious Burgundian youth. His clever but indolent brother, Theophile, leaves home before he is twenty, but returns from the 'brilliant dissipations of Parisian life' to meet their orphaned cousin, Adrienne, who is visiting. Both brothers fall in love with her, but it is Theophile who wins her hand, and Paul leaves their Burgundian chateau in a black mood of melancholy gloom. He travels to Heidelberg, where he meets a young Englishman, Norman Seabrook. During their travels in the Rhineland they meet the *prima donna* Madame Therese Vogelsang, and later an eccentric musician named Fletcher, a gambler and an opium addict, who on his deathbed asks Paul to care for his daughter Margaret, a music teacher at a school in Brussels. Paul takes rooms in Brussels, and feels a growing affection for Margaret. Theophile and Adrienne arrive, and Paul is horrified to learn that his brother is now enamoured of Therese Vogelsang, and they run away together. Madame Vogelsang's lover, Alphonse Lemaitre, pursues them and murders Theophile. Paul discovers the body in a wood, alerts the police, and Alphonse is sentenced to death. Madame Vogelsang disappears, and her husband, bent on retribution but incurably ill, commends his young sister in Brussels to Paul. She turns out to be none other than Margaret, whom Paul takes home to his mother, together with the widowed Adrienne. His friend, Norman Seabrook, joins them, and wins Adrienne's hand, while Paul marries Margaret. Therese Vogelsang is reduced to singing ballads in the street, and finally throws herself into the Thames at London Bridge.

For all the improbability of the plot, there is much in the novel to hold the interest of the reader. Amelia excels at describing scenes which she could expect would be new and strange to many of her readers, and draws such scenes into the story even when not germane to the plot, as for example the visit to the Kursaal at Ems: 'All looked serious and interested; but there were none of those violent emotions of which we read in books … They won and lost with the utmost composure.' She adds, with a clever irony, 'It is only in novels that ruined gamblers rush wildly from tables, with distraction in their faces. Here a man will lose his last florin with a smile that looks, at least, sufficiently natural.'[7] Far more serious is her description of the Paris morgue to which the search for Theophile and Therese leads Paul:

> There was a crowd of ouvriers, soldiers, women, and children gathered round the entrance … A fearful place indeed! There on a black marble slab, exposed to the idle gaze of every eye, lay the body of a young, fair boy, a mere child. His long bright hair fell in wet masses on the stone couch; his eyes and mouth were closed …

'Suicide!' murmured the people at the grating. 'Suicide!' I turned
to a soldier standing by the door. 'Is it possible that this child can
have purposely destroyed himself?' 'We cannot tell, monsieur; but
it is most likely. They often do.'[8]

There are numerous 'thumbnail' sketches of people who appear only
briefly as part of the passing scene, such as the 'tall lady with a long
waist, and long neck, and a long nose' who arrived at a soirée in the
house of Theophile and Adrienne, looking 'like a stork with a turban
on'.

'What a terrible woman!' I exclaimed, when we were out of
hearing. 'Terrible species, but common' replied Seabrook,
laconically. '*Order*: Aristocratic; *Generic character*: Detestable;
Locality: Unexceptionable; *Habits*: Gregarious; *Family*: the Bores.' 'I
am glad, at all events,' I said, laughing, 'to find that the species is
not dangerous.' 'Not dangerous? On the contrary, it belongs to a
genus of the most unparalleled ferocity, especially when providing
for its young. The *heir*, indeed, is its natural prey.'[9]

Such sketches are amusing but superficial; even the main characters are
not portrayed in depth: the interest lies in what befalls them.

In this first novel, however, it is interesting to note a feature which
was to recur in all Amelia's fiction: a fascination with books and
literature and an admiration for the studious nature. Paul

made the early Romance languages my study ... I studied all the
varieties of the Provencal dialect ... the strange, fantastic mysteries
and miracle plays which preceded the drama throughout Europe
... Legends, serventes, canzones or black-letter pamphlets were
my recreation and delight.[10]

The first insight into Adrienne's taste comes in a long conversation with
Paul on modern Italian literature.[11] Of a later novel the *Sunday Times*
reviewer wrote of Amelia: 'Perhaps she may be a little pedantic or ostentatious in the display of her erudition',[12] but it is questionable whether
she introduced such passages out of ostentation: she was more probably
reproducing the topics of conversation which she had herself shared
with companions during her travels. As Joan Rees comments, the book
'reflects its author as ... a young woman eager for adventure and drama
in her life and filled also with excitement at the intellectual and cultural
pastures open to her to explore.'[13]

The Ladder of Life *(1856)*

The Ladder of Life[14] appeared within two years, in December 1856. Again the novel is set on the continent, but this time told in the person of a young woman, Natalie Metz, orphaned at the age of eleven, growing up in Switzerland, where she is cared for by her teacher, Madame de Wahl, whom she adores. Her playmates are the son, Louis de Wahl, and Laurent, nephew of a local toy-maker who was once in love with her mother. Louis goes off to university in Heidelberg, and Laurent to Lyons to seek employment as a wood-carver. Laurent departs, declaring that she is as far above him 'as the bright stars of heaven', leaving with her a carving, his best work, as a parting gift; Louis returns from university to find her a woman, and declares his love, but his mother is distressed at the prospect of what she sees as an 'unequal relationship' and urges Natalie to go abroad, out of his way.

There follows an adventurous journey to England, during which she is robbed by a Mrs Jones, in whose company she was travelling, of all but the wood carving given her by Laurent. She is eventually rescued by a Swiss musician and composer, Mr Vaughan, who lives with his infant daughter, Alice, and she earns her keep by helping him catalogue his music and by teaching Alice. Finding that she has a fine voice, he offers to train her, and she is engaged as a soprano at Drury Lane. There she receives the unwanted attentions of a violinist, Silvio Romani, who has strange beliefs on 'pre-existence, double-being, predestination and the like.' Mr Vaughan's fortunes improve when his opera is accepted and in the unexpected absence of the prima donna, Madame Malibran, Natalie plays the leading role to a rapturous house – but is dismayed to see in the audience the face of Mrs Jones.

Then come worrying times for Natalie, with fears of a stalker, a robbery at the house, and the importunity of Signore Romani. She resigns her position and escapes to a seaside cottage with Mr Vaughan and Alice. There they live an idyllic existence, and make friends with a neighbour and her delicate daughter, Constance. When their neighbour's friend the Baron von Oetiker, a well-known sculptor, arrives, Natalie immediately recognises him as Laurent. She does not disclose her identity at once, believing Constance is in love with him, but Laurent recognises her and declares his love. Natalie hesitates, however, out of concern for Constance who is growing weaker; when the dying girl's aunt and cousin come to visit, they prove to be none other than Madame de Wahl and Louis. Anxious and sleepless, Natalie is walking alone on the beach one night when she stumbles on smugglers whom she recognises as Silvio Romani and his accomplice, Mrs Jones. As Silvio carries her off to his boat, Louis arrives and shoots him. Mrs Jones is sentenced to transportation. The book ends with the death of Constance and the betrothal of Laurent and Natalie.

The Ladder of Life is yet more melodramatic and improbable than *My Brother's Wife*, but Amelia was drawing for many of the scenes on her own experience, for example, of her own early success as a singer, and her own travels in Europe. There is nothing remarkable about the main characters, but there are numerous instances of felicitous descriptions of behaviour which reveal Amelia as an acute observer of human nature as well as of landscape and of art. Such is the description of Alice, the 'baby housekeeper', setting the table and

> supping bread by the fireside … while the cat (with its forepaws resting on her knees) watched the spoon as it travelled backwards and forwards between the cup and her rosy little mouth. Now and then he would utter a plaintive little remonstrance, and this never failed to bring him a morsel. Sometimes he would put up one paw and try to arrest the hand that held the spoon, which act of undecorous greediness was sure to be reproved.[15]

Sometimes humour replaces sentiment, as in the description of the mean Mrs Wigglesworth who 'wore a light front of exceedingly loose disposition' and explained to Natalie:

> We generally buy our own provisions when we are travelling … Bye the bye, have you any soap with you? My dear young lady, if you only touch their soap at these hotels, they make you pay for the entire cake! We always carry our own soap when we are travelling.

Before leaving each hotel, she

> replenishes her ink-bottle, wafer-box and paper-case at the expense of her host; she likewise 'gets up' pocket handkerchiefs, false collars, and other trifles in the seclusion of her own chamber and hangs them out to dry on fine nights from the bedroom window.[16]

Amelia is able to convey a significant message in a few oblique words; thus Laurent's gallantry and at the same time his modesty when he appears as Baron von Oetiker is learnt from 'a fragment of scarlet ribbon at his buttonhole … where his decoration would be worn.' The personalities of Amelia's characters are revealed not so much by their actions or by their emotions as by their thinking; thus Silvio Romani is suspect from the start because of his strange beliefs, and Laurent, chided by

Constance for denying that man is the monarch of creation, replies: 'Nature can but own one king, her Creator … Nature is the associate, not the slave of man, and man is the reasonable and labouring dweller in nature.' Amelia may well have been putting her own modern, scientific view into Laurent's mouth, while not rejecting an essentially theocratic outlook. Fascinated though she was by mysteries, her feet were firmly planted in mainstream tracks, and unorthodox theories were taken to indicate a suspicious if not sinister character.

Hand and Glove *(1859)*

Hand and Glove was Amelia's third novel, and the last of the three which she later dismissed as 'juvenile efforts'. The book begins with a death scene. The part of the narrator is taken by Gartha, who watches her father die in chapter one. She learns from the kindly Dr Bryant that he died a ruined man and has left her nothing. She decides to go abroad, learn a language, and take a post as a teacher, housekeeper or companion. The journey to London–Paris–Lyon is described with Amelia's familiar enthusiasm and vividness. Gartha is transported from the beleaguered station at Meersault to the home of M. and Mme Delahaye and their young daughter, Marguerite, by a gruff and uncommunicative man whom she later knows as Uncle Alexander. Marguerite has been engaged to her cousin, Charles Gautier, since she was three years of age, but his love for her is not returned. Soon after Gartha's arrival, the whole family drives into the village to hear the new Protestant minister, M. Hamel, preach his first sermon. He causes a sensation with his passionate oratory, and the congregation is divided in its reactions. Uncle Alexander thinks him a charlatan, Charles dislikes him too, but Marguerite is fascinated, soon falls in love with him, and is quick to respond to his proposal. There is gossip about him in the village, however, and people notice that he never ungloves his hand. On the eve of his wedding to Marguerite, Dr Bryant arrives from England, and recognises in M. Hamel the husband of Gartha's aunt and denounces him as the cause of her father's ruin.

M. Hamel is unmasked: he is no clergyman, but was once imprisoned in Rio de Janeiro and branded on the hand; hence the glove. Learning the truth, Marguerite collapses with 'brain-fever'. Uncle Alexander and Gartha hope to get M. Hamel out of the country, for Marguerite's sake, but they find him dead in a loft, poisoned by his own hand. Marguerite has been changed by the tragedy and begins to love Charles Gautier after all. Their betrothal is soon followed by that of Gartha and Uncle Alexander.

Hand and Glove shares with *My Brother's Wife* an atmosphere of mystery and foreboding. This mood is set at the outset, with Gartha waiting in the porch, watching the mist on the moors, afraid to go back into the house where her father lies dead. The same mood pervades the description of a visit to an ancient Roman columbarium where Marguerite puts her hand into an urn, feels the dust within, and is told by Charles that she holds in her hand 'one who was once a being like yourself'.[17] A morbid interest in domestic danger is revealed when a young boy is accidentally locked in a vault where grapes are fermenting, is overcome by the fumes, and only rescued at the eleventh hour by Uncle Alexander, at great risk to his own life.

As in the earlier novels, there are humorous sketches. The dandy M. Delahaye, 'a little withered old gentleman in a flaxen wig, a flowered dressing gown, an embroidered smoking cap and velvet slippers', rises at four-thirty to practise his singing.[18] There is some development of character in the course of the book: Marguerite is little more than a capricious child at the start, and a wiser woman at the end; her fiancé, Charles, behaves to her more as a tutor to a pupil at the start, but becomes tolerant and understanding towards her at the end. Uncle Alexander retains his gruff, unpolished habit throughout, but Gartha's attitude towards him changes: at the start she is annoyed at his pipe smoke blowing in her face; at the end she notices only his generosity, his kindness and his courage.

The most interesting character is undoubtedly M. Hamel. The contradictions in his behaviour are apparent from his very first sermon, on the text: 'I come not to bring peace but a sword'.

> It was a history of Christianity – a history of its darkest and most
> woful side, drawn by an iron hand, and delivered not only with
> the profoundest knowledge of 'effect', but at times with something
> of a splendid yet terrible irony … He spared neither side. He dealt
> by Christian and Pagan with crushing impartiality.[19]

M. Hamel concludes that Christianity 'has destroyed much, and it has reaped little … Despair, again, I say, despair.' His sermon causes consternation among his hearers. Most hail him as a genius: 'Every word *extempore* … The best thoughts in the best language!' Amelia was no doubt satirising the dramatic style of preachers of her day, but to her educated readers the language of the sermon would have been recognised as a travesty of the gospel, and would have marked him as a villain. M. Hamel's stylish and extravagant way of life, his love of the gaming tables, and not least his recommendation of George Sand's novels to the impressionable Marguerite, confirm his true nature. Amelia, who had enjoyed Sand only a year or two earlier, along with cigar-smoking and pistol-shooting, was no longer deceived by such tempting fruit. After the oratory of the sermon, 'the blessing was pronounced, but pronounced so indistinctly, that I no longer recognised the impassioned tones of the preacher'.[20] It is his insincerity which condemns him. M. Hamel is in many respects Amelia's finest villain.

Joan Rees sees *Hand and Glove* as unique among Amelia's novels in

> exploring sexual passion, and [it] even daringly hints at its existence in a young girl, but … what was acceptable for the French George Sand was not acceptable to the English audience … Melodrama was acceptable to the Victorians and Amelia was always ready to supply that; passion was not.[21]

Certainly Amelia was more concerned with the situations in which her characters became entangled than with their emotional response to them, although she was fully aware that emotions could determine situations as well as responses.

Barbara's History *(1863, imprint 1864)*
Barbara's History appeared after a gap of five years, and Amelia described it as 'a lucky novel.[22] It was indeed a successful novel, in spite of the mixed reviews. The ingredients which had proved so effective in the hands of the Brontë sisters could be used in new recipes to good effect. The storyteller is a young girl, Barbara Churchill, one of three motherless sisters, whose father has little time for them. When their rich great-aunt, Mrs Shandyshaft, invites Barbara to stay with her at Stoneycroft Hall in Suffolk, she is glad to leave home. She learns from her aunt of their absentee neighbour, Hugh Farquhar, who went off on the Grand Tour and has not returned. Her aunt disapproves of him, but Barbara imagines him a romantic hero, and when he unexpectedly returns and she meets him, she falls 'as much in love as a child of ten years old could be'.[23] She idolises him, and when he is injured by a falling picture, she attends him in his convalescence. To him she is 'a formidable little girl … and my most especial friend, nurse, playmate and companion'.[24] In spite of the difference in their ages, they have in common a love of art. When he asks her if she will be his wife in seven years' time, she agrees, not knowing whether he is in jest or earnest. He gives her a ring to wear secretly round her neck.

Shortly afterwards she has to leave her great-aunt's house and return to her father. One of her sisters has just died, and her father sends her, with her other sister, Hilda, to school at Zollenstrasse in Germany, where she excels in painting. One day her father arrives with a new wife, a woman of the world, and Hilda leaves with them for the gaiety of Paris, but Barbara remains in Germany, and wins the prize at the local art festival for the best historical painting. One of the visitors to the exhibition is none other than Hugh Farquhar, who advises her to devote herself to her art, to 'wed it; live in it; die for it'.[25] He offers to escort her to Paris for Hilda's wedding, but this is considered quite contrary to accepted convention. Nevertheless, he appears on the Rhine steamer, and after an evening of conversation about literature and travel, he suddenly clasps her in his arms and kisses her 'so wildly, so passionately, so strangely, that I could neither speak nor move, then releasing me as suddenly "Child! child!" he exclaimed, "forgive me! I am not myself tonight … I am old enough to be your father."'[26]

In Paris, Hugh is welcomed by Barbara's father and stepmother on account of his wealth and position. He makes himself agreeable, and strolling one day in the forest of Vincennes with their party, he and Barbara fall behind, and he stoops to kiss her. She rests in his arms willingly 'only for a moment, and yet in that moment the sense of the mystery grew clear to me, and life became earnest … In the morning a whole world of feeling had been revealed to me … I had passed in a few hours from childhood to womanhood.'[27] They become engaged, but the mystery about his past deepens: he loves her, but says that her love is the curse of his life. They marry, and he wants to settle in Italy for the summer, but Barbara wishes to return to England, and take her place at Broomhill. He agrees, but insists on making a preliminary visit alone. When she eventually reaches his home she is perplexed that he seems to find no pleasure there. On their first night she sees a dark shadow on the stairs, but he denies that there is anyone there. When he is showing her the treasures of his library she hears a door shut, but there is no door. He treats her to every luxury; much to Barbara's distress, the extravagance and ostentation shock her aunt when she visits Broomhill. One day Barbara accidentally discovers a false door in the library, and passing through, finds herself in a sitting room with a fire burning, and a book on the table inscribed 'Hugo à Maddalena'. Hugh tells Barbara that Maddalena was a stowaway in his boat, on whom he took pity, but later she overhears him one night addressing her as 'my wife'.

Barbara flees from the house, and travels abroad with her old nurse, Goody. She falls ill with fever, and their funds are low, but her former art teacher, Professor Metz, shows kindly concern and pays for their keep and for comforts during her illness. When she recovers he proposes to her, but she explains that she is not free to accept. She discovers that she is pregnant, and her baby gives her a new purpose in life. She earns enough to keep herself, her child and Goody by painting and copying old masters. She paints a picture of a street singer, and discovers that he is Maddalena's brother. She is overjoyed to learn from him that Maddalena could not be Hugh's wife, because she was married to another; she was his mistress, but the love was all on her side. Hugh, he says, loves Barbara, and has grown grey in the search for her. Learning that he is very ill, she returns to Broomhill and watches by his bedside. In the knowledge of her presence he recovers, while the wretched Maddalena dies on the threshold.

The survival of a draft of the plot of the novel in Amelia's diary of 1857 gives a rare opportunity to compare the first plan with the final publication of 1864. She began the draft on 5 April 1857 when she was staying in Venice, with a list of the characters which she intended, including 'Jessie (indolent… fond of novels)' and 'Myself Larine (Etty's

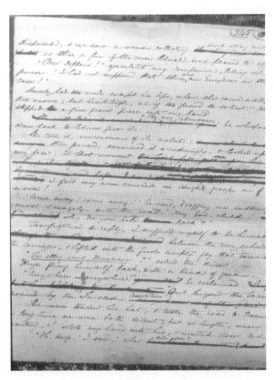

Fig. 37: A page of the manuscript of Barbara's History, *written on blue paper.*

appearance & character) … Romantic', presumably a reference to her childhood friend, Etty Du Bois.[28]

The main character, Hugh, is not yet named, but described:

> Character irresolute, amiable, affectionate, with occasional bursts of surliness. Comes either as a visitor for the shooting season or to his neighbouring estate. We love; I admire his accomplishments, taste, refined mind, etc., he seems to love me with a strange mixture of daring, hesitation & incertitude … Sometimes seems to give way to passion.[29]

He is already recognisable as the Hugh Farquhar of the published book.

The secret wife is also present in the first plan, but in her husband's Harley Street home, not in a Suffolk mansion: 'In library is a singular looking person dressed in black, worn, eager-looking, & with a strange passion in her face.'[30] In the plan she is introduced as the housekeeper, and not confined to a secret room. Amelia presumably on second thoughts considered the latter arrangement, immediately reminiscent of the secret wife in *Jane Eyre*, more plausible. In the plan, the woman begs to be called 'wife' but is refused.

In the plan Barbara flees to Rome with her boy and 'exercises her talent for art as a copyist of the old masters'. The boy is evidently not the mere baby of the book. A stranger 'takes notice of the boy when playing in the Pincio under nurse's care. Gives him presents: This happens frequently & I am curious to see the person … When at Borghese, the child runs up to the gentleman familiarly …' The gentleman is her husband's friend who tells her that her husband is 'dying & longing to see me & the child. I consent to go. Journey. Find *her* dark form outside the door. Hugh dies, and so does the strange woman. So end these two unhappy creatures.'[31] Barbara is well provided for, and her son is rich.

It is clear that Amelia changed her mind about the ending. At one stage she apparently intended both Hugh and Barbara to die. In the final version of the plan she intended Hugh and Barbara to die in the same year. In the book only Maddalena dies. Hugh Farquhar survives, like Mr Rochester in *Jane Eyre*, but unlike Mr Rochester he is not blinded; nor has he rescued his mistress from a blazing building. Hugh is not the romantic hero that Mr Rochester was; indeed Uncle Alexander in *Hand and Glove* more closely matches up to Mr Rochester. In some respects the earlier, tragic end in Amelia's plan would have been more appropriate in terms of 'poetic justice' for a character with such a chequered past as Hugh. He is by no means the perfect hero. In the early chapters he annoys Barbara in treating her as the child that she was, and years later, in the forest of

Vincennes, he is short-tempered with her: 'What can you recognise of any power of passion that is in me? You neither know how I can love nor how I can hate.'[32] Above all, he deceives her.

Joan Rees, commenting on the relationship between Hugh and the child Barbara, writes that

> No doubt his fondling and his lover-like speeches were intended to be nothing but innocent but the underlying sexuality of the relation between man and child, evident enough to modern eyes, adds to the impression of some sexual turbulence in Amelia herself during these years when she was moving from her late twenties to her early thirties.[33]

As we know from the diary, of which Joan Rees was apparently unaware, Amelia was not quite twenty-six when she planned the novel, although thirty-three when it was published. The relationship between Hugh's friend and Barbara's boy in the plan might in the same spirit also be interpreted as a sexual one, but it is more probable that it was 'intended to be nothing but innocent': Barbara is curious rather than anxious about it.

As in the earlier novels, there is satire and humour in the minor characters. Even Professor Metz makes jokes: ' 'That cherub', said he to [one of his art students] 'has the scarlet fever'... To a fourth, 'Your Madonna is a coquette.'[34] Again, there are the humorous thumbnail sketches, as of the second Mrs Churchill, who was

> what is generally called a fine woman. That is to say, she was large, well-defined, and of a comely presence ... She spoke seldom, and never unless she really had something to say. That something, if clever, was not original; and, if original, was not clever ... [She] was, beyond all doubt, well accustomed to the ways, means and appliances of that little corner of society called 'the world'.[35]

There are signs in *Barbara's History* of Amelia's concern for the position of women, and in particular, for their opportunities for employment. Barbara represents the new woman who looks for a career, if need be, instead of a marriage. As Natalie in *The Ladder of Life*, Barbara aims to earn her living: 'If you do not marry, what will become of you?', asks her father, when he visits the art school. Barbara replies:

> 'I should hope, Sir, that my profession will at all times enable me to live.' He looked fixedly at me, as if scarcely comprehending the

sense of my words. 'Your what?' he said at length, 'Your ... say that again.'

'My profession, sir,' I repeated, with a strange fluttering of my heart.

'Your profession!' he exclaimed, flushing scarlet. 'Upon my soul, I was not aware that you had one! What is it, pray? The church, the law or the army? ... I suppose that because you have been daubing here for the last few years you fancy yourself a painter? ... Do you suppose that I ... will allow my daughter to earn her bread like a dressmaker?'[36]

Half a Million of Money *(1865)*

Amelia's next novel, *Half a Million of Money*,[37] received, as has been seen, a poor press. She thought this unjust, not without reason. The story is of Saxon Trefalden, a young Swiss farmer of Cornish extraction, who by the bizarre will of his great-grandfather a hundred years earlier inherits the accumulated sum of half a million pounds. His scheming cousin, William Trefalden, a lawyer in his late thirties, travels to Switzerland to acquaint him of his good fortune. He finds Saxon to be a good sportsman, well-read and well-educated, but quite innocent in the ways of the world. He offers to take him in hand, bringing him to London and introducing him to city life. There Saxon falls in with a young man of his own age, Gervase Wynnecliffe, Lord Castletowers, and his set. News of Saxon's riches soon spreads, and he finds himself spending freely, entertaining, bestowing gifts, and setting himself up as a gentleman. He has a generous nature, and helps one of his new friends out of debt by buying his mare and cab. Gervase invites him to Castletowers, his estate in the country, and on the way he rescues a poor girl, Miss Helen Rivière, who has lost her railway ticket. His cousin William discovers that he is proposing to invest half his fortune with a banker in a critical financial position, and narrowly manages to persuade him to stop the cheque. Saxon insists, however, on giving the banker the smaller sum which he needs to see himself through the crisis. William makes him promise not to dispose of any large sum without his advice, and persuades him to invest in a speculative proposal for an overland railway route via Palmyra to India.

At Castletowers Saxon meets an Italian activist, Signor Colonna, and his daughter Olimpia, who are guests there. They are ardent in the cause of Italian liberty, and have set up an operations room in the tower. They are in a fever of excitement, as Garibaldi is preparing to invade Sicily, but the cause needs money. Signor Colonna persuades his daughter to win

Saxon's affections and thereby access to his fortune. Flattered by her attentions, he gives her a blank cheque, but is then smitten by remorse, remembering his promise to William. In an anxious frame of mind he takes a walk in the park and wanders into a mausoleum, where he accidentally overhears a vain plea from a young girl to the dowager Lady Castletowers for help for her ailing mother. He recognises the girl as none other than Miss Rivière, and longs to help her without her knowing. Being about to leave with Gervase on a cruise to Norway in his newly acquired yacht, he asks William to find a way of providing for the girl and her mother and helping them to return to their home in Nice. Left with a free hand on Saxon's fortune while he is away, William wins Helen Rivière's affections by buying her dead father's bad paintings at inflated prices, and proposes marriage.

Saxon and Gervase, meanwhile, change their minds about cruising to Norway, and sail instead for Sicily, where they become involved in the fight for freedom. Saxon displays skill and courage during the siege of Milazzo, and has a hero's reception. Gervase is wounded and necessarily out of the fray, so they cruise to Alexandria, where Saxon learns to his dismay that the proposed overland railway route to India is a fiction. He is appalled to realise William's deceit, and travels back to England to confront his cousin. On the way they receive a cry for help from Signor Colonna, and rescue him and Olimpia, disguised as a boy, from the island of Cumae, but Colonna dies of his wounds. They reach Nice, expecting to find Miss Rivière and her mother comfortably settled there, as Saxon had arranged, but they have never arrived. Back in England, Saxon learns that Helen Rivière's mother has died, and that William is about to marry her, and leave for America with his fortune.

He confronts his cousin with his falsehood and robbery, but William escapes in the night and flees with Helen to France. Saxon catches up with them and sees Helen at the Château de Peyrolles, where her wedding to his cousin, whom she knows as 'Mr Forsyth', is planned for the following day. He reveals to her William's treachery, and forthwith proposes to her himself. When William arrives in an intoxicated state to claim his bride, he is again confronted by Saxon. Rejecting the thousand pounds which Saxon offers to enable him to emigrate to America, he stumbles out into the stormy night and his body is found in a pond the next day. Gervase, with the security of a post in the Perquisite Office, is accepted by Olimpia, while Saxon and Helen live in rural contentment in Switzerland.

The contemporary criticisms of *Half a Million of Money* revolved in part around the unseemly central place of the improbably large sum of

Fig. 38: Cover of Half a Millon of Money, *4th edition, 1892*
(London: Routledge, 1892).

money which Saxon inherited, but when making fun of the extravagances of polite society Amelia found exaggeration an invaluable device.
She well contrasts the scheming nature of the apparently benevolent
William and the ease with which the naive but genuinely benevolent
Saxon is duped. Once Saxon learns the deceit, he loses no time in seeking
William out and confronting him. He remains the hero of the book,
generous, kind, brave and intelligent, although this last quality is
demonstrated only by his familiarity with a wide range of literature and
of languages; Amelia does not poke fun at his naiveté. In the first volume
interest is well sustained by the humorous descriptions of the landed
gentry at home in the country and in their London clubs.

The major part of the second volume is taken up by the campaign in
Sicily, and here Amelia clearly indulges her interest in military history.

The cause of freedom is portrayed as a noble ideal, but Signor Colonna's treatment of Olimpia in requiring her to feign love which she does not feel for Saxon, shows the depths to which his fanaticism and hers will stoop. Colonna's death is the death of a hero in a noble cause, but it is not of tragic consequence in the plot. The Battle of Milazzo in which Saxon displays his courage took place on 24 July 1854, and precisely dates the action of the novel, eleven years before Amelia was writing. At that time she may well have been acquainted with the cause of Italian liberty. Correspondence in the Somerville Archive from Giuseppe Mazzini to his friend and hers, Sarah Braysher, shows him writing very much as Signor Colonna would have done: 'The time has arrived for all those who sympathise with our suffering & for our cause to do what they can towards giving our nation practical help...'[38] The skilful description of the confusion of battle, and the young men's light-hearted and eager involvement are well portrayed, but Saxon's tedious pursuit of his villainous cousin in the third volume, and his precipitate declaration of love for Helen, within moments of revealing to her his cousin's deceitfulness, cannot fail to remove any suspension of disbelief which the reader may have maintained.

Joan Rees describes the novel as 'a positive brantub of stories, containing six or seven narrative lines squashed together'[39] and this is indeed a fair comment, not only on *Half a Million of Money* but on Amelia's novel-writing in general. She moves from scene to scene, forwarding the adventures of first one group of characters and then another. Occasionally she introduces a character who plays no obvious part in the story; such is the rich Miss Hatherton, whose way was 'to be always talking – and somewhat loudly too'.[40] Her characters rarely develop during the course of the novel, but William Trefalden is something of an exception. He is portrayed as a benevolent 'uncle' to Saxon in the early chapters, giving him genuinely good advice, sympathetic to his initial extravagances. Deceit was part of his nature almost from the first, but it was falling in love with Helen Rivière which drove him to abuse Saxon's trust and his fortune to the consummate extent that he did. The scenes in which he befriends Helen and her mother are delicately written. Although 'gifted ... with a manner which was in itself a passport to good society ... he traded unscrupulously on their love for the husband and father whom they had lost ... and before many weeks the widow and orphan believed in William Trefalden as if he were an oracle.'[41] Mrs Rivière discerns a fondness for Helen in his behaviour almost before the reader appreciates it, but Helen denies that she loves him. For William, however, 'it was delightful to see the book and the embroidery laid aside as he came in – to meet such looks of confidence and gladness – to be listened to when he spoke, as if all his words were wisdom – listening to Helen's gentle voice, and dreaming delicious dreams of days to come. For William Trefalden was more than ever in love.'[42]

Debenham's Vow *(1870)*

Debenham's Vow[43] was the third of Amelia's novels to begin with a death scene, this time in a wayside inn on a wild Welsh mountain pass, in a misty twilight, in a room suggesting 'a whole history of well-born poverty and homeless wandering'.[44] The dying man is Lord De Benham, formerly of Benhampton Hall, who lost his estates under the influence of a young Oxford gambler. His wife and eight-year-old son, Temple, watch him die. By the next chapter Temple Debenham, as he is now known, is a successful organist. With a friend, Archibald Blyth, he visits the home of his friend's cousins, Mr Josiah Hardwicke, a wealthy merchant, and the haughty Claudia Hardwicke, by whom he feels snubbed.

On a holiday tour of the Wye Valley, Temple and Archie are staying one night in a village inn, and meet an artist, Mr Alleyne, and his daughter Juliet, to whom both young men are attracted. Juliet is enchanted by Temple's organ playing in a neighbouring church. Temple declares his love for her and gives her a ring, but is reluctant to tell her father, by whose design she has been betrothed to another from an early age. Archie is not pleased at Temple's hasty action, having set his heart on his friend marrying his cousin Claudia.

On their tour, Temple receives a letter from his mother, telling him that he is close to the family estate of Benhampton, and she expresses the hope that he will visit his father's grave there. Temple is excited, and vows to visit Benhampton and learn the full story. In his excitement he forgets to say goodnight to Juliet. From that time on his chief ambition is to make money and recover the old family estate. He offers his services to Josiah Hardwicke, and becomes a highly successful agent, travelling first to Russia, and then to America, where he runs the blockade of Charleston harbour, to his own and Josiah Hardwicke's financial gain. He returns to a hero's welcome, but he has been wounded during the battle, and suffers from 'brain-fever' – not the first of Amelia's characters to succumb to the illness which afflicted her more than once.

When he recovers, Temple begins to use the old form of his name, and is forced to reveal his lineage to the Hardwickes. He tells them of his desire to recover the family estate. Claudia, who covets the status of a title, now seeks to win his mother's friendship; Josiah Hardwicke offers him joint partnership in his ship, and suggests marriage to his sister as an alternative method of acquiring wealth. Seeing no other way of acquiring sufficient money to buy back the family estate, he woos Claudia. He makes a new will, remembering in it his friend Archie, his mother, and – Juliet. He has a sudden picture of his life as it might have been with Juliet, and feels desolate. He purchases the Benhampton estate and arranges a little home nearby for his mother. Claudia shows him no romantic love, although when his wound re-opens on his travels with her on the Continent, she nurses him with 'that rare pity that is not merely akin to, but is a vital part of love'.[45] His mother arrives, and gradually assumes control. He suggests to Claudia that his mother should accompany them henceforth on their journey, and misconstrues her reply 'if you please' as indifference; for Claudia has grown to love him, though he does not recognise it. He feels aggrieved, while she realises that she will never be alone with her husband again.

Amelia eloquently justified this strange and unsatisfactory ending in the last paragraph of her book:

> To those who may object that such ending is unsatisfactory, and that the heroes and heroines of romance should either die or be happy according to the received order of things, it may be answered that life is unsatisfactory, and death still more so; and that those men and women who neither die nor are happy constitute the great overwhelming majority upon earth … Prosperity is not all success; conquest is not all triumph … We have seen how Temple De Benham desired riches and Claudia Hardwicke rank; and how both attained the summit of their ambition. If, being successful, they were not also happy, then their story adds but another testimony to the truth of that maxim which tells us that to those whom the gods chastise they grant the desires of their hearts.[46]

It may be that Amelia was wishing to prove to herself, after the failure of *Half a Million of Money*, that she could write a successful romantic novel which turned on the acquisition of wealth. Temple marries Claudia for her money, but cannot believe that she loves him in spite of it. It is significant that Amelia uses the phrase 'pity akin to love', reminiscent of the heading of the chapter 'What pity is akin to' in the earlier novel, to which critics had taken exception. There is, however, a marked difference between the two novels: whereas Saxon Trefalden is essentially a sympathetic character, there is in *Debenham's Vow*, as Lord Lytton rightly wrote, 'a want of sympathy with Debenham'.[47] Debenham is rude to the young organ-blower: 'Your business here is to blow – not to think.'[48] He is jealous of his friend Archie, and abrupt with him: when Archie asks 'Isn't Miss Alleyne a little beauty?' Debenham shuts the door in his face.[49] When compelled to jettison part of a cargo of cotton, his personal loss of 'ten to twelve thousand pounds ... was as nothing compared with ... the loss of prestige, of future opportunities, of his employer's confidence.'[50] His treatment of Juliet is inexcusable.

Although the tone of the novel is essentially serious there are as in all Amelia's work the usual brilliant 'thumbnail' sketches and humorous touches, as for instance the description of two of Debenham's pupils in Finsbury Square,

> where he administered piano lessons to the infant daughters of one of his churchwardens, ... a meat salesman in the parish of St Hildegarde ... They were excellent people; vulgar; ostentatious; good-natured ... Their well-meant hospitality irritated him. Their English made him shudder. Their guineas weighed him down with a crushing sense of humiliation.[51]

As always, Amelia drew on her own experience – in this case as an organist and piano teacher – and when personal experience failed she spared no pains in research. Writing to the publisher, Richard Bowker, some years later she explained:

> As regards technicalities, I do my best to go to the proper sources, and to have reliable data. For instance, in writing the American scenes of 'Debenham's Vow', I took no little trouble to post myself up in all the collateral details. Among those who assisted me with documentary and oral data were Mr Moran for the North, and for the South a distinguished officer who commanded a volunteer regiment at Charleston, and also a gentleman who was a foremost agent for the Confederates in London, and who lent me bills of loading, etc... and I had an intelligent fireman, who had been a seaman on board a blockade-runner, from Regent Street Fire Brigade Depot, in my library for two afternoons, from whom I learnt all the signals ... The *Saturday Review* said that Miss Edwards' seamanship and naval details were of course ludicrously wrong, like ladies' seamanship in general... Sir Thos. Hastings and Capt. Hamilton were both indignant, and said they would stake their naval reputation on the fact that there was not an error from beginning to end ... I am painstaking, and of the unsparing trouble I take to be accurate, I own I am a little vain.[52]

To these truths she did not add another, that she could not bear to be wrong.

In the Days of my Youth *(1872)*

For her next novel, *In the Days of my Youth*,[53] published late in 1872 with the imprint 1873, Amelia returned to her earlier practice of writing in the first person. Basil Arbuthnot is a studious youth, son of a doctor in the village of Saxonholme. As a boy he goes to a soirée fantastique in the Red Lion Hotel there, to watch the 'Wizard of the Caucasus' perform. For one of his tricks the boy hands over his watch, but the wizard has a heart-attack during his performance, and the watch cannot be found. At twenty Basil is sent to Paris to train as a doctor, but has gone no further than Rouen when he falls in with a 'gentleman of leisure', Oscar Dalrymple, who has bought himself out of the Enniskillen Dragoons, and his friend, Frank Sullivan. They gate-crash a bridal party, flirt with a guest, pick an argument with her fiancé, let off the fireworks, and row off down the river in a merry state singing 'God save the Queen'.

The next day Basil reaches Paris, falls asleep in a church, gets drunk again, and is carried back to his hotel. Thereafter he lives 'a very sober, studious life for three weeks', before looking Dalrymple up again. Dalrymple introduces him to Rachel, an actress, and Madame Maugnan, 'a lady', who flatters him with her attentions; he is her slave for three weeks. He acts as witness at Dalrymple's wedding, a private occasion, since his bride is already betrothed (and financially bound) to another. The happy pair part, and the two young men go with Franz Mueller, an artist, to an all-night party in the Latin Quarter, where Basil takes a fancy to a pretty grisette, Josephine. He soon tires of his friend's flirtations and returns to his lodgings, only to be dragged away by Dalrymple to the Ecole de Natation, then to the Café Procope, once frequented by Voltaire. Mueller sketches a stranger without his knowledge, and provokes a fight, which is broken up by the police. The stranger vanishes with his sketchbook which is later returned, but the portrait is missing.

Dalrymple longs for the life of a soldier and has almost forgotten his wife. Basil visits her, and becomes her knight. He has tired of the life of society and longs for that of a student. He meets Hortense Dufresnoy, a language teacher, in a neighbouring lodging, and falls hopelessly in love. He learns that she has won the Biennial Prize of the Académie Française for a poem that she has written. But other friends have a more powerful influence: he visits a Vaudeville theatre with Mueller, and a gambling house with Dalrymple, who accuses another player of cheating and is challenged to a duel. Dalrymple calls on Basil to be his second. He mortally wounds his rival, and is slightly wounded himself.

Basil then receives news from home that his father has died. He leaves for England, but not before declaring his love for Hortense. He finds himself now with adequate means, and gives up the thought of a medical career. He returns to Paris looking for Hortense, but she is gone. He tries to drown his sorrow with travel, but returns eventually to Saxonholme. One day a veiled lady arrives, seeking records of her father, a conjurer. It is Hortense. Basil marries her, and they plan to join Dalrymple and his wife in Italy, On clearing the old home in Saxonholme, they discover the conjurer's magic table, title deeds to his chateau in France, and Basil's lost watch.

This strange tale received, as was shown above (see pp. 109–10) a poor press. In tone it is much more like Amelia's early novels *My Brother's Wife* and *the Ladder of Life* than her more recent ones. It lacks the seriousness of *Barbara's History*, the mystery of *Hand and Glove*, the racy excitement of *Half a Million of Money* and *Debenham's Vow*. The first two volumes contain little more than a catalogue of escapades in and around Paris on the part of the aimless Basil in the company of idlers. Amelia draws on scenes and experiences of her own early travels, invoking imagination, maybe, when experience and booklore fail. Every now and then Basil is recalled to his senses, and vows to take his studies seriously, but when his father's death leaves him with an adequate fortune even that purpose fades, in favour of the one serious love of his life, Hortense.

The scenes in the bath-house, the fair and the Vaudeville theatre may have shocked conservative critics, but they gave Amelia an opening for many amusing sketches. In the theatre 'nuts and apple-parings fly hither and thither; oranges describe perilous parabolas between the pit and the gallery; adventurous *gamins* make daring excursions round the upper rails'.[54] The plot does little more than bind together pictures of characters who pass fleetingly across the path of Basil and his friends, such as the artist who replaces 'two centuries of family portraits reduced to ashes' by painting 'multiple likenesses of the surviving lordship'.[55] The commonplace scenes of home also come in for Amelia's caricature: there is, for instance, the hamlet of Saxonholme, with its

> fine new suburb of Italian and gothic villas, … a new church in the medieval style … and a new cemetery laid out like a pleasure-garden; a new school-house, where the children are taught upon a system with a foreign name; and a Mechanics Institute, where London professors come down at long intervals to propound

popular science, and where agriculturalists meet to discuss popular grievances.[56]

The book has much of the same kind of humour as that which she displayed in her childhood cartoons of Mrs Roliston and Patrick Murphy, and it may be that she was reviving an idea for a novel first planned at an early stage in her writing career, but there is no record of when and where it was written. In spite of the critics, it appears to have been successful, for it was reprinted twice, and translated into German.

Lord Brackenbury *(1880)*

Lord Brackenbury[57] appeared after a gap of six years in novel writing, with the success of her two books of travel coming between. The story opens with Cuthbert, Lord Brackenbury, buying a large quantity of diamonds and other jewels from a banker in Genoa, and proposing to take them on his person to Rome. With his valet, Mr Prouting, he sets out in a cab, but when they are delayed at Borghetto he impatiently leaves the cab to walk the last ten kilometres to La Spezzia. When he does not turn up there as expected, Mr Prouting becomes concerned, and eventually a major search is put in hand, but in vain.

Having aroused the reader's interest with a mystery, Amelia then explains the story of the Brackenbury fortune: The family had bought land in the North country on which coal was discovered, and it brought them wealth. The Langtreys, from whom they had bought the land, took them to law on the ground that they had not sold the coal, but failed in their case, and the law suit ruined them. Herbert, Lord Brackenbury, Cuthbert's father, had to forgo any thought of marriage to Mabel Langtrey in view of the family feud, and married an Italian woman instead, settling in Italy. When she died, he returned to England with his sons, Cuthbert and Lancelot, and built an Italian villa on his estate. He felt the ruin of Stephen Langtrey somewhat on his conscience, and hoped that Cuthbert would settle down and marry Mabel's daughter Winifred, who lived with her aunt Miss Langtrey. While Cuthbert was away, he wooed Winifred on his son's behalf, and it was arranged that they would marry when she was twenty. Before that time, however, he died suddenly, and Cuthbert inherited the title. When Winifred's twentieth birthday came she did not wish to leave her aunt, and the couple agreed to wait for two further years. Cuthbert returns to Italy, and disappears.

After a while Lancelot is advised to prove his brother's will, in fairness to Winifred, who stands to benefit. He takes his friend, Horace Cochrane, who was 'a bit of an antiquary', to see Langtrey Grange. Horace is moved to 'a sort of antiquarian rapture' at the sight of it.[58] They meet Winifred, who is grateful to learn of the £12,000 legacy which will transform their situation. Lancelot then takes Horace for a tramp across the moors, where they come across the 'dark folk': 'now and then… a sand-carrier trudging beside his laden ass; or an old man stooping under a bundle of cut furze; or a horde of shy little flaxen-polled savages beating the bushes in quest of a few late blackberries.'[59] They are disconcerted to hear one old woman, known to Lancelot, speak in a trance of Cuthbert being alive. 'I'd ha' seen his corps in my dreams gin he war dead'.[60]

Shortly afterwards Winifred's aunt dies, and she is overwhelmed with grief. Lancelot 'felt an immense longing to take the hand in his – to hold it fast; but he turned away instead, and went to the window'.[61] She decides to go away for a while, and Lancelot makes arrangements for a stay in Germany and offers to accompany her there – with a maid. In Munich he stays longer than he had at first intended, and takes her round the art galleries. She confesses to him that she was not in love with Cuthbert. Within weeks they declare their love for one another, and that they had always been in love.

The scene changes to Verona. 'The writer who essays to weave into a single narrative the facts by which the destinies of many persons have been governed', comments Amelia, with ingenuous detachment, 'must occasionally shift his scenes, and move the hands of the clock.'[62] A sailor, Cesare Donato, wins the affection of a girl, Giulietta, and takes her, with her father, to Venice. They plan a new life in the south, but Cesare is assaulted by a stranger and wounded. He recovers, and they plan their wedding. He gives her a ring – Cuthbert Brackenbury's ring.

Meanwhile Lancelot and Winifred plan their wedding, and their life together. Lancelot proposes to give up painting, run the estate, and establish the 'moor folk' in decent homes. They make a wedding tour to Italy, and visit Lancelot's childhood home in the south. Lancelot thinks that he sees Cuthbert there. They experience an eruption of Vesuvius, during which he sees a sailor rescuing a child. He believes it is Cuthbert, and tells Winifred: 'I have seen him – Cuthbert – my brother – face to face.'[63]

Twelve years later, an impostor claims the Brackenbury fortune, producing personalia as evidence. Mr Marrables, the Brackenbury solicitor, is disconcerted and asks the claimant to appear. Then the real Cuthbert arrives, and indicates that he wishes Lancelot to be confirmed in the title, but this can only be effected if Lancelot believes Cuthbert dead. Cuthbert identifies the impostor as Mr Prouting. He then leaves for Italy without seeing his brother. 'Looking back at the fast-receding lights of the great city, he tells himself that this last is the hardest sacrifice of all. 'Good-bye, Lancelot!' The night is dark, and there are none to see his tears.'[64] Thus the novel ends.

Many of the elements of the novel have been encountered before. There is the usual wit in the apt turn of phrase, such as 'the many-dollared American'.[65] The minor characters are well-drawn. Mr Prouting, for example, 'prided himself on his Conservatism. In Mr Prouting's eyes, a lord was a lord; a valet was a gentleman; a fisherman in shirt-sleeves was low society',[66] and when the cab-driver 'lit a fresh cigarette, Mr Prouting followed suite with a cigar.'[67] Similarly Mrs Bridget, a servant at Langtrey Grange who came to announce the midday meal, 'had a keen sense of the family dignity, and finding Lancelot in the porch ... judiciously translated "dinner" as "luncheon"'.[68]

Winifred is more credibly portrayed than some of Amelia's heroines: when meeting with Cuthbert she

> naturally regarded him with awe, and was on her best behaviour ... but there was another Winifred of whom he knew nothing – a Winifred not of the schoolroom, but of the poultry-yard ... whom the cow-boy would have died for; who was never so happy as when ... running in and out of poor folk's cottages ... and who could cry in secret over a foolish old romance as bitterly as if Miss Langtrey had never preached that novels and plays, circulating libraries and theatres, were among the choicest inventions of the devil.[69]

What is new in *Lord Brackenbury* is the sympathetic description of the 'moor folk' or 'dark folk', and Lancelot's concern for their well-being. His interest is not sentimental: 'They are charming people,' he tells Horace, 'but a little of them goes a long way ... Be prepared to see a brood of lawless settlers just a shade more respectable than gipsies.'[70] His interest was partly intellectual: he was fascinated by their vocabulary, and by the theory that they were descended from the Saracen captives brought over at the crusades; but it also stemmed from his conscientiousness in what he regarded as his duty. He was giving up his art – just as Amelia was giving up her novel writing – for more serious things:

> 'I don't mean my Parliamentary duties', he said, smiling, 'though they must, of course, count for something. I mean my duties as a landlord ... I must do what Cuthbert would have done.' ... There is his pet project of reclaiming the Danebury marshes ... Above all, there are those wretched 'dark-folk', who need reclaiming more than the Marshes.[71]

His plans to 'compel his "dark-folk" to settle into something like a community' sound autocratic and even patronising today, but Lancelot is unique among Amelia's heroes in displaying public spirit and a social conscience.

Amelia took great pains with *Lord Brackenbury*. She wrote of it to Richard Bowker:

> I never describe scenery that I have not seen, nor yet buildings. My descriptions are from notes taken on the spot, and from my own skeletons. I made a special journey to Cheshire to study the mise-en-scène of 'Lord Brackenbury' I spent days wandering about Biddulph Moor, sketching the scenery, going into the cottages of the 'dark folks', &c. The graphic illustration of Langtrey Grange was simply a photographic reproduction of my large water colour drawing[72] of Old Moreton thrown, I believe, on the woodblock, and then worked up in pencil by the draughtsmen. Mr Fildes only put in three little figures and some pigeons, and the subject appeared as 'By Luke Fildes, A.R.A.' Rather hard on A.B.E.[73]

Amelia never intended *Lord Brackenbury* to be her last novel. In 1883 she drafted a note to the *Literary World* headed 'A voice from the tomb' in which she wrote:

> You add … that I am 'too far lost to have turned my pen to novel-writing', which is undeniably correct; but then I have never been a frequent novel-writer … You will see that between each of my fictions there intervene years of silent penitence. That I shall sin again some day in the way of story telling I do not doubt; but I venture to think that, for the present, I am more usefully employed.[74]

Notes

[1] In 2000 the Rubicon Press published two: *Hand and Glove* and *Barbara's History*, and announced its intention to publish *Debenham's Vow* and *Lord Brackenbury*.

[2] Published anonymously in *Chambers's Journal*, New Series 20, 511 (15 October 1853), pp. 246a–50b, and New Series 21, 512 (22 October 1853), pp. 261b–66b.

[3] SCO Edwards 438.

[4] Amelia B. Edwards, *Pharaohs, Fellahs and Explorers* (London: Osgood, McIlvaine, 1891).

5 Amelia B. Edwards, 'The Art of the Novelist', *The Contemporary Review*, 66 (1894), pp. 224–42.

6 SCO Edwards 351.

7 Amelia B. Edwards, *My Brother's Wife* (London: Hurst & Blackett, 1855), p. 90.

8 Ibid., p. 224.

9 Ibid., p. 167.

10 Ibid., p. 7.

11 Ibid., p. 20.

12 *Sunday Times*, (London), 25 December 1864.

13 Joan Rees, *Amelia B. Edwards, Traveller, Novelist and Egyptologist* (London: Rubicon Press, 1998), p. 72.

14 Amelia B. Edwards, *The Ladder of Life: a heart history* (London: Routledge, 1857).

15 Ibid., p. 131.

16 Ibid., p. 103.

17 Amelia B. Edwards, *Hand and Glove* (London: J & C. Brown, [1859]), p. 133.

18 Ibid., p. 70.

19 Ibid., p. 97.

20 Ibid., p. 100.

21 Rees, *Amelia B. Edwards*, p. 73.

22 SCO Edwards 351.

23 Amelia B. Edwards, *Barbara's History* (London: Hurst & Blackett, 1864), p. 50.

24 Ibid., p. 83.

25 Ibid., p. 161.

26 Ibid., p. 202.

27 Ibid., p. 231.

28 SCO Edwards 515, 5 April 1857.

29 Ibid.

30 Ibid.

31 Ibid., 7 April 1857.

32 Edwards, *Barbara's History*, p. 230.

33 Rees, *Amelia B. Edwards*. p. 78.

34 Edwards, *Barbara's History*, p. 131.

35 Ibid., p. 137.

36 Ibid., p. 147.

37 Amelia B. Edwards, *Half a Million of Money: a novel*, 3 vols (London: Tinsley Brothers, 1866).

38 SCO Edwards 218.

39 Rees, *Amelia B. Edwards*, p. 73.

40 Edwards, *Half a Million of Money*, vol. 1, p. 73.

41 Ibid., vol. 3, p. 63.

42 Ibid., vol. 3, p. 66.

43 Amelia B. Edwards, *Debenham's Vow*, 3 vols (London: Hurst & Blackett, 1870).

44 Ibid., vol. 1, p. 3.

45 Ibid., vol. 3, p. 222.

46 Ibid., vol. 3, p. 276.

47 SCO Edwards 318.

48 Edwards, *Debenham's Vow*, vol. 1, p. 35.

49 Ibid., vol. 1, p. 132.

50 Ibid., vol. 2, p. 214.

51 Ibid., vol. 1, p. 31.

52 SCO Edwards 438.

53 Amelia B. Edwards, *In the Days of my Youth*, 3 vols (London: Hurst & Blackett, 1873).

54 Ibid., vol. 3, p. 193.

55 Ibid., vol. 2, p. 93.

56 Ibid., vol. 1, p. 3.

57 Amelia B. Edwards, *Lord Brackenbury: a novel*, 3 vols (London: Hurst & Blackett, 1880).

58 Ibid., vol. 1, p. 250.

59 Ibid., vol. 1, p. 295.

60 Ibid., vol. 1, p. 314.

61 Ibid., vol. 2, p. 115.

62 Ibid., vol. 2, p. 214.

63 Ibid., vol. 3, p. 270.

64 Ibid., vol. 3, p. 332.

65 Ibid., vol. 1, p. 4.

66 Ibid., vol. 1, p. 66.

67 Ibid., vol. 1, p. 74.

68 Ibid., vol. 2, p. 150.

69 Ibid., vol. 1, p. 164.

70 Ibid., vol. 1, p. 299.

71 Ibid., vol. 3, p. 73.

72 The painting survives: SCO Edwards W16.

73 SCO Edwards 438.

74 SCO Edwards 565.13.

Index

Fields, Annie, 225–6
Fields, James, 53
Fildes, Luke, 159–60, 306
First Cataract, 125–6, 128, 147–8
First Poor Traveller's Story, The, 22, 253
Fitzgerald, Captain, 17, 240
'Fostat' (dahabiah), 125
Foster, Birket, 61, 280
Four-Fifteen Express, The, 72, 259–60
Fowles, E.F., 72
Fraser, George Willoughby, 235
French in Egypt, 177–8
Frith, William Powell, 60, 71

Galbraith, Mrs, 49
Gardner, Ernest Arthur, 167, 169, 192
Gascon, The, 20
Gaskell, Elizabeth, 2
Gibson, Mr, 36
Ghedina, Guiseppe, 98–102
Gilbertson, E, 184, 188–9, 199, 201, 204–5
Gill, Miss, 36, 39
Girga, 130; *119*
Globe, The, 27
Gladstone, William Ewart, 139
Giza, 117, 131; *194*
Good Words, 73, 159
Goss, Sir John, 14
Gosselin, Helier, 204–5, 211, 213
Graphic, The, 159
Great Western Laundry, 156–7
Greenwell, Canon, 183, 184
Griffith, Francis Llewellyn, 199–200, 202, 204, 213–14, 235, 241
Griffith, Kate *see* Bradbury, Kate
Griffith Institute, Oxford, 223, 241

Half a Million of Money, 1–2, 64, 69, 73, 258–9, 294–8; *298*
Hand and Glove, 1, 42, 255, 287–9
'Happy Couple', 116, 123, 125, 126–7, 131, 132, 146–7
Harper's Weekly, 64
Harper's New Monthly Magazine, 153, 168–9, 222, 266
Harris, Selima, 176
Harrison, Jane Ellen, 171
Hathaway, George, 224, 226
Hawara, 215
Haworth, Jesse, 215, 218–19, 237, 239–40
Hays, Emily, 35, 37, 39